Leonard Solomon (1963)
Robert Chin (1960–1965)
John Harding (1956–1959)
M. Brewster Smith (1951–1955)
Harold H. Kelley (1949)
Ronald Lippitt (1944–1950)

2012 Vol. 68, No. 2

The Reality of Contemporary Discrimination in the United States: The Consequences of Hidden Bias in Real World Contexts

Issue Editors: Jason A. Nier and Samuel L. Gaertner

Journal of Social Issues, Vol. 68, No. 2, 2012, pp. 207–220

The Challenge of Detecting Contemporary Forms of Discrimination

Jason A. Nier[*]
Connecticut College

Samuel L. Gaertner
University of Delaware

While the persistent and widespread racial and gender inequalities that exist in the United States are almost certainly due to a combination of many different factors, one likely source of inequality is discrimination. As decades of research in social psychology suggest, this discrimination is often subtle and difficult to detect, and in some instances, may be unintentional. Although this type of discrimination is subtle, it is nonetheless damaging to those who are its victims and the cumulative effects of such discrimination may be substantial. In the domains of race and gender, in which individuals are presumably legally protected from discrimination, people are deprived of their civil rights when they face such behavior. Therefore, an important goal for research and practice in intergroup relations is to develop techniques that allow such discrimination to be reliably detected and to distinguish discriminatory conduct from behavior that is not influenced by subtle racial and gender biases.

From its earliest roots, the *Journal of Social Issues (JSI)* has been at the forefront of the study of discrimination. Prejudice, as a pressing societal issue to be addressed by social science, was the focus of the very first issue of *JSI*, which was titled "Racial and religious prejudice in everyday living" (Weltfish, 1945a). Indeed, with so much to say on the matter, the editorial board of *JSI* decided to devote much of the second issue of *JSI* to the topic as well (Weltfish, 1945b). Contributors to these first two volumes included some of the most influential social scientists of the era, such as Gordon Allport, Kenneth Clark, and Margaret

---

[*]Correspondence concerning this article should be addressed to Jason A. Nier, Department of Psychology, Box 5305, Connecticut College, 270 Mohegan Avenue, New London, CT 06320. Tel: 860 439 5057 [e-mail: janie@conncoll.edu].

Mead. Kurt Lewin himself also offered a commentary on one of the articles. In reading their works, one is immediately struck by their timeliness. They dealt with some of the most significant forms of bigotry of their times, such as anti-Semitism, racism directed at Black Americans, and sexism against women.

They also saw that while discrimination could often be overt, as in the case of Jim Crow style racism directed at Black Americans, it also could be subtle. The editor of that first *JSI* issue, Gene Weltfish, wrote that "[t]he Negro has been selected as an illustration of [employment discrimination] because the situation applies most stringently to him. But Jews, Catholics, and Foreign-Born are in no sense immune to this type of discrimination. People are less open about the fact that they have a discriminatory policy toward these groups; the discrimination comes in more subtle forms, but it is there nevertheless. This means that a considerable part of our American people suffer one of the most serious kinds of discrimination that there is." (Weltfish, 1945a, p. 11).

Since that time, much has changed and, yet, much also remains the same. Some of these social and cultural changes, many of which were wrought by the civil rights movement, were foreseen by the editor of that first issue of *JSI*. She wrote, "[i]f we take no practical steps to clear away prejudice [against Black Americans], and if jobs are hard to get after the war, the previous situation will recur. All jobs will be difficult for Negroes to get, not on the basis of inability to do the work or lack of need, but on the basis of race prejudice. The Negro will then demand his rights in no uncertain terms." (Weltfish, 1945a, p. 11). African Americans and other groups did, of course, demand their rights in the ensuing decades, and with the passage of the Civil Rights Act of 1965, many of those rights became legally protected. Yet, over 65 years after the first *JSI* issue dealing with discrimination, subtle prejudice remains. Just as religious minorities were sometimes a target of subtle, rather than overt, discrimination in the United States in 1945, racial minorities and women (and other groups as well) must still sometimes face subtle bias in the present day.

Since contemporary forms of discrimination can often times appear, ironically, to be nondiscriminatory, detecting the subtle manifestations of discrimination, and understanding the true consequences of these behaviors, has proven difficult. In an attempt to better understand the tangible impact of these subtle biases, the objective of this issue is to examine the consequences of contemporary forms of race and gender discrimination in several different naturalistic domains—the workplace, law enforcement, academia, and well-being. Toward that end, this issue will focus on the procedures that may be employed to detect the operation of subtle biases in these contexts, including the use of experimental field studies of discrimination, in which adverse decisions toward members of legally protected classes (e.g., deciding not to hire a particular individual because of his/her race or gender) are observed in the actual contexts in which they normally occur (Bendick, Jackson,

& Reinoso, 1994; Bertrand & Mullainathan, 2004; Pager, 2007). The practical significance of identifying everyday discrimination will also be addressed, including a discussion of the different ways in which research examining contemporary forms of discrimination can be integrated into the litigation of discrimination cases (e.g., Borgida, Hunt, & Kim, 2005).

Racial and Gender Disparities

Racial and gender disparities are widespread in many different countries, including the United States. For example, according to the U.S. Department of Labor (2012), rates of unemployment are over twice as high for Black Americans relative to Whites, and unemployment rates are also significantly higher for Latinos compared to Whites. Similar disparities also exist in income as well; on average Black households earn about $22,500 less per year than White households, and Latino households earn about $16,500 less than do Whites (DeNavas-Walt, Proctor, & Smith, 2011). Income inequities also persist in the domain of gender. While unemployment rates are similar for women and men, according to Census Bureau statistics (DeNavas-Walt et al., 2011), women workers averaged $33,900 per year whereas male workers averaged $47,700 per year. Alarming disparities exist in the realm of law enforcement practices. For example, Black males are six times more likely to be incarcerated than White males, and Latinos are twice as likely to be in prison than are White males (U.S. Department of Justice, 2007). And although reliable data on police shootings are difficult to obtain, by one estimate Blacks are about five times more likely to be killed by police officers than are Whites (Sadler, Correll, Park, & Judd, 2012), and a growing body of research has begun to indicate that individuals, including law enforcement professionals, are likely to react more swiftly to non-Whites in the application of deadly force (Correll, Park, Judd, & Wittenbrink, 2002; Correll et al., 2007; Payne, 2006).

Perhaps the most disconcerting inequities are the disparities in the health and well-being of various racial and ethnic groups in the United States. These racial disparities often times remain sizable even after controlling for other variables for which race may serve as a proxy, such as insurance status and income. This finding led the Institute of Medicine to conclude that the subtle biases of White health care providers against Black patients may be partially responsible for many health care disparities (Smedley, Stith, & Nelson, 2002).

Subtle Forms of Contemporary Discrimination

Although most racial and gender disparities are likely due to a combination of many factors, one potential source, both in the United States and in other countries as well, is discrimination. Following the passage of Title VII of the

1965 Civil Rights Act discrimination based on race and gender was outlawed in the United States. During and after this period, overtly racist and sexist attitudes and discrimination decreased significantly. So how can research reconcile the persistent racial and gender inequalities with the decline in overtly racist and sexist behavior? One possible explanation is that prejudice and discrimination continue to exist in a form that is more subtle and difficult to detect. Consistent with this interpretation, a number of different forms of subtle race and gender bias have been identified by social psychologists, including Symbolic Racism (Sears & Henry, 2005), Aversive Racism (Dovidio & Gaertner, 2004; Gaertner & Dovidio, 1986), Modern Sexism (Swim, Aikin, Hall, & Hunter, 1995), and Ambivalent Sexism (Glick & Fiske, 1996, 2001). Although these forms of subtle bias differ in important ways, they also share some features in common. Perhaps most significantly, many theories of subtle bias focus on the idea that different kinds of attitudes and beliefs sometime conflict with one another, which in turn results in subtle (rather than overt) discrimination. In short, subtle bias is often the product of ambivalence.

In the domain of race, the Aversive Racism perspective proposes that ambivalent attitudes sometimes result in subtle discrimination (Dovidio & Gaertner, 2004; Gaertner & Dovidio, 1986). According to this perspective, the explicit racial attitudes of many White Americans are presumed to positive and egalitarian, whereas their implicit attitudes are often negative. As a result of these negative implicit attitudes and their seemingly contradictory egalitarian values, Whites may discriminate against African Americans in some situations, but not in others. In situations where their explicit egalitarian values are salient, they will not discriminate. However, when their egalitarian values are not salient, their negative implicit attitudes toward African Americans may guide their behavior and often result in discrimination.

According to the research examining Ambivalent Sexism (Glick & Fiske, 1996), prejudicial attitudes toward women may, at times, simply reflect hostility, but perhaps more commonly, sexism likely reflects a mix of positive and negative beliefs about women. These conflicting positive and negative beliefs are referred to as Hostile Sexism, on the one hand, and Benevolent Sexism, on the other. According to this perspective, Women who conform to traditional gender roles will typically evoke a positive reaction associated with Benevolent Sexism, whereas those who do not conform to tradition are likely to evoke the negative reactions associated with Hostile Sexism. Thus, both racial attitudes and gender attitudes are often characterized by ambivalence, which suggests that beliefs about race and gender may manifest themselves in subtle and complex ways during the course of everyday interactions (i.e., in "the real world"). The manner in which race and gender may influence behavior may be so subtle, in fact, that it precludes actors from recognizing their differential behavior toward the targets of such beliefs, such as African Americans and women.

Detecting Contemporary Discrimination: Challenges and Critiques

Despite its subtle and often unintentional nature, contemporary forms of discrimination can nonetheless have a significant impact on the lives of those who are presumably legally protected from such behavior. But how may such discrimination, which may even be hidden from the individual who is actually discriminating, be detected outside the laboratory, where investigators do not have such tight control over different variables that may be responsible for disparate outcomes? This is a significant challenge indeed, because in addition to reliably detecting the presence of discriminatory behavior, it is equally important to detect nondiscriminatory behavior as well. Many adverse decisions made toward members of legally protected classes may be relatively free from the influence of racial and gender biases, and whatever approach is employed to detect discriminatory conduct must also be able to detect these negative, but nonetheless nondiscriminatory decisions, and distinguish them from adverse decision that are based on discriminatory factors.

In order to distinguish discriminatory behavior from nondiscriminatory behavior, a growing number of researchers are turning to field experiments, conducted outside of the laboratory, which are sometimes referred to as "audit" or "testing" studies of contemporary discrimination. For example, Pager & Western (2006) conducted an audit study of workplace discrimination in New York City. In this study, members of a research team, some of whom were White, some of whom were Latino, and some Black, applied for entry level positions at 252 different companies. All members of the research team (referred to as "testers") who applied for one of these positions had undergone training in order to standardize the manner in which they presented themselves to prospective employers. After applying for these positions, the results were examined to see whether the race of the tester had an impact on the likelihood of receiving a job offer or a "callback." The employers' responses to the testers demonstrated a consistent pattern of discrimination; overall 23% of White testers received either a job offer or a callback, whereas only 19% of Latino and 13% of Blacks testers received an offer or a callback. Also, these negative outcomes faced by Latino and Black testers were typically veiled by racially neutral explanations. This is precisely the type of discrimination that would be expected to occur, according to the subtle bias perspective; discriminatory employment decisions were rationalized on the basis of ostensibly fair criteria. Moreover, this discriminatory conduct would likely have gone undetected if employment decisions were only examined on a case-by-case basis.

Although audit studies of real-world discrimination do indeed document the type of discrimination that is predicted by the subtle bias perspective, such studies do have weaknesses and limitations. For example, despite the training that testers of different races receive to present themselves in a uniform manner to employers, testers may subtly and perhaps unintentionally respond in a manner that elicits a negative response from prospective employers. In other words, Latino and Black testers may anticipate receiving a cooler reception than their White counterparts, and may interact with prospective employers in a manner that is less warm and friendly, and the employers may then respond more negatively toward this behavior. If racially disparate outcomes were produced by this process, a form of self-fulfilling prophecy, then no actual discrimination would have occurred.

However, other audit procedures have addressed this limitation and provide further evidence that the disparate treatment generally found in audit studies does reflect discrimination. For example, one variation of audit studies relies upon resumes rather than face-to-face interviews. In studies such as these, resumes of fictitious individuals with equivalent (although not identical) qualifications are sent to prospective employers. The race of the hypothetical job applicants is varied through the use of race typed names. An employer may receive similar resumes from Greg and Jamal, or from Lakisha and Emily. The results of studies employing such resume methodologies are similar to those obtained while using the face-to-face techniques. For example, Bertrand and Mullainathan (2004) found that resumes with White-sounding names were about 50% more likely to receive callbacks for interviews than were resumes with Black-sounding names. However, studies employing this resume procedure are imperfect as well and have their own limitations (for a review, see Pager, 2007). But when one simultaneously considers the results of audit studies using face-to-face interviews and resume procedures, discrimination is clearly the most parsimonious explanation for the results that are typically observed. Although it is possible that some audit studies may overestimate the impact of race and gender on employment decisions (Pager, 2007), it seems quite unlikely that all of the disparate treatment observed in such audit studies is simply a consequence of these methodological concerns.

While the idea that subtle bias persists in the face of declining overt biases is well accepted within the social psychological literature, there are some who are critical of the subtle bias perspective. Many of these critics have come from outside the discipline of social psychology (e.g., Wax, 1999; Zuriff, 2002), but some have also come from within the field of social psychology (Mitchell & Tetlock, 2006; Tetlock & Mitchell, 2008, 2009). These critics argue that subtle bias has not been convincingly demonstrated to result in discriminatory behavior. However, reviews of the implicit bias literature indicate that discriminatory behavior has indeed been linked to different forms of subtle bias. For example, Dasgupta (2004) examined the relationship between implicit bias and behavior in a number of previous studies. She concluded that while implicit bias does not invariably lead to discriminatory behavior, the link between implicit beliefs and discriminatory behavior has been empirically demonstrated and replicated in numerous studies. More recently, Greenwald, Poehlman, Uhlmann, and Banaji (2009) examined the relationship between one particular measure of subtle bias (the Implicit

Association Test or IAT) and a variety of different criterion variables, such as nonverbal behavior. When combining the results of over 50 different empirical studies, they found that scores on the IAT did tend to be associated with criterion variables. Taken together these results strongly suggest that there is indeed a predictable relationship between implicit measures of subtle bias and discriminatory conduct.

Despite this substantial evidence, critics of the subtle bias perspective (Mitchell & Tetlock, 2006) argue that there is no evidence linking implicit bias to "real-world" discriminatory conduct, since the studies that have examined this link are typically conducted in laboratory contexts. That is, no study has linked implicit bias to discrimination in a truly naturalistic setting (e.g., an actual, rather than simulated, employment setting). While such a study has not been conducted in the United States, a study recently conducted in Sweden has indeed examined the link between implicit bias and actual employment decisions (Rooth, 2010, Experiment 1). This study employed a resume methodology in which two resumes with similar qualifications were sent in response actual employment advertisements, which had been placed by job recruiters. One of these resumes ostensibly belonged to an individual with a native Swedish surname and another resume was ostensibly from an individual with an Arab/Muslim surname. Researchers then recorded whether the resume received a callback for an interview from each of the job recruiters. In the bulk of the cases, neither resume received a callback from the job recruiter; however, in 522 cases at least one of the resumes received a callback. In 239 of these cases, both hypothetical applicants received a callback. Of those cases in which only one of the applicants received a callback, 217 calls were returned for the native Swedish applicant, whereas only 66 calls were returned for the Arab/Muslim applicant. Thus, consistent with previous studies conducted in the United States that have employed a similar methodology, a pattern of discrimination did emerge such that native Swedish applicants were significantly more likely to receive a callback than the Arab/Muslim applicants.

Later these job recruiters, who either called back the hypothetical applicant or failed to call the hypothetical applicant, were contacted and asked to complete implicit and explicit measures of their stereotypes of native Swedes and of Arab/Muslims, over the internet. Then the implicit and explicit beliefs of these individuals were examined to determine whether these beliefs were significant predictors of the call-back decision. The results revealed that implicit stereotypes were indeed a significant predictor of the callback decision, even after controlling for a number of other variables, including explicit attitudes and stereotypes. Rooth also conducted a second, similar study and was able to replicate this finding; he again found that IAT scores were able to predict discriminatory employment behavior. These studies demonstrate that there is indeed a link between implicit bias and discriminatory conduct in actual employment settings. Thus the consequences of implicit bias should no longer be viewed as a laboratory artifact, but as a phenomenon that has been linked to actual discriminatory employment-related decisions. Furthermore, this line of research suggests, as do a number of other studies, that subtle bias may be an international phenomenon that extends beyond the United States, and that similar forms of prejudice and discrimination may exist in a number of different countries (Dovidio & Gaertner, 2007; Hodson, Dovidio, & Gaertner, 2002; Nosek et al., 2007).

But since Rooth's research (2010) was conducted outside of the United States, does it tell us anything about subtle discrimination in the United States? While similar research has yet to be conducted in the United States, we would point out that there is a significant amount of literature that documents precisely the type of discrimination that would be expected based on the subtle bias perspective. For example, audit studies indicate that the pattern of discrimination that exists in the United States often conforms to the pattern that would be predicted by the subtle bias perspective (Bertrand & Mullainathan, 2004; Pager & Western, 2006). Thus, even though the link between measures of subtle bias and "real-world" employment discrimination has not yet been directly observed in the United States, research does nonetheless indicate that discrimination in the United States often follows the pattern predicted by the subtle bias perspective.

Despite evidence such as this, critics of the subtle bias perspective argue that there is good reason to expect that discrimination will be less likely to occur in "real-world" contexts, relative to laboratory contexts in which the bulk of research has been conducted. Specifically, Mitchell and Tetlock (2006) reason that many real-world contexts have institutionalized safeguards, such as equal employment opportunity policies, which greatly reduce the likelihood that discriminatory conduct will occur. Since laboratory contexts typically lack such safeguards, the link between implicit bias and discrimination, which occurs in lab, does not accurately reflect the dynamics of real-world decision making. For example, in employment settings many organizations have official policies and procedures in place that strongly discourage discriminatory conduct, and as a result, the subtle forms of prejudice that may express themselves in laboratory contexts may not express themselves in such employment contexts. Whether this is actually the case remains an empirical question that has not been directly tested. However, audit studies of discrimination strongly suggest that discrimination still occurs, despite such safeguards; recall that audit studies reveal a consistent pattern of differential treatment in the contexts in which these institutional safeguards are presumably in place. If such safeguards actually prevented the expression of discriminatory conduct in actual employment contexts, then one would expect to see little evidence of disparate treatment in audit studies. Thus, while the hypothesis that institutional safeguards prevent the expression of subtle discriminatory conduct has not been rigorously tested, the available evidence does not seem to support such an interpretation and suggests that discrimination does commonly occur in naturalistic settings.

Burden of Proof in Applied Settings

Since the purpose of this issue is to examine the consequences of contemporary discrimination in everyday contexts, we should point out that the existence of race and gender disparities alone do not convincingly demonstrate that such disparities are due to subtle discrimination. At the very least, any procedure used to draw an inference of discrimination must provide evidence that other plausible explanations for disparate outcomes cannot fully account for such disparities. Therefore in this volume, the authors will address the evidence that suggests that group disparities are manifestations of discrimination, rather than factors unrelated to race or gender. Authors will also address how alternative explanations for disparate outcomes can (or cannot) be ruled out.

Although each selection will discuss the evidence that points to subtle bias as a cause of disparate outcomes, the burden of proof required in order to draw an inference of discrimination should not be set unrealistically high either. Although it is more difficult to isolate subtle bias as a cause of discrimination in real-world contexts, it is important to note that antidiscrimination laws typically involve a different burden of proof than that which is commonly required in the social sciences. For example, Title VII of the Civil Rights Act does not require absolute proof of discrimination or even proof "beyond a reasonable doubt" in order for an inference of discriminatory conduct to be drawn. As in other types of civil court procedures, only a preponderance of evidence is required to demonstrate discrimination. In other words, only more evidence supporting an inference of discrimination than that which refutes an inference of discrimination is required. Thus while social scientific evidence alone may not prove discriminatory conduct in applied settings with 100% confidence, such strong evidence is not required in order to draw a legally actionable inference of discrimination. Indeed such a high burden of proof is not required in any area of law, and in many instances there is likely to be at least some ambiguity in the motives that underlay the bulk of real-world discriminatory behavior. Despite this ambiguity, in some domains the available social scientific data strongly suggest that discrimination is at least partially responsible for the disparate outcomes faced by those who belong to groups that are legally protected under Title VII. And in many cases, evidence from social psychology may be of value to demonstrate the presence or absence of legally actionable discrimination.

Organization of the Issue

The first section of the issue will examine workplace discrimination. A significant and growing number of social psychologists, sociologists, and legal scholars have focused specifically on workplace discrimination as perhaps the most damaging form of subtle discrimination. This section will begin with a chapter by Devah

Pager and Bruce Western who will discuss the need for experimental research conducted outside of the laboratory. Since lab research documenting implicit bias and discrimination is typically conducted in artificial settings, its applicability to hiring decisions made in actual organizations, is open to debate. Pager and Western report that field studies of racial discrimination indicate that Blacks are significantly less likely to be hired than similarly qualified Whites. Moreover, they present qualitative data that point to subtle, rather than overt, discrimination as the source of this differential treatment. For example, Black testers, who are less likely to receive callbacks from prospective White employers, do not typically report that they have been treated more negatively by their prospective employers. In other words, the process by which discriminatory treatment occurred is so subtle, that the targets of the discriminatory conduct cannot accurately detect it.

In the same spirit as Pager and Western, Marc Bendick and Ana Nunes will discuss the use of paired comparison techniques to detect discrimination in the workplace. These procedures, in which pairs of research assistants with equivalent credentials apply for an actual position in a real workplace, have demonstrated that somewhere between 20% and 40% of employers discriminate against members of a legally protected class. Although a significant number of paired comparison studies have been conducted in the past decade, there has not been a concerted effort to systematically employ such techniques on a broader scale. Bendick and Nunes also believe that the use of such techniques can enhance social scientists' understanding of the psychological mechanisms that are responsible for subtle bias.

Mina Cikara, Susan Fiske, and Laurie Rudman describe how subtle gender bias may be present in academia and within the field of social psychology. They point out that despite the preponderance of women in the field, women are underrepresented at the highest levels of the professional hierarchy. This disparity is perhaps most evident in the publications appearing in social psychology's flagship journal, *The Journal of Personality and Social Psychology*. Cikara and her colleagues test a number of nondiscriminatory explanations for the existence of the gender gap in publications in this journal, and find that these gender neutral explanations cannot fully account for the disparity. They therefore conclude that the disparity may be due, at least in part, to a subtle form of gender discrimination.

The second section of this issue will address the implications of subtle bias in legal contexts. Melody Sadler, Joshua Correll, Bernadette Park, and Charles Judd explore the role that subtle bias may play in law enforcement contexts. They specifically examine whether the "shooter bias" (i.e., the tendency for Whites to more quickly shoot Black targets, relative to White targets) extends to a multiethnic context. They report data that suggest that the shooter bias is not unique to Black–White relations. For example, they observe that many Whites, including police officers, are quicker to shoot at Latino targets, relative to White targets. They also observe that Asian targets show a reverse shooter bias; Whites were more quick to fire on other Whites relative to Asian targets. These results have potentially significant consequences for the some of the split second decisions that those in the law enforcement community must make in the application of deadly force.

Jerry Kang will examine the different ways in which evidence of implicit bias may facilitate the enforcement of antidiscrimination law. He argues that some have been alarmist in presuming that measures of implicit bias will be used to "read the minds" of individuals who are accused of discrimination; some fear that individual acts discrimination will be proven in the future by requiring individuals to complete measures of implicit bias. Despite this fear, no psychologists have suggested that measures of implicit bias be used in this way. He points out that implicit bias can still nonetheless improve compliance with antidiscrimination law by focusing on the prevention of such biases, rather than focusing on litigation that occurs after discrimination has already taken place.

Two of the chapters in this volume will examine the role of subtle bias in health and well-being. Louis Penner, Susan Eggly, Jennifer Griggs, Willie Underwood, Heather Orom, and Terrance Albrecht will discuss the implications of subtle racial discrimination in the treatment of cancer. They discuss the evidence that indicates that racial disparities in survival rates for cancer are significant, even after controlling for a number of nonracial variables. They argue that physician's biases and stereotypes about Black patients play a key role in the different outcomes faced by Black and White cancer patients. They also discuss how these biases may influence the quality of physician–patient interactions, such that Black patients typically have lower quality interactions with their physicians than do White patients, and how the nature of these interactions may contribute to disparate outcomes.

Elizabeth Brondolo, Madeline Libretti, Luis Rivera, and Katrina Walsemann will discuss the role that implicit and subtle bias may play in social and physical well-being. They review the literature that suggests that different forms of subtle bias may serve to undermine the social capital of people of color. They argue that this diminished social capital is associated with a host of negative outcomes, and that it may therefore contribute to a number of economic, social, and health-related inequalities.

Emily Fisher and Eugene Borgida will contribute one of two concluding chapters by focusing on the most widely used measure of implicit prejudice, the Implicit Association Test, and its role in the litigation of employment discrimination cases. The IAT has faced on a number of critics who have focused on the presumed methodological shortcomings of the test (e.g., Blanton & Jaccard, 2006), as well as those who have questioned its application to the specific domain of employment litigation (e.g., Mitchell & Tetlock, 2006). Fisher and Borgida contend that while the IAT does have a number of shortcomings, the IAT and other measures of implicit bias still have relevance for understanding discrimination that occurs outside of the laboratory.

Nilanas Dasgupta and Jane Stout will offer a concluding chapter that summaries the findings contained in our issue. They point out that questions about the external validity of laboratory research are indeed legitimate; at the same time however, the authors discuss how research has now begun to move from the laboratory into the field. They will also describe how the other selections in this issue illustrate the significance of implicit bias for "real-world" behavior, and call for greater collaboration between researchers and practitioners. They conclude by discussing the possible remedies for implicit bias, and argue that both perceivers and targets must take action in order to minimize the impact of the implicit bias.

Conclusion

While the consistent and widespread racial and gender inequalities that exist in many different domains are likely due to a combination of many different factors, one likely source of these inequalities is discrimination. In many cases, this discrimination is likely to be subtle and difficult to detect, and in some instances, may be unintentional. Although this type of discrimination is subtle, it is nonetheless damaging to those who are the targets of discriminatory conduct, and the cumulative effects of such discrimination may be substantial. In the domains of race and gender, in which individuals are presumably legally protected from discrimination, people are deprived of the civil rights when they face such behavior. Therefore, an important goal for research and practice in intergroup relations is the development of techniques that allow such discrimination to be reliably detected, and to distinguish discriminatory conduct from behavior that is not influenced by subtle racial and gender biases.

References

Bendick, M., Jackson, C. W., & Reinoso, V. A. (1994). Measuring employment discrimination through controlled experiments. *Review of Black Political Economy*, *23*, 25–48. doi:10.1007/BF02895739.

Bertrand, M., & Mullainathan, S. (2004). Are Emily and Greg more employable than Lakisha and Jamal? A field experiment on labor market discrimination. *American Economic Review*, *94*, 991–1013. doi:10.1257/0002828042002561.

Blanton, H., & Jaccard, J. (2006). Arbitrary metrics in psychology. *American Psychologist*, *61*, 27–41. doi:10.1037/0003-066X.61.1.27.

Borgida, E., Hunt, C., & Kim, A. (2005). On the use of gender stereotyping research in sex discrimination litigation. *Journal of Law and Policy*, *13*, 613–628.

Correll, J., Park, B., Judd, C. M., & Wittenbrink, B. (2002). The police officer's dilemma: Using ethnicity to disambiguate potentially hostile individuals. *Journal of Personality and Social Psychology*, *83*, 1314–1329. doi:10.1037//0022-3514.83.6.1314.

Correll, J., Park, B, Judd, C. M., Wittenbrink, B., Sadler, M. S., & Keesee, T. (2007). Across the thin blue line: Police officers and racial bias in the decision to shoot. *Journal of Personality and Social Psychology*, *92*, 1006–1023. doi:10.1037/0022-3514.92.6.1006.

Dasgupta, N. (2004). Implicit ingroup favoritism, outgroup favoritism, and their behavioral manifestations. *Social Justice Research, 17*, 143–169. doi:10.1023/B:SORE.0000027407.70241.15.

DeNavas-Walt, C., Proctor, B. D., & Smith, J. (2011). *Income, poverty, and health insurance coverage in the United States: 2010*. Washington, DC: U.S. Government Printing Office.

Dovidio, J. F., & Gaertner, S. L. (2004). Aversive racism. In M. P. Zanna (Ed.), *Advances in experimental social psychology* (Vol. *36*, pp. 1–51). San Diego, CA: Academic Press.

Dovidio, J. F., & Gaertner, S. L. (2007). New directions in aversive racism research: Persistence and pervasiveness. In C. W. Esqueda (Ed.), *Nebraska symposium on motivation: Motivational aspects of prejudice and racism* (pp. 43–67). New York: Springer.

Gaertner, S. L., & Dovidio, J. F. (1986). The aversive form of racism. In J. F. Dovidio & S. L. Gaertner (Eds.), *Prejudice, discrimination, and racism* (pp. 61–89). Orlando, FL: Academic Press.

Glick, P., & Fiske, S. T. (1996). The ambivalent sexism inventory: Differentiating hostile and benevolent sexism. *Journal of Personality and Social Psychology, 70*(3), 491–512. doi:10.1037/0022-3514.70.3.491.

Glick, P., & Fiske, S. T. (2001). An ambivalent alliance: Hostile and benevolent sexism as complementary justifications of gender inequality. *American Psychologist, 56*, 109–118. doi:10.1037//O003-066X.56.2.1O9.

Greenwald, A. G., Poehlman, T. A., Uhlmann, E., & Banaji, M. R. (2009). Understanding and using the Implicit Association Test: III. Meta-analysis of predictive validity. *Journal of Personality and Social Psychology, 97*, 17–41. doi:10.1037/a0015575.

Hodson, G., Dovidio, J. F., & Gaertner, S. L. (2002). Processes in racial discrimination: Differential weighting of conflicting information. *Personality and Social Psychology Bulletin, 28*, 460–471. doi:10.1177/0146167202287004.

Mitchell, G., & Tetlock, P. E. (2006). Antidiscrimination law and the perils of mindreading. *Ohio State Law Journal, 67*, 1023–1121.

Nosek, B. A., Smyth, F. L., Hansen, J. J., Devos, T., Lindner, N. M., Ranganath, K. A., Smith, C. T., Olson, K. R., Chugh, D., Greenwald, A. G., & Banaji, M. R. (2007). Pervasiveness and correlates of implicit attitudes and stereotypes. *European Review of Social Psychology, 18*, 36–88. doi:10.1080/10463280701489053.

Pager, D. (2007). The use of field experiments for studies of employment discrimination: Contributions, critiques, and directions for the future. *The Annals of the American Academy of Political and Social Science, 609*, 104–133. doi:10.1177/0002716206294796.

Pager, D., & Western, B. (2006). *Race at work: Realities of race and criminal record in the New York City job market*. Report prepared for the 50th Anniversary of the New York City Commission on Human Rights. (Retrieved October 22, 2011 from http://www.princeton.edu/p̄ager/race_at_work.pdf).

Payne, B. K. (2006). Weapon bias: Split-second decisions and unintended stereotyping. *Current Directions in Psychological Science, 15*, 287–291. doi:10.1111/j.1467-8721.2006.00454.x.

Rooth, D. (2010). Automatic associations and discrimination in hiring: Real world evidence. *Labour Economics, 17*, 523–534. doi:10.1016/j.labeco.2009.04.005.

Sadler, M. S., Correll, J, Park, B., & Judd, C. M. (2012). The world is not Black and White: Racial bias in the decision to shoot in a multiethnic context. *Journal of Social Issues, 68*(2), 286–313. doi:10.1111/j.1540-4560.2011.01749.x

Sears, D. O., & Henry, P. J. (2005). Over thirty years later: A contemporary look at symbolic racism. In M. P. Zanna (Ed.), *Advances in experimental social psychology* (Vol. *37*, pp. 95–150). San Diego, CA: Academic Press. doi:10.1016/S0065-2601(05)37002-X.

Smedley, B. D., Stith, A. Y., & Nelson, A. R. (2002). *Unequal treatment: Confronting racial and ethnic disparities in health care*. Washington DC: National Academies Press.

Swim, J. K., Aikin, K. J., Hall, W. S., & Hunter, B. A. (1995). Sexism and racism: Old fashioned and modern prejudices. *Journal of Personality and Social Psychology, 68*, 199–214. doi:10.1037/0022-3514.68.2.199.

Tetlock, P. E., & Mitchell, G. (2008). Calibrating prejudice in milliseconds. *Social Psychology Quarterly, 71*, 12–16. doi:10.1177/019027250807100104.

Tetlock, P. E., & Mitchell, G. (2009). Implicit bias and accountability systems: What must organizations do to prevent discrimination? *Research in Organizational Behavior, 29*, 3–38. doi:10.1016/j.riob.2009.10.002.

U.S. Department of Justice. (2007). *Prison inmates at mid year 2007*. Bureau of Justice Statistics. (Retrieved June 10, 2008 from http://www.ojp.usdoj.gov/bjs/).
U.S. Department of Labor. (2012). *The employment situation: December 2011*. (Retrieved January 6, 2012 from http://www.bls.gov/cps/).
Wax, A. L. (1999). Discrimination as accident. *Indiana Law Journal, 74*, 1129–1231.
Weltfish, G. (Ed.). (1945a). Racial and religious prejudice in everyday living—First of two issues. *Journal of Social Issues* [Special Issue], *1*(1).
Weltfish, G. (Ed.). (1945b). Racial and religious prejudice in everyday living—Second of two issues. *Journal of Social Issues* [Special Issue], *1*(2).
Zuriff, G. E. (2002). Inventing racism. *Public Interest, 146*, 114–128.

JASON A. NIER is an Associate Professor of Psychology at Connecticut College in New London, Connecticut. He received his undergraduate degree from the Pennsylvania State University and his masters and doctorate in psychology from the University of Delaware. Dr. Nier is a social psychologist who specializes in the study of intergroup relations. Within the field of intergroup relations his research has focused primarily on the measurement of intergroup attitudes and stereotypes, the development of techniques to detect subtle bias in applied settings, and the study of interventions that reduce bias and conflict between groups. He has authored or coauthored numerous articles and book chapters, which have appeared in journals such as the *Journal of Personality and Social Psychology*, *Personality and Social Psychology Bulletin*, and *Group Processes and Intergroup Relations*. Nier also coauthored a book chapter, along with Samuel Gaertner, John Dovidio and their colleagues, which won the Gordon Allport Intergroup Relations Prize, awarded annually to the best paper in the field of intergroup relations.

SAMUEL L. GAERTNER (BA., 1964, Brooklyn College; PhD, 1970, The City University of New York: Graduate Center) is Professor of Psychology at the University of Delaware. His research interests involve intergroup relations with a focus on understanding and reducing prejudice, discrimination and racism. He has served on the editorial boards of the *Journal of Personality and Social Psychology*, *Personality and Social Psychology Bulletin*, and *Group Processes and Intergroup Relations*. Currently, Professor Gaertner is coeditor (with Rupert Brown, Sussex University, UK), of *Social Issues and Policy Review*, a journal of the Society for the Psychological Study of Social Issues. Professor Gaertner's research has been supported by grants from the Office of Naval Research, the National Institutes of Mental Health and the National Science Foundation. Professor Gaertner was awarded the Gordon Allport Intergroup Relations Prize in 1985 and 1998, as well as the Kurt Lewin Memorial Award (a career award, in 2004) from the Society for the Psychological Study of Social Issues, Division 9 of the American Psychological Association.

Journal of Social Issues, Vol. 68, No. 2, 2012, pp. 221–237

Identifying Discrimination at Work: The Use of Field Experiments

Devah Pager[*]
Princeton University

Bruce Western
Harvard University

Antidiscrimination law offers protection to workers who have been treated unfairly on the basis of their race, gender, religion, or national origin. In order for these protections to be invoked, however, potential plaintiffs must be aware of and able to document discriminatory treatment. Given the subtlety of contemporary forms of discrimination, it is often difficult to identify discrimination when it has taken place. The methodology of field experiments offers one approach to measuring and detecting hiring discrimination, providing direct observation of discrimination in real-world settings. In this article, we discuss the findings of two recent field experiments measuring racial discrimination in low wage labor markets. This research provides several relevant findings for researchers and those interested in civil rights enforcement: (1) it produces estimates of the rate of discrimination at the point of hire; (2) it yields evidence about the interactions associated with discrimination (many of which reveal the subtlety with which contemporary discrimination is practiced); and (3) it provides a vehicle for both research on and enforcement of antidiscrimination law.

Antidiscrimination law offers protection to workers who have been treated unfairly on the basis of their race, gender, religion, or national origin. In order for these protections to be invoked, however, potential plaintiffs must be aware of and able to document discriminatory treatment. In the case of unequal pay or wrongful termination, employees are often able to gather sufficient evidence based on information about coworkers or through interactions with the employer to identify

*Correspondence concerning this article should be addressed to Devah Pager, Department of Sociology, Princeton University, Princeton, NJ 08544 [e-mail: pager@princeton.edu].

This research was supported by generous grants from NIH (K01HD53694) and NSF (CAREER 0547810).

and document unfair treatment. In the case of hiring discrimination, by contrast, applicants have very little information with which to assess the legitimacy of employers' decision-making. With little or no information about the qualifications of other applicants, the relevant needs of the employer or requirements of the job, applicants who may have been unfairly dismissed on the basis of their race or gender are often left unaware or unable to take action (see also Bendick & Nunes, 2012).

Indeed, trends in the composition of antidiscrimination enforcement show that, in stark contrast to the composition of claims filed in the 1970s, claims today are far more likely to emphasize wrongful termination or on-the-job discrimination than to target instances of discrimination at the point of hire. In the mid-1960s charges of discrimination in hiring outnumbered charges of wrongful termination by 50%; by the mid-1980s this ratio had reversed by more than 6 to 1 (Donohue & Siegelman, 1991, p. 1015). This changing pattern of claims could reflect a change in the distribution of discrimination, indicating a reduction in discrimination at the point of hire relative to increases (relative or absolute) in wage discrimination or wrongful termination. The bulk of evidence, by contrast, suggests that declines in claims of hiring discrimination result from changing standards of legal evidence and the difficulties facing plaintiffs in acquiring the necessary information to pursue a successful claim (Nielsen & Nelson, 2005). In fact, changing patterns of enforcement may have the perverse effect of increasing the relative importance of discrimination at the point of hire. Declining enforcement of discrimination at the point of hire lowers the risk to employers who discriminate at this stage; the simultaneous increase in the rate of claims for wrongful termination increases the risks associated with firing minority workers (see Donohue & Siegelman, 1991, p. 1024; Posner, 1987, p. 519). Thus, despite the fact that claims of employment discrimination at any stage are rare, their relative distribution implies far less vulnerability for employers over decisions made at the initial-hiring stage. It may be the case, then, that even if overall levels of racial discrimination have declined, the relative importance of hiring discrimination (compared to discrimination at later stages) may be increasing in importance.

Like applicants, researchers face similar difficulties in identifying discrimination in labor markets. Social psychological studies demonstrate the persistence of stereotypes and biases and their effects on conscious and unconscious decision-making, but lab-based studies often have limited generalizability to real-world outcomes (Levitt & List, 2007) Survey-based analyses more typical of research in sociology and economics can identify race or gender gaps in employment or wages, but residual estimates from statistical models leave open the possibility of omitted variables that may inflate estimates of discrimination (see, for example, the debate between Cancio et al., 1996 and Farkas & Vicknair, 1996).

Direct measures of hiring discrimination are few and far between. Particularly in the contemporary United States where acts of discrimination are likely to be subtle and covert, it is extremely difficult to measure discrimination directly.

Fortunately, the methodology of field experiments offers one approach to the study of hiring discrimination which allows researchers to directly observe discrimination in real-world settings. In this article, we discuss the findings of two recent field experiments measuring racial discrimination in low wage labor markets. Complementing Bendick and Egan (2012)—which offers a review of the broader potential of field experiments—this article focuses on the use of field experiments to reveal both gross-hiring inequities and extremely subtle processes of bias in decision-making. Providing both quantitative evidence of hiring discrimination and qualitative evidence of bias in the hiring process, field experiments represent a powerful tool for researchers and those interested in civil rights enforcement. In the following discussion, we illustrate three desirable features of the field experiment: (1) it produces estimates of the rate of discrimination at the point of hire; (2) it yields evidence about the interactions associated with discrimination (many of which reveal the subtlety with which contemporary discrimination is practiced); and (3) it provides a vehicle for both research on and enforcement of antidiscrimination law.

Field Experiments for Measuring Discrimination

The basic design of an employment audit involves sending matched pairs of individuals (called testers) to apply for real job openings in order to see whether employers respond differently to applicants on the basis of selected characteristics. The appeal of the audit methodology lies in its ability to combine experimental methods with real-life contexts. This combination allows for greater generalizability than a lab experiment, and a better grasp of the causal mechanisms than what we can normally obtain from observational or correlational data. Indeed, for those with an interest in studying discrimination in real-world settings, the audit methodology provides an ideal tool.

The audit approach has been applied to numerous settings, including mortgage applications, negotiations at a car dealership, housing searches, and hailing a taxi (Ayres & Siegelman, 1995; Bendick et al., 1994; Cross et al., 1990; Massey & Lundy, 2001; Neumark, 1996; Ridley et al., 1989; Turner et al., 1991; Turner & Skidmore, 1999; Yinger, 1995). In the employment context, researchers have studied hiring discrimination by presenting employers with equivalent applicants who differ only by their race or ethnicity, either via resumes (known as "correspondence studies") or through in-person applicants ("in-person audit studies"). Marian Betrand and Sendhill Mullainathan (2004), for example, prepared two sets of matched resumes reflecting applicant pools of two skill levels. Using racially distinctive names to signal the race of applicants, the researchers mailed out resumes to more than 1,300 employers in Chicago and Boston, targeting job ads for sales, administrative support, and clerical and customer-services positions. The results of their study indicate that White-sounding names were 50% more likely to elicit positive responses from employers relative to equally qualified applicants with "Black" names (9.7% vs. 6.5%). Moreover, applicants with White names received a significant payoff to additional qualifications, while those with Black names did not. The racial gap among job applicants was thus higher among the more highly skilled applicant pairs than among those with fewer qualifications.

The primary advantage of the correspondence-test approach is that it requires no actual job applicants (only fictitious paper applicants). This is desirable for both methodological and practical reasons. Methodologically, the use of fictitious paper applicants allows researchers to create carefully matched applicant pairs without needing to accommodate the complexities of real people. The researcher thus has far more control over the precise content of "treatment" and "control" conditions. Practically, the reliance on paper applicants is also desirable in terms of the logistical ease with which the application process can be carried out. Rather than coordinating job visits by real people (creating opportunities for applicants to get lost, to contact the employer under differing circumstances), the correspondence test approach simply requires that resumes be sent out at specified intervals. Additionally, the small cost of postage or fax charges is trivial relative to the cost involved in hiring individuals to pose as job applicants.

At the same time, while correspondence tests do have many attractive features, there are also certain limitations of this design that have led some researchers to prefer the in-person audit approach. First, because correspondence tests rely on paper applications only, all relevant target information must be conveyed without the visual cues of in-person contact. This can pose complications for certain signals. The correspondence study discussed above, for example, used names like "Jamal" and "Lakisha" to signal African Americans. While these names are reliably associated with their intended race groups, some critics have argued that the more distinctive African American names are also associated with lower socioeconomic status, thus confounding the effects of race and class. Indeed, mother's education is a significant (negative) predictor of a child having a distinctively African American name (Fryer & Levitt, 2004). Directly assessing these connotations/associations is thus an important first step in developing the materials necessary for a strong test of discrimination.

In addition to signaling complexities, the correspondence-test method is also somewhat limited with respect to the types of jobs available for testing. The type of application procedure used in correspondence tests—sending resumes by mail—is typically reserved for studies of administrative, clerical, and other white-collar occupations. The vast majority of entry-level jobs, by contrast, often require in-person applications. For jobs such as busboy, messenger, laborer, or cashier, for example, a mailed-in resume would appear out of place.

Finally, as we discuss below, correspondence studies are limited in the information they provide about the evaluation process that precedes the hiring decision. The ability to observe the level of attention, encouragement, or hostility applicants elicit can provide important information about the subtle and contingent aspects of hiring process. For many of these reasons, some researchers have turned to the use of in-person audit studies.

Though in-person audits are time consuming and require intensive supervision, the approach offers several desirable qualities. In-person audits allow for the inclusion of a wide range of entry-level job types (which often require in-person applications); they provide a clear method for signaling race, without concerns over the class connotations of racially distinctive names (e.g., Fryer & Levitt, 2004); and they provide the opportunity to gather both quantitative and qualitative data, with information on whether or not the applicant receives the job as well as how he or she is treated during the interview process. Unfortunately, in part because of taxing logistical requirements, the use of in-person audit studies of employment remains quite rare, with only a handful of such studies conducted over the past 20 years (Bendick et al., 1991; Bendick et al. 1994; Cross et al. 1990; Pager, 2003; Turner et al. 1991; for a recent summary, see Pager 2007a).

The current article discusses the results from two recent field experiments that used an in-person audit approach to study racial and ethnic discrimination in the low wage labor markets of Milwaukee and New York City. In both studies, young men between the ages of 21 and 24 were hired to play the role of job applicants. These young men (called testers) were matched on the basis of their physical appearance (height, weight, attractiveness), verbal skills, and interactional styles (level of eye-contact, demeanor, and verbosity). Testers were assigned fictitious resumes indicating identical educational attainment, work experience (quantity and kind), and neighborhood of residence. Resumes were prepared in different fonts and formats and randomly varied across testers, with each resume used by testers from each race group. Testers presented themselves as high school graduates with steady work experience in entry-level jobs. Finally, the testers passed through a common training program to ensure uniform behavior in job interviews. While in the field, the testers dressed similarly and communicated with teammates by cell phone to anticipate unusual interview situations. In Milwaukee, racial comparisons are based on between-team comparisons, as Black and White testers applied to separate employers (the effect of a criminal record was measured within same-race pairs (see Pager, 2003). In New York City, Black, White, and Latino testers applied to the same set of employers for racial comparisons based within team.

Entry level job listings, defined as jobs requiring no previous experience and no education greater than high school, were randomly selected each week from the classified sections of the major city newspapers. Job titles included restaurant jobs, retail sales, warehouse workers, couriers, telemarketers, customer-service positions, clerical workers, stockers, movers, delivery drivers, and a wide range of other low-wage positions. Jobs were randomly assigned across teams, with testers in each team randomly varying the order in which they applied for each position. Eight testers in the Milwaukee study visited 350 employers; 10 testers in

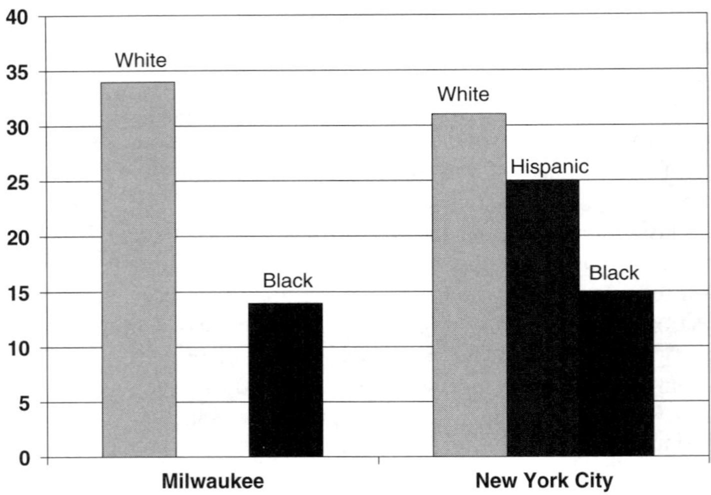

Fig. 1. Percent of applicants receiving a callback or job offer, by race.

Source. Pager, 2003; Pager, Western, and Bonikowski, 2009.

the New York City study visited 340 employers. The dependent variable in each study recorded any positive response in which a tester was either offered a job or called back for a second interview. Callbacks were recorded by voicemail boxes set up for each tester.

Results

Figure 1 presents the percent of applicants receiving a callback or job offer, by race of the applicant. The results across the two cities are highly consistent, with Whites receiving positive responses at roughly twice the rate of equally qualified Black applicants. In the Milwaukee study, Whites received callbacks or job offers in 34% of cases relative to 14% for equally qualified Black applicants ($p < .01$). In New York City, Whites received callbacks or job offers in 31% of cases, relative to 25% of Latino applicants and 15% for Blacks (for Black–White comparison, $p < .01$). The remarkable consistency of Black–White disparities across the two cities suggests that racial discrimination in hiring is not the product of distinctive local cultures or labor market dynamics but rather a more generalized phenomenon. Milwaukee and New York are quite distinct in their demographics, industrial composition, segregation patterns, and histories of racial conflict. Despite these differences, the prevalence and magnitude of discrimination in both cities is nearly identical.

Perceptibility of Discrimination

Despite the frequency of differential treatment recorded in these data, few of the incidents were noticeable from the job applicant's perspective. In the Milwaukee experiment, more than three fourths of applications were submitted with little or no personal contact with the employer. In such cases, applicants have virtually no information with which to assess their reception by employers, and employers make first-round cuts on the basis of superficial impressions (if they see the applicant), a name on the resume, or the brief information provided on the application form. Testers in Milwaukee generally reported cordial treatment by employers and, apart from a few notable exceptions, Black testers did not feel unwelcome submitting their applications.

In the New York City experiment, testers more often had the opportunity to talk with employers, with such conversations occurring in roughly half of the firms to which they applied. But even in these cases it was difficult to decipher the employer's preferences or biases based on a single interaction. Indeed, in many cases it was only after the side by side comparisons of test partners that evidence of possible bias could be detected. In one case from the New York City study, for example, the three testers inquired about a sales position at a retail clothing store. The employer spoke with each of the applicants and appeared to treat each one fairly.

> Joe, one of our African-American tester, reported: "[The employer] said the position was just filled and that she would be calling people in for an interview if the person doesn't work out." Josue, his Latino-test partner, was told something very similar: "She informed me that the position was already filled, but did not know if the hired employee would work out. She told me to leave my resume with her." By contrast, when Simon, their White-test partner, applied last, his experience was notably different: "... I asked what the hiring process was—if they're taking applications now, interviewing, etc. She looked at my application. 'You can start immediately?' Yes. 'Can you start tomorrow?' Yes. '10 a.m.' She was very friendly and introduced me to another woman (White, 28) at the cash register who will be training me."

When evaluated individually, these interactions would not have raised any concern. All three testers were asked about their availability and about their sales experience. The employer appeared willing to consider each of them. But when it came down to it, it was the White applicant who walked out with the job.

Indeed, in the majority of applications testers did not detect signs from employers that anticipated the differential treatment we observed. As a way of gauging testers' subjective experiences, we had testers in the New York City study fill out "treatment thermometers" recording their perception of how they were treated by an employer after each visit. On a scale of 1 to 100, the average rating for Blacks was 69.6 overall, and among Blacks experiencing differential treatment, 67.5. This small and statistically insignificant decrease in perceived treatment suggests that employers' preferences and biases were largely concealed in the interview process, with the majority of Black applicants unaware that their candidacy was in question.

Some have argued that Blacks are quick to interpret ambiguous interactions as evidence of racism (Ford, 2008), a concern particularly relevant to a study that relies on the performance of testers who are aware of the intended focus of the research (Heckman, 1998). Quite unlike expectations that testers would be vigilant in perceiving the slightest hint of foul play, the present research suggests that testers were rarely able to identify discrimination at work. Indeed, this research is more consistent with social psychological studies that suggest targets of discrimination often underestimate the significance of discrimination in their own lives, even as they recognize it as a problem facing their group (Crosby, 1984; Taylor et al., 1990).

In addition to testers' weak ability to perceive discrimination in action, testers' perceptions of their treatment by employers did little to predict their actual likelihood of employment. There was essentially zero correlation between testers' ratings on the "treatment thermometer" and their likelihood of getting a callback. Excluding those cases in which testers were offered the job on the spot (and therefore, the tester had concrete feedback regarding the employers' approval), the correlation between the "treatment thermometer" score and the likelihood of a callback was .02 for Whites and .05 for Blacks. The friendliness or gruffness of an employer thus did little to signal actual-hiring intentions. Even among these "professional applicants"—in the sense that our testers were being paid to monitor the application process and had significant experience with a wide range of employment interactions—their ability to detect racial preferences at work was extremely limited.

In most cases, it is only by comparing the experiences of similar applicants side by side that we observe the ways in which race appears to shape employers' evaluations in subtle but systematic ways. These patterns have significant implications for the enforcement of antidiscrimination law. The reliance on individual plaintiffs to come forward with evidence of discrimination represents a bar that few incidents of hiring discrimination can meet. In contrast to cases of wage discrimination or wrongful termination, in which victims presumably have access to better information about the comparative treatment of other similarly situated employees, job applicants have access to very little information with which to gauge suspicions of discrimination. Moreover, because acts of discrimination are themselves typically subtle and covert, the applicant's suspicions are unlikely to be aroused even when systematic or regularly occurring forms of bias are solidly in place. Under these conditions, we would expect the vast majority of incidents of hiring discrimination to go undetected. The difficulty in identifying and enforcing discrimination at the point of hire leaves this stage of the employment process particularly vulnerable to the influences of persistent racial bias.

Are Employers Hiding Racist Beliefs?

Employers are adamant that race does not affect their decisions about who to hire; they speak about looking for the best-possible candidate whether "White, Black, Yellow or Green" (employer at a retail clothing store). In order to better understand employers' perspectives on hiring, we conducted in-depth interviews with 55 employers in New York City (Pager & Karafin, 2009). When asked what his sense was of how African American men are doing in terms of employment compared to other groups, the manager of a supply company simply said, "Skip that question because that has nothing to do with me. I just hire people based on their abilities." Another employer for a retail sales company expressed a common sentiment of universality: "Number one, they are all the same to me. When I look, I don't look at religion, I don't look at what color you are because we are all human beings." These employers, like many we spoke with, appear committed to an evaluation process that is blind to race or color.

At the same time, when asked to step back from their own hiring process to think about race differences more generally, employers were surprisingly willing to express strong opinions about the characteristics and attributes they perceive among different groups of workers. Indeed, the plurality of employers we spoke with, when considering Black men independent of their own workplace, charac-terized this group according to three common tropes: as lazy or having a poor work ethic; threatening or criminal; or possessing an inappropriate style or demeanor (Pager & Karafin, 2009). For example, one employer at a retail store said simply, "I will tell you the truth. African Americans don't want to work." An employer at a local garment factory commented, "I find that the great majority of this minority group that you are talking about either doesn't qualify for certain jobs because they look a little bit more, they come on as if, well, they are threatening." Previ-ous studies have found similar characterizations by employers in the context of open-ended interviews (Kirschenman & Neckerman, 1991; Moss & Tilly, 2001; Waldinger & Lichter, 2003; Wilson, 1996).

One possible interpretation of this discrepancy, between employers' charac-terization of their own color-blind hiring philosophy and their strong negative portrayals of Black men, is simply that employers work to conceal the ways that their own biases result in discriminatory hiring practices. Surely employers who hold such negative stereotypes about African Americans are unlikely to give them a fair shake in the hiring process. And yet, a puzzling finding in attempts to match employer attitudes with hiring behavior is the striking lack of consistency between the two (Moss & Tilly, 2001; Pager & Quillian, 2005; see also LaPiere, 1934). In some cases, employers expressing strong negative attitudes about Black men appear more likely to hire Black-male applicants. Indeed, Moss and Tilly (2001) report the surprising finding that "businesses where a plurality of managers com-plained about Black motivation [and other negative characteristics] are more likely to hire Black men" (p.151). These results point the fact that hiring decisions are influenced by a complex range of factors, conscious racial attitudes being only one. The stated preferences of employers, then, leave uncertain the degree to which negative attitudes about Blacks translate into active forms of discrimination.

Indeed, it is difficult to know exactly what is going through employers' minds as they evaluate candidates of different races. Based on the evidence we can glean from the interactions between testers and employers in our field experiments, it seemed that only in rare cases were employers categorically unwilling to hire African Americans (see Pager et al., 2009, p. 787–788). Rather, employers often seemed genuinely interested in evaluating the qualifications of a given candidate, irrespective of their race in an effort to identify the best candidate for the job. Unfortunately, these evaluations themselves appeared influenced by race. Indeed, in analyzing the interactions between employers and our testers, we noticed a pattern in which employers appeared to perceive real-skill or experience differences among applicants despite the fact that the testers' resumes were designed to convey identical qualifications (for additional discussion and analyses of these interactions see Pager, Western, and Bonikowski, 2009). In one case from NYC, for example, the testers applied for a job at a moving company.

> Joe, the African American applicant, spoke with the employer about his prior experience at a delivery company. Nevertheless, "[the employer] told me that he couldn't use me because he is looking for someone with moving experience." Josue, his Latino partner, presented his experience as a stocker at a delivery company and reports a similar reaction: "He then told me that since I have no experience . . . there is nothing he could do for me." Simon, their White-test partner, presented his identical qualifications to which the employer responds more favorably: "'To be honest, we're looking for someone with specific moving experience. But because you've worked for [a storage company], that has a little to do with moving.' He wanted me to come in tomorrow between 10 and 11 for an interview."

The employer is consistent in his preference for workers with relevant prior experience, but he is willing to apply a more flexible, inclusive standard in evaluating the experience of the White applicant than in the case of the minority applicants.

When applying for a job as a line cook at a midlevel Manhattan restaurant, the three testers encountered similar concerns about their lack of relevant experience.

> Josue, the Latino tester, reported, "[The employer] then asked me if I had any prior kitchen or cooking experience. I told him that I did not really have any, but that I worked alongside cooks at [my prior job as a server]. He then asked me if I had any 'knife' experience and I told him no . . . He told me he would give me a try and wanted to know if I was available this coming Sunday at 2 p.m." Simon, his White-test partner, was also invited to come back for a trial period. By contrast, Joe, the Black tester, found that "they are only looking for experienced-line cooks." Joe wrote, "I started to try and convince him to give me a chance but he cut me off and said I didn't qualify."

None of the testers had direct experience with kitchen work, but the White and Latino applicants were viewed as viable prospects while the Black applicant was rejected because he lacked experience. The shifting standards used by employers, offering more latitude to marginally skilled White applicants than similarly qualified minorities, suggests that even the evaluation of "objective" information can be affected by underlying racial considerations (see Pager, Western, & Bonikowski, 2009).

The shifting standards we witness in these interactions are less consistent with a model of traditional prejudice than with a more contingent and subtle conceptualization of racial attitudes. According to Dovidio and Gaertner's (2004) theory of aversive racism, for example, many individuals in contemporary society experience few conscious anti-Black sentiments, and traditional measures of prejudice have substantially declined. At the same time, there remains a high level of generalized anxiety or discomfort with Blacks that can shape interracial interaction and decision-making. Fueled largely by unconscious negative associations rather than overt forms of prejudice, aversive racism represents a more subtle and difficult-to-identify form of bias. Aversive racists believe in equality and consciously eschew distinctions on the basis of race; unconscious bias, however, leads to situations in which subtle forms of discrimination persist without the actor's awareness (see also Gaertner & Dovidio, 1986). In a laboratory experiment simulating a hiring situation, for example, the authors found little evidence of discrimination in cases where Black and White applicants were either highly qualified or poorly qualified for the position. When applicants had acceptable but ambiguous qualifications, however, participants were nearly 70% more likely to recommend the White applicant than the Black applicant (Dovidio & Gaertner, 2000; see also Hodson, Dovidio, & Gaertner, 2002). Few of the participants seemed to categorically believe that Whites were better employees than Blacks; in the context of uncertainty, however, race provided a kind of tie-breaker. Assessments of person-specific traits or characteristics, then, can take on different meanings when evaluated in the context of group-based expectations. Particularly in assessing characteristics with some degree of ambiguity—something that characterizes many of the qualities or skills expected of low-wage workers—employers may be more heavily influenced by prior expectations or unconscious stereotypes in forming their evaluations (see also Biernat & Kobrynowicz, 1997; Darley & Gross, 1983).

The fact that employers' preferences and biases are more often manifested through subtle and dynamic interactions, rather than outright rejection of minority candidates, itself poses problems for the enforcement of antidiscrimination law. It is extremely difficult to find evidence of intent—often a prerequisite to a successful antidiscrimination case—when an employer does not consciously intend to exclude Blacks, but instead selectively attends to information that presents a more favorable impression of White candidates. This complex process of discrimination is far more difficult to document in legal cases, leaving a more limited range of possible remedies for subtle and unconscious discrimination. Indeed, with both job seeker and employer often unaware that any systematic bias is in effect, it becomes difficult to remedy subtle forms of discrimination without more proactive efforts at monitoring and enforcing the requirements of antidiscrimination law.

Field Experiments for the Purposes of Enforcement

The use of field experiments in research on discrimination represents an important tool for informing both social science and public opinion. The experimental method offers a clean design with which to assess causal effects, while simultaneously providing simple and straightforward measures of discrimination that can be easily understood by a lay audience. Given recent public-opinion surveys that demonstrate widespread skepticism over the persistence of discrimination, research of this kind can play an important role by providing "clear and convincing evidence" that discrimination remains an important feature of contemporary U.S. labor markets. Indeed, more than 80% of White respondents indicate that Blacks have "as good a chance as White people . . . to get any kind of job for which they are qualified," and similar proportions believe that Blacks are not discriminated against in access to housing or managerial jobs. Respondents are more evenly split when asked about whether Blacks are treated fairly by the police (53% agree) (Schuman et al., 1997, p. 159–160). To the extent that public opinion concerning the relevance of discrimination shapes support for public policy efforts to address racial bias, the existence of reliable and accessible evidence on this question can play a potentially important role in shaping policy discussions.

At the same time, the field experimental approach can also play a more active role in support of antidiscrimination law and policy. Indeed, the audit method was initially designed for the enforcement of antidiscrimination law. Testers have been used to detect racially discriminatory practices among real estate agents, landlords, and lenders, providing evidence of differential treatment for use in litigation. In these discrimination cases, testers serve as the plaintiffs. Despite the fact that the testers themselves were not in fact seeking employment (or housing) at the time their application was submitted, their treatment nevertheless represents an actionable claim. This issue has received close scrutiny by the courts, including rulings by the highest federal courts (e.g., Havens Realty Corp. v. Coleman, 455 U.S. 363, 373, 1982).

The differences between audit studies for research purposes and those used for enforcement are subtle, but are worth careful attention. Audit studies for research purposes are oriented not toward a specific intervention, but rather to obtaining accurate measures of the prevalence of discrimination across a broad sector or metropolitan area. The interest is in average treatment effects rather than in isolating discriminatory treatment at any single firm or agency. Studies of this kind typically include no more than a single audit per employer, with discrimination detected through systematic patterns across employers, rather than repeated acts of discrimination by a single employer. The design of research-based audit studies has important implications for what kinds of conclusions we can draw from their results. From research based audit studies, it is not possible to draw conclusions about the discriminatory tendencies of any given employer. Indeed, even a nondiscriminatory employer, when forced to choose between two equally qualified candidates, will choose the White applicant half the time. Only by looking at generalized patterns across a large number of employers can we determine whether hiring appears systematically influenced by race or other stigmatizing characteristics. The point of research based audit studies, then, is to assess the prevalence of discrimination across the labor market, rather than to intervene in particular sites of discrimination.

Testing for litigation, by contrast, requires multiple audits of the same employer (or real estate agent, etc.) to detect consistent patterns of discrimination by that particular individual and/or company. Recognizing that single-audit outcomes may be affected by chance or circumstance, building a case against an individual employer requires repeated measures of differential treatment that systematically bias one group relative to another. This approach often requires the recruitment of a much larger number of testers (and/or resume pairs) so that multiple unique-tester pairs can visit the employer without arousing suspicion. The conceptual underpinnings across audit types are very similar, but their design and implementation diverges considerably. Remaining cognizant of the goals and possibilities of each approach is important in constructing an appropriate study design.

Why isn't Testing Used More?

Testing has been used as a research tool and an enforcement mechanism by the Department of Housing and Urban Development (HUD) to address discrimination in housing markets since the early 1970s. As recently as 1998, HUD allocated $7.5 million to fund a 20-city testing study measuring racial and ethnic discrimination in housing rental, sales, and lending markets, and to track changes over time according to testing measures of discrimination collected over the preceding two decades (Turner et al., 2002). Testing has been widely viewed as an effective vehicle for enforcing Fair Housing laws and for reducing the degree of active discrimination in housing markets (Turner et al., 2002; Yinger, 1995).

The case of employment has followed a very different path. In addition to the logistical concerns discussed above, employment testing has further been stymied by a hostile political environment that has limited the resources available for "testing" the prevalence of discrimination in labor markets. In 1997, the Equal Employment Opportunity Commission (EEOC) announced a plan to launch a series of pilot employment audits across the country to support a more proactive model of enforcement of antidiscrimination law (http://www.eeoc.gov/press/12–5-97.html). Congressional leadership, at that time controlled by conservative house speaker Newt Gingrich, objected vehemently to this strategy of enforcement. According to Gingrich, "The use of employment testers, frankly, undermines the credibility of the EEOC. The government should not sanction applicants' misrepresentation of their credentials to prospective employers. The use of testers not only causes innocent businesses to waste resources (interviewing candidates not interested in actual employment), but also puts a government agency in the business of entrapment. It assumes guilt where there has been no indication of discriminatory behavior (Gingrich, 1998)" That year's budget appropriations bill provided funding for the EEOC conditional on eliminating of the use of testing. Unlike the arena of housing discrimination, in which dozens of federally sponsored testing studies have taken place, the use of the audit methodology for both research and litigation in the area of employment discrimination has thus remained negligible.

The ethical concerns raised by Gingrich are important and should not be dismissed out of hand. Indeed, audit studies require that employers are unwittingly recruited for participation and then led to believe that the testers are viable job candidates. Time spent reviewing applications and/or interviewing applicants will therefore impose a cost on the subject. Most employment audit studies limit their samples to employers for entry-level positions—those requiring the least intensive review—in part to minimize the time employers spend evaluating phony applicants. The field experiments reported in this article further limited imposition on employers by restricting audits to the first stage of the employment process. Candidate reviews in these cases typically consisted of no more than a short review of the application and/or resume and, in a smaller fraction of cases, a short interview (Pager, 2003; Pager et al., 2009; see Pager 2007 for a more extensive discussion of ethical issues related to audit research).

While the costs to employers should not be overlooked, they must also be examined relative to the possible benefits resulting from this approach. As noted earlier, in the absence of some form of proactive investigation, hiring discrimination remains extremely difficult to identify or address. Job applicants typically have too little information at their disposal to make credible claims, and employers can easily come up with reasonable post hoc justifications for hiring decisions in individual cases. It is only through repeated observation of systematic hiring bias that discrimination at the early stages of the hiring process can be reliably identified and remedied. Recently, the EEOC has shown signs of renewed interest in pursuing a testing program. It remains to be seen whether, within the prevailing political climate, this preliminary agenda can be realized.

Discussion

By focusing on discrimination at the point of hire, field experiments uncover an important and much under-investigated source of racial disadvantage in the labor market. According to the results of our experiments, Blacks are less than half as likely to receive consideration by employers relative to equally qualified Whites across a wide range of low-wage jobs. Though the subtle nature of contemporary discrimination in most cases leaves applicants unaware of differential treatment, the ultimate distribution of employment opportunities across equally qualified applicants reveals a process of decision-making very much shaped by race. This research emphasizes the need for direct measures of discrimination in real-life settings; and suggests that enforcement efforts that rely on reactive claims will miss much of the discrimination that takes place in labor markets today.

Of course field experiments are not appropriate for measuring all types of discrimination. Discrimination at higher levels of the corporate hierarchy and among jobs filled through personal networks is less identifiable using this methodology. Likewise, the many informal channels through which preferences and biases are enacted in the workplace are difficult to document using an audit methodology (Collins, 1989). For a complete picture of discrimination in labor markets, then, we require a range of methodological approaches and perspectives. This essay focuses on the merits of the audit methodology as a tool for both research and enforcement of discrimination in employment. Complementing other approaches, this methodology has much to offer in pursuing the goal of equal access to employment.

References

Ayres, I., & Siegelman, P. (1995). Race and gender discrimination in bargaining for a new car. *American Economic Review, 85*, 304–321.

Bendick, M. Jr., Jackson, C., Reinoso, V., & Hodges, L. (1991). Discrimination against Latino job applicants: A controlled experiment. *Human Resource Management, 30*, 469–484. doi: 10.1002/hrm.3930300404

Bendick, M. Jr., Jackson, C., & Reinoso, V. (1994). Measuring employment discrimination through controlled experiments. *Review of Black Political Economy, 23*, 25–48.

Bendick, M. Jr., & Nunes, A. (2012). Developing the research basis for controlling bias in hiring. *Journal of Social Issues, 68*(2), 238–262. doi: 10.1111/j.1540-4560.2011.01747.x

Bertrand, M., & Mullainathan, S. (2004). Are Emily and Greg more employable than Lakisha and Jamal? A field experiment on labor market discrimination. *The American Economic Review, 94*, 991–1013. doi: 10.1257/0002828042002561

Biernat, M., & Kobrynowicz, D. (1997). Gender and race-based standards of competence: Lower minimum standards but higher ability standards for devalued groups. *Journal of Personality and Social Psychology, 72*, 544–557. doi: 10.1037//0022-3514.72.3.544

Cancio, A., Silvia, T., Evans, D., & Maume, D. (1996). Reconsidering the declining significance of race: Racial differences in early career wages. *American Sociological Review, 61*, 541–56. doi: 10.2307/2096391

Collins, S. (1989). The marginalization of Black executives. *Social Problems, 36*, 317–331.

Crosby, F. (1984). The denial of personal discrimination. *American Behavioral Scientist. 27*, 371–386. doi: 10.1177/000276484027003008

Cross, H., Kenney, G., Mell, J., & Zimmerman, W. (1990). *Employer hiring practices: Differential treatment of hispanic and Anglo job seekers.* Washington, DC: Urban Institute Press.

Darley, J., & Gross, P. (1983). A hypothesis-confirming bias in labeling effects. *Journal of Personality and Social Psychology, 44*, 20–33. doi: 10.1037/0022-3514.44.1.20

Donohue, III John J., & Siegelman P. (1991). The changing nature of employment discrimination litigation. *Stanford Law Review, 43*, 983–1033

Dovidio, J., & Gaertner, S. (2000). Aversive racism and selection decisions. *Psychological Science, 11*, 315–319. doi: 10.1111/1467-9280.00262

Dovidio, J., & Gaertner, S. (2004). Aversive racism. In M. P. Zanna (Ed.), *Advances in experimental social psychology* (Vol. 36, pp. 1–52). San Diego, CA: Academic Press.

Fryer, R. Jr., & Levitt, S. (2004). The causes and consequences of distinctively Black names. *The Quarterly Journal of Economics, 119*, 767–805.

Gaertner, S. L., & Dovidio, J. F. (1986). The aversive form of racism. In J. F. Dovidio & S. L. Gaertner (Eds.), *Prejudice, discrimination, and racism* (pp. 61–89). Orlando, FL: Academic Press.

Gingrich, N. (1998). Testimony of House Speaker Newt Gingrich before the House Subcommittee on Employer-Employee Relations on "The Future Direction of the Equal Employment Opportunity Commission," March 3, 1998. Retrieved from: http://www.house.gov/ed_workforce/hearings/105th/eer/eeoc3398/gingrich.htm

Heckman, J. (1998). Detecting discrimination. *The Journal of Economic Perspectives, 12*, 101–116. doi: 10.1257/jep.12.2.101

Farkas, G., & Vicknair, K. (1996). Appropriate tests of racial wage discrimination require controls for cognitive skill: Comment on Cancio, Evans, and Maume. *American Sociological Review, 61*, 557–60.

Ford, R. (2008). *The Race Card*. New York: Picador.

Hodson, G., Dovidio, J., & Gaertner, S. (2002). Processes in racial discrimination: Differential weighting of conflicting information. *Personality and Social Psychology Bulletin, 28*, 460–471. doi: 10.1177/0146167202287004

Kirschenman, J., & Neckerman, K. (1991). We'd love to hire them, but . . . : The meaning of race for employers. In C. Jencks & P. Peterson (Eds.), *The Urban Underclass* (pp. 203–234). Washington, DC: Brookings Institution.

LaPiere, R. (1934). Attitudes versus actions. *Social Forces, 13*, 230–237.

Levitt, S., & List, J. (2007). What do laboratory experiments measuring social preferences reveal about the real world? *Journal of Economic Perspectives, 21*, 153–174. doi: 10.1257/jep.21.2.153

Massey, D., & Lundy, G. (2001). Use of Black English and racial discrimination in urban housing markets: New methods and findings. *Urban Affairs Review, 36*, 452–469. doi: 10.1177/10780870122184957

Moss, P., & Tilly, C. (2001). *Stories employers tell: Race, skill, and hiring in America*. New York: Russell Sage Foundation.

Neumark, D. (1996). Sex discrimination in restaurant hiring: An audit study. *Quarterly Journal of Economics, 111*, 915–941. doi: 10.2307/2946676

Nielsen, L., & Nelson, R. (2005). Scaling the pyramid: A sociolegal model of employment discrimination litigation. In L.B. Nielsen & R.L. Nelson (Eds.), *Handbook of employment discrimination research* (pp. 3–34). Dordrecht, Netherlands: Springer.

Pager, D. (2003). The mark of a criminal record. *American Journal of Sociology, 108*, 937–975.

Pager, D., & Quillian, L. (2005). Walking the talk: What employers say versus what they do. *American Sociological Review, 70*, 355–380. doi: 10.1177/000312240507000301

Pager, D. (2007). The use of field experiments for studies of employment discrimination: Contributions, critiques, and directions for the future. *Annals of the American Academy of Political and Social Science, 609*, 104–133. doi: 10.1177/0002716206294796

Pager, D., Western, B., & Bonikowski, B. (2009). Discrimination in a low wage labor market: A field experiment. *American Sociological Review, 74*, 777–799. doi: 10.1177/000312240907400505

Pager, D., & Karafin, D. (2009). Bayesian bigot? Statistical discrimination, stereotypes, and employer decision-making. *Annals of the American Academy of Political and Social Sciences, 621*, 70–93. doi: 10.1177/0002716208324628

Posner, R. (1987). The efficiency and efficacy of Title VII. *University of Pennsylvania Law Review, 136*, 513–21.

Ridley, S., Bayton, J., & Outtz, J. (1989). *Taxi service in the district of Columbia: Is it influenced by Patrons' race and destination?* Washington, DC: Washington Lawyers' Committee for Civil Rights under the Law.

Schuman, H., Steeh, C., Bobo, L., & Krysan, M. (1997). *Racial attitudes in America: Trends and interpretations*. Cambridge, MA: Harvard University Press.

Taylor, D., Wright, S., Moghaddam, F., & Lalonde, R. (1990). The personal/group discrimination discrepancy: Perceiving my group, but not myself, to be a target for discrimination. *Personality and Social Psychology Bulletin, 16*, 254–262. doi: 10.1177/01461672901620006

Turner, M., Fix, M., & Struyk, R. (1991). *Opportunities denied, opportunities diminished: Racial discrimination in hiring*. Washington, DC: Urban Institute Press.

Turner, M., & Skidmore, F. (1999). *Mortgage lending discrimination: A review of existing evidence*. Washington, DC: Urban Institute Press.

Turner, M., Ross, S., Gaister, G., & Yinger, J. (2002). *Discrimination in metropolitan housing markets: National results from Phase 1 HDS 2000*. Washington, DC: Urban Institute, Department of Housing and Urban Development. Retrieved from: http://www.huduser.org/intercept.asp?loc=/Publications/pdf/Phase1_Report.pdf

Waldinger, R., & Lichter, M. (2003). *How the other half works: Immigration and the social organization of labor*. California: The University of California Press.

Wilson, W. (1996). *When work disappears: The world of the new urban poor*. New York: Vintage Books.

Yinger, J. (1995). *Closed doors, opportunities lost: The continuing costs of housing discrimination*. New York: Russell Sage Foundation.

DEVAH PAGER is an Associate Professor of Sociology and Co-Director of the Joint Degree Program in Social Policy at Princeton University. Her research focuses on institutions affecting racial stratification, including education, labor markets, and the criminal justice system. Pager's recent research has involved a series of field experiments studying discrimination against minorities and ex-offenders in the low wage labor market. Her book, *Marked: Race, Crime, and Finding Work in an Era of Mass Incarceration* (University of Chicago, 2007), investigates the racial and economic consequences of large-scale imprisonment for contemporary U.S. labor markets. Pager holds Masters Degrees from Stanford University and the University of Cape Town, and a PhD from the University of Wisconsin–Madison.

BRUCE WESTERN is Professor of Sociology and Director of the Malcolm Wiener Center for Social Policy at the Harvard Kennedy School of Government. His research interests are in the field of social stratification and inequality, political sociology, and statistical methods. He is the author of Punishment and Inequality in America, a study of the growth and social impact of the American penal system. His first book, *Between Class and Market*, examined the development and decline of labor unions in the postwar industrialized democracies. He is currently studying the social impact of rising-income inequality in the United States. Western taught at Princeton from 1993 to 2007 and received his PhD in sociology from UCLA.

Journal of Social Issues, Vol. 68, No. 2, 2012, pp. 238–262

Developing the Research Basis for Controlling Bias in Hiring

Marc Bendick, Jr.[*]
Bendick and Egan Economic Consultants, Inc.

Ana P. Nunes
Institute of Social Sciences of the University of Lisbon

Discrimination based on race, ethnicity, national origin, gender, age, disability, gender orientation, and other characteristics continues to distort employers' hiring decisions and thereby limit employment opportunities for historically excluded groups. Research in psychology, sociology, economics, and management provides insights concerning the mechanisms of bias and interventions to mitigate their effects, but important questions remain. The innovative research technique of matched pair testing offers laboratory-like controlled conditions in quasi-experiments in real-world hiring situations. We propose seven types of testing studies to advance conceptual understanding of hiring bias and improve hiring practices.

Employers in America's private sector decide who to hire 60 million times a year—more than 250,000 times each work day (U.S. Bureau of Labor Statistics, 2009). For successful job candidates, the hiring process provides employment and determines initial job titles, work assignments, and wages, which, in turn, often influence that employee's career for years thereafter. For successful and unsuccessful job applicants, it also provides job-seeking experience, career information, and encouragement or discouragement. Few human resource management processes rival hiring in impact on the distribution of employment opportunities and rewards.

---

[*]Correspondence concerning this article should be addressed to Marc Bendick, Jr., Bendick and Egan Economic Consultants, Inc., 4411 Westover Place NW, Washington, DC 20016 [e-mail: bendickegan@mindspring.com].

The authors contributed equally to this article.

An earlier version was presented at the Monash University Conference on Field Experiments on Discrimination in Markets, Prato, Italy (2005).

Controlling bias that potentially distorts these high-stakes decisions has long been a goal of American society as reflected in federal, state, and local laws against hiring discrimination and requiring affirmative action. It has also motivated many employers to adopt highly structured hiring procedures (Bielby, 2000), train hiring decision makers (Bendick, Egan & Lofhjelm, 2001), and actively "manage workforce diversity" (Kochan et al., 2003).

Drawing primarily on studies in the United States and other industrialized economies, Section I of this article documents that research in psychology, sociology, economics, and management offers many insights into the mechanisms of bias and the likely interventions to mitigate their effects. However, as Sections II and III document, despite considerable progress, a mix of covert and overt bias continues to pervade the American hiring system. Accordingly, this article proposes additional research to support further changes in hiring practices. Section IV proposes four types of studies to expand conceptual understanding of hiring bias, while Section V proposes three types to enhance the influence of such research on hiring practitioners.

Other publications synthesize research on employment bias and identify future research needs (e.g., Brief, 2008; Dipboye & Colella, 2005; Stockdale & Crosby, 2004). The present article differs from these by focusing on hiring and one innovative research methodology—matched pair testing—with unique potential for studying hiring. This technique is described in Section III.

Section I: Research-Based Predictions about Hiring Bias

The Civil Rights Movement of the 1960s was a reaction to widespread, blatant, and sometimes legally codified discrimination against African Americans and other groups. Correspondingly, ensuing antidiscrimination legislation—prominently, the Civil Rights Act of 1964 (mandating equal opportunity), Executive Order 11246 (establishing affirmative action), the Age Discrimination in Employment Act, the Americans with Disabilities Act, and counterpart state and local laws—aimed foremost at employers' *conscious* behavior. Violations of these statutes are most commonly proven through documentation of discriminatory acts (e.g., use of racial epithets in the workplace) or measurement of employment outcomes (e.g., few minority employees when many qualified minority job applicants are available).

Behavioral science research raises important concerns about the limitations of this approach. In particular, it questions the effectiveness of seeking to change employer behavior without explicitly addressing the often-unconscious attitudes and perceptions underlying that behavior (Gaertner & Dovidio, 2005). Equally, it suggests the need to improve specific employment processes (such as interviewing, performance evaluation, or succession planning), not simply the employment outcomes they help to shape. At least three lines of research raise such concerns explicitly or implicitly.

Stereotypes Infect Us All

The first line of research explores stereotypes and their role in discriminatory behavior. *Implicit bias*—unconscious association of traits with members of a demographic group (Greenwald, McGhee, & Schwartz, 1998; Nosek, Greenwald, & Banaji, 2005)—has been demonstrated and these associations shown to correlate with biased behavior (Dovidio, Kawakami, & Gaertner, 2002). When these associations are activated in the hiring process, their predominantly negative content about traditionally excluded groups (e.g., African Americans are uneducated; women are not career-committed) handicap members of these groups in competing for jobs.

Decades of related research have further elucidated how stereotypes unconsciously influence perceptions and evaluations, and process central to employment decisions such as hiring. For example, studies have documented that in evaluating members of a stereotyped group, individuals pay more attention to information consistent with a stereotype than to inconsistent information (Koomen & Dijker, 1998), interpret ambiguous information to confirm stereotypes (Hilton & Van Hippel, 1996), seek information confirming stereotypes at a greater rate than that contradicting them (Erber & Fiske, 1984), and are unaffected by information that a stereotype is invalid (Nelson, Acker, & Manis, 1996). Individuals also make memory errors consistent with stereotypes (Eberhardt, Dasgupta, & Banaszynski, 2003), even when recalling objective facts such as test scores (Darley & Gross, 1983). Together, such processes explain how hiring decision makers may honestly perceive themselves as making unbiased decisions reflecting objective differences in applicants' qualifications when, in fact, they have not.

Individuals Cannot Readily Counter Stereotypes

A second line of research demonstrates the difficulties that stigmatized groups face when attempting to ameliorate the adverse effects of negative stereotypes. For example, when an individual performs in a way inconsistent with a stereotype, that performance gets discounted as reflecting exceptional circumstances such as luck (Swim & Sanna, 1996). Furthermore, social congruity theory (Eagly & Karau, 2002; see also Fiske, Bersoff, Borgida, Deaux, & Heilman, 1991) predicts that members of a stereotyped group who behave or occupy social roles inconsistent with a stereotype experience stronger adverse reactions than if they conform.

Compounding these difficulties, biased treatment itself or anticipation of it, can adversely affect the actual performance of employees or job applicants. For example, Word, Zamma, & Cooper (1974; see also Shelton, Richeson, &

Salvatore, 2005) demonstrated that White job interviewers sat further away from African American job applicants than White applicants, made less eye contact, and made more speech errors during interviews, and that this interviewer behavior caused applicants to perform less well during interviews. That is, these situations may elicit *stereotype threat* (Roberson & Kulik, 2007; Steele & Aronson, 1995) leading minorities and women to perform less well when they are aware that their performance may confirm a negative stereotype (e.g., when gender is made salient prior to a math exam).

Shared Traits Confer Advantage

A third line of research focuses on *in-group bias*, or the tendency for individuals to prefer members of their own group or derogate those of other groups, as part of maintaining a positive social identity (Brewer, 1979; Tajfel, 1982). Operating consciously or unconsciously, this process then leads to employment decisions not based on applicants' abilities to perform the job, but rather categorization. Its presence has been empirically demonstrated in the laboratory with even minimal or fabricated groups (Hertel & Kerr, 2001; Tajfel, Billig, Bundy, & Flament, 1971). The same processes are likely to operate even more powerfully when based on more salient traits such as race, gender, age, or social class. For instance, Finkelstein, Burke, and Raju (1995) concluded that young persons with authority to hire tended to rate young job applicants more favorably than older ones.

Employment advantages reflecting shared traits may also be created by social patterns outside the workplace. Many relationships in American society today remain highly segregated, with racial, ethnic, and class groups tending to reside in separate neighborhoods and attending different schools and churches. Different genders and ages tend to socialize in different groups and social networks (Alba, Logan, & Stutts, 2000). But social relationships created through such interactions are resources in the labor market (Adler & Kwon, 2002; Granovetter, 1995; Ibarra, 1995). Many job vacancies are never publicly advertised in newspapers or on Internet job boards, so they become known primarily to the friends, relatives, neighbors, classmates, or colleagues of current employees (Kuhn & Skuterud, 2000). Similarly, in preemployment skill testing and interviewing, informal coaching and insider information may equip applicants who have ties to current employees to perform better than their competitors (Hulett, Bendick, Thomas, & Moccio, 2008). Limited access to information-rich social networks helps to keep traditionally excluded groups excluded.

Bias May Evolve Rather than Disappear

Over the four decades since the Civil Rights Movement, antidiscrimination legislation has reduced many blatant forms of employment discrimination, such as the once-traditional advertising of job vacancies as "Help Wanted-Male" or "Help Wanted-Female." Over the same period, public opinion polls reflected downward trends in individuals' self-reported prejudice. For example, in 1965, 59% of Americans agreed that they would vote for a qualified African American presidential candidate, but by 2005, that figure had risen to 93%; parallel questions concerning a qualified woman elicited 55% agreement in 1965 but 87% in 2005 (Gallup, 2005; see also Smith, 2000).

However, these developments may not translate into substantially reduced bias. Rather, blatant discriminatory behavior may have simply evolved into what McConahay, Hardee, and Batts (1981) label *modern racism*—a shift in social norms making explicit expression of prejudiced attitudes rarely seen yet remaining in more covert forms.

Consistent with this model, researchers have documented covert prejudice in the behavior of actual supervisors and managers. For example, Moss & Tilly (2002) and Rooth (2007) describe how, in rejecting minority job applicants, hiring decision makers now often cite applicants' deficiencies in "soft skills" ("inability to communicate," "lack of work commitment") as a socially acceptable proxy for an applicant's race. Moss and Tilly's work is consistent with Dovidio and Gaertner's (2000) findings that discrimination against minorities is most evident when qualifications are ambiguous rather than very strong or very weak; ambiguous qualifications allow bias to influence hiring decisions while leaving hiring decision makers feeling justified in their choices. Other researchers have described some employers' equal employment initiatives as primarily symbolic, appearing to comply with legal and social norms without intending to change employment outcomes substantially (Bendick & Egan, 2009; Edelman & Petterson, 1999).

Hiring Is Particularly Vulnerable to Bias

Of course, such cognitive and organizational processes can lead to biased outcomes in *post*-hiring employment processes such as performance evaluations, promotions, raises, and terminations. However, hiring decisions differ from post-hiring decisions in ways that tend to make bias more influential in hiring than in those other processes.

The first way is the limited information on which hiring decisions are based (Altonji & Pierret, 2001). Post-hiring decisions tend to be made by supervisors who have observed employees' performance over months or years. Hiring, in contrast, typically requires assessing job applicants who are virtual strangers. Resumes, applications, and work samples typically provide only a sketch of their qualifications and require judgment about relevance to the positions for which they are being hired. Job interviews tend to be brief—for entry-level positions, often as short as 10 minutes (Bendick, Rodriguez, & Jayaraman, 2010). Interviews also tend to be subject to "impression management," deliberate self-presentation to create impressions not sustained post-hiring (Giacalone & Rosenfeld, 1989; Higgins & Judge, 2004). For these and other reasons, traditional job interviews have limited power to predict post-hiring job performance (Le, Oh, Shaffer, & Schmidt, 2007).

Another factor negatively impacting stigmatized groups is the time pressure under which managers often operate. Stereotypes exercise particular influence in time-pressured situations (Macrae, Bodenhausen, & Milne, 1998). Concurrently, limited contact between job applicants and hiring decision makers imbues every interaction with intense pressure to perform that tends to enhance stereotype threat.

Another circumstance enhancing bias in hiring is differences in opportunities to correct errors. Many post-hiring decisions are part of ongoing or repeated processes in which errors can be corrected later. For instance, a too-generous raise in one year may be brought back into line by a smaller raise the next year, or employees passed over for one promotion may be considered for others. In fact, the continued visibility of minority employees who are not progressing may itself pressure managers to act (Stangor, Sechrist, & Jost, 2001; Zitek & Hebl, 2007). In hiring, in contrast, applicants who are not hired tend immediately to go elsewhere to find employment, eliminating opportunities for employers to reconsider.

External pressure from antidiscrimination laws is also less likely to correct bias in hiring decisions than post-hiring decisions. Employees who feel aggrieved about a post-hiring decision often have information on which to base a complaint (e.g., who was promoted instead of me?) and a sufficient stake in the outcome to seek redress. In contrast, job applicants who suspect discrimination often lack sufficient information to determine if discrimination has occurred (e.g., when the company said the job vacancy was already filled, was that an excuse?), and are more likely to pursue other opportunities than to dispute the decision. For such reasons, hiring complaints comprise only 6% of formal discrimination complaints filed with the Equal Employment Opportunity Commission (EEOC) (Bendick, Jackson, & Reinoso, 1994).

Section II: Empirical Evidence of Employment Bias

The research reviewed in Section I translates into a testable hypothesis: bias continues to adversely affect hiring outcomes for historically excluded groups in the American labor market today. Does empirical evidence support this hypothesis?

Certainly, research documents substantial progress toward employment equality over recent decades. Women now constitute 51% of managerial and professional workers in the American labor force, and race/ethnic minorities more than 22% (U.S. Bureau of Labor Statistics, 2008), a very different situation from the early 1960s, when their numbers in most such occupations were so small that essentially every individual was a highly visible exception. Women's earnings, which averaged about 60% of men's until the 1970s, rose to nearly 80% by the 1990s (Blau & Kahn, 2007), and over the same period, African Americans' average earnings rose from 57% of Whites' to more than 73% (Smith & Welch, 1989).

Yet, such measures document remaining problems as much as progress. Earnings ratios of 73% or 80% are still far below the 100% that would signal simple equality. Worse, in recent years, upward movement of race and gender wage ratios has slowed or stopped (Rodgers, 2006). Concurrently, the number of women and minorities remains very limited in many occupations, especially more prestigious, well paid ones—patterns of occupational segregation often referred to as "glass walls" and "glass ceilings" (Altonji & Blank, 1999; Reskin & Bielby, 2005). For example, although Hispanics now constitute 11.6% of police patrol officers, they are only 6.1% of police sergeants and lieutenants. African Americans are 7.7% of construction laborers but only 2.2% of structural steel workers (U.S. Bureau of Labor Statistics, 2008; see also Bendick, 2000). And although women now are 31% of medical doctors, they are only 4% of orthopedic surgeons. Moreover, female physicians earn an average of 18% less than male physicians with matching credentials, medical specialties, years in practice, and work hours per week (HRSA, 2010).

Research in the form illustrated by these findings on physicians' earnings— showing different employment outcomes among demographic groups not explained by differences in education, experience, other measures of qualifications, or work effort—provides the most rigorous evidence that substantial bias remains in the American labor market. Such studies have been conducted on many different occupations, industries, localities, and demographic groups, producing results such as the following:

- After controlling for education, age, work experience, residence, and criminal records, dark-skinned black males had a 52% lower chance of being employed than lighter skinned black males (Johnson, Bienenstock, & Stoloff, 1995).
- Although surgery did not alter their job qualifications, when transgender individuals who were men transformed into women, their earnings fell 12%, while women who transformed into men had their earnings rise 8% (Schilt & Wiswall, 2008).
- Among American professionals and managers working in international business, an additional year of international experience raised men's annual earnings $2,500 but women's only $1,300; working an extra 8 hours a week increased men's earning $7,300 but women's only $4,300 (Egan, Bendick, & Miller, 2002).
- Leading symphony orchestras auditioning musicians behind screens so that judges could not see the applicants hired more women players than those conducting auditions in the open (Golden & Rouse, 2000).

Such findings are consistent with perceptions of bias reported by adversely affected individuals. In one typical survey with a nationally representative sample, 81% of African Americans, 60% of Hispanics, and 53% of Asian respondents felt that they would have a lower chance of promotion to a managerial position than an equally qualified White (Smith, 2000). In another national survey, 31% of Asians, 26% of African Americans, 18% of Hispanics, and 22% of women reported having been discriminated against in their workplace during the previous year (Gallup, 2005). In narrower examples, in a survey of self-identified transgender adults in San Francisco, 40% of respondents reported having been discriminated against in applying for jobs, and 24% reported having been sexually harassed at work (Guardian, 2006); and in a nationwide survey of women firefighters, 85% reported having been treated adversely at work, including hostile comments, sexual advances, and being placed in unnecessary danger (Hulett et al., 2008).

Finally, evidence of perceived discrimination is provided by formal legal complaints filed with the United States, which in 2008 numbered 93,000 (U.S. EEOC, 2010). In parallel, thousands of antidiscrimination lawsuits by public antidiscrimination agencies or private litigators continue to be filed each year, with some resolutions including tens of millions of dollars in damages (Bendick & Egan, 2009; Darity & Mason, 1998).

Section III: Testing Provides Direct Evidence of Hiring Bias

Although the previous section provides considerable evidence of continuing bias, this evidence often does not separate hiring from post-hiring processes; may be based on perceptions rather than objectively verified; requires extrapolation from laboratory settings to behavior of actual employment decision makers; or is inferred from differences in employment outcomes that remain after other explanations have been eliminated. Since 1990, an additional research technique has been increasingly used that uniquely provides *direct, objective* observation of *hiring* bias in *real-world* settings under controlled, quasi-experimental conditions. This technique is matched pair testing.

Matched pair testing (also referred to as situation testing, paired comparison testing, employment auditing, field experiments, or employment testing) is a systematic procedure creating controlled experiments analyzing employers' candid responses to employees' personal characteristics (Bendick, 2007; Pager & Western, 2012). Economists define employment discrimination as valuation in the labor market of workers' characteristics not related to productivity (Arrow, 1998). In testing, pairs of research assistants apply for the same actual job vacancy. Within each pair, applicant characteristics related to a worker's productivity on the job—education, work experience, professional certifications, and technical skills—are equalized by selecting, training, and credentialing testers to appear equally qualified for the positions they seek. Simultaneously, personal characteristics unrelated to job performance are experimentally manipulated by pairing testers who differ in one characteristic—a White paired with an African American, a male with a female, or a person age 32 with one age 57. If testers within a pair experience substantially different responses to their job-seeking efforts, it is then presumed that this differential treatment is due to the employers' reaction to the manipulated characteristic. Thus, testing addresses Kang's (2012) *Axis of Specificity* by documenting both specific discrimination perpetrated by an employer that may be used in litigation and general information regarding levels of discrimination in broader circumstances that may be used to develop public policy.

Of course, interpretation of testing outcomes as discrimination is appropriate only if employers are presented with pairs of job candidates who truly appear equally qualified. This condition is relatively easy to achieve in testing that involves resumes mailed, faxed, or e-mailed to employers (Bendick, Jackson, & Romero, 1996; Bertrand & Mullainathan, 2004). In these studies, the resumes describe equivalent education, work experience, and job skills while varying formats and details to avoid appearing obviously similar. The resumes communicate applicants' demographic characteristics through gender-specific names, ethnically related activities, or age-revealing graduation dates. In nations where resumes customarily include applicant photographs, these images can also communicate demographic characteristics.

Resume testing can probe only the initial stages of the hiring process, ending with employers' decision to invite candidates for in-person interviews. To study the complete hiring process, "live" testers are required to file applications, return messages, take skills tests, and be interviewed. Ensuring that the testers in each pair appear equally qualified throughout those processes requires substantial care and effort (Bovenkerk, 1992; Lodder, 1994).

The first step is to recruit research assistants who meet a daunting set of requirements: ability to play the job seeker role convincingly while accurately observing the hiring process; willingness to approach the study objectively; similarities between testing partners in general appearance and demeanor; and the demographic characteristics required by the study design. Recruiting individuals meeting all these requirements is often a time-consuming, painstaking process; in one typical study, 93 potential testers were interviewed before four were selected to form two testing teams (Nunes & Seligman, 1999). College students, professional actors, actual job seekers, and community volunteers have all served as testers.

The second step is training, which typically requires at least three days, to make pairs of testers equally credible job applicants. During training, testers develop and memorize their false resumes, receive coaching on effective interviewing techniques, and rehearse similar answers to common interview questions.

Concurrently, testers are trained to remember important details of their testing experiences.

A third step in maintaining tester equivalence involves closely supervising testers' actions. The testers within each pair usually present themselves to employers in random order, with the second tester applying shortly after the first. Testers document their experiences as soon as practical after each event without knowing the experiences of their testing partners. They typically use structured questionnaires and are constantly reminded to focus on facts rather than interpretations. Such careful management requires continuous, hands-on monitoring by a trained "Test Coordinator," who can usually supervise no more than three teams concurrently.

Testing studies typically repeat their quasi-experiment for dozens or hundreds of job vacancies, to "average out" random circumstances that may affect the outcome in single tests. In analyzing outcomes, one key summary statistic is the *net rate of discrimination*, the proportion of job applications in which testers with the characteristic hypothesized to be disfavored is successful minus the proportion of applications in which testers with the characteristic hypothesized to be favored is successful. Another important measure is the ratio of the proportion of tests in which testers with the disfavored characteristic are successfully divided by the proportion of tests in which the other tester is successful. "Successful" is typically defined as reaching an identifiable milestone in the hiring process, such as being offered an interview or a job.

Given the 20–40% net rates of discrimination observed in typical testing studies, statistically significant main effects in the experiment can be obtained with as few as 40–50 completed tests. Samples of about 100 tests have proved sufficient to observe statistically significant effects of mediating factors on net rates of discrimination. Analyses applying multivariate techniques, such as regression analysis (Kenney & Wissoker, 1994), often require larger samples.

The following are examples of hiring outcomes that testing studies have identified as biased:

- A major newspaper carried an advertisement for a restaurant supervisor in an affluent neighborhood. An African American tester who presented himself at the restaurant was told that he would be called if the restaurant wished to pursue his application. Minutes later, a White tester whose resume showed the same level of education and restaurant experience followed the same procedure. He was called later that day to schedule an interview, and subsequently offered the position. The African American tester made four follow-up calls to reiterate his interest, including shortly after the White tester declined the job offer, with no response (Bendick et al., 1994).

- A vacancy for a receptionist in an optometrist's office was advertised in a local newspaper in an affluent neighborhood. When a tester with a Latina name and slight accent telephoned the following day, she was put on hold, called Carmen when she had given her name as Juanita, and told that the office was not taking any further applications. When her testing partner with an Anglo name and no accent called 13 minutes later, she received an interview appointment for the following morning (Bendick, Jackson, Reinoso, & Hodges, 1991).

- An employment agency advertised for an executive recruiter. Two White males, whose resumes and appearance portrayed ages 32 and 57, respectively, responded by telephone and were granted interviews. The older tester's interview lasted 48 minutes, during which he was cautioned against making a precipitous career change and instructed to call back if he was still interested after reading books on sales techniques. The younger tester's interview lasted 85 minutes, with the interviewer discussing work and nonwork topics in a friendly manner and commenting enthusiastically on the tester's responses. This tester was invited back for a second interview, after which he was offered a job (Bendick, Brown, & Wall, 1999).

- An automobile service shop advertised in a newspaper for a technician to lubricate and repair automobiles. When a female applicant whose resume showed experience in physically demanding jobs applied for the position, the manager told her that "the auto lube job is hard for a woman," said that he liked her smile, and offered a lower paying position in the on-premise coffee kiosk. When her male testing partner applied several hours later, he was interviewed for the advertised technician position (Nunes & Seligman, 2000).

The most frequent criticism of testing studies is by "free market" economists who reason that, because employers are forced by a competitive labor market to consider only productivity-related characteristics of job applicants, differences in hiring outcomes between paired testers must signal failure by the researchers to match the testers on some subtle productivity-related characteristics (e.g., Heckman, 1998; see also Pager, 2007). Such criticism is tautological as well as contradicted by research reviewed throughout this article. However, it provides an important caution that only researchers committed to methodological rigor should undertake testing.

Over the past two decades, several dozen testing studies have examined hiring in labor markets from Boston to Los Angeles and occupations from entry-level retail sales to professional and managerial positions (Bendick, 1999; Bendick, 2007; Pager, 2007). Several dozen additional studies have been conducted in other industrialized nations, from the Netherlands to Australia (European Commission, 2006; ILO, 1998; Riach & Rich, 2002). Demographic groups whose experiences were analyzed have included women, older workers, persons with disabilities, transgender individuals, and race/ethnic minority groups ranging from African Americans and Hispanics in the United States to immigrant Turks, North Africans, West Indians, and South Asians in Europe.

These studies have been essentially unanimous in documenting considerable hiring bias. As mentioned previously, typical net rates of discrimination range between 20% and 40%. Equivalently, these studies estimate that bias infects the hiring decisions of 20–40% of employers. Such estimates are striking consistent with the nontesting evidence reviewed in Sections I and II.

One obvious direction for future testing is to continue "mapping" the prevalence of discrimination in different locations (urban centers vs. suburban areas), occupations and industry (professional occupations vs. entry-level jobs), and demographic groups (women vs. African Americans). Such studies would be particularly useful if they were repeated using a consistent methodology on a nationally representative sample to generate a recurrent "national report card" tracing trends over time (Fix & Turner, 1999). Another particularly useful form of "mapping" involves testing for bias on bases other than the "usual" race, gender, and age characteristics; innovative studies have involved, for instance, Arab Americans facing backlash after September 11, 2001 (Discrimination Research Center, 2004), persons with a criminal record (Pager & Western, 2012), transgender individuals (Make the Road, 2010), and overweight persons (Rooth, 2009).

However, testing has typically revealed relatively modest variation in the prevalence of discrimination among demographic groups, locations, and occupations, suggesting that exploration of how rates of discrimination vary across demographic groups or labor markets should not command high priority. Furthermore, although these studies typically capture media attention when released, there is little evidence that they have powerful or lasting impact on public opinion or public policy. For example, although testing results were discussed in debates about California's Proposition 209 to abolish affirmative action (Bendick, 1995), the proposition passed.

Accordingly, matched pair testing is likely to address bias more effectively if, rather than primarily measuring the prevalence of hiring bias, studies seek to advance fundamental understanding of bias and its remedies. Compared to past testing studies, research in this spirit would be more grounded in behavioral science theory, coordinated with nontesting research on the same issues, and designed to provide data analyzable with other methodologies. In short, future research should "test deeper" rather than "test broader."

Section IV: Testing to Understand Hiring Bias

This section presents four research proposals illustrating that "test deeper" approach.

Study Employer–Job Candidate Interactions

The first proposal concerns using testing to analyze employer–candidate interactions, particularly job interviews. Behavioral science research suggests that bias, especially when unconscious, is often embodied in small, subtle but crucial differences in words or actions referred to as *microinequities* (Valian, 1998). These small differences often leave perpetrators of bias unaware of these unconscious processes and their cumulative impact. Equally, they pose measurement challenges to researchers seeking to understand exactly how bias operates.

To date, research on the details of employer–employee interactions has primarily examined written materials such as letters of recommendations and performance evaluations (Bison-Rapp, 1999; Trix & Psenka, 2003). These studies have documented systematic differences in statements about equally qualified individuals of different demographic backgrounds. For example, a comparison of performance evaluations for men and women professionals who all received high-performance ratings at a financial services firm found that women were praised primarily for activities within their own work group and men for external activities; criticisms of men tended to be accompanied by mitigating explanations but those for women were not; and men were commonly recommended for advancement, while women were described as valuable in their current position (Townsend, 1997). Other studies have revealed *Linguistic Intergroup Bias,* language describing in-group and out-group behavior that itself perpetuate stereotypes—for instance, by describing out-group positive behavior and in-group negative behavior in concrete terms suggesting situational traits, while reporting out-group negative behavior and positive in-group behavior in abstract terms suggesting persistent qualities (Maas, Salvi, Acuri, & Semin, 1989; Semin & Fiedler, 1992).

Only a few studies in this tradition have examined face-to-face interactions rather than written materials (Binning, Goldstein, Garcia, & Scattereregia, 1988; Shelly & Shelly, 2009). This research requires samples of the exact words used to describe demographically different individuals who are equivalent in actual qualifications or performance—precisely what testing can provide. Through miniature technology, voice and video recordings of conversations can be collected without making employers aware of being tested or recorded. Transcripts of these encounters could then be analyzed using psycholinguistic techniques.

Some testing studies have examined employer and employee behavior in job interviews. For example, Bendick et al. (1994) analyzed interviews of African American and White applicants for entry-level positions. They observed that although the two groups received very different numbers of job offers, applicants experienced no substantial differences in treatment during interviews such as interview length, proportion of the interview devoted to job-relevant topics, and rank of the interviewer. Another study examined interviews of Whites and Persons of Color applying for waitstaff positions in upscale restaurants (Bendick, Rodriguez,

& Jayaraman, 2010). It documented that interviewers tended to accept White applicants' claims of past restaurant experience without probing but skeptically questioned non-Whites. Such studies suggest the insights that more sophisticated analyses of interview transcripts could uncover.

Coordinate Testing Studies of Multiple Out-Groups

Our second research proposal is to study patterns of bias against multiple out-groups by the same employer.

Many analyses of discrimination focus on issues specific to demographic groups, for example, the residual effects of segregation on African Americans, the relationship between family responsibilities and women's careers, or the effect of English language requirements on recent immigrants (Bell, 2007). But other threads in behavioral science research suggest a fundamentally different approach. More than 50 years ago, psychologists began to consider prejudice as a consistent characteristic of an individual so that a person harboring bias against women would also tend to be prejudiced against minorities (Bierly, 1985; Peterson, Doty, & Winter, 1993). In parallel, some sociologists have argued that the essence of workplace discrimination is not adverse attitudes toward specific out-groups but rather *social closure* to preserve the power, status, and privilege of a dominant in-group against *all* alternative claimants (Freshman, 1990; Moore, 1990; Murray, 1988; Sidanius & Pratto, 2001; Tomaskovic-Devey, 1993).

This debate is important not only to social theory but to practical antidis-crimination efforts. The first perspective implies that it is important to contradict stereotypes adverse to individual out-groups. In contrast, the second perspective considers stereotypes primarily *ex post* rationales for negative treatment of out-groups rather than independent causes and suggests controlling the generic process of stereotyping rather than the content of specific stereotypes (Bendick et al., 2001; Egan & Bendick, 2008).

To date, testing has typically examined one out-group per study. However, studies could be organized to, for example, field teams of males and females, African Americans and Whites, and older and younger workers to apply to the same employers. Positive correlations in bias against multiple out-groups would support the social closure model, while zero or negative correlations would support the alternative (Fiske, Cuddy, Glick, & Xu, 2002).

Behavioral science research also suggests other ways in which an employer's behavior toward an out-group may differ depending on a context that includes other out-groups. For instance, *moral credentialing* (Monin & Miller, 2001) suggests that employers who have hired an applicant from one stigmatized group, and therefore feel that they have adequately demonstrated egalitarian values, may be less favorable to subsequent candidates from other stigmatized groups. Again, test-ing studies could be designed to test this hypothesis, in this case, by appropriately sequencing multiple tests of the same employer and analyzing the relationship between each test outcome and that of preceding tests.

Evaluate Strategies for Minimizing Bias

Practical advice routinely offered to out-group job seekers often includes suggestions concerning how to minimize bias they may encounter. For example, some advisors counsel explicitly refuting stereotypes about groups to which the job seeker belongs (Kawakami, Dovidio, Moll, Hermsen, & Russin, 2000); others suggest using individuating information to counter the applicability of the stereotype to the job seeker (Beckett & Park, 1995; Glick, Zion, & Nelson, 1988); and still others advise emphasizing alternative, positive stereotypes associated with those groups (Gawronski, Deutsch, Mbirkou, Seibt, & Strack, 2008). Some advisors suggest implementing such strategies proactively—in anticipation that stereotypes inevitably bias hiring decisions—while others suggest doing so only if some indication suggests a problem. Matched pair testing could be designed to provide evidence-based advice to job seekers rather than the current, largely intuitive guidance.

To date, only rare testing studies have examined alternative strategies for combating bias. One study of age discrimination using mailed resumes randomly assigned different cover letters to accompany the older workers' resume. In one letter, older applicants described themselves as career-committed, energetic, and technologically up-to-date—positive attributes stereotypically associated with younger applicants; in an alternative letter, older applicants described themselves as experienced, mature, and stable—positive attributes stereotypically associated with older workers; and a third letter contained neither statement. The first cover letter generated a substantially higher rate of favorable employer responses than the other two (Bendick et al., 1996).

Employers also have implemented a variety of initiatives designed to minimize bias. Most prominently, the majority of U.S. employers today invest in "workforce diversity training" for their employees, despite research that questions the effectiveness of many of these efforts (Bendick et al., 2001; Kalev, Dobbin, & Kelly, 2006). Testing could be structured to provide assessments of these efforts. For example, tests could be conducted in a workplace prior to a diversity training program and then again subsequently. Or a multiestablishment firm could implement training in one subset of its establishments and not in a matched subset, and then conduct hiring tests in both experimental and control locations. Here, testing could measure the effect of the training on overall rates of discrimination and specific hiring practices that employees were trained to adopt or avoid.

Testing could also improve guidance for employers on other antibias efforts. For example, in sincere efforts to avoid violating social norms, some hiring interviewers consciously avoid any reference to race. However, Apfelbaum, Sommers, and Norton (2008) demonstrate that such *strategic colorblindness* may backfire, leading to nonverbal unfriendliness interpreted by Black observers as negative and prejudiced. Similarly, Chartrand and Bargh (1999) discuss a *chameleon effect* in which interviewees unconsciously mirror the behavior of interviewers, generating awkward behavior not representative of their potential post-hiring performance. Testing could be used to study the prevalence in actual job interviews of these hypothesized effects and whether they vary among different demographic combinations of interviewers and interviewees, and findings could be translated into practical guidance to interviewers.

Study the Effects of Hiring Rejection

Research has long documented the negative psychological and social consequences of unemployment, including increased physical and mental illness, loss of self-esteem, family stress, and discouragement (Clark, Georgellis, & Sanfey, 1999; Linn, Sandifer, & Stein, 1985). A few studies have focused on these effects when bias was a factor (Goldsmith, Sedo, Darity, & Hamilton, 2004). These studies employ a range of techniques, including epidemiological studies of morbidity and mortality, surveys utilizing scales of self-efficacy and psychological well-being, laboratory studies tracking physiological responses to disappointment, and diaries tracking attitudes and perceptions over time (Bolger, Davis, & Rafieli, 2003).

Matched pair testing offers an additional methodology for measuring these effects. It provides unusually detailed information about the rejection experience. It allows examining hiring separately from other aspects of workers' unemployment experiences, such as the duration of their unemployment. And by forming appropriate tester teams, it can isolate differences in the responses of different types of workers—for instance, youth just entering the workforce compared to mid-career workers.

Using such measures, researchers might study, for example, whether the effects of failing to be hired are different when the decision was biased or unbiased; the cumulative effects of multiple job disappointments; and whether the same disappointing experience creates different effects on different demographic groups. For example, it might be hypothesized that because greater expectations of eventual employment create a greater sense of *self-efficacy* (Bandura, 1997), White males might experience smaller adverse effects than women or minorities. Testing could also be used to examine the efficacy of strategies to minimize the adverse effects of job disappointment. For example, *self-affirmation theory* (Steele, 1988) suggests that individuals frustrated in one endeavor (e.g., job seeking) might preserve their self-image by success in a different domain (e.g., volunteer work). Explicitly measuring testers' perceptions of themselves as well as attitudes toward in-group and out-group members' pre- and posttesting experiences may provide information into how hiring experiences may be internalized differently by different groups. However, this research would require that testers be actual job seekers who really want jobs and who would be allowed to accept positions offered.

Testing could also be used to study the effect on individuals' attitudes and empathy of being exposed to the reality of discrimination that they otherwise might not encounter. Research (Batson et al., 2003; Gaertner & Dovidio, 2005) suggests that putting an individual "in the shoes of others" expands the range of persons about whose well-being they feel concerned, and Fogelman (1994) has documented the role of striking personal incidents in persuading bystanders to act on behalf of victims of persecution. It can be hypothesized that, in this spirit, White or male testers who observe their testing partners encounter bias may become more empathetic. This hypothesis could be studied by measuring the attitudes and behavior of in-group testers before and after their testing experience.

Section V: Using Testing to Change Employer Behavior

A perennial challenge in the behavioral sciences is to mobilize research findings to influence real-world practices. How can employers be convinced and assisted to incorporate the research findings discussed throughout this article into their firm's employment practices? Testing offers new approaches for doing so, of which this section outlines three proposals.

Testing on Behalf of Employers

Employers commonly monitor their own staff using unobtrusive data gathering techniques. For example, retailers often employ "mystery shoppers" to pose as customers and record their interactions with sales staff (www.mysteryshop.org). The employers use these data to improve customer service. Most employment testing studies have been conducted without employers being aware of being tested or presented with findings about their individual firms. Our first proposal suggests testing by employers as a means of self-audit.

One example of which we are personally aware took place in 2009 at the teaching hospital of a major medical school. This employer desired to offer jobs to residents of its surrounding community as well as employ staff who could relate to its demographically diverse patients, and therefore wanted to ensure that its hiring practices were not biased. To support this goal, the hospital required all supervisors to be trained to conduct job interviews in a job-related structured manner (Le et al., 2007). However, the hospital had never measured the extent to which these supervisors subsequently followed those procedures. Accordingly, the hospital's vice president of human resources secretly arranged with a nonprofit organization to send matched pairs of White and minority applicants to apply for positions at the hospital and two comparable hospitals in the same city.

Businesses currently invest huge numbers of staff hours and many millions of dollars each year to address bias and increase staff diversity. However, 62% of them collect no information on the impact of these efforts (Esen, 2005). This lack of data limits their ability to improve these initiatives as well as to hold managers accountable for following prescribed practices (Bendick, 2008). As the hospital example illustrates, testing conducted by or with employers can provide direct data about the extent to which initiatives effectively modify employment practices "on the shop floor" and the extent to which those modifications change hiring outcomes.

Testing for Training

When testing results are presented to audiences of nonresearchers—for example, in legislative hearings or the mass media—their attention-grabbing power is immediately evident. This power reflects testing's combination of rigorously controlled statistical evidence and vivid anecdotes that put a human face on those statistics (Cialdini, 2000).

This persuasive power has yet to be extensively harnessed in practical employee training. Among larger employers, more than 90% provide some form of antidiscrimination or prodiversity training, often enrolling everyone from senior executives and mid-level supervisors to nonmanagerial employees (Esen, 2005; Kalev et al., 2006). The most effective forms of this training use vivid examples from real workplaces to persuade trainees of the continued presence of discrimination and communicate desired changes in employee behavior (Adamson, 2000; Bendick et al., 2001). Testing is ideally structured to provide specific vivid examples for use in training, especially if tests are documented through audio or video recording. In addition, posttraining testing could be used to assess whether training is effective.

Testing for Litigation

U.S. employers who violate equal federal or state employment laws can be sued either by government agencies, such as the federal EEOC, or in private litigation brought by the victims of discrimination. If the plaintiffs prevail, the employer may be liable for substantial damage payments as well as mandatory court-supervised changes in employment practices. Since the late 1960s, such litigation—or employers' desire to avoid it—has been a major motivator for reductions in employment bias (Blumrosen, 1993).

American law grants matched pair testing potential roles in enforcement of these laws. Individual testers and nonprofit organizations employing testers have "standing" to become plaintiffs in litigation based on testing evidence alone (Boggs, Sellers, & Bendick, 1993; Yelnosky, 2010). In addition, if an employer is sued based on evidence other than testing, testing-based documentation of an employer's discriminatory behavior can be used as corroborative evidence.

Despite this potential, only a handful of testing-based enforcement actions have been brought. One pioneering lawsuit, *Fair Employment Council et al. v. BMC Marketing,* was filed in the District of Columbia in 1990. In it, the plaintiffs were two African American university students and the nonprofit organization that employed them as testers. The defendant was a local office of one of the nation's largest job placement agencies. The agency had interviewed, coached, and found entry-level office jobs for two White testers, while failing to do so for the African Americans who were their testing partners. This litigation was settled with payment of damages to the nonprofit organization and commitments by the defendant to retrain its staff and eliminate discriminatory practices (Boggs et al., 1993).

That lawsuit involved plaintiffs from a stigmatized group—African Americans—for whom testing is only one of several ways to generate evidence of discrimination. For other groups, however, testing-based evidence may be the only feasible basis for litigation. For example, in antidiscrimination litigation, statistics from sources such as the Census are often used to demonstrate that an employer has fewer female or race/ethnic minority employees than would be expected based on their availability in the local labor market. However, such Census data are not collected for many historically excluded groups—for instance, persons with psychiatric disabilities (Tal, Moran, Rooth, & Bendick, 2009) or gay, lesbian, transgender, and bisexual individuals (Make the Road, 2010). In that circumstance, direct evidence of employer discrimination obtained by testing may be the only feasible source of legally viable evidence of hiring discrimination.

Litigation is only one adversarial approach in which testing can be used to influence employers. To date, publicly released results from testing studies have typically not named employers against whom incriminating findings were obtained. However, the results of tests on specific employers could be released to the general public, news media, insurers, investors, unions, customers, and others, providing information by which these stakeholders can induce discriminating employers to change their behavior (Egan, Mauleon, Wolff, & Bendick, 2009).

Section VI: Summary

The seven types of matched pair testing studies discussed here form an ambitious research agenda for any society attempting to reduce bias in hiring. However, these examples by no means exhaust the potential of testing to generate theoretical and practical advances. It is time for researchers in the social, behavioral, and managerial sciences to mobilize the power of this technique creatively to advance this important societal goal.

References

Adamson, J. (2000). *The Denny's story: How a company in crisis resurrected its good name and reputation.* New York: John Wiley.

Adler, P., & Kwon, S. (2002). Social capital: Prospects for a new concept. *Academy of Management Review, 27*(1), 17–40.

Alba, R., Logan, J., & Stutts, B. (2000). How segregated are middle-class African Americans? *Social Problems, 47*(4), 543–558.

Altonji, J., & Blank, R. (1999). Race and gender in the labor market. In O. Aschenfelter & D. Card (Eds.) *Handbook of labor economics*, (Vol. *1*, pp. 3243–3259). Amsterdam: Elsevier.

Altonji, J., & Pierret, C. (2001). Employer learning and statistical discrimination. *Quarterly Journal of Economics, 116*, 313–350.

Apfelbaum, E., Sommers, S., & Norton, M. (2008). Seeing race and seeming racist? Evaluating colorblindness in social interactions. *Journal of Personality and Social Psychology, 95*, 918–932. doi: 10.1037/a0011990.

Arrow, K. (1998). What has economics to say about racial discrimination? *Journal of Economic Perspectives, 12*, 91–100.

Bandura, A. (1997). *Self-efficacy: The exercise of control.* New York: Freeman.

Batson, C., Lishner, D., Carpenter, A., Dulin, L., Harjusola-Webb, S., Stocks, E., Gale, S., Hassan, O., & Sampat, B. (2003). "As you would have them do unto you": Does imagining yourself in the other's place stimulate moral action? *Personality and Social Psychology Bulletin, 29*, 1190–1201. doi: 10.1177/0146167203254600.

Beckett, N., & Park, B. (1995). Use of category versus individuating information: Making base rates salient. *Personality and Social Psychology Bulletin, 21*, 21–31. doi: 10.1177/0146167295211004.

Bell, M. (2007). *Diversity in organizations.* Mason, OH: Thomson South-Western.

Bendick, M., Jr. (1995). Research evidence on racial/ethnic discrimination and affirmative action in employment. In *Discrimination and affirmative action: Are there any facts out there?* (pp. A58-A78). Sacramento: Assembly Judiciary Committee, California State Legislature.

Bendick, M., Jr. (1999). Adding testing to the nation's portfolio of information on employment discrimination. In M. Fix and M. Turner (Eds.) *A national report card on discrimination: The role of testing* (pp. 47–68). Washington, DC: The Urban Institute.

Bendick, M., Jr. (2000). Using EEO-1 data to analyze allegations of employment discrimination. *Presented at American Bar Association National Conference.*

Bendick, M., Jr. (2008) Measure inclusion, not diversity. *Presented at Society for Human Resource Management National Diversity Conference.*

Bendick, M., Jr., Brown, L., & Wall, K. (1999). No foot in the door: An experimental study of employment discrimination against older workers. *Journal of Aging and Social Policy, 10*, 5–23.

Bendick, M., Jr., & Egan, M. (2009). *Research perspectives on race and employment in advertising.* Washington, DC: Bendick and Egan Economic Consultants, Inc. for the Madison Avenue Project.

Bendick, M., Jr., Egan, M., & Lofhjelm, S. (2001). Diversity training: From anti-discrimination compliance to organization development. *Human Resource Planning, 24*, 10–25.

Bendick, M., Jr., Jackson, C., Reinoso, V., & Hodges, L. (1991). Discrimination against Latino job applicants: A controlled experiment. *Human Resource Management, 30*, 469–484.

Bendick, M., Jr., Jackson, C., & Reinoso, V. (1994). Measuring employment discrimination through controlled experiments. *Review of Black Political Economy, 23*, 25–48.

Bendick, M., Jr., Jackson, C., & Romero, J. (1996). Employment discrimination against older workers: An experimental study of hiring practices. *Journal of Aging and Social Policy, 8*, 25–46.

Bendick, M., Jr., Rodriguez, R., & Jayaraman, S. (2010). Race-ethnic employment discrimination in upscale restaurants: Evidence from paired comparison testing. *Social Science Journal, 47*, 802–818.

Bertrand, M., & Mullainathan, S. (2004). Are Emily and Brendan more employable than Lakisha and Jamal? A field experiment on labor market discrimination. *American Economic Review, 113*, 991–1001.

Bielby, W. (2000). Minimizing workplace gender and racial bias. *Contemporary Sociology, 29*, 120–129.

Bierly, M. (1985). Prejudice toward contemporary outgroups as a generalized attitude. *Journal of Applied Social Psychology, 15*, 189–199. doi: 10.1111/j.1559-1816.1985.tb02344.x.

Binning, J., Goldstein, M., Garcia, M., & Scattereregia, J. (1988). Effects of preinterview impressions on interviewer questioning strategies in same- and opposite-sex employment interviews. *Journal of Applied Psychology, 73*, 30–37. doi: 10.1037/0021-9010.73.1.30.

Bison-Rapp, S. (1999). Bulletproofing the workplace: Symbol and substance in employment discrimination law practice. *Florida State University Law Review, 26*, 959–1047.

Blau, F., & Kahn, L. (2007). The gender pay gap: Have women gone as far as they can? *Academy of Management Perspectives, 21*, 7–23.

Blumrosen, A. (1993). *Modern law: The law transmission system and equal employment opportunity.* Madison: University of Wisconsin Press.

Boggs, R., Sellers, J., & Bendick, M., Jr. (1993). Use of testing in civil rights enforcement. In M. Fix and R. Struyk (Eds.), *Clear and convincing evidence: Measurement of discrimination in America* (pp. 345–376). Washington, DC: Urban Institute Press.

Bolger, N., Davis, A., & Rafieli, E. (2003). Diary methods: Capturing life as it is lived. *Annual Review of Psychology, 54*, 579-616. doi: 10.1146/54.101601.145030.

Bovenkerk, F. (1992). *Testing discrimination in natural experiments: A manual for international comparative research on discrimination on the grounds of "race" and ethnic origin.* Geneva: International Labour Office.

Brewer, M. (1979). In-group bias in the minimal intergroup situation: A cognitive motivational analysis. *Psychological Bulletin, 86*, 307–324. doi: 10.1037/0033-2909.86.2.307.

Brief, A. (Ed.) (2008). *Diversity at work.* New York: Cambridge University Press.

Chartrand, T., & Bargh, J. (1999). The chameleon effect: The perception-behavior link and social interaction. *Journal of Personality and Social Psychology, 76*, 893–910. doi: 10.1037/0022-3514.76.6.893.

Cialdini, R. (2000). *Influence: Science and practice.* Boston: Allyn & Bacon.

Clark, A., Georgellis, Y., & Sanfey, P. (1999). Scarring: The psychological effect of past unemployment. *Economica, 68*(2), 221–241.

Darity, W., & Mason, P. (1998). Evidence on discrimination in employment: Codes of color, codes of gender. *Journal of Economic Perspectives, 12*, 63–90.

Darley, J., & Gross, P. (1983). A hypothesis-conforming bias in labelling effects. *Journal of Personality and Social Psychology, 44*, 20–33. doi: 10.1037/0022-3514.44.1.20.

Dipboye, R., & Colella, A. (2005). *Discrimination at work: The Psychological and Organizational Bases.* Mahwah, NJ: Lawrence Erlbaum.

Discrimination Research Center (2004). *Names make a difference: The screening of resumes by temporary employment agencies in California.* Berkeley, CA: Discrimination Research Center of the Impact Fund.

Dovidio, J., & Gaertner, S. (2000). Aversive racism and selection decisions: 1989 and 1999. *Psychological Science, 11*(4), 315–319. doi: 0.1111/1467-9280.00262.

Dovidio, J., Kawakami, K., & Gaertner, S. (2002). Implicit and explicit prejudice and interracial interaction. *Journal of Personality and Social Psychology, 82*, 62–68. doi: 10.1037/0022-3514.82.1.62.

Eagly, A., & Karau, S. (2002). Role congruity theory of prejudice toward female leaders. *Psychological Review, 109*, 573–598. doi: 0.1037/0033-295X.109.3.573.

Eberhardt, J., Dasgupta, N., & Banaszynski, T. (2003). Believing is seeing: The effects of racial labels and implicit beliefs on face perception. *Personality and Social Psychology Bulletin, 29*, 360–370. doi: 10.1177/0146167202250215.

Edelman, L., & Petterson, S. (1999). Symbols and substance in organizational response to civil rights law. *Research in Social Stratification and Mobility, 17*, 107–136.

Egan, M., & Bendick, M., Jr. (2008). Combining multicultural management and diversity into one course on cultural competence. *Academy of Management Learning and Education, 7*, 387–393.

Egan, M., Bendick, M., Jr., & Miller, J. (2002). US firms' evaluation of employee credentials in international business. *International Journal of Human Resource Management, 13*, 78–88.

Egan, M., Mauleon, F., Wolff, D., & Bendick, M., Jr. (2009). France's Mandatory "Triple Bottom Line" Reporting: Promoting sustainable development through informational regulation. *International Journal of Environmental, Cultural, Economic, and Social Sustainability, 7*, 27–47.

Erber, R., & Fiske, S. (1984). Outcome dependency and attention to inconsistent information. *Journal of Personality and Social Psychology, 47*, 709–726. doi: 10.1037/0022-3514.47.4.709.

Esen, E. (2005). *2005 workplace diversity practices: Survey report.* Alexandria, VA: Society for Human Resource Management.

European Commision (2006). *Equality and non-discrimination annual report.* Brussels: Commission of the European Union.

Finkelstein, L., Burke, M., & Raju, N. (1995). Age discrimination in simulated employment contexts: An integrative analysis. *Journal of Applied Psychology, 80*, 625–663. doi: 10.1037/0021-9010.80.6.652.

Fiske, S., Bersoff, D., Borgida, E., Deaux, K., & Heilman, M. (1991). Social science research on trial: The use of sex stereotyping research in Price Waterhouse v. Hopkins. *American Psychologist, 46*, 1049–1060. doi: 10.1037/0003-066X.46.10.1049.

Fiske, S., Cuddy, A., Glick, P., & Xu, J. (2002). A model of (often mixed) stereotype content: Competence and warmth respectively follow from perceived status and competition. *Journal of Personality and Social Psychology, 82*, 878–902. doi: 10.1037/0022-3514.82.6.878.

Fix, M., & Turner, M. (Eds.) (1999). *A national report card on discrimination: The role of testing.* Washington, DC: Urban Institute Press.

Fogelman, E. (1994). *Conscience and courage, rescuers of Jews during the Holocaust.* New York: Anchor Doubleday.

Freshman, C. (1990). Beyond atomized discrimination: Use of acts of discrimination against "other" minorities to prove discriminatory motivation under federal employment law. *Stanford Law Review, 43*, 241–273.

Gaertner, S., & Dovidio, J. (2005). Understanding and addressing contemporary racism: From aversive racism to the common ingroup identity model. *Journal of Social Issues, 61*, 615–639. doi: 10.1111/j.1540-4560.2005.00424.x.

Gallup (2005). *Employee discrimination in the workplace.* Washington, DC: The Gallup Organization.

Gawronski, B., Deutsch, R., Mbirkou, S., Siebt, B., & Strack, F. (2008). When 'Just say no' is not enough: Affirmation vs. negation training and the reduction of automatic stereotype activation. *Journal of Experimental Social Psychology, 44*, 370–377. doi: 10.1016/j.jesp.2006.12.004.

Giacalone, R., & Rosenfeld, P. (1989). *Impression management in the organization.* Hillsdale, NJ: Lawrence Erlbaum.

Glick, P., Zion, C., & Nelson, C. (1988). What mediates sex discrimination in hiring decisions? *Journal of Personality and Social Psychology, 55*, 178–186. doi: 10.1037/0022-3514.55.2.178.

Golden, C., & Rouse, C. (2000). Orchestrating impartiality: The impact of "blind" auditions on female musicians. *American Economic Review, 90*, 715–741.

Goldsmith, A., Sedo, S., Darity, W., & Hamilton, D. (2004). The labor supply consequences of perceptions of employer discrimination during search and on-the-job: Integrating neoclassical theory and cognitive dissonance. *Journal of Economic Psychology, 25, 15–39.* doi: 10.1016/S0167-4870(02)00210-6.

Granovetter, M. (1995). *Getting a job, A study of contacts and career.* Chicago: University of Chicago Press.

Greenwald, A., McGhee, D., & Schwartz, J. (1998). Measuring individual differences in implicit cognition: The implicit association test. *Journal of Personality and Social Psychology, 74*, 1464–1480. doi: 10.1037/0022-3514.74.6.1464.

Guardian (2006). *Good jobs NOW! A snapshot of the economic health of San Francisco's transgender communities.* San Francisco, CA: The San Francisco Bay Guardian.

Heckman, J. (1998). Detecting discrimination. *Journal of Economic Perspectives, 12*, 101–116.

Hertel, G. & Kerr, N. L. (2001). Priming in-group favoritism: The impact of normative scripts in the minimal group paradigm. *Journal of Experimental Social Psychology, 37*, 316–324. doi: 10.1006/jesp.2000.1447.

Higgins, C., & Judge, T. (2004). The effect of applicant influence tactics on recruiter perceptions of fit and hiring recommendations: A field study. *Journal of Applied Psychology, 89*, 622–632. doi: 10.1037/0021-9010.89.4.622.

Hilton, J., & Von Hippel, W. (1996). Stereotypes. *Annual Review of Psychology, 47*, 237–271. doi: 10.1146/annurev.psych.47.1.237.

HRSA (2010). *The physician workforce: Projections and research into current issues affecting supply and demand.* Washington, DC: U.S. Department of Health and Human Services, Health Resources and Services Administration.

Hulett, D., Bendick, M., Jr., Thomas, S., & Moccio, F. (2008). Enhancing women's inclusion in firefighting in the USA. *International Journal of Diversity in Organizations, Communities, and Nations, 8*, 1–24.

Ibarra, H. (1995). Race, opportunity, and diversity of social circles in managerial network. *Academy of Management Journal, 38*, 673–703.

ILO (1998). *Discrimination in access to employment on grounds of foreign origin: The case of Belgium.* International Migration Paper 23. Geneva: International Labour Organisation.

Johnson, J., Jr., Bienenstock, E., & Stoloff, J. (1995). An empirical test of the cultural capital hypothesis. *Review of Black Political Economy, 23*, 7–27.

Kalev, A., Dobbin, F., & Kelly, E. (2006). Best practices or best guesses? Diversity management and the remediation of inequality. *American Sociological Review, 71*, 589–617.

Kang, J. (2012). The missing quadrants of anti-discrimination: Going beyond the "Prejudice Polygraph". *Journal of Social Issues, 68*(2), 314–327. doi: 10.1111/j.1540-4560.2011.01750.x

Kawakami, K., Dovidio, J. F., Moll, J., Hermsen, S., & Russin, A. (2000). Just say no (to stereotyping): Effects of training in the negation of stereotypic associations on stereotype activation. *Journal of Personality and Social Psychology, 78*, 871–888. doi: 10.1037/0022-3514.78.5.871.

Kenney, G., & Wissoker, D. (1994). An analysis of the correlates of discrimination facing young Hispanic job-seekers. *American Economic Review, 84*, 674–83.

Kochan, T., Bezrukova, K., Ely, R., Jackson, S., Joshi, A., Jehn, K., Leonard, J., Levine, D., & Thomas, D. (2003). The effects of diversity on business performance: Report of the diversity research network. *Human Resource Management, 42*, 3–21.

Koomen, W., & Dijker, A. J. (1998). Ingroup and outgroup stereotypes and selective processing. *European Journal of Social Psychology, 27*, 589–601. doi: 10.1002/(SICI)1099-0992(199709/10)27:5<589::AID-EJS P840>3.0.CO;2-Y.

Kuhn, P., & Skuterud, M. (2000). Job search methods: Internet versus traditional. *Monthly Labor Review, 123*, 3–11.

Le, H., Oh, I., Shaffer, J., & Schmidt, F. (2007). Implications of methodological advances for practices of personnel selection: How practitioners benefit from meta-analysis. *Academy of Management Perspectives, 21*, 6–15.

Linn, M., Sandifer, R., & Stein, S. (1985). Effects of unemployment on mental and physical health. *American Journal of Public Health, 75*, 507–512.

Lodder, L. (1994). *Employment testing for civil rights enforcement: An operations manual.* Chicago: Legal Assistance Foundation of Chicago.

Maass, A., Salvi, D., Acuri, L., & Semin, G. (1989). Language use in intergroup contexts: The linguistic intergroup bias. *Journal of Personality and Social Psychology, 57*, 981–993. doi: 10.1037/0022-3514.57.6.981.

Macrae, C., Bodenhausen, G., & Milne, A. (1998) Saying no to unwanted thoughts: Self-focus and the regulation of mental life. *Journal of Personality and Social Psychology, 74*, 578–590. doi: 10.1037/0022-3514.74.3.578.

Make the Road (2010). *Transgender need not apply: Gender identity job discrimination in New York City's retail sector.* New York: Make the Road New York.

McConahay, J., Hardee, B, & Batts, V. (1981). Has racism declined in America? It depends on who is asking and what is asked. *Journal of Conflict Resolution, 25*, 563–579.

Monin, B., & Miller, D. (2001). Moral credentials and the expression of prejudice. *Journal of Personality and Social Psychology, 81*, 33–43. doi: 0.1037/0022-3514.81.1.33.

Moore, R. (1990). *The formation of a persecuting society: Power and deviance in Western Europe* (pp. 950–1250). Oxford: Blackwell.

Moss, P., & Tilly, C. (2002). *Stories employers tell: Race, skill, and hiring in America.* New York: Russell Sage Foundation.

Murray, R. (1988). *Social closure: The theory of monopolization and exclusion.* Oxford: Oxford University Press.

Nelson, T., Acker, M., & Manis, M. (1996). Irrepressible stereotypes. *Journal of Experimental Social Psychology, 32*, 13–38. doi: 10.1006/jesp.1996.0002.

Nosek, B. Greenwald, A., & Banaji, M. (2005). Understanding and using the implicit association test: II. Method variables and construct validity. *Personality & Social Psychology Bulletin, 31*, 166–180. doi: 10.1177/0146167204271418.

Nunes, A., & Seligman, B. (1999). *Treatment of Caucasian and African-American applicants by San Francisco Bay Area employment agencies: Results of a study utilizing "testers."* Berkeley, CA: Discrimination Research Center of the Impact Fund.

Nunes, A., & Seligman, B. (2000). *A study of the treatment of female and male applicants by San Francisco Bay Area auto service shops.* Berkeley, CA: Discrimination Research Center of the Impact Fund.

Pager, D. (2007). The use of field experiments for studies of employment discrimination: Contributions, critiques, and directions for the future. *Annals of the American Academy of Political and Social Science, 609*, 104–133.

Pager, D., & Western, B. (2012). Identifying discrimination at work: The use of field experiments. *Journal of Social Issues, 68*(2), 221–237. doi: 10.1111/j.1540-4560.2011.01746.x

Peterson, B., Doty, R., & Winter, D. (1993). Authoritarianism and attitudes toward contemporary social issues. *Personality and Social Psychology Bulletin, 19*, 174–184. doi: 10.1177/0146167293192006

Reskin, B., & Bielby, D. (2005). A sociological perspective on gender and career outcomes. *Journal of Economic Perspectives, 19*, 71–86.

Riach, P., & Rich, J. (2002). Field experiments in discrimination in the market place. *The Economic Journal, 112*, F480–F518.

Roberson, L., & Kulik, C. (2007). Stereotype threat at work. *Academy of Management Perspectives, 21*, 24–40.

Rodgers, W., III (Ed.) (2006). *Handbook on the economics of discrimination.* Northampton, MA: Edward Elgar.

Rooth, D. (2007). *Implicit discrimination in hiring: Real world evidence.* Discussion Paper 2764. Berlin: IZA.

Rooth, D. (2009) Obesity, attractiveness, and differential treatment in hiring: A field experiment. *Journal of Human Resources, 44*, 710–735.

Schilt, K., & Wiswall, M. (2008). Before and after: Gender transitions, human capital, and workplace experiences. *The Bell Economic Journal of Economic Analysis and Policy, 8*, 1–26.

Semin, G., & Fiedler, F. (Eds.) (1992). *Language, interaction, and social cognition.* Newberry Park, CA: Sage Publications.

Shelly, R., & Shelly, A. (2009). Speech content and the emergence of inequality in task groups. *Journal of Social Issues, 65*, 307–333. doi: 10.1111/j.1540-4560.2009.01602.x.

Shelton, J., Richeson, J., & Salvatore, J. (2005). Expecting to be the target of prejudice: Implications for interethnic interactions. *Personality and Social Psychology Bulletin, 31*, 1189–1202. doi: 10.1177/0146167205274894.

Sidanius, J., & Pratto, F. (2001). *Social dominance: An intergroup theory of social hierarchy and oppression.* Cambridge: Cambridge University Press.

Smith, J., & Welch, F. (1989). Black economic progress after Myrdal. *Journal of Economic Literature, 27*, 519–564.

Smith, T. (2000). *Taking America's Pulse II, NCCJ's 200 survey of intergroup relations in the United States.* New York: National Conference for Community and Justice.

Stangor, C., Sechrist, G., & Jost, J. T. (2001). Changing racial beliefs by providing consensus information. *Personality and Social Psychology Bulletin, 27*, 486–496. doi: 10.1177/0146167201274009.

Steele, C. (1988). The psychology of self-affirmation: Sustaining the integrity of the self. In L. Berkowitz (Ed.) *Advances in experimental social psychology* (Vol. *21*, pp. 261–302). Orlando, FL: Academic Press.

Steele, C., & Aronson, J. (1995). Stereotype threat and the intellectual test performance of African Americans. *Journal of Personality and Social Psychology, 9*, 797–811. doi: 10.1037/0022-3514.69.5.797.

Stockdale, M., & Crosby, F. (2004). *The psychology and management of workplace diversity*. Malden, MA: Blackwell.

Swim, J., & Sanna, L. (1996). He's skilled, she's lucky: A meta-analysis of observers' attributions for women's and men's successes and failures. *Personality and Social Psychology Bulletin, 22,* 507–519. doi: 10.1177/0146167296225008.

Tajfel, H. (1982). Social psychology of intergroup relations. *Annual Review of Psychology, 33,* 1–39.

Tajfel, H., Billig, M., Bundy, R., & Flament, C. (1971). Social categorisation and intergroup behaviour. *European Journal of Social Psychology, 1,* 149–178. doi: 10.1002/ejsp.2420010202.

Tal, A., Moran, G., Rooth, D., & Bendick, M., Jr. (2009). Using situation testing to document employment discrimination against persons with psychiatric disabilities. *Employee Relations Law Journal, 35,* 82–102.

Tomaskovic-Devey, D. (1993). The gender and race composition of jobs and the male/female, white/black pay gaps. *Social Forces, 72,* 45–76.

Townsend, B. (1997). *Confidential study of performance evaluations*. New York: Catalyst.

Trix, F., & Psenka, C. (2003). Exploring the color of glass: Letters of recommendation for female and male medical faculty. *Discourse and Society, 14,* 191–220.

U.S. Bureau of Labor Statistics (2008). Employed persons by detailed occupations, sex, race, and hispanic or latino ethnicity(Downloaded February 10, 2010 from www.bls.gov/cps/cpsaat11.pdf).

U.S. Bureau of Labor Statistics (2009). Job openings and labor turnover-August 2009 (Downloaded October 26, 2009 from www.bls.gov/news.release/pdf/jolts.pdf).

U.S. Equal Employment Opportunity Commission (EEOC) (2010). Charge statistics FY 2007 through FY 2009 (Downloaded February 22, 2010 from www.eeoc.gov/eeoc/statistics/enforcement/charges.cfm).

Valian, V. (1998). *Why so slow? The advancement of women*. Cambridge, MA: MIT Press.

Word, C., Zanna, M., & Cooper, J. (1974). The nonverbal mediation of self-fulfilling prophecies in interracial interactions. *Journal of Experimental Social Psychology, 10,* 109–120. doi: 10.1016/0022-1031(74)90059-6.

Yelnosky, M. (2010). *Testers Revisited*. Legal Studies Paper 74. Bristol, RI: Roger Williams School of Law.

Zitek, E. M., & Hebl, M. R. (2007). The role of social norm clarity in the influenced expression of prejudice over time. *Journal of Experimental Social Psychology, 43,* 867–876. doi: 10.1016/j.jesp.2006.10.010.

MARC BENDICK, JR., is a Principal in Bendick and Egan Economic Consultants, Inc., in Washington, DC. He received his PhD from the University of Wisconsin. His 125 scholarly publications concern poverty, employment, and public policies to enhance inclusion of individuals, businesses, and communities in the economic mainstream. He is a consultant on workforce diversity management to major employers, frequent expert witness in discrimination litigation, and has led dozens of matched pair testing studies.

ANA P. NUNES is a post-doctoral social psychology fellow at the Instituto de Ciências Sociais da Universidade de Lisboa (Institute of Social Sciences of the University of Lisbon). She received her Doctorate in social psychology from the University of Colorado Boulder. Her research interests focus on person perception processes and the effect of diversity mandates on judgments and behavior, especially in high-stake decision contexts such as hiring. She formerly directed testing studies of discrimination in housing for Project Sentinel in Palo Alto, CA, and employment for the Discrimination Research Center in Berkeley, CA.

Journal of Social Issues, Vol. 68, No. 2, 2012, pp. 263–285

Dearth by a Thousand Cuts?: Accounting for Gender Differences in Top-Ranked Publication Rates in Social Psychology

Mina Cikara*
Carnegie Mellon University

Laurie Rudman
Rutgers University

Susan Fiske
Princeton University

Publication in the Journal of Personality and Social Psychology, a flagship indicator of scientific prestige, shows dramatic gender disparities. A bibliometric analysis included yoked-control authors matched for PhD prestige and cohort. Though women publish less, at slower annual rates, they are more cited in handbooks and textbooks per JPSP-article-published. No gender differences emerged on variables reflecting differential qualifications. Many factors explain gender discrepancy in productivity. Among top publishers, per-year rate and first authorship especially differ by gender; rate uniquely predicts top-male productivity, whereas career-length uniquely predicts top-female productivity. Among men, across top-publishers and controls, productivity correlates uniquely with editorial negotiating and being married. For women, no personal variables predict productivity. A separate inquiry shows tiny gender differences in acceptance rates per JPSP article submitted; discrimination would be a small-but-plausible contributor,

*Correspondence concerning this article should be addressed to Mina Cikara, Department of Social and Decision Sciences, Carnegie Mellon University, Pittsburgh, PA 15213 [e-mail: mina.cikara@gmail.com].

The authors gratefully acknowledge the support of the Russell Sage Foundation, the Princeton Neuroscience Institute, Princeton's Joint Degree Program in Social Policy, and the Charlotte Elizabeth Procter fellowship, awarded by Princeton University to MC.

263

*absent independent indicators of manuscript quality. Recent productivity rates
mirror earlier gender disparities, suggesting gender gaps will continue.*

This volume discusses the pervasive nature of subtle bias across a variety of
contexts. Given that bias against women is often subtle, perhaps it is evident even
in the practices of those who are arguably at the front lines of efforts to identify and
eradicate it: social psychologists. Here, we examine potential sources of gender
disparity in publication rates within our flagship empirical journal and whether
gender bias may be exhibited in this group, one that would safely be considered
to be against prejudice.

Women have made substantial progress in social psychology, composing the
majority of undergraduate majors and even graduate students in many departments. However, at each higher level of the professional hierarchy, women are
less and less represented, and cohort effects do not account for these patterns; this
pattern is common to many sciences (National Academy of Sciences, 2006). For
example, despite the fact that women now earn 44% of doctoral degrees in science,
engineering, and math fields, the percentage of women who are full professors
in science and engineering has remained at 10% for the past 50 years (Rosser &
Taylor, 2009). Moreover, women are less likely to be chosen as leaders than men
in a variety of academic settings, despite the fact that female leaders are often as
effective, or even more effective, than male leaders (Eagly, Johannesen-Schmidt,
& van Engan, 2003; Rosser, 2003). Finally, women more often than men leave the
field at every stage of their professional careers (National Academy of Sciences,
2006). Many factors could account for this, but one factor might be perceived
scientific impact. We explore here disparities in a top-ranked publication process,
as a case study of one indicator in one academic field. Scientific contributions
are formally and informally measured mainly by publication rate in a field's best
empirical journals. Because publishing in the field's flagship journal increases
one's scientific impact, it is important to consider factors that predict women's
visibility in the journal.

Though subtle bias is a global phenomenon stretching across professional domains and societies, this paper focuses on a particular context—authors published
in the *Journal of Personality and Social Psychology (JPSP)*. In a bibliometric analysis, we counted how many articles the top 30 men and top 23 women
identified by Quiñones-Vidal, Lopez-García, Peñaranda-Ortega, and Tortosa-Gil
(2004) as frequent *JPSP* authors had published in *JPSP* from 1965 to 2004. We
noticed a stark gender difference in *JPSP* authorship identified but not examined
by Quiñones-Vidal et al. (2004): With the exception of Shelley Taylor, there is
no overlap between the men's and women's distributions. Note that a comparable
analysis of the top 20 male and female *Journal of Experimental Social Psychology*
authors showed the same gender divide, with men's publications ranging from

17 to 11, and women's from 8 to 4. Thus, we have evidence that *JPSP* is not unique vis-à-vis gender representation.

The current paper explores potential predictors of this gender disparity in *JPSP* publications. Specifically, we describe publication patterns of male and female authors since *JPSP*'s inception and examine the role of professional and personal variables in predicting *JPSP* visibility as well as other indicators of scientific impact. We stress again that this analysis is specific to this context: social psychologists in the United States. Our hope, however, is that this case study suggests advice for current and future female investigators that could help to narrow the gender gap and to increase women's scientific impact more broadly.

Method

Bibliometric Analyses

Using PsycINFO, we counted how many articles the 30 men and 23 women identified by Quiñones-Vidal et al. (2004) as frequent *JPSP* authors had published in *JPSP* from 1965 to 2004 (to extend Quiñones-Vidal et al.'s analysis, which had stopped at the year 2000). Tables 1 and 2 show the stark sex difference in *JPSP* authorship identified by Quiñones-Vidal et al. (2004). Using data from Tesser and Bau (2002), we noted the standardized ranking of these same authors for citations in the Gilbert, Fiske, and Lindzey (1998) *Handbook of Social Psychology* and in the Higgins and Kruglanski (1996) *Social Psychology: Handbook of Basic Principles*. The original Tesser and Bau list had 160 authors. Any of the 53 *JPSP* top authors not on this list were assigned a value of -1.00.

Using data from Proctor and Bujak (2001), we also noted these authors' rank order for textbook citation frequency (recoded from high to low). Proctor and Bujak used 12 full-length social psychology textbooks published between 1996 and 2001 to determine the 50 most cited social psychologists. Specifically, they collected data from the name index, recording the number of pages on which each author appeared. The number of pages for each author was summed and ranked. To control for bias, textbook authors' scores were based on the other texts. Any of the 53 *JPSP* top authors not on this Proctor-Bujak list were assigned a rank order of zero. The handbook and textbook citations represent the second and third scientific impact variables in Tables 1 and 2, respectively.

We also coded whether authors were APS or APA fellows as an indicator of scientific prestige. There were no sex differences on these variables, both $ts(51) <$ 1.00, *ns*. For male authors, APS and APA fellow status was related, $r(28) = .49$, $p < .01$. They did not covary reliably for women, $r(21) = .27$, *ns*. Because Fellow status did not predict our scientific impact variables, including *JPSP* authorship, for either gender, all $rs < .29$, *ns*, it will not be discussed. Finally, we counted the

Table 1. Scientific Impact of the Most Productive Male Authors in the Journal of Personality and Social Psychology

Author	*JPSP* 1965–2004	Handbook citations	Textbook citations
Wyer, Robert S.	52.00	−0.10	0.00
Petty, Richard E.	39.00	1.77	49.00
Diener, Ed	38.00	−1.00	0.00
Mischel, Walter	34.00	−0.22	0.00
Cialdini, Robert B.	32.00	−0.22	38.00
Insko, Chester A.	31.00	−1.00	0.00
Mikulincer, Mario	31.00	−1.00	0.00
Swann, William B.	30.00	−0.27	0.00
Greenberg, Jeff	30.00	−0.53	7.00
Baumeister, Roy F.	30.00	0.36	40.00
Cacioppo, John	29.00	1.56	42.00
Batson, C. Daniel	28.00	−1.00	27.00
Zuckerman, Miron	28.00	−1.00	0.00
Bandura, Albert	27.00	−.53	12.00
Carver, Charles, S.	27.00	−0.34	0.00
Wegner, Daniel M.	26.00	0.15	0.00
Holmes, David S.	25.00	−1.00	0.00
Komorita, Samuel S.	25.00	−1.00	0.00
Cooper, Joel	25.00	−0.60	0.00
Zanna, Mark P.	25.00	0.65	39.00
Higgins, E. Tory	25.00	3.33	10.00
Lepper, Mark R.	24.00	−1.00	0.00
Snyder, Mark	24.00	0.51	41.00
McCrae, Robert R.	24.00	−1.00	0.00
Ross, Michael	24.00	−0.43	0.00
Pyszczynski, Tom	24.00	−0.76	0.00
Sarason, Irwin	23.00	−1.00	0.00
Tesser, Abraham	23.00	0.13	17.00
Feather, N. T.	22.00	−1.00	0.00
Spanos, Nicholas P.	21.00	−1.00	0.00

Note. Total number of articles = 846.

total number of published papers for these 53 authors, using PsycINFO. Although quantity of output does not necessarily represent quality, we presumed it would positively correlate with (at least) some of the scientific impact variables.

Institutional Status

We used 1997 National Research Council (NRC) scores (available at www.socialpsychologynetwork.org) to code for the status of the authors' graduate

Table 2. Scientific Impact of the Most Productive Female Authors in the Journal of Personality and Social Psychology

Author	*JPSP* 1965–2004	Handbook citations	Textbook citations
Taylor, Shelley E.	24.00	1.89	43.00
Chaiken, Shelly	20.00	2.34	44.00
Park, Bernadette	19.00	−1.00	0.00
Eagly, Alice H.	18.00	1.94	50.00
Berscheid, Ellen	17.00	0.51	29.00
Langer, Ellen	17.00	−1.00	0.00
Major, Brenda	17.00	−1.00	0.00
Fiske, Susan T.	16.00	3.30	48.00
Wortman, Camille	16.00	−1.00	0.00
DePaulo, Bella M.	15.00	−1.00	0.00
Matthews, Karen A.	15.00	−1.00	0.00
Rusbult, Caryl E.	15.00	−1.00	0.00
Dweck, Carol S.	15.00	−1.00	0.00
Harackiewicz, Judith M.	15.00	−1.00	0.00
Rodin, Judith	14.00	−1.00	0.00
Andersen, Susan M.	14.00	−1.00	0.00
McFarland, Cathy	14.00	−1.00	0.00
Cantor, Nancy	13.00	−.64	0.00
Spence, Janet T.	13.00	−1.00	0.00
Walster, Elaine	13.00	−1.00	27.00
Nolen-Hoeksema, Susan	12.00	−1.00	0.00
Grusec, Joan E.	12.00	−1.00	0.00
Mackie, Diane	12.00	−.15	0.00

Note. Total number of articles = 356.

psychology PhD program. These ratings pertained to the top 185 U.S. programs and ranged from a rating of 49 (Boston University) to 72 (Stanford). Data for two authors who obtained foreign PhDs (one male, one female) and one male author who obtained an MD were not available.

Generating the Control Group

We generated a control group of authors, who had published at least once in *JPSP*, for comparison against the 53 *JPSP* top authors. First we generated a list of random numbers between 1 and 7,993 (the number of articles in *JPSP* between 1965 and 2004; #1 being the first editorial by Daniel Katz regarding the launching of *JPSP* and #7,993 being the last article in volume 87, issue 6). From the random number list, we looked up the first author of the corresponding article. The author was included in the control group and yoked to one of the original 53 authors if (1) the two authors received their PhDs within 3 years of one another and (2) their PhD granting institutions were within three points of each other, according to the 1997 NRC ranking score. If those conditions were not satisfied, then the random number was excluded and the next article (according to the next number in the random sequence) was chosen and the process repeated until all 53 authors had a yoked author, controlled for career age and graduate degree quality.

Personal Factors Websurvey

We examined personal factors using a brief websurvey emailed to the original 53 and corresponding control group of authors. We asked about authors' family status (e.g., "Current marital status," "Years married," "Previously married?", "Number of children"), department service (e.g., "Have you ever been Department Chair or served in another major administrative position (Dean, Provost)?"; "If yes, how many years?"), job satisfaction (e.g., "Overall, how would you describe your psychology career satisfaction?" on a 1 (disappointing) to 10 (highly satisfying) scale, and success negotiating with editors ("Consider only your submissions to *JPSP*: To the best of your recollection how often did you negotiate with an editor about a paper (e.g., trying to change a rejection to a revise and resubmit)?", "Of the times you negotiated with a *JPSP* editor, to the best of your recollection how often did it result in acceptance by *JPSP*?"). The number of respondents for the original and control authors was 44 and 36, respectively.

Results

Gender Differences in Scientific Impact for Original 53 Authors

Consistent with Quiñones-Vidal et al. (2004), the gender difference in *JPSP* authorship from 1965 to 2004 was robust ($Ms = 28.20$ vs. 15.47, respectively, for men and women, $t(51) = 9.0$, $p < .001$, $d = 1.57$). However, among these frequently published *JPSP* authors, there were *no* reliable sex differences for the number of handbook citations (standardized $Ms = -.25$ vs. $-.29$ for men and women, $t(51) = .14$, *ns*, $d = .04$), or for the number of textbook citations (rank order $Ms = 10.73$ vs. 10.48 for men and women, $t(51) = .05$, *ns*, $d = .01$). This suggests that *JPSP* visibility serves to ameliorate the large gender discrepancies found by Tesser and Bau's (2002) handbook and Proctor and Bujak's (2001) textbook analyses of scientific citation impact. That is, per *JPSP* article published, top female authors were more cited in handbooks and textbooks than top male authors. Thus, our first counsel to female authors is to publish in the field's flagship journal to increase their scientific impact.

Table 3. Correlates of Scientific Impact for Women and Men

	JPSP (1965–2004)	Textbook citations	Handbook citations	N articles
Women				
Textbook	0.56**			
Handbook	0.55**	0.92**		
N articles	0.29	0.31	0.37†	
Percent	0.09	−0.12	−0.21	−0.79**
Men				
Textbook	0.12			
Handbook	0.15	0.57**		
N articles	0.04	0.19	0.22	
Percent	0.34†	−0.17	−0.20	−0.86**

Note. Percent = the number of *JPSP* articles (1965–2004) divided by *N* Articles (the total of published articles, 1965–2004).
† $p < .10$; ** $p < .01$.

Is there evidence of gender bias in *JPSP* article acceptance? We obtained access to APA's general records of *JPSP* manuscripts submitted to articles published by gender. The gender difference is small, about 4%. Specifically, male authors had 135 articles accepted of 751 submitted (18%) and female authors had 65 articles accepted of 455 submitted (14%); however, it is not clear whether the cause is inferior quality, lack of persistence, or bias. To the extent that bias is a possibility, we recommend blind review for everyone, not the practice during the time period covered by these APA data.

Although not shown in Tables 1 and 2, men published more total articles than did women, resulting in a large effect size; $Ms = 134.57$ versus 74.83, $t(51) = 5.02$, $p < .001$, $d = 1.15$. However, computing the percent of published articles that appeared in *JPSP* (1965–2004) found no sex differences (both $Ms = 23\%$). Thus, men produce more articles but research quality (as measured by *JPSP* acceptance) appears to be equal for both genders. This suggests that women would need to make up the difference in sheer volume, not so much per-article quality, to catch up to male *JPSP* authors. Arguably, women might choose a different model, publishing fewer but higher impact articles, a point we explore next.

Predictors of Scientific Impact Variables

Table 3 shows the relationships among the scientific impact and productivity variables, separately for women and men. The first column presents number of *JPSP* publications (1965–2004). Our first surprise was that *JPSP* authorship is strongly related to textbook and handbook citations, but only for women. This observation buttresses our first counsel to women (that publishing in *JPSP* increases their scientific impact). For men, these correlations were negligible, suggesting that they have more independent sources of scientific impact than do women (that is, *JPSP* and textbook/handbook citations are separate indicators). A second surprise is that women who produce more total articles tend to appear in *JPSP* ($r = .29$, *ns*), whereas men's total output does not at all predict their *JPSP* visibility ($r = .04$, *ns*). Thus, perhaps women may have to work harder than men do to achieve success in the journal. That is, their sheer productivity may have to be higher for their work to appear in *JPSP*. This relationship also supports our second counsel to women (to produce more overall output to close the *JPSP* gender gap).

Tesser and Bau (2002) found the relationship between handbook and textbook citations to be robust, and stronger than the link between sheer number of articles (output) and scientific impact. Table 3 echoes their findings for both genders. However, the magnitude of the handbook and textbook citation correlation for women is nearly twice than that for men ($rs = .92$ vs. $.57$, respectively, $p < .05$), again suggesting that men draw scientific impact from more independent sources than women do.

Finally, men's *JPSP* visibility covaried with how much of their total output was published in the journal (the percent index), $p < .05$. There was no comparable linkage for women. That is, men who appear often in *JPSP* tend to use the journal as a home for their published research, whereas women do not. Thus, our third counsel to women is to submit more of their research to the journal.

Gender Differences in Variables Predicting JPSP Visibility

Because *JPSP* visibility strongly relates to women's scientific impact, it is important to uncover potential predictors of their success in the journal—predictors that might help to explain the gender gap in *JPSP* authorship. For example, possibly men began publishing in *JPSP* earlier, compared with women. However, we found only an unreliable 3-year difference between their initial publications ($Ms = 1972$ vs. 1975, *ns*, $d = .46$). Thus, men did not appear to have a significant "running start." However, and by contrast, men's most *recent* publication marked a later year ($M = 2001$), compared with women ($M = 1996$), resulting in a large effect ($d = .78$). Taking the difference between initial year and most recent year as an index of *JPSP* publishing period, we found that men have been publishing longer in the journal compared with women ($Ms = 28.30$ vs. 20.78 years, $d = 1.08$)—a difference of 7.5 years. This suggests that, although they started around the same time, women tend to end their *JPSP* publishing careers before men do. In addition to length, we computed the *JPSP* publication rate (ratio of *JPSP* publications to length of time publishing in *JPSP*). Men's publication rate was considerably faster, compared to women's ($Ms = .94$ vs. $.76$, $p < .05$, $d = .72$).

Do men and women show differences in *JPSP* authorship order? This would follow just from men publishing a higher quantity in general; however, it is possible the gender gap may vary by authorship position. Analyses revealed that men had more first and second authorships than did women, $t(51) = 5.14$, 2.66, $ps < .05$, $ds = 1.16$ and $.68$ for first and second authorships, respectively; $Ms = 14.76$ versus 7.70 for men versus women for first authorships and 8.43 versus 5.53 for second authorships. Third authorships favored men, but did not reliably differ by sex, $t(51) = 1.38$, ns, $d = .38$; $Ms = 1.80$ versus 1.21. Gender disparity is by far the greatest for first authorship (nearly twice that for second authorship and twice or more for later authorships). From this we can conclude that men are especially often first authors (14.76) compared with later authors (8.43, 1.80, .80), whereas women are also more likely to be first (7.70), but nearly as likely to be second (5.53). Quiñones-Vidal et al. (2004) suggested that men's greater tendency to network could reap an advantage. If so, men may publish more often as "late" (fourth or higher) authors, compared with women. Indeed, combining fourth through highest authorships (seventh was the highest), we found exactly this tendency ($Ms = .80$ vs. $.17$ for men and women, $t(51) = 2.15$, $p < .05$, $d = .58$). Moreover, women never appeared later than fourth author.

We also analyzed demographic variables. On average, marital status ($1 =$ single, $2 =$ married) did not reliably differ by gender; $Ms = 1.80$ vs. 1.74 for men and women, $t(51) = 0.75$, ns, $d = .13$. Although men tended to have more children, this difference was nonsignificant; $Ms = 1.28$ versus $.86$ for men and women, $t(51) = 1.57$, ns, $d = .45$. Plausibly, male authors were older than female authors, and this was borne out. On average, men received their PhDs 5 years earlier; $Ms = 1969$ versus 1974, $t(51) = 2.06$, $p < .05$, $d = .58$; however, as stated above, we found only an unreliable 3-year difference between men's and women's initial *JPSP* publications ($Ms = 1972$ vs. 1975).

Accounting for the Sex Difference in JPSP Success

Initial analyses suggested that publishing longer and faster are two variables that, not surprisingly, predict *JPSP* success, and both showed a gender difference that favors men. Taken together, they might account for the gender difference found by Quiñones-Vidal et al. (2004). Figure 1 shows the results of a mediational analysis (Baron & Kenny, 1986) predicting *JPSP* publications (1965–2004) from publishing rate and length. As can be seen, the substantial link between gender and *JPSP* publications was reduced to nonsignificance after accounting for publication career length and speed. Thus, to eliminate the gender gap in *JPSP* publications, women need to (i) continue to publish in the journal and (ii) publish at a faster rate.

But of course length and rate add up to sheer numbers, and women have less control over when they start to publish than the rate at which they publish in *JPSP*.

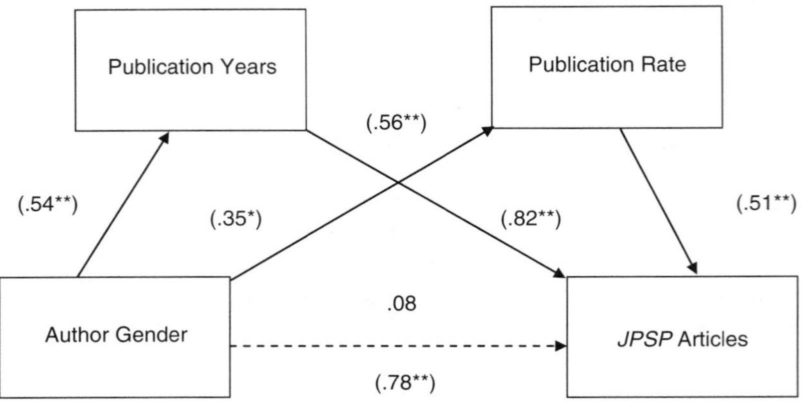

Fig. 1. Regression analyses testing length and rate of publication in *JPSP* as mediators of the relationship between author gender and *JPSP* publications (1965–2004). Coefficients in parentheses reflect a bivariate analysis. A dashed arrow indicates successful mediation. Author gender was coded 2 (male) 1 (female).

Separate mediational analyses for length and rate yielded a decrease in the effect of author gender on *JPSP* articles, but the gender gap remained reliable in each case, both betas $> -.68$, $ps < .001$. Thus, adjusting for the fact that men have been publishing longer in the journal than women was not a sufficient explanation for the overrepresentation of men. Instead, the faster rate at which men publish in *JPSP* is necessary to include to fully account for the gender discrepancy in *JPSP* publications.

Correlates of JPSP Variables

The above analysis is not particularly satisfying with respect to illuminating the gender gap in *JPSP* success. Suggesting to women that they need to publish longer and faster does not explain *why* men have longer publishing careers at *JPSP* or produce *JPSP* papers at a faster rate. In addition, other variables (beyond length and rate) might covary with *JPSP* success. Table 4 shows potential correlates of *JPSP* productivity, as well as length and rate of publishing in the journal, separately by gender. Table 4 includes variables that were derived from *JPSP* publications and demographics taken from the websurvey.

JPSP variables.   As already noted, and as is obvious, length and rate of publishing in *JPSP* predicts sheer number of *JPSP* articles; Table 4 reveals that for women, length was a reliable correlate of total number of *JPSP* articles, whereas rate was not. Thus, women may have to work several years longer to achieve high

Table 4. Correlates of JPSP Articles and *JPSP* Publishing Length and Rate, By Gender

	Women			Men		
	JPSP articles	Publishing length	Publication rate	*JPSP* articles	Publishing length	Publication rate
JPSP variables						
Length	0.55**			0.20		
Rate	−0.15	−0.84**		0.59**	−0.59**	
First author	0.34†	−0.05	0.27	0.43*	0.17	0.37*
Second author	0.21	0.38†	−0.27	0.68**	0.18	0.29
Third author	0.15	0.09	−0.06	0.02	0.19	−0.14
Late author	0.42*	0.09	0.04	−0.17	−0.31†	0.07
Initial year	−0.12	−0.24	−0.04	−0.01	−0.76**	0.42*
Recent year	0.36†	0.57**	−0.69**	0.27	0.22	−0.17
Demographics						
PhD year	0.04	−0.24	0.05	−0.02	−0.57**	0.30†
Marital status	0.10	0.37†	−0.38†	0.34†	0.16	0.12
Children	0.21	0.21	−0.22	0.14	0.26	−0.11

Note. Publishing length = the number of years publishing in *JPSP*. Publication rate = number of *JPSP* articles divided by publication years. Late author = sum of fourth through seventh authorships. Initial year marks the date of authors' first *JPSP* publication. Recent year marks the most recent *JPSP* publication year. Marital status was coded 1 = single, 2 = married. Children = number of children. † $p < .10$; *$p < .05$; **$p < .01$.

JPSP visibility. By contrast, for men, rate was a reliable correlate, whereas length was not. Thus, men who work quickly achieve success in the journal, and they do not necessarily have to earn their status over a long period time. Not surprisingly, publishing length and rate were negatively related for both genders, $p < .05$, suggesting that a longer publishing career covaried with slowing down.

Table 4 also reveals correlations between authorship order and *JPSP* visibility. First and second authorships correlated positively with men's *JPSP* success. Surprisingly, first authorship covaried marginally positively with women's success, whereas second authorship showed only a weak positive link. Presuming that first authorship demands more time and energy than second authorship, this is an indication that women may have to work harder than men to achieve *JPSP* success. Interestingly, "late" authorship was negatively linked to *JPSP* success for men, albeit weakly. However, it was positively related to *JPSP* success for women. As a result, cultivating networks appears to be good advice for women, because it may promote women's *JPSP* visibility. Finally, authorship order was not reliably related to publishing length or rate for either gender, with one exception. Men showed a positive relationship between first authorship and publication rate, whereas for women, this link was unreliably positive. In addition, men showed a marginally negative relationship between late authorship and publishing length, suggesting greater networking among younger male authors. Women showed a marginally positive link between second authorship and publishing length, suggesting that teamwork may extend women's *JPSP* publication career.

Demographic variables.   As noted, men tended to obtain their doctoral degrees earlier than women did. Table 4 shows that date of degree was related to neither men's nor women's *JPSP* success. However, younger men are more likely to produce faster, whereas PhD year and rate are not at all related for women. This suggests that younger women are not likely to close the gender gap. Rather, for women, it is a career-long process.

Might family demands hinder women's *JPSP* success? As can be seen, marital status and family size (number of children) were unreliably related to *JPSP* success for either gender, although there was a tendency for married men to publish more often in the journal, compared with unmarried men. For women, marital status positively covaried with publishing length, but negatively covaried with publishing rate, albeit marginally so in each case. To the extent that marriage slows down women's rate of *JPSP* publishing, it may augment the gender gap. The positive link between marriage and publishing length may also reflect the fact that older women (as measured by PhD year) tend to be married ($r = .42, p < .05$), whereas age and marriage are unrelated for men ($r = .17, ns$).

Institutional status.   Another possible explanation for the gender gap in *JPSP* authorship concerns the institutional status of our authors. If men graduated from more prestigious programs, they may be better equipped for an academic career. Unexpectedly, results showed that women graduated from more prestigious programs than men did, $t(48) = 2.33, p < .05$ ($Ms = 67.00$ vs. $63.71, d = .66$). However, PhD program status was unrelated to *JPSP* authorship variables, including number of publications, publishing years, and rate, for both genders (all $ps > .30$). Thus, although women tended to graduate from more prestigious programs, this difference cannot inform the gender gap in *JPSP* publications. Readers may find it noteworthy that 30% of the authors graduated from prestigious private institutions (five from Stanford, four from Yale, four from Harvard, and three from Princeton). Three authors each graduated from some of the most prestigious public universities—University of Michigan, Ohio State University, and University of North Carolina–Chapel Hill—resulting in an additional 17%.

A second possibility was that men might tend to be hired at more prestigious institutions, compared with women. Assuming that institutional prestige reflects greater publishing resources (e.g., collaborations with other faculty, internal research funds, and graduate students), it might have explanatory power. However, we found no gender differences in the status of authors' first or most recent departments, both $ts < 1.00, ns$. (Status was not coded for five male and two female authors housed in foreign institutions or government agencies.) In addition,

Table 5. Percent of Top-Published *JPSP* Authors Serving as *JPSP* Editors by Decade and Gender

	Men			Women		
Time span	Editor	Associate editor	Consulting editor	Editor	Associate editor	Consulting editor
1965–1974	0%	3%	17%	0%	0	4%
1975–1984	0%	7%	53%	0%	4%	26%
1985–1994	3%	3%	47%	0%	9%	57%
1995–2004	7%	3%	70%	0%	4%	52%

Note. Men $N = 30$; Women $N = 23$. Authors were counted as new editors each decade even if they were already counted in the previous decade.

institutional prestige, whether first or most recent, was unreliably related to the authors' number of *JPSP* publications, as well as their rate of production, all $ps > .31$. However, men's most recent status predicted their publishing length at *JPSP*, $r(22) = .43$, $p < .05$. By contrast, women did not show this relationship, $r(19) = .20$, *ns*. Thus, being housed in a prestigious institution may help men (but not women) to sustain their *JPSP* publishing career.

Finally, to examine whether men tended to gravitate, over time, to departments with higher status more often than women, we computed the difference in status between authors' first and most recent institution. This analysis yielded no sex difference, $t(51) < 1.00$, *ns*. That is, men did not show greater upward mobility than women. However, upward mobility tended to covary with number of *JPSP* publications, but only for men, $r(22) = .39$, $p = .06$. Women did not show this link, $r(19) = .13$, *ns*. One implication of this finding, as well as the relationship between men's most recent status and their *JPSP* career length, is that men may make greater use of the institutional resources available to them. Alternatively, these results could reflect that men's upward mobility is more dependent on their *JPSP* publication record, compared with women's. The latter seems unlikely, given the importance of women's *JPSP* publications for predicting other career status indicators (e.g., handbook and textbook citations). In either case, the fact that institutional status variables did not differ by sex preclude them as mediators of the gender gap in *JPSP* authorship. Although they may shed some light on why men outperform women at the journal, they cannot account for the gap.

JPSP editorial status.   Although to date, there have only been two female editors at *JPSP* (Patricia Devine and 2009 incoming editor, Laura A. King), the higher influx of women into the field from 1965 to the present ought to be reflected in greater female editorial positions, including associate and consulting editors.

We computed the percent of men and women from the original 53 who had served as editor, associated editor, or consulting editor for *JPSP*, across four decades (Table 5). While the percent of highly productive men serving as editor has increased a miniscule amount over time (from 0% to 7%), none of the most productive women have served as *JPSP* editor. The percent of productive men and women serving as associate editors has remained fairly stable over time (3–7% for men, and 4–9% for women). However, the percent serving as consulting editors increased for both men and women between 1965 and 2004. Collapsing across all four decades, the years served by an individual as an associate or consulting editor correlates with scientific impact for both genders. For men, years spent as an associate editor marginally relates to total number of *JPSP* articles, $r(28) = .33, p = .07$; years spent as a consulting editor positively correlates with handbook citations, $r(28) = .59, p < .05$, and textbook citations, $r(28) = .52, p < .05$, both of which are indicators of scientific impact. Similarly, for women, years spent as a consulting editor positively relates to total number of *JPSP* articles, $r(21) = .46$, as well as handbook citations, $r(21) = .57$, and textbook citations, $r(21) = .59$, all $ps < .05$. This suggests that accepting invitations to become a consulting editor at *JPSP* may be beneficial for women's productivity and visibility in the field. Alternatively, perhaps women are only asked to serve as consulting editors once they have become successful. Correlations that account for a lag demonstrated that for women, total number of *JPSP* articles in decade 1 positively related to years spent as consulting editor in decade 2, $r(21) = .59, p < .05$, and number of *JPSP* articles in decade 3 positively related to years spent as consulting editor in decade 4, $r(21) = .44, p < .05$; however, this relationship disappeared for female consulting editors who served from 1985 to1994. That said, we see a similar pattern for men: total number of *JPSP* articles in decade 1 positively related to years spent as consulting editor in decade 2, $r(21) = .36, p < .05$, number of *JPSP* articles in decade 2 positively related to years spent as consulting editor in decade 3, $r(21) = .45, p < .05$, but, this relationship disappeared for male consulting editors who served from 1995 to 2004. Overall, the lagged correlations suggest that being a consulting editor comes as a result of productivity.

JPSP Authorship by Decade.   To examine whether the gender gap in *JPSP* publications might be modified by decade, we measured authors' publication frequency over four decades (1965–1974, 1975–1984, 1985–1994, and 1995–2004). The first column of Table 6 shows the results in effect sizes, collapsed across authorship order. In each time period, men outscored women in total number of *JPSP* publications. However, the first decade showed only a marginally significant sex difference, $p = .05$. The next two decades revealed an increased gender gap, which has not been diminished in the most recent decade (all $ps < .01$). In fact, the difference between the first and last decade's gender gap is modest ($d = .16$).

Table 6 also shows effect sizes for gender differences as a function of *JPSP* authorship order, by decade. Gender differences in first authorship occur in every time period, but have decreased steadily since the second decade, resulting in a marginal difference for the most recent decade, $p = .08$. By contrast, the gender

Table 6. Effect Sizes for the Gender Gap in *JPSP* Publications by Decade and Author Order

Time span	Authorship combined	First author	Second author	Third author	Fourth or more author
1965–1974	0.53†	0.60*	0.19	0.19	0.32
1975–1984	0.88**	0.73**	0.59*	0.18	0.09
1985–1994	0.74**	0.65*	0.38	0.18	0.18
1995–2004	0.69**	0.48†	0.42	0.38	0.51†
1965–2004	**1.57****	**1.16****	**0.68***	**0.38**	**0.58**†

Note. Effect sizes are Cohen's *d*. Positive effects indicate that men published more than women. By convention, small, medium, and large effect sizes correspond to 0.20, 0.50, and 0.80, respectively (Cohen, 1988). Bold values indicate effect across all 4 decades.
† $p < .10$. * $p < .05$. ** $p < .01$.

Table 7. Mean *JPSP* Publications as a Function of Gender, Time Period, and Authorship Order

	1965–1974	1975–1984	1975–1984	1995–2004
Women				
Total	2.13[a]	4.76[b,c]	5.04[b,c]	3.87[a,b]
First author	1.22[a]	3.09[b]	2.48[a,b]	1.09[a]
Second author	0.74[a]	1.39[a,b]	1.96[b]	1.78[b]
Third author	0.17[a]	0.26[a]	0.48[a]	0.56[a]
Late author	0.00[a]	0.04[a]	0.13[a]	0.08[a]
Men				
Total	4.86[a]	8.53[b]	7.76[b]	7.03[b]
First author	3.63[a]	5.43[a,b]	4.17[a,b]	2.37[a]
Second author	0.87[a]	2.63[b]	2.77[b]	2.90[b]
Third author	0.30[a]	0.40[a,b]	0.60[a,b]	1.10[b]
Late author	0.06[a]	0.06[a]	0.23[a,b]	0.67[b,c]

Note. Means not sharing a superscript differ within rows at the $p < .05$ level or higher. Late author = sum of fourth through seventh authorships.

gap in late authorship—a possible indicator of networking—has increased in the most recent decade, resulting in a marginal advantage for men, $p = .07$. Third authorship is the only variable that has not yet shown a reliable sex difference, but the gender gap has doubled in the most recent decade, compared with earlier time periods. Thus, while women appear to be closing the gap when it comes to first authorship, the networking gap has grown.

Finally, Table 7 shows tests of within-decade differences in *JPSP* publication for women and men. The top row for each gender reflects the total number of papers, collapsed across authorship order. As can be seen, compared with the first time period, women produced more papers in the second and third decades.

However, the most recent decade shows a return to the publication level of the first. That is, the first and fourth decades do not reliably differ for women. Although women's fourth decade average is not different from the second's, it is reliably smaller than their output in the third decade. By contrast, men produced more papers in all time periods, compared with the first. Moreover, their output in the most recent time period is comparable to their second and third decade's averages. This is another sign that the gender gap is not on the wane.

The remaining rows in Table 7 indicate *JPSP* publications as a function of authorship order, for each time period. For women, first authorship rose in the second decade, but reverted to the initial figure in the third and fourth decades. Men showed a similar pattern. For both genders, second authorship increased by the third decade and remained steady in the fourth. However, third and late authorship show gender discrepancies. In each case, women's averages remained steady across the time periods. By contrast, men's averages have reliably increased by the fourth decade. In concert, Tables 6 and 7 suggest that men counteract their decrease in first authorship publications by networking, resulting in a steady output of *JPSP* papers over time, whereas women have not used this strategy as effectively.

Gender Differences in Comparison to Control Group

Is the gender gap unique to the 53 authors identified as top publishers by gender? To address this question, a 2 (male/female author) $\times$ 2 (original/yoked-control authors) ANOVA tested whether these groups differed in publication success and professional and personal factors. The main effects of author group demonstrated that the original 53 authors had higher values than the control authors on the following variables: handbook citations, textbook citations, number of APS fellows, total articles, total *JPSP* articles, percent of total articles that appeared in *JPSP*, length of career, rate of publication in *JPSP* (in general and adjusted for length of career), first author, second author, third author *JPSP* articles, and recent *JPSP* articles (published between 2001 and 2004), all $Fs(1, 105) > 6.35, p \leq .01$. The original 53 also had earlier dates of first *JPSP* article and later dates of last *JPSP* article, $Fs(1, 105) > 5.82, p < .05$.

Gender main effects revealed that control-group men had higher values than women on the following variables: total articles, total *JPSP* articles, first, second, third, and fourth or later author *JPSP* articles, recent *JPSP* articles (published between 2001 and 2004), length of *JPSP* career, rate of JPSP publication, and rate of JPSP publication in the last decade, all $Fs(1, 105) > 8.20, p < .01$. Men also had earlier PhD dates, and earlier dates for their first *JPSP* articles, all $Fs(1, 105) > 5.58, p < .05$.

The following effects were qualified by a significant group $\times$ gender interaction (means, highest to lowest: Men in Table 1 > women in Table 2 > control men > control women): total articles, total *JPSP* articles, first author *JPSP* articles, and recent *JPSP* articles, all Fs(1, 105) > 6.60, $p < .01$. These interactions all followed the same pattern: the difference between men in Table 1 and women in Table 2 was greater than the difference between control men and control women. Interestingly, we observed a slightly different pattern for the per-year *rate* of publication in *JPSP*, such that the productive men (Table 1) published at a greater rate than the productive women (Table 2), but that the control women published at a greater rate than the control men (who both published at a slower rate than the productive women in Table 2), $F(1,105) = 4.61, p < .05$. All of these interactions held when we reanalyzed these data using an ANCOVA controlling for PhD year, indicating these effects are not driven solely by length of career.

We also examined differences in personal variables between the two author groups. The original 53 authors were more likely to be married that than control authors, $F(1, 79) = 18.88, p < .01$; they also, however, had marginally fewer children than the control authors ($M_{original} = 1.49, SD = 1.24; M_{control} = 1.93, SD = 0.94$), $F(1, 79) = 3.33, p < .10$. Female authors (in general) tended to have fewer children than male authors ($M_{female} = 1.26, SD = 1.10; M_{male} = 1.91, SD = 1.12$), $F(1, 79) = 3.22, p < .10$. None of the other personal variables varied as a function of author group or gender.

Collapsing across author groups, their gender, marital status, number of children, and self-reported tendency of negotiating with editors correlated with *JPSP* publication outcomes: total number *JPSP* articles, rate of publication in *JPSP* (adjusted for length of career), number of first author *JPSP* articles, and number of recent *JPSP* articles (1995–2004). We were interested in examining the extent to which marital status, number of children, and tendency to negotiate with editors predicted these publication outcomes for men and women separately. We ran separate regressions for the four publication outcomes, for men and women, respectively (Table 8). We always entered the following variables stepwise in this order: number of children, marital status, and tendency to negotiate with editors. For men, being married (controlling for number of children and tendency to negotiate) is related to higher numbers of JPSP articles, greater rate of publication, more first author *JPSP* articles, and higher numbers recent *JPSP* articles (1995–2004). Men's tendency to negotiate with editors (controlling for marital status and number of children) also predicted total number of *JPSP* articles and marginally predicted number of first author *JPSP* articles. None of the personal factors significantly predicted JPSP publication outcomes for women.

Discussion

Clearly, publishing in *JPSP* matters to a social psychologist's career. Women's publication status in *JPSP* is especially linked to their citation frequency indices, whereas men apparently have other independent sources of scientific impact. As

Table 8. Personal Factors Predicting *JPSP* Publication Outcomes

	Men				Women			
	Total # *JPSP*	*JPSP* adj. rate	First author	Recent *JPSP*	Total # *JPSP*	*JPSP* adj. rate	First author	Recent *JPSP*
Predictor								
Number of children	−0.37(1.12)	0.02(0.05)	−0.79(0.82)	−0.47(0.65)	−0.75(0.83)	−0.05(0.04)	−0.69(0.56)	0.25(0.52)
Marital status	14.97**(2.53)	0.25*(0.12)	7.61**(1.85)	6.17**(1.47)	0.53(1.86)	0.01(0.10)	−1.43(1.24)	−0.44(1.17)
Negotiate with ed.	1.13*(0.52)	0.02(0.03)	0.70†(0.38)	−0.30(0.29)	1.03(0.79)	−0.03(0.04)	0.63(0.53)	−0.12(0.50)

Note. Unstandardized betas, standard error appears in parentheses. Predictors were entered simultaneously; table displays last model including all three predictors. Regression includes original 53 authors and yoked-control authors. Recent JPSP = number of JPSP articles 1995–2004. Marital status was coded 1 = single, 2 = married.
† *p* < .10; *p* < .05; ** *p* < .01.

a result, publishing in *JPSP* is particularly important for women. Taken together, these findings illuminate potential factors underlying the gender gap in *JPSP* publications. Moreover, there are reasons to suspect that the gender gap is not likely to decrease—at least, not among these productive authors.

First, authors' age, as indexed by PhD year and year of initial publication in *JPSP*, predicted both length and rate of *JPSP* publications, but only for men. Male authors who started later (and are, presumably, younger) not surprisingly have shorter publishing careers, but they also produce at a faster rate than more experienced authors. However, women did not echo these observations. That is, younger women are not necessarily faster, or likely to have shorter *JPSP* publishing careers, compared with experienced women. This suggests that a "running start" does not predict *JPSP* publishing length for women, and youth is not advantageous vis-à-vis their speed. Second, marriage is linked to age and a slower productivity rate for women (but not for men), suggesting that older women are likely to marry, but spousal duties may slow women down. Third, recent female *JPSP* authors tend to be experienced (i.e., success for women breeds success), but they also produce *JPSP* papers less often, whereas there is no matching maturity or slowing down effect for recent male authors.

Are there signs of burnout for women? Yes. First, women and men started publishing at approximately the same time in their careers, but men continue to publish longer in *JPSP*. Second, although length and rate were negatively linked for both genders (suggesting a slower rate for experienced authors; see Table 4), this relationship was stronger for women than for men, $z = 1.93, p = .05$. Thus, experienced men appear to have more stamina than their female counterparts.

Are there signs that younger women can pick up the slack? No. On the contrary, men who recently started to appear in the journal are publishing fast, but this is not so for younger women. Moreover, men's career span at *JPSP* does not predict their more recent publications. By contrast, women with longer track records are more likely to have authored recently in the journal. So while women need *JPSP* more than men do to ensure scientific impact, the indications are that women have to work longer to achieve a track record at *JPSP*, including recent authorship, but this achievement slows them down (more so than men), suggesting that the gender gap is not likely to decrease in the future.

In fact, when publications were examined by decade, there were two disturbing trends that buttress this conclusion. First, the gender gap started out as marginally significant, became reliable in the second decade and has remained so up to the most recent time span (1994–2004). In other words, the gap does not show a trend toward closing. Second, men have outpaced themselves in every decade, compared with the first. After an initial publication increase in the second decade, their numbers have remained steady. By contrast, women have declined in their output when the third and fourth decades are compared so that, most recently, their numbers have reverted back to the first decade. A possible reason for this is that men have widened the gender gap in networking (third or later authorship) in recent times, even while women have begun to catch up to men vis-à-vis first authorship. Nonetheless, the most compelling explanation is that men produce papers in the journal for a longer time period and at a faster rate; together, these two variables fully account for the male advantage in *JPSP* authorship. Our advice to women as individual scholars, then, is to submit early and often to *JPSP*, to network and collaborate, and above all to persist.

How can the field, as a whole, address the gender disparity? First, we reiterate the following: to the extent that bias is a possibility, we recommend double-blind review for everyone. Subtle bias may operate at every stage of evaluation and targets of discrimination are often unaware of the role it has played in the rejection or acceptance of their work (see Bendick & Nunes, 2012, and Pager & Western, 2012, for empirical approaches that bring subtle discrimination to light). Even among social psychologists—many of whom are dedicated to eradicating bias and discrimination, but who are also responsible for reviewing their peers' work— knowledge of the existing biases may not be sufficient to inoculate the evaluators (see Kang, 2012, for a discussion of evaluators' self-analysis with regard to bias). Second, the field needs to recognize multiple indicators of quality, such as textbook and handbook citations, as well as sheer numbers of articles. Current promotion trends acknowledge this by examining journal impact and article citation rates. Finally, as a career strategy, woman may be deciding to submit only their best work to a flagship journal such as *JPSP* because they perceive their research to be a trade-off with other nonwork roles, so it had better be worth the sacrifice. This quality-over-quantity strategy is an adaptive model, and the field needs to recognize it as a viable option.

We examined personal factors by a brief questionnaire emailed to all authors highly published in *JPSP* and to a control group of authors who also publish in *JPSP* but not as often. We asked about authors' family status, department service, job satisfaction, and success negotiating with editors. We predicted that negotiating with editors ought to increase publication outcomes for both genders, whereas marriage and children might decrease women's productivity more than men's (e.g., Eagly, 1987). Surprisingly, negotiation and being married were only reliable predictors for men (not for women). Specifically, men have marginally better self-rated negotiation success with editors, men have published longer in the journal, and men are more likely to be married. Of these predictors uncovered by our analyses that favor men (negotiation success, years publishing in the journal, and being married), only negotiation success accounted for unique variance when predicting *JPSP* success. We can just speculate as to why this pattern emerged. First, negotiation is often more successful for men than for women (Babcock & Laschever, 2003), and some evidence indicates that this is due to a double standard (i.e., women, but not men, who negotiate are perceived as "pushy" and "demanding"; Bowles, Babcock, & Lai, 2007). Second, having a spouse may afford men more time to concentrate on their careers, given that wives are typically more helpful than husbands regarding domestic responsibilities, even in dual-career families (e.g., Biernat & Wortman, 1991). Future research may determine what accounts for men's greater effectiveness when negotiating with editors and their success at publishing in *JPSP* when married.

Several potential explanations for the gender gap were not supported by our research. First, although sex differences in networking appeared, with men appearing as fourth (or later) authors more than women, this variable was not linked to *JPSP* success. Second, the idea that women's greater domestic demands undermine success was not supported; marital status and number of children were weak and not unique predictors of women's *JPSP* success. Third, men were not likely to receive their degrees from institutions with higher status than women. In fact, the reverse was true, although this advantage was not a predictor of *JPSP* success. Also surprising was the absence of gender differences in authors' first and most recent institutional status.

Finally, our analyses showed no sign that the gender gap in *JPSP* authorship is a function of cohort. Despite a steady increase in female reviewers and editors over time, women remain at a disadvantage in *JPSP* publications. In fact, when publications were examined by decade, we found that the gender gap started out as marginally significant, became reliable in the second decade, and has remained so up to the most recent time span (1994–2004). That is, there does not appear to be even a trend toward closing the gap.

Whatever the additional explanations, we have evidence of a gender gap in productivity overall, including in the sheer number (though not the proportion) of articles in top-ranked journals. A number of small effects all contribute: years married, length of time publishing in the journal, and negotiation with editors. In addition, we have evidence of a small amount of gender disparity in acceptance rate per article submitted. Absent an independent indicator of article quality, we cannot call this discrimination, but other measures suggest that women's articles are not of inherently lower quality (if anything, the reverse, considering impact per *JPSP* article published); the gender discrepancy in articles published does not diminish women's impact (as measured by textbook and handbook citations). Though our analysis is specific to social psychologists within the United States, given the pervasiveness of subtle bias, we suspect that a similar pattern of findings might emerge in other scientific disciplines and nonacademic domains in which an individual's success is determined in large part by the sheer quantity of her productivity and visibility in the field. If the disparity is caused by discrimination, it is discrimination by a thousand little cuts. There is no single, quick fix.

References

Babcock, L., & Laschever, S. (2003). *Women don't ask: Negotiation and the gender divide*. Princeton, NJ: Princeton University Press.

Baron, R., & Kenny, D. (1986). The moderator–mediator variable distinction in social psychological research: Conceptual, strategic, and statistical considerations. *Journal of Personality and Social Psychology, 51*, 1173–1182. doi: 10.1037/0022-3514.51.6.1173.

Bendik, M., & Nunes, A P. (2012). Developing the research basis for controlling bias in hiring. *Journal of Social Issues, 68*(2), 238–262. doi: 10.1111/j.1540-4560.2011.01747.x

Biernat, M., & Wortman, C. B. (1991). Sharing of home responsibilities between professionally employed women and their husbands. *Journal of Personality and Social Psychology, 60*, 844–860. doi: 10.1037/0022-3514.60.6.844.

Bowles, H. R., Babcock, L., & Lai, L. (2007). Social incentives for gender differences in the propensity to initiate negotiations: Sometimes it does hurt to ask. *Organizational Behavior and Human Decision Processes, 103*, 84–103. doi: 10.1016/j.obhdp.2006.09.001.

Cohen, J. (1988). *Statistical power analysis for the behavioral sciences* (2nd ed.). Hillsdale, NJ: Erlbaum.

Eagly, A. (1987). *Sex differences in social behavior: A social-role interpretation*, Hillsdale, NJ: Erlbaum.

Eagly, A. H., Johannesen-Schmidt, M. C., & van Engen, M. L. (2003). Transformational, transactional, and laissez-faire leadership styles: A meta-analysis comparing women and men. *Psychological Bulletin, 129*, 569–591. doi: 10.1037/0033-2909.129.4.569.

Gilbert, D. T., Fiske, S. T., & Lindszey, G. (Eds.) (1998). *Handbook of social psychology*. New York: McGraw-Hill.

Higgins, E. T., & Kruglanski, A. (Eds.) (1996). *Social psychology: Handbook of basic principles*. New York: Guilford.

Kang, J. (2012). The missing quadrants of anti-discrimination: Going beyond the "prejudice polygraph". *Journal of Social Issues, 68*(2), 314–327. doi: 10.1111/j.1540-4560.2011.01750.x

National Academy of Sciences (2006). *Beyond bias and barriers: Fulfilling the potential of women in academic science and engineering*. Washington, D.C.: The National Academies Press.

Pager, D., & Western, B. (2012). Identifying discrimination at work: The use of field experiments. *Journal of Social Issues, 68*(2), 221–237. doi: 10.1111/j.1540-4560.2011.01746.x

Proctor, D. L., & Bujak, A. (2001, June). *Coverage of core concepts by introduction to psychology textbooks*. Poster session presented at the 13th annual meeting of the American Psychological Society, Toronto, Ontario, Canada.

Quinones-Vidal, E., Lopez-Garcia, J. J., Penaranda-Ortega, M., & Tortosa-Gil, F. (2004). The nature of social and personality psychology as reflected in JPSP, 1965–2000. *Journal of Personality and Social Psychology, 86*, 435–452. doi: 10.1037/0022-3514.86.3.435.

Rosser, V. J. (2003). Faculty and staff members' perceptions of effective leadership: Are there differences between men and women? *Equity and Excellence in Education, 36*, 1–25. doi: 10.1080/10665680303501.

Rosser, S. V., & Taylor, M. Z. (2009). Why are we still worried about women in science? *Academe, 95*(3), 6–10.

Tesser, A., & Bau, J. J. (2002). Social psychology: Who we are and what we do. *Personality and Social Psychology Review, 6*, 72–85. doi: 10.1207/S15327957PSPR0601_4.

MINA CIKARA is currently a NIH Ruth L. Kirschstein postdoctoral fellow at MIT. She received her PhD in social psychology and social policy from Princeton University in 2010. Cikara is a social cognitive neuroscientist who studies how competition, stereotypes, and prejudice disrupt the processes that allow people to see one another as human and to empathize with others. She uses a wide range of tools—standard laboratory experiments, implicit and explicit behavioral measures, fMRI, and psychophysiology—to study how misunderstanding, failures of empathy, and dehumanization unfold in the brain, as well as the behavioral consequences of these processes. She will begin a tenure-track faculty appointment in the department of social and decision sciences at Carnegie Mellon University in Fall 2012.

LAURIE A. RUDMAN is a Professor of psychology at Rutgers University in New Brunswick, New Jersey. Her research interests are intergroup relations and social justice issues, with a focus on predicting behavior from implicit attitudes and beliefs. The author of over 60 professional publications, she serves on several editorial boards and is currently a Senior Associate Editor of *Personality and Social Psychology Bulletin*. Her honors and awards include a National Science Foundation Fellowship, a National Research Service Award (National Institutes of Health), and she has twice been awarded (with Eugene Borgida and Julie Phelan) the Gordon Allport Prize for the best paper on intergroup relations, given annually by the Society for the Psychological Study of Social Issues. She is a fellow of the American Psychological Association, the Association for Psychological Science, and an honorary member of the Society for Experimental Social Psychology (SESP), for whom she served as representative to the Federation of Behavioral, Psychological, and Cognitive Sciences. Her current NSF-funded program of research aims to discover the factors that promote or hinder negative reactions to counterstereotypicality on the part of both perceivers and actors. The downstream consequences of these reactions include cultural stereotype maintenance and human capital issues. The author of *The Social Psychology of Gender: How Power and Intimacy Shape Gender Relations* (with Peter Glick), Dr. Rudman has frequently served as an expert witness in gender discrimination cases.

SUSAN T. FISKE is Eugene Higgins Professor of psychology, Princeton University (PhD, Harvard University; honorary doctorates, Université Catholique de Louvain-la-Neuve, Belgium; Universiteit Leiden, Netherlands). She investigates social cognition, especially cognitive stereotypes and emotional prejudices, at cultural, interpersonal, and neuroscientific levels. Author of over 250 publications and winner of numerous scientific awards, she has edited most recently, *Beyond Common Sense: Psychological Science in the Courtroom* (2008) and the *Handbook of Social Psychology* (2010, 5/e). Currently an editor of *Annual Review of Psychology, Psychological Review,* and the forthcoming *Behavioral Science and Policy*, she wrote *Social Beings: Core Motives in Social Psychology* (2010, 2/e) and *Social Cognition: From Brains to Culture* (2008, 3/e). Sponsored by a Guggenheim, her 2011 Russell-Sage-Foundation book is *Envy Up and Scorn Down: How Status Divides Us*.

Journal of Social Issues, Vol. 68, No. 2, 2012, pp. 286–313

The World Is Not Black and White: Racial Bias in the Decision to Shoot in a Multiethnic Context

Melody S. Sadler*
San Diego State University

Joshua Correll
University of Chicago

Bernadette Park and Charles M. Judd
University of Colorado at Boulder

We examined implicit race biases in the decision to shoot potentially hostile targets in a multiethnic context. Results of two studies showed that college-aged participants and police officers showed anti-Black racial bias in their response times: they were quicker to correctly shoot armed Black targets and to indicate "don't shoot" for unarmed Latino, Asian, and White targets. In addition, police officers showed racial biases in response times toward Latinos versus Asians or Whites, and surprisingly, toward Whites versus Asians. Results also showed that the accuracy of decisions to shoot was higher for Black and Latino targets than for White and Asian targets. Finally, the degree of bias shown by police officers toward Blacks was related to contact, attitudes, and stereotypes. Overestimation of community violent crime correlated with greater bias toward Latinos but less toward Whites. Implications for police training to ameliorate biases are discussed.

As the country becomes increasingly diverse, attempts to address overt and subtle forms of prejudice and discrimination based on race and/or ethnicity take on a new importance. The U.S. Census Bureau (2008) projects that by 2050, racial and ethnic minorities combined will constitute 54% of the population, the numerical

*Correspondence concerning this article should be addressed to Melody S. Sadler, Department of Psychology, San Diego State University, San Diego, CA 92182 [e-mail: msadler@sciences.sdsu.edu].

This work was supported by a grant from the Russell Sage Foundation. The authors wish to thank the police officers who took part in the study and Calibre Press whose cooperation was integral to completing the research. They also thank Kyle Jensen and Christopher Blankenship for their tireless effort and assistance in the research.

majority. The largest changes to the racial/ethnic composition of the country are expected in the decrease of non-Latino, single-race Whites, and corresponding increase in Latinos and Asians. Whites are expected to decrease from 66% to 46% of the population. In contrast, Latinos are expected to increase from 15% to 30% and Asians are expected to increase from approximately 5–9% of the population. The representation of Blacks is expected to remain relatively stable, constituting about 15% of the population.

In understanding the racial and ethnic transition the country will face, two implications seem evident. First, research on stereotyping, prejudice, and discrimination should increase its attention to bias toward people of Latino or Asian descent (Martinez, 2007; Peterson & Krivo, 2005). Second, researchers should anticipate that the shift of Whites from the numerical majority to a minority is likely to strain relations among racial/ethnic groups within the United States. In fitting with this special issue, the current research examined how implicit racial biases toward Blacks, Latinos, and Asians may be evidenced in the decision to open fire on suspects in the United States.

From this point forward, we use "race" rather than "race/ethnicity" for simplicity because most available national sources record race or ethnicity, but not both (the census is an exception). Our choice of race is meant to represent physical attributes such as skin color, hair, etc., that facilitate categorization. It should be noted that it is possible that race and ethnicity each contributes independently to biases, or that the differences attributed to race are at least in part due to ethnic differences.

Race and Law Enforcement

Data drawn from national sources such as the U.S. Department of Justice (DOJ; 2001) and Bureau of Justice Statistics (BJS; 2007) provide evidence that some minorities, especially young Black males, are incarcerated at disproportional rates. Compared to their proportion of the general population, Blacks are grossly overrepresented and Whites are underrepresented as inmates. Latinos, in contrast, are incarcerated at rates approximately equal to their representation in the population.

Equally disturbing is the fact that some minorities are overrepresented in the suspects shot and killed by police officers. The DOJ (2001) reports that Black suspects were killed by police at a rate about five times greater than White suspects in the period from 1976 to 1998. Information on the rates of justifiable homicide for Asians and Latinos are less clear. Asians are designated simply as "other" (a category encompassing multiple races) and at a maximum account for 2 or 3% of those shot. The prevalence rates for Latinos cannot be directly discerned from the DOJ data because Latinos are included in the racial category "White." Some sources report, however, that Latinos are shot and killed more often by police than Whites but less than Blacks (for a review, see Geller, 1982).

The available national-level data clearly point to Blacks being killed by police more often, and Whites and Asians less often, than would be expected given the percent of the population they represent in the United States. It should be noted that evidence for disparate treatment of ethnic minorities, immigrants, or "foreigners" by the criminal justice system has been found cross-culturally (Albrecht, 1997; Johnson, van Wingerden, & Nieuwbeerta, 2010). However, the focus of the current work is on implicit racial biases that may underlie differential treatment in the United States.

It is one thing to document the discrepancy in treatment of racial/ethnic minorities by police and/or the criminal justice system in the United States, and it is quite another to understand why it exists. A major debate in the criminology literature involves the degree to which this discrepancy reflects bias in the justice system, the tendency for minorities to engage in more criminal activity, or both (Cureton, 2001; Goldkamp, 1976). In other words, are minorities more likely than Whites to participate in criminal behavior (justifying the differences in incarceration) or is the law differentially enforced for suspects as a function of their race?

Evidence on this point is mixed. The subculture of violence (Wolfgang & Ferracuti, 1967) and danger perception (MacDonald, Kaminski, Alpert, & Tennenbaum, 2001) theories suggest that minorities are more likely than Whites to commit crime due to the history of each group in the United States, cultural variations in response to minor affronts, and/or distrust in the justice system to resolve disputes. The overrepresentation of minorities in prison, especially Blacks, is often cited in support of this view. However, survey research has found no evidence that African Americans endorse violence as more acceptable than other races (Parker, 1989; Smith, 1992). Further, Hannon (2004) reviewed 950 cases of nonjustifiable homicide and found no evidence that victim provocation patterns differed by offender race. Thus, African Americans perpetrators were no more or less likely than White perpetrators to react with lethal force to minor transgressions.

Perhaps, the most researched theory of law enforcement in the United States, conflict theory, proposes that the purpose of law is to sustain the position of the majority in society (Turk, 1969) building an inherent bias into the system. Historically, in the United States, this has meant buttressing the position of Whites against the "threat" of minority groups based on race and socioeconomic and immigrant status (Holmes, 2000). This theory lends itself to two immediate corollaries: First, police officers may label or "criminalize" minorities unfairly and police them differently than Whites (Cureton, 2001) and second, as the ethnic composition of the country changes, minorities should pose a greater threat to the majority and attempts to police and control them will intensify (this has been labeled the threat hypothesis, MacDonald et al., 2001). Given the current climate of concern over racial bias, it seems unlikely that blatant, intentional discrimination of the sort proposed by conflict theory is responsible for differential outcomes experienced by racial groups in the criminal justice system at present. Instead, it is more likely that stereotypes insidiously influence behavior without awareness or intention. Nevertheless, as called for by Kang (2012), it will be the charge of law and law enforcement to adjust to the shifting basis of discrimination.

Whatever the "cause" of the overrepresentation of minorities in the criminal justice system at the national level, we propose that knowledge of this racial/ethnic discrepancy may impact perceptions and conduct of police officers in encounters with civilians. To be clear, the current research does not and cannot determine whether or not disproportionate minority involvement with law enforcement is justified. But regardless of its cause, we suggest that the mere association between minorities (particularly Black and Latino groups) and crime at the societal level may have consequences for police behavior at the individual level.

In some encounters, police officers must make life-or-death decisions quickly. In these moments, prior expectations—be they fact or fiction, personally endorsed or simply prevalent in the culture—may influence how information is processed. Knowledge that racial minorities, and Blacks in particular, are overrepresented in prison and jail (BJS, 2007) and are more likely to use a firearm in commission of a crime (DOJ, 2001) may contribute to an increased perception of minorities as threats. Also relevant are characteristics of the neighborhood served. Violent crime rates and the proportion of non-White people in an area have been associated with increased perception of threat (Cureton, 2001). Taken in sum, these factors may influence the level of threat officers expect in interactions with minorities. Couple with this, the distrust racial/ethnic minorities report toward police (Locke, 1996), and fodder for a self-fulfilling prophecy of aggressive encounters is laid. Awareness of a societal-level phenomenon, whatever its underlying cause, may thus be associated with implicit biases that impact cognitive processing or behavior (Fisher & Borgida, 2012). Applied to the context of race and law enforcement, the mere association of race and criminality at the societal level may impact, for example, the speed with which stimuli are processed and the likelihood of a decision to open fire.

Race and the Decision to Shoot

It is difficult to determine whether or not race influences the course of encounters between police officers and suspects. In the real world, minority status is (on average) associated with a number of factors such as poverty, living in disadvantaged neighborhoods, and living within disorganized family structures (Sampson & Lauritsen, 1997), making a clear attribution difficult (e.g., were the officers responding to the suspect's race or to the threatening neighborhood?). However, experimental research that isolates the effect of race on shoot/don't shoot decisions demonstrates that race alone can influence responses to threatening objects. Correll, Park, Judd, and Wittenbrink (2002) asked college-aged participants to perform a first-person-shooter (FPS) task, so-called because the participants take the first-person perspective of an officer who must make rapid judgments about whether or not to shoot Black and White male suspects (targets) who appear on the screen holding either a gun or a nonthreatening object (such as a wallet or cell phone). Participants were faster to shoot armed Black targets than armed White targets, and they were faster to decide not to shoot unarmed White targets than unarmed Blacks. Further, this effect transferred into mistaken decisions or behaviors when participants were forced to respond extremely quickly. Importantly, the degree of racial bias against Black targets did not differ between White and Black participants.

In these simulations, target race is not diagnostic of the presence or absence of a weapon. This is important because it allows the investigators to conduct a direct examination of the impact of racial cues, *per se*, on the tendency to shoot. Given the time pressure and complexity of stimuli employed, the ability to exert control over responses was diminished, making it likely that observed racial biases in behavior were implicit or operating outside of conscious control. Although compelling, demonstrations of implicit racial bias among college students in the laboratory lack external validity. Examining the phenomenon among police officers provides a better gauge of the extent to which implicit racial bias may impact the decision to open fire and thus contribute to the disparity in rates of minorities versus Whites shot and killed by police.

Two groups of researchers have investigated the effect of race on decisions to shoot with police officers (Correll et al., 2007; Peruche & Plant, 2006; Plant & Peruche, 2005). Correll et al. (2007) found that police officers and community members both showed bias in the speed of their responses (responding more quickly to stereotypic targets). Consistent with prior work, the extent of racial bias in response times did not differ between White and non-White officers. But in spite of this bias in reaction time, police officers were no more likely to shoot an unarmed Black target than they were to shoot an unarmed White. In other words, despite the influence of race on the time taken to make correct decisions, police officers were able to overcome the impact of race and choose whether or not to "open fire" as a function of the weapon held, not the race of the person holding it. Using a different paradigm, Plant and Peruche (2005) found that although police officers initially exhibited racial bias in the decision to shoot, bias decreased with practice. Thus, college students, community members, and police officers all evidenced an implicit racial bias in the time taken to make a decision to shoot; however, police officers were able to overcome this bias when instigating a behavioral response.

The Current Research

No prior research has investigated bias toward Latinos and Asians in a shoot/don't shoot scenario. In light of differential minority contact with law enforcement and the profound demographic changes taking place in the

United States, such an investigation is both timely and important. The current research examined implicit racial bias in the decision to shoot White, Black, Latino, and Asian male targets in a FPS task in two studies. In the first study, we investigated the performance of college students on two primary outcomes. First, we examined the average response times needed to *correctly* determine if targets of each race were armed or unarmed. Racial bias in reaction times is indicated by faster responses to stereotypic combinations (e.g., armed Black target) than counter-stereotypic combinations (e.g., unarmed Black target). Second, we examined whether target race influenced the pattern of correct versus incorrect responses. Both racial bias measures are assumed to reflect the influence of cultural stereotypes; however, our previous work suggests that they may reflect different components of cognitive processing (Correll et al., 2007). Although stereotypes may impact the speed with which correct responses are made, whether or not they affect the ultimate decision to shoot may depend on the extent to which perceivers can exert control over their behavioral response.

In the second study, we examined implicit racial bias in reaction times and errors among police officers, and whether these biases varied as a function of community characteristics and personal or cultural beliefs. For example, one might expect that officers who serve areas in which the predominant criminal element is Latino should show a greater bias toward Latinos than they do toward Blacks. To allow for sufficient variability in types of communities and personal beliefs, we recruited police officers from the Southeast, Southwest, and Northwest regions of the United States.

The present research thus exemplifies "full-cycle social psychology" (Cialdini, 1980; Dasgupta & Stout, 2012) wherein the phenomenon of interest was borne of real-life events (i.e., mistaken shootings of unarmed minority suspects by police officers) and examined both in the laboratory and with experts from the field. Inclusion of both samples allows for an investigation of whether or not implicit racial bias findings from the lab converge with those of officers who are accountable for decisions to use deadly force on the job. Another benefit of an investigation of police officers may be that "...implicit bias in decision-making from these studies can be directly connected to societal-level disparities" (Dasgupta & Stout, 2012).

Study 1: Overview

To examine the effect of different race/ethnic groups on the decision to shoot, we created a multiethnic environment in a computer task. We employed a four-group FPS task with target race randomly varying from trial to trial between Black, White, Latino, and Asian males.

Participants

Sixty-nine undergraduate students from the University of Colorado at Boulder participated in exchange for partial credit toward a course requirement. Participants were approximately equally divided on gender (34 males, 30 females, and 5 missing) and predominantly White (75% White, 2% Black, 5% Asian, 3% Latino, 3% Native American, and 8% other). Although there were too few Black participants in Study 1 to examine if Black and White participants performed differently on the FPS task, previous work found no evidence that bias varied between these groups (Correll et al., 2002).

Video Game Simulation

The original FPS task, developed by Correll and colleagues (see Correll et al., 2002), focused on bias in the decision to shoot Black compared to White males. To make a multiethnic version of the task, Latino and Asian American male targets were added. Latino and Asian college-aged males, recruited from three college campuses in the Denver metropolitan area, were paid $8 to be photographed holding four plastic guns (silver and black revolvers and automatic handguns) and four nonthreatening objects (black wallet, black cell phone, silver cell phone, and silver soda can) in each of five poses (e.g., standing with hand holding object positioned near the shoulder). Consent was obtained from all men to use their photographs in future research.

We chose new targets to be included in the shooter task based on a pilot study in which their race was correctly identified by a majority of police officers and community members.

Design

The multiethnic FPS task was based on the 4 (Target Race: Black vs. Latino vs. Asian vs. White) × 2 (Object: Gun vs. No Gun) within-participant design. During each trial, one to three preceding empty background scenes (e.g., a bus terminal or a city park) was presented for 200 to 500 ms each. The number of preceding backgrounds and the duration of the backgrounds were randomly determined per trial. Next, the target background appeared for 500–800 ms before the target photo appeared on the background. From stimulus onset, participants were required to respond within an 850 ms time window. Participants were instructed to "shoot" targets holding guns and to indicate "don't shoot" for targets holding innocuous objects. Responses were made on button boxes with the leftmost button labeled "don't shoot" and the rightmost button labeled "shoot" (the button box orientation was reversed for left-handed participants in order to have all participants "shoot" with their dominant hand). Participants were instructed to leave their thumbs or forefingers over the buttons in between trials.

A point structure for trial-by-trial performance was used to make the game and its potential consequences, personally relevant for participants. Mirroring real life, the cost of mistakes was greater than the reward of accurate responses, especially the error of failing to shoot a threatening target. Correct responses earned five points (not shooting an unarmed target) or 10 points (shooting an armed target). Incorrect responses were more heavily weighted and cost 20 points (mistakenly shooting an unarmed target) or 40 points (failing to shoot an armed target). A time-out, or failing to respond within the 850 ms window, resulted in a 10-point deduction. At the end of each trial, participants received auditory and on-screen feedback regarding the points earned or lost during the trial and a cumulative point total.

The multiethnic FPS task included 20 targets for each racial group, each presented once armed and once unarmed. Thus, there were 40 test trials per race group and 160 test trials overall. Twenty-four practice trials were also included. The sequence of trials was randomly determined within practice and test trials. Reaction time and whether or not the decision was correct were recorded per trial.

Procedure

An experimenter met participants and guided them to individual cubicles for the duration of the study. The experimenter explained that participants were to quickly and accurately respond to photographs of males on-screen based on the type of object they held. Detailed instructions and the FPS task were presented using Psyscope software (Cohen, MacWhinney, Flatt, & Provost, 1993) on iMac desktop computers. Participants wore headphones to receive auditory feedback and reduce interference from participants in neighboring rooms. Finally, the experimenter instructed participants to fill out a questionnaire packet that was left in a manila envelope in the room after they finished the video game. Participants were thanked and debriefed at the end of the session.

Results and Discussion

Reaction Time

Reaction times for trials on which participants responded correctly (94.8% of trials across participants) were log-transformed. An average log-transformed reaction time was then computed for each participant for each type of target (e.g., Black with gun and White with no gun). Log-transformed reaction times were analyzed by a Target Race (Black or Latino or White or Asian) × Object (Gun or

Table 1. Reaction Time and Sensitivity as a Function of Object and Target Race (Study 1)

| | Target race | | | | | | | |
| | Black | | Latino | | Asian | | White | |
Variable	M	SD	M	SD	M	SD	M	SD
Reaction time (ms)								
Gun	543_a	43	537_b	38	558_c	37	552_d	41
No gun	623_a	38	593_b	41	617_a	40	605_c	42
Average	583_a	36	565_b	36	588_c	35	579_a	37
Sensitivity (d')	3.55_a	.51	3.61_a	.52	3.39_b	.51	3.41_b	.58

Note. Differing subscripts within a row indicate significant differences, $p < .05$, except for the comparison between Black/unarmed and Asian/unarmed, $p < .06$. All sensitivity means significantly differed from zero, $p < .05$. $N = 69$.

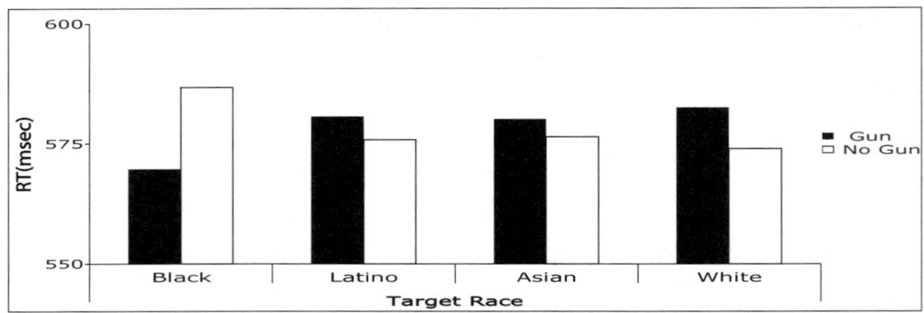

Fig. 1. Reaction time as a function of object and target race (Study 1).

Note. Reaction times were mean polished.

No Gun) repeated measures ANOVA. Means backtransformed to the millisecond metric are presented in Table 1 and Figure 1. Reported effect sizes are PREs that reflect the proportional reduction in error due to a predictor or planned contrast (Judd, McClelland, & Ryan, 2008). In the analyses we report, PRE is equivalent to a partial eta-squared.

There was a significant main effect of object, $F (1, 68) = 299.00, p < .001$, PRE $= .81$. Participants correctly responded more quickly, on average, to gun ($M = 548$) than no gun trials ($M = 610$). There was also a significant main effect of race, $F (3, 204) = 51.24, p < .001$. We tested all possible pairwise comparisons among target groups. On average, across the object held by targets, participants responded more quickly when making the correct decision for Latino targets ($M = 565$) than Black targets ($M = 583$), $F (1, 68) = 108.16$, PRE $= .61$, $p < .001$; White targets ($M = 579$), $F (1, 68) = 54.91$, PRE $= .447, p < .001$; and

Asian targets ($M = 588$), F (1, 68) = 17.22, PRE = .20, $p < .001$. Participants responded *more slowly* overall when making the correct decision to Asian targets than White targets, F (1, 68) = 17.22, PRE = .20, $p < .001$, or Black targets, F (1, 68) = 7.67, PRE = .10, $p = .007$. As in our previous work, the comparison in mean reaction times for Black versus White targets was not significant, F (1, 68) = 2.72, PRE = .035, *n.s.*

Of primary interest were the Race × Object interactions that gauge racial bias in the decision to shoot. The omnibus Race × Object interaction was significant, F (3, 204) = 16.81, $p < .001$. We tested all pairwise "simple" Race × Object interactions to examine the patterns of bias as a function of specific pairwise race comparisons. For example, we tested if responses to gun versus no-gun trials differed when the objects were held by Black versus Latino targets. Further, to interpret the Race × Object interactions, we applied a mean polish transformation to the reaction time data within each pairwise comparison. Rosnow and Rosenthal (1989) noted that researchers often misinterpret interactions by looking at simple effect tests among original cell means. This approach is problematic because differences in the original cell means also reflect lower order effects (e.g., main effects) thereby obscuring the nature of the higher order interaction. The advantage of using the mean polish transformation is that it expresses the mean reaction time for each cell of the Race × Object design as a residual from the average reaction time to that particular race and that particular object. For example, in the Latino/gun cell, the mean polished Latino/gun average is computed per participant as:

$$\mathrm{RT}_{\text{Latino/gun mean polished}} = \left(\mathrm{RT}_{\text{Latino/gun}}\right) - \left(\mathrm{RT}_{\text{gun}}\right) - (\mathrm{RT}_{\text{Latino}}) + (\mathrm{RT}_{\text{Grand Mean}})$$

where values are averages calculated per participant and per cell of the design. The mean polished cell value yields the difference in how a participant responds to Latinos who are armed removing both the main effect to respond faster overall to gun trials, and faster overall to Latino targets. We chose the mean polish transformation to aid in interpretation of racial bias effects because for the first time in this line of research, we found differences in how quickly participants responded to different races, across the type of object held (i.e., main effect of race).

Black targets versus all others groups.   All Race × Object interactions involving Black targets were significant: Black versus White interaction, F (1, 68) = 45.83, PRE = .40, p < .001, Black versus Latino interaction, F (1, 68) = 22.18, PRE = .25, $p < .001$, and Black versus Asian interaction, F (1, 68) = 32.14, PRE = .32, $p < .001$. These effects demonstrate bias such that participants were especially likely to favor the "shoot" response over the "don't shoot" response when the target was Black rather than any other race.

Latino targets versus Asians and Whites.   There were no significant Race ×
Object interactions comparing Latino and White targets or Latino and Asian
targets, Fs $(1, 68) < 1$, *PRE*s $< .01$, *n.s.*

Asian targets versus Whites.   The Race × Object interaction for Asians and
Whites was not significant, F $(1, 68) = 1.40$, PRE $= .02$, *n.s.*

Thus, in Study 1, we found consistent evidence of the interactive influence of
race and object on reaction times only toward Black targets compared to targets of
other races. As shown in Figure 1, we replicated the implicit racial bias found in
previous research for Black versus White targets. Participants correctly responded
more quickly on gun trials to Black than White targets but correctly responded
more slowly on no-gun trials to Black than White targets. A strikingly similar
pattern of bias emerged for Black compared to Latino or Black compared to Asian
targets.

Signal Detection Analyses

We next examined if race influenced the pattern of errors versus correct
decisions made based on the object that targets held. On average, participants made
incorrect responses on 3.3% of trials and time-outs on 2.5%. Overall, participants
performed quite well on the task, a pattern consistent with previous work with the
FPS task that employed extended response windows (850 ms; Correll et al., 2002).

The number of correct and incorrect responses for a given target race was
submitted to signal detection theory (SDT) analysis. SDT extrapolates two normal
curves on a continuous judgment dimension from correct and incorrect responses
to targets holding guns versus nonguns. For the FPS task, we conceive of this
dimension as the amount of threat posed by targets. Placed on the dimension is
one curve that represents the distribution of responses on no-gun trials (low threat)
and another curve that represents the distribution of responses on gun trials (high
threat). Two statistics are computed. First, the d' statistic, or *sensitivity,* assesses
the degree of separation between the gun and no-gun curves. Higher d' values
indicate that the curves do not overlap much, i.e., participants are able to discriminate between gun and no-gun trials and to make accurate responses in general
(fire on armed targets, do not shoot unarmed targets). Lower d' values indicate that
the curves overlap more and that participants mistakenly shoot when they should
not (false alarm) or fail to shoot when they should (miss). The more overlapping the curves, the greater difficulty perceivers have in discerning weapons from
nonthreatening objects. Second, the c statistic, or *decision criterion,* reflects the
threshold at which targets are perceived as threatening enough to shoot. Although
racial bias in the placement of the criterion has previously been found with the FPS
task (e.g., Correll et al., 2002; Correll et al., 2007), there was only one significant
pairwise race comparison on the decision criterion across studies. However, in

Table 2. Reaction Time and Sensitivity as a Function of Object and Target Race (Study 2)

| | Target race | | | | | | | |
| | Black | | Latino | | Asian | | White | |
Variable	M	SD	M	SD	M	SD	M	SD
Reaction time (ms)								
Gun	548_a	41	537_b	40	575_c	37	573_d	37
No gun	640_a	36	615_b	37	629_a	39	639_c	37
Average	595_a	35	577_b	34	607_c	34	594_d	34
Sensitivity (d')	3.53_a	.51	3.66_b	.55	3.44_c	.59	3.46_c	.60

Note. Differing subscripts within a row indicate significant differences, $ps < .001$. Except average reaction difference between Black and White targets, $p < .10$. All sensitivity means significantly differed from zero, $ps < .05$. $N = 224$.

previous research, this result generally emerges when the response window for the task is 630 ms or less. Thus, the failure to find effects on the criterion in the current studies, which use an 850-ms time window, is not surprising. Analyses of this measure are not discussed further.

We computed d' values separately for each target group and found that the mean sensitivity (d') toward each group significantly differed from zero, all ts (68) > 48.84, $ps < .001$. The positive d' values in Table 2 indicate that participants distinguished guns from nonthreatening objects and, on average, were able to make appropriate decisions based on the object.

ANOVA. Sensitivity scores were submitted to a repeated measures ANOVA with Target Race (Black or Latino or White or Asian) as the within-participant factor. There was a main effect of target race, F (3, 204) $= 6.20$, PRE $= .03$, $p < .001$. More pertinent for our purposes were the pairwise comparisons of sensitivity between target groups. Results showed that accuracy was significantly higher toward Blacks and Latinos than toward Whites and Asians (Blacks vs. Whites, t (68) $= 2.23$, PRE $= .07$, $p = .029$, Blacks vs. Asians, t (68) $= 2.73$, PRE $= .10$, $p = .008$, Latinos vs. Whites, t (68) $= 3.46$, PRE $= .15$, $p < .001$, and Latinos vs. Asians, t (68) $= 3.49$, PRE $= .15$, $p < .001$). There was no evidence that participants were able to better discriminate guns from nonthreatening objects for Blacks than Latinos, t (68) $= 1.12$, *n.s.*, nor was there a difference between Whites and Asians, $t < 1$.

Racial bias in the amount of time needed to correctly determine whether or not to shoot Blacks perseveres in a multiethnic context. Participants were faster to correctly "shoot" a Black armed target than a White, Latino, or Asian armed target but slower to correctly "not shoot" a Black unarmed target than a White, Latino, or Asian unarmed target. There was no evidence, however, of race impacting the time to respond to Latino versus White or Asian targets, or White versus Asian targets regardless of the object held. Thus, the perceived threat Blacks pose appears to overwhelm any potential threat from other groups. In Study 2, we investigate the extent to which such bias is found among police officers, and if the degree of bias varies as a function of community characteristics and individual differences in officer beliefs about the groups.

Study 2: Overview

Police officers are among a selected few whose job it is to make shoot/don't shoot decisions. Although guidelines exist to limit when deadly force may be used, there are nonetheless allowances for officer discretion to open fire. Chief among these is the perceived imminent threat posed by the suspect to innocent bystanders, fellow officers, or the officer himself/herself.

Factors that may be associated with threat, such as stereotypes about suspect race and aggression, may influence how a potentially deadly encounter unfolds. Prior work with the shooter task found that police officers were prone to the same bias in reaction times toward Black than White targets shown by college students and community members, though, importantly, their ultimate decision of whether or not to shoot was not affected by target race (Correll et al., 2007). One purpose of Study 2 was to investigate if the pattern of racial biases toward Blacks versus Latinos, Asians, and Whites found with college-aged participants in Study 1 would similarly be replicated among police officers.

The second purpose of Study 2 was to investigate if characteristics of the community and explicit personal beliefs and attitudes of officers might be affiliated with implicit multiethnic racial biases in the shooter task. Our prior work showed that the degree of racial bias in reaction times toward Black versus White targets in a sample of police officers from a variety of cities was associated with several characteristics of the community served. In particular, bias was larger for officers from larger cities, those cities with higher minority and/or Black populations, and for officers who perceived greater violent crime in the community served (Correll et al., 2007). Using a similar computer simulation, Peruche and Plant (2006) found that police officers with general negative expectations about Blacks tended to show more racial bias in reaction times on early task trials. Thus, research has shown that differences in racial bias toward Blacks than Whites may be related to both community characteristics and individual officer beliefs. The present study will extend prior work by examining the factors related to multiethnic racial bias toward Latinos and Asians.

To obtain variation in officers' experiences with Black, Latino, or Asian suspects, we recruited police officers from the Southeast, Southwest, and Northwest regions of the United States. Officers completed the four-group multiethnic FPS task and provided information about the community in which they served, their history of service in law enforcement, and their beliefs and attitudes toward each of the four racial groups.

Method

Participants and Design

Police officers attending a voluntary two-day training seminar in the Southeast, Southwest, and Northwest were recruited. Officers were compensated $50 for their time. Two hundred and twenty-four officers participated (41% from a seminar in Florida, 35% from a seminar in New Mexico, and 24% from a seminar in Washington). Although many officers were from the state in which the seminar was held, 11 states were represented across the seminars. Most participants were patrol officers (61%) and male (86%). The majority of officers were Caucasian (53%) and Latino (31%). Fewer than 3% of the officers reported being African, Asian, or Native American (5% missing). Note that we found no evidence in Study 2 that officer race (minority versus White, or Latino versus White) was associated with differential racial bias in response times or accuracy, Fs (1, 214) < 1, *n.s.*

Police officers completed the 160 trial multiethnic FPS task with Black, Latino, Asian, and White male targets. The study was a Race (4: Black or Latino or Asian or White) × Object (2: Gun or No gun) within-participants design.

Materials

Intergroup attitudes. The discrimination scale (Wittenbrink, Judd, & Park, 1997) is an 11-item scale that gauges the extent to which people believe that discrimination toward African Americans is currently a problem. The scale was modified to address racial discrimination, in general, by substituting "ethnic minorities" for "Blacks." Example items included, "Members of ethnic minorities often exaggerate the extent to which they suffer from racial inequality," and "In the United States, people are no longer judged by their skin color." Ratings were made on a 1 (strongly disagree) to 9 (strongly agree) response scale. The scale was found to be reliable ($\alpha = .86$).

Stereotypes. The *stereotype rating scale* consisted of three items measuring the extent to which a group was viewed as aggressive, violent, or dangerous (Correll et al., 2002). For each item, participants marked an "X" on a 5-inch line with 12 evenly spaced tick marks, including endpoints. The line was anchored with not having the trait (e.g., not aggressive) to having the trait (e.g., aggressive). The *percent estimate task* also consisted of three items to assess the aggressiveness of a group, however, in this task, ratings were of the percent of people in the group who were believed to participate in specific behaviors. Participants rated what percent of the group commits violent crimes, owns a handgun, and dies at the hands of an in-group member. Participants completed these stereotype measures twice, once for their personal stereotypes and once for cultural stereotypes. In the former case, they were asked to report their own personal beliefs. In the latter case, they were asked to rate how they believed "people in general in the United States would respond."

Intergroup contact was measured with three items for each group. Participants were asked the amount of contact they had with each racial/ethnic group in the neighborhood in which they spent the most time growing up, at the high school from which they graduated, and with childhood friends. Responses on each item could range from 1 (none) to 7 (many).

Community characteristics and demographics.   Officers were asked to provide information about their history in law enforcement and the community they served. Officers reported the total number of years on the police force and in the department in which they were currently assigned. Officers estimated the rate of violent crime in their community relative to the FBI 2000–2002 rate of 500 offenses per 100,000 people. They chose between five options ranging from "much lower than average" to "much higher than average." In addition, we generated the extent to which officers over- or underestimated the amount of violent crime in their community by comparing the self-report percentages to those we gathered from the Uniform Crime Reports (2007) per city (or county, if city information was not available). Both variables were standardized, and then a difference score was computed ($Z_{self-report} - Z_{UCR}$).

The ethnic makeup of the community was also derived from two sources. Police officers estimated the percent of African, Asian, Latino, Native, and European Americans in the area. We also obtained U.S. Census Bureau (2000) information on the racial/ethnic makeup of the area served. Both variables were standardized and a difference score ($Z_{self-report} - Z_{Census}$) reflecting the degree to which officers over- or underestimated the percentage of a group in the community.

Officers also provided demographic information including their gender, ethnicity, education, and political orientation.

Procedure

Police officers were recruited to participate through announcements made each day as the seminar reconvened from lunch break. Officers reported to a room in the hotel in which the seminar was held. Participation took place in the evenings after the seminar concluded for the day. Although we could not isolate officers in individual cubicles, no more than two officers were seated at a table at a time and officers did not face each other during the study. To reduce disruption from other participants, officers wore headphones. Officers completed the FPS task on

Macintosh iBook laptop computers with 13-inch screens. The button boxes were the same ones used to collect responses in the laboratory in Study 1. Following the FPS task, officers completed the questionnaire packet and sealed it in a manila envelope. Officers were paid, thanked, and fully debriefed.

Results and Discussion

Reaction Time

Log-transformed reaction times for correct trials were analyzed by a Target Race (4: Black or Latino or White or Asian) $\times$ Object (2: Gun or No Gun) repeated measures ANOVA. All pairwise comparisons among target race groups (e.g., Black vs. Latino) and between target race pair and object (e.g., Black vs. Latino by Object interaction) were tested. Means backtransformed to the millisecond metric are presented in Table 2. There was a significant main effect of object, $F(1, 223) = 1970.62, p < .001$, PRE $= .90$. Participants were faster, on average, to gun ($M = 553$) than no gun trials ($M = 631$). There was also a significant main effect of race, $F(3, 669) = 256.41, p < .001$, PRE $= .53$. On average, across gun and no gun trials, participants were faster to correctly respond to Latino targets ($M = 575$) than Black targets ($M = 592$), $F(1, 223) = 250.27$, PRE $= .53$, $p < .001$, White targets ($M = 591$), $F(1, 223) = 221.12$, PRE $= .50$, $p < .001$, and Asian targets ($M = 605$), $F(1, 223) = 795.80$, PRE $= .78, p < .001$. Participants responded more slowly to Asian targets than White targets, $F(1, 223) = 163.33$, PRE $= .42, p < .001$, or Black targets, $F(1, 223) = 141.61$, PRE $= .39$, $p < .001$. There was no significant difference in mean reaction times for Black versus White targets, $F(1, 223) = 1.23$, PRE $= .01$, *n.s.* This pattern of results parallels that found in Study 1.

The omnibus Race $\times$ Object interaction was significant, $F(3, 669) = 52.35$, $p < .001$, as were all pairwise race $\times$ Object interactions (described below). As in Study 1, we used mean-polished values to aid in interpretation of the interactions.

Black targets versus all others groups. As shown in Figure 2, implicit racial bias was found toward Black versus White targets, $F(1, 223) = 81.90$, PRE $= .27, p < .001$, Black versus Latino targets, $F(1, 223) = 22.47$, PRE $= .09$, $p < .001$, and Black versus Asian targets, $F(1, 223) = 189.06$, PRE $= .46, p < .001$. As in Study 1, police officers correctly responded more quickly to guns, but more slowly to nonguns, held by Black targets than by targets of any other race.

Latino targets versus Asians and Whites. In addition, the Latino versus White, $F(1, 223) = 16.00$, PRE $= .67, p < .001$, and Latino versus Asian interactions were significant, $F(1, 223) = 90.82$, PRE $= .29, p < .001$. Officers showed racial bias in the decision to shoot Latinos relative to Whites and Asians.

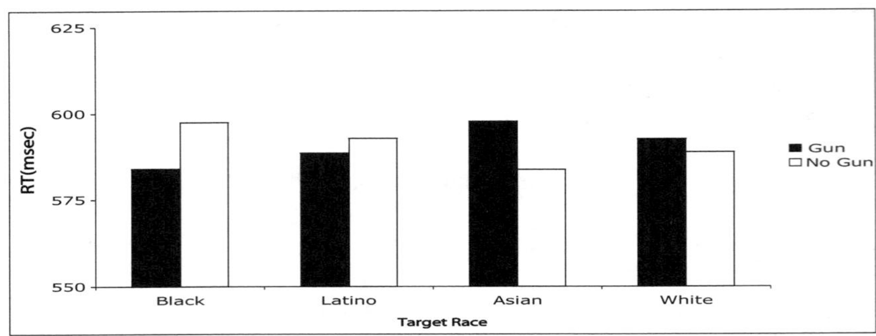

Fig. 2. Reaction time as a function of object and target race (Study 2).

Note. Reaction times were mean polished.

Asian targets versus Whites.   We also found a significant Asian versus White $\times$ Object interaction, F (1, 223) = 24.90, PRE = .10, p < .001. Opposite to the typical pattern of bias toward racial/ethnic minorities, police officers were faster to shoot White than Asian armed targets, but slower to decide not to shoot White than Asian unarmed targets. In other words, racial bias was shown as a bias in favor of shooting Whites rather than Asians.

Signal Detection Analysis

Police officers performed well on the four-group FPS task with incorrect responses on 2.9% of the trials and time-outs on 2.6% of the trials. Sensitivity (d') scores were submitted to a repeated-measures ANOVA with target race (Black or Latino or White or Asian) as a within-participant factor. The means appear in Table 2. The main effect of target race was significant, F (3, 669) = 18.48, p < .001.

Black targets versus all others groups.   Pairwise comparisons revealed that police officers were better able to discriminate weapons from nonthreatening objects when they were held by Black than White targets, F (1, 223) = 4.88, p = .028, PRE = .02, or Asian targets, F (1, 223) = 7.29, p = .007, PRE = .03. These results suggest that if minorities are policed differently than nonminorities (as posited by conflict theory), such differences are not due to poorer sensitivity toward Blacks. Unlike the results in Study 1, there was also a significant difference in sensitivity toward Black versus Latino targets among police officers, F (1, 223) = 24.40, p < .001, PRE = .10. Police officers evidenced higher levels of accuracy based on object for Latinos than Blacks.

Latino targets versus Asians and Whites. Similarly, sensitivity was higher to Latino than White targets, $F(1, 223) = 40.45$, $p < .001$, PRE $= .15$, or Asian targets, $F(1, 223) = 51.98$, $p < .001$, PRE $= .19$.

Asian targets versus or Whites. Overall accuracy to Asian and White targets was not found to differ, $F < 1$.

In sum, the pattern of sensitivity to objects as a function of target race found for police officers replicates the previous study reported herein, with one exception: police officers show higher accuracy to Latino than Black targets. Finally, it is interesting to note that reaction time bias and sensitivity bias were generally uncorrelated. The only exception was a significant negative relationship for White targets, $r(223) = -.16$, $p < .05$. The more bias in reaction times to White targets is, the less accurately participants responded to the objects White targets held.

Racial Bias Correlates

We were interested in the extent to which characteristics of the community and officers' experiences with, and beliefs about, Blacks, Latinos, Whites, and Asians related to bias in the FPS task. We correlated the composite score for each questionnaire measure with two variables computed from the FPS task: racial bias in reaction times and sensitivity in the task. Because we wanted to examine correlations separately for each target race, we calculated the simple effect of object type on the mean-polished reaction times per group (e.g., Object Effect$_{Black}$ = Black RT$_{No Gun}$ − Black RT$_{Gun}$), which represents the tendency to respond correctly to armed targets more quickly than to unarmed targets. This effect is important because it represents a predisposition to shoot: shooting armed targets quickly and choosing not to shoot an unarmed target slowly. The simple object effect was chosen because it can be examined for each group alone, rather than relative to another group (e.g., differences in reaction times toward Blacks by type of object rather than racial bias in reactions to Blacks versus Whites). Mean-polished values were used to isolate the effect of object for a particular target race, once the main effects of object and race were removed.

The bivariate correlations of beliefs and community characteristics to reaction time and sensitivity per target race and FPS task outcome are presented in Table 3. We also tested the partial relationships between individual beliefs and racial bias in reaction times and sensitivity controlling for community characteristics and vice versa. The pattern of effects was the same as with the bivariate correlations, indicating that the individual and community characteristics reported were uniquely related to bias.

Table 3. Correlations between Bias in Reaction Times, Accuracy, and Community Characteristics and Police Officer Beliefs

	Object effect (RT)				Sensitivity (d')			
	Black	Latino	Asian	White	Black	Latino	Asian	White
Community characteristics								
Population of city officer serves	−.03	−.07	.04	.08	.04	.05	−.09	.02
Census% of race group	−.02	.06	.02	.04	−.04	.02	−.18*	.00
Self-reported violent crime	.05	.07	−.01	−.12+	−.07	.01	.00	.05
UCR violent crime	−.02	.01	.04	−.02	.03	.01	.11	−.14*
Violent crime difference	−.05	.16*	.04	−.13+	−.07	.03	−.02	.05
Police officer beliefs								
Personal stereotype rating	.06	.12+	−.02	−.03	.02	.04	.07	−.02
Personal stereotype percent estimate	.05	.13+	.07	−.11	.05	−.12+	.00	.03
Cultural stereotype rating	.01	−.05	.08	−.05	.17*	−.06	.11+	−.08
Cultural stereotype percent estimate	−.04	.04	.15*	−.10	.09	−.10	.10	.06
Contact with race group	.21*	−.04	−.01	−.01	.12+	−.04	.00	−.04
Discrimination scale	.14*	−.10	.04	−.05	.03	−.08	−.01	.05

Note. The object effect ($RT_{\text{no gun}} - RT_{\text{gun}}$) per target race was mean polished. Due to missing data, correlations are based on Ns of 208 to 218. $^{*}p < .05$, $^{+}p < .10$.

Reaction Time Correlates

Community characteristics. We examined the reaction time bias to shoot as a function of community characteristics including measures of city population, the percentage of a target race in the community, and violent crime. Across target races, violent crime indices were often related to the bias to shoot. There was a tendency for the object effect (the bias to shoot) to decrease as perceptions of violent crime in an area increased, r (206) $= -.12$, $p = .083$. The violent crime difference was significantly positively related to the degree of bias to shoot Latino targets, r (194) $= .16$, $p = .025$, and marginally negatively related to the bias to shoot White targets, r (194) $= -.13$, $p = .063$. These correlations indicate that the more officers overestimated the amount of violent crime in their area compared to the Uniform Crime Reports (2007), he more bias shown toward Latinos, but the less bias shown toward Whites. There were no significant correlations regarding the overall size of the city or the number of members of a target race in the area, all rs $< .10$.

Officer beliefs. The officer beliefs we examined included personal and cultural stereotypes, attitudes toward racial/ethnic minorities in general, and the amount of contact with a target race. Reaction time bias to shoot Black targets increased as a function of both reported contact with Blacks, r (206) $= .21$,

$p = .002$, and prejudice reported on the discrimination scale, r (206) $= .14$, $p = .042$. Bias to shoot Latino targets was marginally associated with personal stereotypes as reported on the rating scale, r (205) $= .12, p = .079$, and the percent estimate task, r (204) $= .13, p = .068$. The more officers endorsed stereotypes of Latinos as violent and dangerous, the faster they tended to respond to armed than unarmed Latino targets. Racial bias toward Asian targets as a function of object was significantly higher, the more officers rated the cultural stereotype of Asians to be aggressive on the percent estimate task, r (205) $= .15, p = .033$. We found no significant relationships between beliefs about Whites and reaction time bias to shoot.

In summary, racial bias in reaction time across target races was associated with the extent to which officers overestimated the amount of violent crime in a community. As violent crime increased, bias to shoot Latino targets increased, but bias to shoot White targets decreased. Further, for Black targets, contact and discrimination predicted racial bias, whereas personal stereotypes were related to bias toward Latinos and cultural stereotypes were related to bias toward Asians. Though not wholly consistent, these observed relationships suggest that attitudes and/or stereotypes can affect bias in latencies among officers.

Sensitivity Correlates

Community characteristics.   We also examined the relationships between racial bias in sensitivity and community characteristics. The amount of violent crime in an area was related to the ability to correctly distinguish a gun from a nonthreatening object. The more violent crime according to the Uniform Crime Reports (2007), the less able officers were to distinguish objects held by White targets, r (206) $= -.14, p = .041$. New in the accuracy data was a significant correlation between the proportion of Asians according to census data and discriminability for Asian targets, r (206) $= -.18, p = .008$. As the number of Asians increases in an area, accuracy in determining the object an Asian target held during the shooter task decreases.

Officer beliefs.   Across target races, the pattern of significant relationships between officer beliefs and sensitivity was similar to that found for reaction times. For Black targets, the correlation between sensitivity and contact was marginally significant, r (213) $= .12, p = .068$. Officers who reported more contact with Blacks showed a tendency toward higher accuracy in distinguishing guns from nonthreatening objects. Although general discrimination was not related to the accuracy of responses to Black targets, there was a significant association between sensitivity and cultural stereotypes of Blacks, r (212) $= .17, p = .013$. The more violent and aggressive police officers perceived the cultural stereotype of Blacks to be, the more accurate they were in decisions of whether or not a Black target was armed. For Latino targets, personal stereotypes on the percent estimate task were marginally related to sensitivity, $r\ (211) = -.12, p = .073$. The more aggressive their personal stereotype of Latinos, the less able officers were to accurately distinguish objects. For Asian targets, accuracy was marginally related to cultural stereotypes on the rating task, $r\ (213) = .11, p = .093$. As cultural stereotypes of Asians as aggressive increase, accuracy increases. None of the officer beliefs correlated significantly with accuracy toward White targets.

In summary, the community characteristics and officer beliefs associated with accuracy are similar to that found for reaction time bias, although the relationships are not always in the same direction and tended to be smaller in magnitude. Violent crime in an area was related to the ability to discriminate objects held by White targets. Greater sensitivity for Black targets was associated with more contact and sensitivity for Asian targets with higher cultural stereotypes, whereas sensitivity for Latino targets decreased for officers who more highly endorsed personal stereotypes.

General Discussion

We examined implicit racial bias in the decision to shoot Blacks, Latinos, Asians, and Whites. Replicating prior research, racial bias in response times to decide whether or not to shoot Black targets was pervasive. Interestingly, this was the only reaction time bias to emerge among college-aged participants. However, police officers showed additional racial biases in reaction times, on average, toward Latinos relative to Asians and Whites, and toward Whites relative to Asians, suggesting racial bias in the decision to shoot is not simply an anti-Black phenomenon.

To our knowledge, the current research is the first to find a differential pattern of racial bias in reaction times between participant samples, which highlights the importance of substantiating evidence garnered from convenience samples with field samples (Dasgupta & Stout, 2012). The multiethnic shooter task posed a greater challenge to participants, given that there were more irrelevant racial cues present in the task, and no predictability about which racial cue would occur from trial to trial. The difficulty of the task for college participants may have resulted in a tendency to default to the stereotype of Blacks as most aggressive. On the other hand, cultural stereotypes and local norms germane to the likelihood that groups will aggress may be more available and practiced among police officers. After all, police officers must constantly evaluate the potential threat posed by people. Several officers across conferences we attended spoke of searching for the "wolves" among the "sheep."

The second outcome considered was the accuracy of the decision to shoot. In contrast to the differential pattern of bias found for reaction times, both college participants and police officers were better able to distinguish weapons from nonthreatening objects when held by Black and Latino targets than by Asian and White targets, an unexpected effect given our previous work (Correll, et al., 2002; Correll et al., 2007). We suspect that in the more challenging multiethnic shooter task, both participant samples may have shifted attention to Blacks and Latinos, the groups potentially more associated with threat. This result is consistent with recent evidence that suggests that threat-based attentional biases may serve as a mechanism for the impact of race on such decisions (Donders, Correll, & Wittenbrink, 2008; Trawalter, Todd, Baird, & Richeson, 2009). The P200, an event related potential (ERP) that reflects orientation to threatening stimuli in the environment, is greater in response to Black than White faces (Ito & Urland, 2005). Further, Correll, Urland, and Ito (2006) found that the more threatening Blacks were than Whites (as indexed by the P200), the greater the impact of race on the decision to shoot. If perceived threat differences can be inferred from racial bias in the FPS task (Correll et al., 2007), our results suggest that Blacks and Latinos may be more stereotypically associated with violence than Whites and Asians.

Finally, we examined if the degree of racial bias in reaction time and accuracy in the decision to shoot was related to community characteristics and personal beliefs reported by police officers. There was evidence that individual beliefs were related to the extent of bias, though the specific individual differences that correlated with beliefs depended on target groups. Officers who overestimated the amount of violent crime in a community showed a greater bias toward Latinos and less toward Whites. The personal beliefs most associated with racial bias varied with the target group, but were generally strongest for Blacks. Contact, discriminatory attitudes, and cultural stereotypes of aggressiveness and danger were related to bias toward Blacks. There was a trend for relationships between racial bias toward Latinos and personal stereotypes of Latino aggressiveness, and between bias toward Asians and cultural stereotypes about Asians. There was no evidence that bias toward Whites was related to personal beliefs.

Training

Although we cannot speak definitively to the genesis of the stereotypic association between violence and certain minority groups, such as Blacks and Latinos, our results suggest that even when race is not diagnostic for the task at hand, expectations regarding the danger posed by some groups, and further, individual variation in such beliefs, can affect response time. Stated differently, Black, Latino, Asian, and White targets were equally likely to appear armed or unarmed in the shooter task but the association of Blacks and Latinos with danger in U.S. culture may have led to faster correct responses to armed than unarmed targets from these groups compared to Whites and Asians, who are not associated with danger to the same degree. It is interesting to note that biases in reaction times toward Blacks and Latinos were overcome by the time a decision was made, and in fact, there was no evidence that target race biased a police officer's ability to correctly shoot armed targets and to not shoot unarmed targets.

Our accuracy results seemingly bode well for police officers in that implicit racial biases affected the speed of responses but not behavior, but there is reason to temper the optimism in generalizing the results to officers in the field. First, a relatively long response window was used, possibly allowing both college students and police officers sufficient time to enact control over their decisions of whether or not to shoot. It is possible that participants were able to enact distraction-inhibiting goals to avoid basing decisions on race or response-facilitating goals to shoot only if they see a gun (Mendoza, Gollwitzer, & Amodio, 2010). In the field, however, the luxury of time and ability to focus on implementation intentions is far from guaranteed. Second, the environmental conditions under which police officers complete the FPS task may foster relatively high levels of accuracy. Officers are seated comfortably, distractions are reduced, and there is no possibility of imminent physical threat. In contrast, conditions vary greatly in the field that may compromise the performance. For instance, the average accuracy rate with which shots fired at suspects find their target is only about 20% (Geller, 1982). Factors that amplify the perceived threat in an encounter result in even lower accuracy such as a suspect with a firearm (Schade, Bruns, & Morrsion, 1989). Presumably, the average threat level is significantly higher on the job than in the lab. If so, the controlled processes needed to compensate for racial bias may not be implemented as easily. It is conceivable that race-based perceptions of threat (which seem to affect reaction times in the lab) may, in the real world, translate into the decision to open fire. If this is the case, racial biases may, in fact, play a role in encounters between police officers and suspects.

It may prove useful to broaden training considerations from how police officers react to suspect behavior ("passive" role of officers) to how they themselves behave as a situation unfolds (proactive role of officers). Mere expectation that a suspect will be violent may engender a self-fulfilling prophecy: the officer may behave in such a way to elicit aggressive behavior from the suspect resulting in an escalation of the situation. Binder and Scharf (1980) suggested that decisions made in early stages of an encounter predict whether an officer is likely to open fire as the encounter unfolds. Fridell and Binder (1992) found that a crucial stage leading to a decision to open fire is that of information exchange between officer and suspect. Situations in which an officer was unable to ascertain pertinent information, or when suspects were agitated or noncompliant, were more likely to end with use of deadly force.

We argue that it is precisely in the early stages of an encounter that expectations police officers hold based on race, neighborhood, gender, etc., may unintentionally influence officer behavior and contribute to an escalation of the situation. A poignant anecdote comes from a conversation the first author had with a young Black male officer. He relayed a conflict between the Black culture in which he was raised and the police training he received regarding how to interact with a suspect. In his neighborhood, making eye contact with someone, particularly in a tense situation, was a sign of aggression. Compliance, on the other hand, was accomplished by avoiding eye contact. In dramatic contrast, as a police officer he was trained that lack of direct eye contact by a suspect was suspicious and associated with noncompliance. Such differences in the interpretation of nonverbal cues are likely to have marked effects on the progression of an encounter. To reduce the influence of such factors in escalation of police-community encounters, it may be beneficial for police departments to assign officers to districts in which they grew up whenever possible. We do not intend to suggest that it is necessary for officers to be of the same race as the community they serve, only that officers from the district are likely to be familiar with the neighborhood norms for verbal and nonverbal cues to aggression. It should be noted that our data cannot speak directly to this issue, but nonetheless, it may be fruitful for future research to pursue.

Another avenue for police departments to pursue is simulation training. Research has shown that those officers trained with a combination of video and "live fire" simulation training took more preventive actions to avoid escalation in subsequent encounters (Helsen & Starkes, 1999). It is possible that implementing such training would reduce the impact of suspect race on how an encounter progresses (cf. Reisig, McCluskey, Mastrofski, & Terrill, 2004).

Limitations and Extensions

An advantage of implementing an experimental approach to the study of race and the decision to shoot is the ability to manipulate race independently of other factors that may covary with race in the real world. Targets were presented on a common set of backgrounds, their dress was similar (e.g., no ball caps, jackets), and they stood or kneeled in select stances. Because race was not diagnostic of weapon held, we could determine if prior expectations on the part of perceivers were associated with bias in the FPS task. However, the control was achieved at the cost of external validity. We are currently conducting research using a video simulation method that police departments across the country use to provide interactive training to officers. This research brings us one step closer to emulating the psychological and physiological stress officers experience in encounters with suspects, and thus, to an examination of the impact of suspect race in the field.

Our investigation of racial bias provided an extension to prior work through inclusion of three distinct minority groups as targets rather than solely African Americans. We demonstrated that the extent to which bias was present depended on the subject population. College students were biased against African–Americans, whereas police officers evidenced bias toward Latinos in addition to African Americans, and to a differential degree depending on individual differences, such as level of contact or stereotype endorsement. A limitation of this work, however, derives from the fact that it was conducted with U.S. participants. Although our intuition is that treatment of specific minority groups would depend both on the cultural context, i.e., on the stereotypes regarding dangerousness of particular groups in a culture, and variations in belief in the beliefs propagated within that context, it will be the charge of future studies to determine what factors contribute to racial bias cross-culturally (Sampson & Lauritsen, 1997).

Conclusion

Most social psychological work on racial biases in the United States has focused on African Americans and how they are discriminated against in the context of a society dominated by Whites. Our own previous reports of implicit racial bias are very much in this tradition. The present work is based on the premise that an increasingly diverse American society demands that we assess patterns of bias toward multiple ethnic and racial target groups. Doing so highlights the ubiquity of bias in the FPS paradigm against African Americans relative to Whites. But it also brings to light some evidence of bias against Latinos, and bias in favor of Asians (again, relative to Whites). Given that the United States continues to evolve into an increasingly multiethnic nation, research that speaks to such complexity becomes ever more important.

References

Albrecht, H. J. (1997). Ethnic minorities, crime, and criminal justice in Germany. *Ethnicity, Crime, and Immigration, 21*, 31–99. doi: 10.1086/449249.

Binder, A., & Scharf, P. (1980). The violent police-citizen encounter. *Annals of the American Academy of Political and Social Science, 452*, 111–121. doi: 10.1177/000271628045200111.

Bureau of Justice Statistics (2007). Prison and jail inmates at midyear 2006. (Downloaded June 27, 2007 from http://www.ojp.usdoj.gov/bjs/abstract/pjim06.htm).

Cialdini, R. B. (1980). Full-cycle social psychology. *Applied Social Psychology Annual, 1*, 21–47.

Cohen, J. D., MacWhinney, B., Flatt, M., & Provost, J. (1993). PsyScope: A new graphic interactive environment for designing psychology experiments. *Behavioral Research Methods, Instruments, and Computers, 25*(2), 257–271. doi: 10.3758/BF03204507.

Correll, J., Park, B., Judd, C. M., & Wittenbrink, B. (2002). The Police Officer's Dilemma: Using ethnicity to disambiguate potentially threatening individuals. *Journal of Personality and Social Psychology, 83*(6), 1314–1329. doi: 10.1037//0022-3514.83.6.1314.

Correll, J., Urland, G., & Ito, T. (2006). Event-related potentials and the decision to shoot: The role of threat perception and cognitive control. *Journal of Experimental Social Psychology, 42*, 120–128. doi: 10.1016/j.jesp.2005.02.006.

Correll, J., Park, B., Judd, C. M., Wittenbrink, B., Sadler, M., & Keesee, T. (2007). Across the thin blue line: Police officers and racial bias in the decision to shoot. *Journal of Personality and Social Psychology, 92*(6), 1006–1023. doi: 10.1037/0022-3514.92.6.1006.

Cureton, S. R. (2001). An empirical test of the social threat phenomenon—Using 1990 census and uniform crime reports. *Journal of Criminal Justice, 29*(2), 157–166. doi: 10.1016/S0047-2352(00)00091-X.

Dasgupta, N., & Stout, J. G. (2012). Contemporary discrimination in the lab and field: Benefits and obstacles of full-cycle social psychology. *Journal of Social Issues, 68*(2), 399–412. doi: 10.1111/j.1540-4560.2011.01754.x

Donders, N., Correll, J., & Wittenbrink, B. (2008). Danger stereotypes predict racially biased attentional allocation. *Journal of Experimental Social Psychology, 44*(5), 1328–1333. doi: 10.1016/j.jesp.2008.04.002.

Fisher, E. L., & Borgida, E. (2012). Intergroup disparities and implicit bias: A commentary. *Journal of Social Issues, 68*(2), 385–398. doi: 10.1111/j.1540-4560.2011.01753.x

Fridell, L. A., & Binder, A. (1992). Police officer decision making in potentially violent confrontations. *Journal of Criminal Justice, 20*(5), 385–399. doi: 10.1016/0047-2352(92)90075-K.

Geller, W. A. (1982). Deadly force–What we know. *Journal of Police Science and Administration, 10*(2), 151–177.

Goldkamp, J. S. (1976). Minorities as victims of police shootings–interpretations of racial disproportionality and police use of deadly force. *Justice System Journal, 2*(2), 169–183.

Hannon, L. (2004). Race, victim precipitated homicide, and the subculture of violence thesis. *Social Science Journal, 41*(1), 115–121. doi: 10.1016/j.soscij.2003.10.010.

Helsen, W., & Starkes, J. (1999). A new training approach to complex decision making for police officers in potentially dangerous interventions. *Journal of Criminal Justice, 27*(5), 395–410. doi: 10.1016/S0047-2352(99)00012-4.

Holmes, M. D. (2000). Minority threat and police brutality: Determinants of civil rights criminal complaints in US municipalities. *Criminology, 38*(2), 343–367. doi: 10.1111/j.1745-9125.2000.tb00893.x.

Ito, T., & Urland, G. (2005). The influence of processing objectives on the perception of faces: An ERP study of race and gender perception. *Cognitive, Affective & Behavioral Neuroscience, 5,* 21–36. doi: 10.3758/CABN.5.1.21.

Johnson, B. D., Van Wingerden, S., & Nieuwbeerta, P. (2010). Sentencing homicide offenders in the Netherlands: Offender, victim, and situational influences in criminal punishment. *Criminology: An Interdisciplinary Journal, 48*(4), 981–1018. doi: 10.1111/j.1745-9125.2010.00210.x.

Judd, C. M., McClelland, G. H., & Ryan, C. R. (2008). *Data analysis: a model comparison approach* (2nd ed.). New York: Routledge.

Kang, J. (2012). The missing quadrants of anti-discrimination: Going beyond the "prejudice polygraph". *Journal of Social Issues, 68*(2), 314–327. doi: 10.1111/j.1540-4560.2011.01750.x

Locke, H. G. (1996). *The color of law and the issue of color: Race and the abuse of police power.* New Haven: Yale University Press.

MacDonald, J. M., Kaminski, R. J., Alpert, G. P., & Tennenbaum, A. N. (2001). The temporal relationship between police killings of civilians and criminal homicide: A refined version of the danger-perception theory. *Crime & Delinquency, 47*(2), 155–172. doi: 10.1177/0011128701047002001.

Martinez, R. (2007). Incorporating latinos and immigrants into policing research. *Criminology & Public Policy, 6,* 57–64.

Mendoza, S. A., Gollwitzer, P. M., & Amodio, D. M. (2010). Reducing the expression of implicit stereotypes: Reflexive control through implementation intentions. *Personality and Social Psychology Bulletin, 36*(4), 512–523. doi: 10.1177/0146167210362789.

Parker, R. N. (1989). Poverty, subculture of violence, and type of homicide. *Social Forces, 67,* 983–1007. doi: 10.2307/2579711.

Peruche, B., & Plant, E. (2006). The correlates of law enforcement officers' automatic and controlled race-based responses to criminal suspects. *Basic and Applied Social Psychology, 28*(2), 193–199. doi: 10.1207/s15324834basp2802_9.

Peterson, R., & Krivo, L. (2005). Macrostructural analyses of race, ethnicity, and violent crime: Recent lessons and new directions for research. *Annual Review of Sociology, 31,* 331–356. doi: 10.1146/annurev.soc.31.041304.122308.

Plant, E., & Peruche, B. (2005). The consequences of race for police officers' responses to criminal suspects. *Psychological Science, 16*(3), 180–183.

Program, Uniform Crime Reports (2007). Retrieved from http://www.fbi.gov/ucr/cius2007/offenses/violent_crime/index.html on June 29, 2009.

Reisig, M., McCluskey, J., Mastrofski, S., & Terrill, W. (2004). Suspect disrespect toward the police. *Justice Quarterly, 21*(2), 241–268. doi: 10.1080/07418820400095801.

Rosnow, R. L., & Rosenthal, R. (1989). Definition and interpretation of interaction effects. *Psychological Bulletin, 105*(1), 143–146. doi: 10.1037//0033-2909.105.1.143.

Sampson, R. J., & Lauritsen, J. L. (1997). Racial and ethnic disparities in crime and criminal justice in the United States. *Ethnicity, Crime, and Immigration, 21*, 311–374. doi: 10.1086/449253.

Schade, T. V., Burns, G. H., & Morrison, G. (1989). Armed confrontations: Police shooting performance in threatening environments. *American Journal of Police, 8*, 31–48.

Smith, M. D. (1992). Variations in correlates of race-specific urban homicide rates. *Journal of Contemporary Criminal Justice, 8*(2), 137–149. doi: 10.1177/104398629200800206.

Trawalter, S., Todd, A., Baird, A., & Richeson, J. (2008). Attending to threat: Race-based patterns of selective attention. *Journal of Experimental Social Psychology, 44*(5), 1322–1327. doi: 10.1016/j.jesp.2008.03.006.

Turk, A. T. (1969). *Criminality and legal order*. Chicago: Rand McNally.

U.S. Census Bureau (2000). Retrieved from http://www.census.gov/main/www/cen2000.html on August 9, 2007.

U.S. Census Bureau (2008). An older and more diverse nation by midcentury.

U.S. Department of Justice (2001). Policing and homicide, 1976–98: Justifiable homicide by police, police officers murdered by felons: Bureau of Justice Statistics.

Wittenbrink, B., Judd, C., & Park, B. (1997). Evidence for racial prejudice at the implicit level and its relationship with questionnaire measures. *Journal of Personality and Social Psychology, 72*(2), 262–274. doi: 10.1037/0022-3514.72.2.262.

Wolfgang, M. E., & Ferracuti, F. (1967). *The subculture of violence*. London: Social Science Paperbacks.

MELODY S. SADLER is an Assistant Professor of Psychology at San Diego State University. Her interests include topics in social and quantitative psychology. Her research has examined the emotional and cognitive underpinnings of prejudice based on race/ethnicity, mental health status, gender, and sexual orientation.

JOSHUA CORRELL is an Assistant Professor at the University of Chicago. His work focuses on stereotyping, with particular emphasis on the association between racial outgroups and threat, including the effects of racial cues on attention, face processing, and defensive behavior. He also studies the psychological value of group membership.

BERNADETTE PARK is Professor of Psychology and Neuroscience at the University of Colorado. Her research interests broadly defined concern stereotyping and intergroup relations, and person perception and impression formation. She has participated in collaborative work on the role of race in decisions to shoot armed and unarmed targets, and in particular how expertise can facilitate cognitive control over such decisions. In more recent work, she has examined implicit role associations between gender, parenting, and career roles, arguing that the stereotypic content of these roles leads women to experience them in a conflicting and oppositional manner, much more so then men. She is currently examining the effects of such conflicts in the self-concept for decisions about whether to stay or to leave professional careers.

CHARLES M. JUDD is College Professor of Distinction in the Department of Psychology and Neuroscience at the University of Colorado. He is the past editor of the *Journal of Experimental Social Psychology* and the *Journal of Personality and Social Psychology*. His interests lie broadly in social cognition and judgment. He has also published extensively on data analytic methods for the behavioral sciences.

Journal of Social Issues, Vol. 68, No. 2, 2012, pp. 314–327

The Missing Quadrants of Antidiscrimination: Going Beyond the "Prejudice Polygraph"

Jerry Kang[*]
UCLA School of Law

Behavioral realists urge the law to respond to new scientific discoveries about the reality of contemporary discrimination. But in thinking about how the law might respond, it is easy to frame the question as: When should evidence from scientific instruments, such as the Implicit Association Test, be admissible in a discrimination lawsuit. In other words, should we admit into evidence the results of some "Prejudice Polygraph"? But this framing, which focuses on specific facts, found ex post is too narrow and obscures a much broader range of potential legal responses. Indeed, by considering both specific and general facts, as well as both ex post and ex ante time orientations, four separate quadrants of analysis emerge. Psychologists, legal scholars, and policymakers should not miss these other quadrants of antidiscrimination.

Embedded within the laws of every nation are models of how human beings think, make judgments, and behave. These models were not, however, selected through some rigorous scientific competition. Instead, they reflect the intuitive understandings of legislators and judges who made and interpreted the law based on their lay psychological theories of how people work. The law of antidiscrimination in the United States is no exception. It too relies on models of how human beings think and behave, especially across salient social categories such as race and gender. The conventional wisdom was that people made instrumentally rational choices through cognitions that were conscious and self-transparent. In other words, when people discriminated against others, they did so purposefully and with full self-knowledge. But in the past three decades, such traditional "common sense" models have seriously frayed. Modern findings in the cognitive

---

[*]Correspondence concerning this article should be sent to Jerry Kang, ULCA School of Law, 405 Hilgard Ave., Box 951476, Los Angeles, CA 90095-1476 [e-mail: kang@law.ucla.edu].

Research support for this article was provided by the UCLA School of Law and the Korea Times-Hankook Ilbo Chair in Korean American Studies. Helpful research assistance was provided by Jonathan Feingold.

and behavioral sciences have demonstrated that what we thought we knew isn't quite right, sometimes dramatically so. This burgeoning scientific consensus has triggered calls for the law to become more "behaviorally realistic" (Symposium on Behavioral Realism, 2006).

In the past decade, the branch of science that has arguably most destabilized antidiscrimination law is implicit social cognition (ISC). In rough terms, implicit social cognitions are stereotypes and attitudes that we are unaware of and do not necessarily endorse, but nevertheless exist in our minds, activate automatically, and influence our behavior. These cognitions are measured not through self-reports, but through instruments such as reaction-time latencies. The findings in ISC alloyed with findings from audit studies, field experiments, and statistical analyses (Bendick & Nunes, 2012; Pager & Western, 2012) threaten our self-understandings as self-conscious, rational beings who treat others fairly and on-the-merits. Not surprisingly, such self-critical discoveries have triggered anxiety and even backlash (Fisher & Borgida, 2012). For example, critics warn against overreading the evidence. They raise the specter that some instrument that measures, for instance, automatic associations will be treated as a "prejudice polygraph," failure of which triggers immediate legal liability. Skeptics strongly caution against the "perils of [such] mind reading" (Mitchell & Tetlock, 2006).

Given popular culture's obsession with gadgets, trial drama, and gotcha moments, it should not be surprising that the prototype that is readily activated is a mind-reading "prejudice polygraph," introduced as smoking gun evidence in high-stakes litigation. But this framing unduly narrows our understanding of law and the various ways that law might respond to new scientific discoveries about discrimination. In fact, this framing exemplifies only one out of four possible quadrants worth investigating.

To get a sense of these other quadrants, first consider changing the level of specificity. In other words, instead of trying to determine whether a particular person has a particular implicit bias that on a particular occasion caused a particular behavior that harmed a particular victim, imagine answering a far more general question: Do implicit biases generally exist and influence behavior? Consider, second, changing when we ask the question. Instead of asking after the fact (ex post), to blame someone, imagine asking before the fact (ex ante), in order to design preventative strategies and best practices. If we take broader views of both fact specificity (particular to general) and time orientation (ex post to ex ante), and intersect them, we see that four quadrants of possibility emerge. And a "prejudice polygraph," which is both particular and ex post, represents just one of those quadrants. The details including application to American law are worked out below, but the central conceptual payoff is this: By systematically analyzing all four quadrants of possible legal intervention, we can embrace a more comprehensive and robust understanding of how law in whatever society can take into account new understandings of contemporary discrimination.

Lay Psychology and Behavioral Realism

Before working through the four quadrants, it will be useful first to summarize how the social cognitive and behavioral sciences are destabilizing the law of equality and prompting reformist calls for behavioral realism.

Law relies on "common sense" understandings of how human beings make judgments, including those about people who belong to various social categories. This "common sense" is, in turn, based on lay psychology. Accordingly, as Linda Hamilton Krieger has repeated, law cannot opt out of psychology (Krieger & Fiske, 2006). It is already everywhere in the law. Thus the question is not whether to accept psychology; rather, the question is what kind of psychology the law should accept. On the one hand, we have lay psychology rampant in the status quo. On the other hand, we have more scientifically vetted understandings that often support lay views but sometimes reveal their striking errors. Many scholars writing at the interface of law and psychology have advocated for importing more of the latter, and have called for increased "behavioral realism."

As explained by Krieger and Susan Fiske:

> "[B]ehavioral realism, understood as a prescriptive theory of judging, stands for the proposition that as judges develop and elaborate substantive legal doctrines, they should guard against basing their analyses on inaccurate conceptions or irrelevant real-world phenomena." (Krieger & Fiske, 2006, p. 389).

Kristin Lane, Jerry Kang, and Mahzarin Banaji break down behavioral realism into more algorithmic terms:

> First, identify advances in the mind and behavioral sciences that provide a more accurate model of human cognition and behavior.
>
> Second, compare that new model with the latent theories of human behavior and decision-making embedded within the law. These latent theories typically reflect "common sense" based on naïve psychological theories.
>
> Third, when the new model and the latent theories are discrepant, ask lawmakers and legal institutions to account for this disparity. An accounting requires either altering the law to comport with more accurate models of thinking and behavior or providing a transparent explanation of "the prudential, economic, political, or religious reasons for retaining a less accurate and outdated view." (Lane, Kang, & Banaji, 2007).

What happens, for instance, if and when scientists provide convincing evidence that thoughts and feelings that we are not aware of and may not endorse both exist and influence our evaluation of and behavior toward members of various social categories? (Greenwald, Poehlman, Ulhmann, & Banaji, 2009, for meta-analysis). That would mean that the disparate results long evinced by summary statistics across racial and gender groups could not be entirely attributed to merit differences or historical maldistributions of resources. Instead, we would now have reason to believe that these disparate results are also caused—at least in part—by implicit social cognitions operating right now.

How should we respond to such evidence, as is documented in this volume—that we are not as color (or gender, etc.) blind as we supposed? More specifically, how should legal actors respond? Whatever is done, behavioral realists argue that simply ignoring the gap between "what we thought" and "what turns out to be the case" is not an option. Instead, those who make, interpret, and change law must either incorporate these new findings into the law or explain transparently why they cannot.

Four Quadrants of Legal Interventions

But even if lawmakers agree in the abstract that they should incorporate new scientific consensus, what concretely are they supposed to do? For example, should judges embrace "mind reading" and issue orders based on mere fMRIs? Intentionally crude and tendentious, this sentence was meant to demonstrate that focusing too narrowly on such cases can impoverish our understanding of how science can interact with law. To avoid this fate, we should systematically investigate four separate quadrants, produced by intersecting two conceptual axes based on "specificity" and "time."

Axis of specificity. Making new law or applying existing law both require some understanding of the "facts"—either the factual contours of a problem to be solved or the factual particularities necessary to apply general legal principles to a specific case. But as legal scholars have noted, facts can be specific or general (e.g., Faigman, 2008). For instance, we might have a general scientific understanding that cigarette smoking causes lung cancer. However, in a tort lawsuit, the more relevant question is whether the particular victim's lung cancer was specifically caused by smoking a particular brand, which is a different (and much harder) question. Because lung cancer can have other causes, the specific finding must at least rule out confounding causes. In other words, even when there is universal scientific consensus about some general fact—e.g., smoking causes cancer—there can still be doubt about a specific factual allegation—e.g., smoking a particular brand caused this particular cancer in this particular person (Faigman, 2008).

Axis of time. Compared to the axis of specificity, the axis of time has received less scholarly attention. On the one hand, some legal response may have an ex ante time orientation. In other words, it takes place before some future incident of interest, typically some harm to be avoided. The legal act is designed to change behavior to decrease the probability of the incident and/or the magnitude of its harm. On the other hand, the time orientation may be ex post. In other words, the incident of interest has already taken place, and the only question is how to apply existing law to the facts of that incident, to apportion moral responsibility, and legal liability.

		Time Orientation	
		ex post	*ex ante*
Specificity	*specific*	Quadrant I: "Prejudice Polygraph"	Quadrant III: "Self-Analysis"
	general	Quadrant II: "Changing the Frame"	Quadrant IV: "Prevention"

Fig. 1. Four quadrants of legal intervention.

This axis of time may have received less attention because it often aligns with the axis of specificity. For instance, when we think of general facts, we are often in an ex ante orientation, involving law making and prevention. By contrast, when we think of particular facts, we are often in an ex post orientation, involving law applying, accountability, and redress. But as demonstrated below, these pairings are not always so. In order to explore less obvious combinations, we can intersect the two axes, which produces four quadrants (see Figure 1). For easier reference, I give each quadrant a name. Quadrant I is the "Prejudice Polygraph"; Quadrant II is "Changing the Frame"; Quadrant III is "Self-analysis"; Quadrant IV is "Prevention."

Quadrant I: "Prejudice Polygraph"

Quadrant I involves specific facts in an ex post time orientation. The prototypical example is using the scores from some new implicit bias measure, such as the Implicit Association Test (IAT), as evidence to show that a specific employer violated antidiscrimination law. Notice that this is a question about specific facts—did this particular employer have a particular bias that caused a particular employment action. It is also ex post, in the context of a lawsuit alleging past wrongdoing. It is in this Quadrant that the bogeyman of a mindreading "prejudice polygraph" arises.

Mindreading by fortune tellers is not, however, admissible as evidence. Indeed, in American jurisdictions, the results of an actual polygraph is more often than not inadmissible. Whether the results of an IAT or any other instrument, such as neuroimaging, should be admissible turns on the accuracy, reliability, and validity of that instrument. In federal courts, trial court judges act as the gate-keepers for such scientific evidence, in accordance with Federal Rule of Evidence 702, which essentially codifies the Supreme Court's *Daubert-G.E.-Kumho* trilogy of cases (Daubert v. Merrell Dow Pharmaceuticals, Inc., 1993; General Electric Co. v. Joiner, 1997; Kumho Tire Co., Ltd. v. Carmichael, 1999). Under Rule 702, an expert may testify in the form of an opinion or otherwise "if (1) the testimony is based upon sufficient facts or data; (2) the testimony is the product of reliable principles and methods; and (3) the witness has applied the principles and methods reliably to the facts of the case." In rough terms, judges must decide whether the proffered evidence was produced by reliable science. This is a flexible determination that considers various factors, including whether the scientific theory or technique has been reliably tested, has been subjected to peer review, has acceptable error rates, and enjoys general acceptance within the relevant scientific community (Daubert v. Merrell Dow Pharmaceuticals, Inc., pp. 593–94).

Three points are worth noting about this Quadrant, which reframes the question of "How should the law respond to the reality of contemporary discrimination?" into "Should courts admit the result of prejudice polygraphs into evidence?" First, no serious scientist has called for using instruments such as the IAT in this specific, ex post context. In fact, leading implicit bias scientists, such as Mahzarin Banaji, have publicly counseled against it (Vedantam, 2005). Second, although nothing like a prejudice polygraph has ever been admitted, other types of "scientific" evidence are regularly introduced in Quadrant I settings. Consider, for instance, fingerprint, bite mark, and hair specimen analyses regularly admitted by trial courts into evidence to prove that the defendant was at the scene of the crime. What's striking is that according to the recent report from the National Academies of Science, "there is a notable dearth of peer-reviewed, published studies establishing the scientific bases, and validity of many forensic methods." (National Research Council, 2009, p. 8). The final point flows from the first two. Those who passionately object to using something like the IAT in a Quadrant I context (which no serious academic has called for) should consider mobilizing instead against the use of forensic evidence (which is admitted throughout the United States every day). The science validating certain types of forensic evidence is worse—sometimes because it does not even exist—than the science validating implicit bias instruments. Moreover, the stakes in criminal law are much higher, including life imprisonment or death.

In short, although Quadrant I captures much of our attention, it is a red-herring. To repeat, no serious scientist or legal academic is calling for admitting into evidence the specific results of an individual's prejudice polygraph. Those who are genuinely anxious that innocent defendants will be wrongly held liable in a court of law on the basis of shoddy scientific evidence should worry less about those accused of prejudice (implicit social cognition) and more about those accused of murder (forensic evidence). Finally, we should not let the salience of Quadrant I's "Prejudice Polygraph" lead us to ignore the remaining three.

Quadrant II: Changing the Frame

The next quadrant, Quadrant II, keeps the ex post time orientation, but is concerned with general facts. If "prejudice polygraph" captured the sense of Quadrant I, what represents Quadrant II, which I suggest "changes the frame"? I offer two examples.

Social framework evidence.   Social framework evidence "uses general conclusions from tested, reliable, and peer-reviewed social science research and applies them to the case" (Borgida & Fiske, 2008, p. xxxiii). The idea is that social scientists have gained a superior understanding of general facts, especially when science has revealed discrepancies from lay understandings. These general facts can be shared in the form of expert testimony with the jury to inform and guide their deliberations regarding specific facts. Susan Fiske's testimony in the Price Waterhouse v. Hopkins (1989). Title VII gender discrimination trial is the best-known example (Fiske, Bersoff, Borgida, Deaux, & Heilman, 1991). Her expert testimony about sex-stereotyping was discussed by the district court, court of appeals, and the Supreme Court. Countering Price Waterhouse's dismissal of Fiske's testimony as a "chain of intuitive hunches about 'unconscious' sexism," the American Psychological Association's amicus brief supported the credibility of the methodology and literature used by Fiske.

Writing for the D.C. Court of Appeals, Judge Joyce Green pointed out that "unwitting or ingrained bias is no less injurious or worthy of eradication than blatant or calculated discrimination," and "the fact that some or all of the partners at Price Waterhouse may have been unaware of that motivation, even within themselves, neither alters the fact of its existence nor excuses it." (Hopkins v. Price Waterhouse, 1987, p. 469). At the Supreme Court, writing for a plurality, Justice Brennan was "tempted to say that Dr. Fiske's expert testimony was merely icing on Hopkins' cake" and that "no special training" was necessary to discern the sex discrimination (Price Waterhouse v. Hopkins, 1989, p. 256). That said, his opinion displayed a thoroughgoing psychological sophistication.

Structural reform litigation.   Here is another example that is both ex post, yet involves general factual findings. In Farrakhan v. Gregoire (2006), plaintiffs filed a 2 Voting Rights Act (VRA) challenge to Washington state's felon disenfranchisement statute. In order to prevail, a necessary (but not sufficient) requirement was to persuade the federal district court to make a factual finding that the Washington criminal system had engaged in racial discrimination. Notice that this is a general fact-finding, not a specific one focused on specific police officers, prosecutors, juries, and judges. Surprisingly, the court found "compelling evidence of racial discrimination and bias in Washington's criminal justice system." Its finding was not based "solely on [racial disparity] statistics" (Farrakhan v. Gregoire, 2006, p. 17); it was also based on expert testimony that discussed structural, institutional, and implicit social cognitive factors. One of the sources described as helping to "bolster the Court's conclusion" (Farrakhan v. Gregoire, 2006, p. 18) included the expert testimony of Anthony Greenwald, inventor of the IAT, who attached a draft of his work published in a legal symposium calling for Behavioral Realism.

The significance of this case should not be overstated because in the end, the general finding of racial discrimination was insufficient for the trial court to find a VRA violation under a "totality of circumstances" test. And although a three-judge panel of the Ninth Circuit Court of Appeals initially reversed that decision, the entire Circuit sitting en banc ultimately affirmed the district court's judgment (Farrakhan v. Gregoire, 2010/2010). The legal details on appeal are largely beyond the point. What's important here is that Farrakhan demonstrates how the reality of contemporaneous discrimination, described through science, can assist courts in finding general facts that can be legally consequential.

This case can be seen as an example of "structural reform litigation," which is a legal term that can mean many different things. Here, I mean to emphasize litigation requesting a court to provide injunctive relief (not monetary damages) that alters some structural feature of a system, such as prison overcrowding, voting procedures, or school segregation. Often, although not always, structural reform litigation requires finding of general facts.

On one admittedly earnest reading, Brown v. Board of Education (1954) involved just this. The Court explained that: "Whatever may have been the extent of psychological knowledge at the time of Plessy v. Ferguson, this finding [of harm to Black children] is amply supported by modern authority" (Brown v. Board of Education, p. 494). That "modern authority" was a footnote listing various psychological studies that found general facts. (Brown v. Board of Education, p. 11, citing, e.g., the "doll studies" of K. B. Clark). These were not specific facts found of specific plaintiff children by a clinical psychologist. Yet these general facts (regarding stigma), in an ex post setting (constitutional litigation), played some part in crafting a unanimous opinion that signaled the beginning of the end of de jure school segregation.

Social framework and structural reform litigation examples show that even in an ex post orientation of accountability (e.g., adjudicating that some law was broken), general facts can still be relevant. More important, even if one believes that science should not be used in a Quadrant I setting (e.g., as a "prejudice polygraph"), one can believe it appropriate in a Quadrant II setting, to help change the frame. One judgment does not determine the other.

Quadrant III: Self-Analysis

Quadrant III delves into less familiar territory: specific facts but ex ante. Can the recent findings from scientific research examining contemporary forms of discrimination be relevant to this quadrant as well? Consider the practice of self-criticism, in an employment and a policing context. First, suppose a specific person, a manager of some organization, wants to learn more about her implicit biases. The time orientation is ex ante, to prevent implicit biases from infecting important decisions in future hiring and contracting (Bendick & Nunes, 2012, p. 254, discussing testing to change employer behavior). Suppose that that manager takes various tests, including reaction-time measures of implicit bias. Given surprising findings, she takes countermeasures such as anonymizing job applications at initial screening, (Bertrand & Mullainathan, 2004; Rooth, 2007), precommitting to merit criteria (Uhlmann & Cohen, 2005), using more structured interviews, and being less willing to go on gut feelings of likability (Rudman & Glick, 2001).

Now, suppose later that that specific individual is sued for discrimination. This could be by a White male plaintiff who argues that these attempts to avoid discrimination were in fact illegal affirmative action programs. (This hypothetical is inspired by the facts of the recent Supreme Court decision in Ricci v. DeStefano [2009]). Or, the suit could be by a racial minority plaintiff who was hired, but later was denied a promotion.

Here is a second example, in the field of policing. Various studies have revealed the existence of "shooter bias"—the propensity to shoot African Americans faster (and with greater errors) than Whites in a simulation (Correll, Park, Judd, & Wittenbrink, 2002; Sadler, Correll, Park, & Judd, 2012). There is also some evidence that particular training regimens can decrease shooter bias (Plant, Peruche, & Butz, 2005). So, suppose that a socially responsible police chief investigates whether his officers have shooter bias. Finding that they do, he adopts new training that decreases that bias. After a shooting in the field of an African American youth, the victim's family sues and requests the "shooter bias" measures of the accused police officer.

In federal court, under the Federal Rule of Civil Procedure 26(b)(1), discovery is quite broad. As long as the requested information is "nonprivileged matter that is relevant to any party's claim or defense," that information should be turned over. The material requested need not be itself admissible as long as it is "reasonably calculated to lead to the discovery of admissible evidence." Under this standard, the manager's implicit bias score and the police officer's shooter bias score may well be discoverable. But permitting discovery would create perverse incentives to avoid finding out one's biases in the first place – in which case the countermeasures would have never been adopted. If we do not want to penalize self-discovery of biases, what might we do in this setting? We could adopt some sort of self-criticism evidentiary privilege to encourage self-discovery, without threat of that information becoming discoverable in a civil law suit.

Analogous privileges have been recognized in various state jurisdictions. For example, some states have recognized a privilege for medical committee reports and self-evaluations after a medical accident (Flanagan, 1983). The Federal Rules of Evidence 407 also recognize a privilege that covers "subsequent remedial measures": After a product has hurt someone, a manufacturer might want to improve that product's design. But if such remedy will be exploited by a trial lawyer as tacit admission of the product's defect, a manufacturer might think twice. To decrease any such disincentive, the law prevents the evidence of subsequent remedial measures from reaching the jury (to prove negligence or defect).

At least one legal commentator has called for a similar evidentiary privilege covering self-discovery of implicit biases (Pollard, 1999). Given that the leading scientists have not called for Quadrant I application, there seems to be little loss to the goal of truth-seeking in keeping specific implicit bias scores out of the civil litigation process. That said, the argument to create an evidentiary privilege is always complex. My goal here is not to weigh authoritatively the costs and benefits of creating some such privilege. Instead, my modest point is to show how science could help us find specific facts (e.g., our individual biases) that, in turn, prompt ex ante preventative actions (e.g., countermeasures). Again, one's views about Quadrant I's prejudice polygraph says little about the proper analysis of Quadrant III questions.

Quadrant IV: Prevention

Finally, we have reached Quadrant IV—general and ex ante—conceptually most distant from Quadrant I. Within this "Prevention" quadrant lies the possibilities of revising the procedure and substance of law in light of better scientific understanding of our general cognitive tendencies.

The paradigmatic context for this quadrant is not jury trial but legislation. When a legislature enacts legislation to counter some problem, how does it know that the problem exists and that its proposed legislation might help? These questions necessarily turn on some understanding of "facts," but they are not the specific facts of any particular isolated case or adjudication. Instead, they are general facts, similar to the ones that scientists try to discern. For example, if a city wants to ban smoking in bars, specific causation in a particular historical victim of second-hand smoking need not be proven. Instead, the city just needs to be persuaded of the general fact that cigarette smoke is a carcinogen. If such a ban is enacted, it is in an ex ante context. The point here is not to hold someone liable for violating some such ban; instead, it is to create a law that changes prospectively some behavior of interest. Here are two Quadrant IV examples to consider in the context of discrimination.

Eyewitness identification.   Scientists have determined general facts that eyewitness identification—especially across races—is quite poor, and that certain methods of identification produce greater reliability. For example, instead of providing a single suspect, and asking the witness whether he was the perpetrator, greater reliability can be produced by using photo spreads, sequential lineups, or particular identification instructions (Berger, 2008). On the basis of these general facts produced by scientific inquiry, many police departments have reformed their identification practices. (Diamond, 2008).

Debiasing agents.   Jerry Kang and Mahzarin Banaji have reframed parts of the affirmative action controversy into one about "fair measures" (Kang & Banaji, 2006; see also in behavioral economics literatures Jolls & Sunstein, 2006). In that analysis, they raise the possibility of hiring certain individuals because they function as "debiasing agents," whose counter-stereotypical and counter-attitudinal behavior decreases implicit biases of those around them. In the next decade, suppose that scientists accumulate substantial evidence of the following: (i) implicit bias exists against a racial group, (ii) such bias predicts real-world behaviors, and (iii) exposure to debiasing agents decreases implicit bias (Dasgupta & Asgari, 2004; Dasgupta & Greenwald, 2001; for literature review, see Blair, 2002). Such science could lead an institution, such as a public law school, to hire a racial minority applicant (over a comparably qualified White applicant) not as a "role model" but as a debiasing agent. Such a decision would draw an Equal Protection challenge.

Because race was explicitly considered, under current federal constitutional doctrine, this decision would be reviewed under strict scrutiny, which entails a particular type of means-ends analysis. First, the end sought by the state actor has to be "compelling". Second, the means deployed—in this case exposure to a counter-stereotypical exemplar—must be "narrowly tailored" to achieving that compelling interest. As for the ends, the point of this intervention is not to increase minority student self-esteem (connected to the "role model" justification), redistribute wealth between groups, or correct hard-to-measure general "societal discrimination." All three such goals have been rejected by the courts as not compelling. Rather, the point of debiasing is to directly counter (implicit) racial bias that has been found to predict discrimination. And preventing race from influencing behavior—has always been recognized as a compelling interest.

As for narrow tailoring, courts usually look to whether the technique deployed is underinclusive, overinclusive, and whether some other technique that is not facially race conscious could have solved the problem just as well. Here, the particulars of the debiasing intervention will matter greatly, but the debate will turn substantially on the findings of general facts about the magnitude of implicit bias, its behavioral manifestations, and its malleability via the chosen debiasing technique. On the one hand, this seems difficult to demonstrate. On the other hand, in the past, the courts have accepted science with arguably no greater evidence of narrow tailoring. Consider specifically the doll studies in Brown (striking down "separate but equal") and the educational diversity studies in Grutter v. Bollinger (2003) (upholding admissions policy at Michigan Law School). Of course, these opinions could be interpreted as more political compromises than earnest applications of new science.

Again, the goal here is not to discuss in detail the complex merits and legal analysis of any particular policy, such as particular eyewitness-identification procedures or debiasing-agent strategies. Instead, it is to show important examples and opportunities that sit in Quadrant IV.

Conclusion

This volume examines the reality of contemporaneous forms of discrimination. Various articles in this volume provide better pictures of that reality, produced by the traditional application of scientific methods. When a new consensus emerges, behavioral realism asks the law to take account of this (new picture of) reality—or to explain transparently why it cannot. This does not mean, however, that judges should allow in individual IAT scores or PET scans as prejudice polygraph scores. And to focus the debate in that way is to miss inadvertently (or to obscure intentionally) the larger picture. An intersection of the axes of specificity and time produces a total of four-conceptual quadrants worthy of consideration. A "prejudice polygraph" is only Quadrant I; the other three quadrants—Changing the Frame, Self-Analysis, and Prevention–should not be excluded from our field of attention. The simple message for scientists and legal scholars alike is to appreciate the capaciousness of the questions presented. Such an understanding will, in turn, license the creativity necessary to solve modern problems of discrimination with modern tools.

References

Bayern, S. J. (Ed.) (2006). Symposium on behavioral realism. California Law Review. Vol. 94, pp. 945–1190.

Bendick, M. Jr., & Nunes, A. P. (2012). Developing the research basis for controlling bias in hiring. *Journal of Social Issues, 68*(2), 238–264. doi: 10.1111/j.1540-4560.2011.01747.x

Berger, M. A. (2009). Research on eyewitness testimony and false confessions. In E. Borgida, & S. T. Fiske (Eds.), *Beyond common sense: Psychological science in the courtroom* (pp. 315–326). Oxford: Blackwell.

Bertrand, M., & Mullainathan, S. (2004). Are Emily and Greg more employable than Lakisha and Jamal? A field experiment on labor market discrimination. *American Economic Review, 94,* 991–1013. doi: 10.1257/0002828042002561

Blair, I. V. (2002). The malleability of automatic stereotypes and prejudice. *Personality and Social Psychology Review, 6,* 242–261. doi: 10.1207/S15327957PSPR0603_8

Borgida, E., & Fiske, S. T. (Eds.) (2008). *Beyond common sense: Psychological science in the courtroom.* Oxford: Blackwell.

Brown v. Board of Education. (1954). 347 U.S. 483.

Correll, J., Park, B., Judd, C. M., & Wittenbrink, B. (2002). The police officer's dilemma: Using ethnicity to disambiguate potentially threatening individuals. *Journal of Personality and Social Psychology, 83*, 1314–1329. doi: 10.1037//0022-3514.83.6.1314

Dasgupta, N., & Asgari, S. (2004). Seeing is believing: Exposure to counterstereotypic women leaders and its effect on the malleability of automatic gender stereotyping. *Journal of Experimental Social Psychology, 40*, 642–658. doi: 10.1016/j.jesp.2004.02.003

Dasgupta, N., & Greenwald, A. G. (2001). On the malleability of automatic attitudes: Combating automatic prejudice with images of admired and disliked individuals. *Journal of Personality & Social Psychology, 81*, 800–814. doi: 10.1037//0022-3514 81.5.800

Daubert v. Merrell Dow Pharmaceuticals. (1993). Inc., 509 U.S. 579.

Diamond, S. S. (2008). Psychological contributions to evaluating witness testimony. In E. Borgida, & S. T. Fiske (Eds.), *Beyond common sense: Psychological science in the courtroom* (pp. 353). Oxford: Blackwell.

Faigman, D. L. (2008). The limits of science in the courtroom. In E. Borgida, & S. T. Fiske (Eds.), *Beyond common sense: Psychological science in the courtroom* (pp. 303–314). Oxford: Blackwell.

Farrakhan v. Gregoire. (2010). 2006 U.S. Dist. LEXIS 45987, No. CV-96–076-RHW, (E.D. Wash. July 7, 2006), *rev'd* 590 F.3d 989 (2010), *reh'g granted*, 603 F.3d 1072 (9th Cir.).

Farrakhan v. Gregoire. (2010). 623 F.3rd 990 (9th Cir.).

Fisher, E.L., & Borgida, E. (2012). Intergroup disparities and implicit bias: A commentary. *Journal of Social Issues, 68*(2), 385–398. doi: 10.1111/j.1540-4560.2011.01753.x

Fiske, S. T., Bersoff, D. N., Borgida, E., Deaux, K., & Heilman, M. E. (1991). Social science research on trial: Use of sex stereotyping research in Price Waterhouse v. Hopkins. *American Psychologist, 46*, 1049–1060. doi: 10.1037/0003-066X.46.10.1049

Flanagan, J. F. (1983). Rejecting a general privilege for self critical analyses. *George Washington Law Review, 51*, 551–582.

General Electric Co. v. Joiner. (1997). 522 U.S. 136.

Greenwald, A. G., Poehlman, T. A., Uhlmann, E. L., & Banaji, M. R. (2009). Understanding and using the Implicit Association Test: III. Meta-Analysis of predictive validity. *Journal of Personality and Social Psychology, 97*, 17–41. doi: 10.1037/a0015575

Grutter v. Bollinger. (2003). 539 U.S. 982.

Hopkins v. Price Waterhouse. (1989). 825 F.2d 458 (D.C. Cir. 1987), *rev'd*, 490 U.S. 228.

Jolls, C., & Sunstein, C. (2006). The law of implicit bias. *California Law Review, 94*, 969–996.

Kang, J., & Banaji, M. R. (2006). Fair measures: A behavioral realist revision of affirmative action. *California Law Review, 94*, 1063–1118.

Krieger, L. H., & Fiske, S. T. (2006). Behavioral realism in employment discrimination law: Implicit bias and disparate treatment. *California Law Review, 94*, 997–1062.

Kumho Tire Co., Ltd. v. Carmichael. (1999). 526 U.S. 137.

Lane, K., Kang, J., & Banaji, M. (2007). Implicit social cognition and the law. *Annual Review of Law and Social Science, 3*, 19.1–19.25. doi: 10.1146/annurev.lawsocsci.3.081806.112748

Mitchell, G., & Tetlock, P. E. (2006). Antidiscrimination law and the perils of mindreading. *Ohio State Law Journal, 67*, 1023.

National Research Council. (2009). *Strengthening Forensic Science in the United States: A Path Forward*. Washington, DC: National Academies Press.

Pager, D., & Western, B. (2012). Identifying discrimination at work: The use of field experiments. *Journal of Social Issues, 68*(2), 221–237. doi: 10.1111/j.1540-4560.2011.01746.x

Plant, E. A., Peruche, B. M., & Butz, D. A. (2005). Eliminating automatic racial bias: Making race nondiagnostic for responses to criminal suspects. *Journal of Experimental Social Psychology, 41*, 141–156. doi: 10.1016/j.jesp.2004.07.004

Pollard, D. A. (1999). Unconscious bias and self-critical analysis: The case for a qualified evidentiary equal employment opportunity privilege. *Washington Law Review, 74*, 913–1031.

Price Waterhouse v. Hopkins. (1989). 490 U.S. 228.

Ricci v. DeStefano. (2009). 129 S. Ct. 2658.

Rooth, D. (2007). *Implicit discrimination in hiring: Real world evidence* (Discussion Paper No. 2764). Bonn, Germany: Institute for the Study of Labor.

Rudman, L. A., & Glick, P. (2001). Prescriptive gender stereotypes and backlash toward agentic women. *Journal of Social Issues, 57,* 743–762. doi: 10.1111/0022-4537.00239

Sadler, M. S., Correll, J., Park, B., & Judd, C. M. (2012). The world is not Black and White: Shooter bias in a multiethnic context. *Journal of Social Issues, 68*(2), 286–313. doi: 10.1111/j.1540-4560.2011.01749.x

Uhlmann, E. L., & Cohen, G. L. (2005). Constructed criteria: Redefining merit to justify discrimination. *Psychological Science, 16,* 474–480. doi: 10.1111/j.0956-7976.2005.01559.x

Vedantam, S. (2005, January 23). See no bias. The Washington Post, p. W12.

JERRY KANG is Professor of Law at UCLA School of Law. He is also Professor of Asian American Studies (by courtesy) at UCLA, and the inaugural Korea Times—Hankook Ilbo Chair in Korean American Studies. His research interests include race and communications. On race, he has focused on the nexus between implicit bias and the law, with the goal of advancing a "behavioral realism." On communications, Professor Kang has published on the topics of privacy, pervasive computing, mass-media policy, and cyber-race (the techno-social construction of race in cyberspace). At UCLA, he was founding co-Director of the Concentration for Critical Race Studies, the first program of its kind in American legal education. He is also founding co-Director of PULSE: Program on Understanding Law, Science, and Evidence.

Journal of Social Issues, Vol. 68, No. 2, 2012, pp. 328–357

Life-Threatening Disparities: The Treatment of Black and White Cancer Patients

Louis A. Penner*
Karmanos Cancer Institute
Wayne State University
University of Michigan

Susan Eggly
Karmanos Cancer Institute
Wayne State University

Jennifer J. Griggs
University of Michigan

Willie Underwood, III
Roswell Park Cancer Institute

Heather Orom
University of Buffalo,
The State University of New York

Terrance L. Albrecht
Karmanos Cancer Institute
Wayne State University

Cancer mortality and survival rates are much poorer for Black patients than for White patients. We argue that Black–White treatment disparities are a major reason for these disparities. We examine three specific kinds of Black–White treatment

*Correspondence concerning this article should be addressed to Louis A. Penner, 4100 John R, 1026 Harper Professional Building, Karmanos Cancer Center, Detroit, MI 48201 [e-mail: pennerl@karmanos.org].

The work reported here was supported by the following grants and awards to the authors: National Cancer Institute (NCI): U01CA114583 & 1U54CA154606-01 (Albrecht, Penner, & Eggly);

328

disparities: disparities in information exchange in oncology interactions, dispari-
ties in the treatment of breast cancer, and disparities in the treatment of clinically
localized prostate cancer. In the final section, we discuss possible causes of these
disparities, with a primary focus on communication within medical interactions
and the role that race-related attitudes and beliefs may play in the quality of
communication in these interactions.

In this article, we focus on a relatively specific kind of health disparity, racial/ethnic disparities in the treatment of cancer. Our basic thesis is that, although biological, genetic, and physiological factors play significant roles in who develops cancer, how it is treated, and who survives it, social, political, economic, and psychological variables also substantially contribute to cancer racial/ethnic disparities in treatment outcomes. In addition to addressing racial/ethnic disparities in the treatment of cancer, we will also consider disparities associated with socioeconomic status (SES) because, in the United States, SES typically strongly covaries with ethnicity.

Because of the disparities the authors target in their own research, this article focuses on disparities in the treatment of cancer in the United States, but the problem of health care disparities is not unique to the United States. Health care disparities are a persistent and pervasive social problem, found in at least 126 countries, which include 94.4% of the world's population (Dorling, Mitchell, & Pearce, 2007). This includes countries with primarily private payer systems, but health care disparities also exist in countries with single-payer government-supported health care systems, including Canada (Frohlich, Ross, & Richmond, 2006) and Sweden (Rostila, 2010), for example. Furthermore, while we primarily address Black–White disparities, ethnicity/race is not the only group characteristic that has been linked to health care disparities. For example, in the United States and other countries, attributes such as sexual orientation (Dilley, Simmons, Boysun, Pizacari, & Stark, 2010), age (Obeidat et al., 2010), gender (Mobaraki & Söderfeldt, 2010), and developmental disabilities (Linehan, Walsh, van Schrojenstein Lantman-de Valk, Kerr, & Dawson, 2009) have all been associated with disparities in health. In the conclusion to this article, we will briefly consider the implications of the findings discussed in this article for other countries and other groups besides Blacks with cancer in the United States.

A brief word about terminology: Following convention in the public health research literature, the term "Black" describes people who self-identify as Black, African American, or Afro-Caribbean; the term "White" describes people who self-identify as non-Hispanic European American or Caucasian. Also, as "race" is

NCI: R03 CA 130588 (Eggly); NCI: R01 CA 139014 & R01 CA 119202 (Griggs); National Institute of Child Health and Development: 1R21HD050445001A1, SPSSI Sages Award (Penner); NCI: 1R01CA152425-0 (Orom & Underwood); NCI: 1U54CA153598-01, Robert Wood Johnson Foundation's Harold Amos Award; AUA Foundation/Astellas Award (Underwood).

used here it refers to a social construction, not a description of a group's genetic characteristics.

The article includes four separate but overlapping sections on Black–White disparities in the treatment of cancer. In the first, we describe disparities in communication and information exchange between oncologists and patients during oncology interactions; we then summarize a body of research on disparities in the treatment of breast cancer; this is followed by research findings on disparities in the treatment of prostate cancer. These three sections describe the nature of the Black–White treatment disparities, but they do not directly discuss their causes. In the final section, we directly address the critical question of why these disparities occur. To do this, we will draw on the landmark report by the Institute of Medicine on health care disparities ("Unequal Treatment") (Smedley, Stith, & Nelson, 2003) as well as on empirical work from the fields of medicine and psychology on how patients' and physicians' beliefs and attitudes may affect the relative quality of treatment Black and White cancer patients receive.

We believe that race-related attitudes play a significant role in disparities in cancer treatment. In a phrase, race matters. However, our view of how race-related attitudes affect health care disparities begins with the premise that while treatment disparities are quite serious and important, their immediate causes may often involve subtle processes. There is, to be sure, a long, sad, and often shameful history of overt racism and racial discrimination in American medicine (cf. Byrd & Clayton, 2000, 2002); and certainly there are still instances where this "old-fashioned" form of racial bias may produce significant kinds of health care disparities. Today, however, the impact of race-related attitudes on medical interactions more typically involves more subtle and nuanced processes. These include overt conscious processes such as differences in how Black patients and their non-Black physicians interpret their own and each other's behaviors during their interactions and consciously held stereotypes about Blacks that may not involve traditional racial stereotypes but nonetheless create Black–White treatment disparities (cf. van Ryn & Burke, 2000). Perhaps more importantly, implicit and nonconscious affective and cognitive processes can result in significant Black–White treatment disparities (van Ryn & Saha, 2011). Indeed, as we shall discuss later, recent research (e.g., Green et al., 2007; Penner et al., 2010b) suggests that it is often implicit rather than explicit forms of racial bias that are responsible for negative outcomes in racially discordant medical interactions. Thus, while race matters, a contemporary explanation of how racial attitudes may produce disparities in cancer treatment does not necessarily require attributing malevolent conscious intent to the people who hold them. But, of course, this does not make these disparities any more acceptable or their effects less harmful.

Now we turn to cancer treatment disparities. To begin our discussion of these disparities, we need to quite clearly describe the kind of problems that concern us and place cancer treatment disparities in the broader context of overall health disparities.

Disparities versus Differences

A meaningful discussion of the relative health status of Blacks and Whites needs to distinguish health-related differences in health status from health-related disparities. This article is not primarily concerned with differences in cancer health status that are due to biological, genetic, or physiological factors. Such factors are most frequently manifested in differences in the incidence or prevalence of a certain kind of cancer in some specific racial/ethnic group. Two examples of such differences are that men of African ancestry may have a stronger genetic predisposition to develop prostate cancer than men from other populations (Salami, Etukakpan, & Olapade-Olaopa, 2007); and that relative to other groups, Eastern European Jewish women have a substantially higher incidence of mutations of the BRCA 1/2 genes that are believed to be related to the development of breast cancer (Roa, Boyd, Volcik, & Richards, 1996). Such differences are quite distinct from disparities, which Braveman (2006) defines thus:

> Health disparities do not refer to all differences in health. A health disparity is a particular type of difference in health; it is a difference in which disadvantaged social groups— such as the poor, racial/ethnic minorities, women, or other groups who have persistently experienced social disadvantage or discrimination—systematically experience worse health or greater health risks than more advantaged social groups (p. 167).

A critical aspect of Braveman's definition is that health disparities result from social, political, and economic processes and thus, at least theoretically, can be prevented from occurring or can be eliminated once identified. Thus, in this article, we do not discuss the biological, genetic, or physiological aspects of Black–White differences in breast or prostate cancer mortality. Rather, we focus on something that clearly can be prevented or eliminated—disparities in how cancer is treated.

The Institute of Medicine report on the health status of racial/ethnic minorities in the United States (Smedley et al., 2003) concluded that the poorer health status of certain racial/ethnic minorities was due, in large part, to the health care they received; that is, their health status was poorer in large measure because they received poorer treatment for their medical problems. This conclusion provides the basis of a core assumption of this article. Specifically, we believe that for many cancers, a substantial portion of the Black–White differences in rates of mortality are disparities that could be eliminated if disparities in cancer treatment were eliminated. This is not to say that if all treatment disparities were eliminated, the cancer mortality rates for different racial/ethnic groups would also be eliminated; stage at diagnosis and racial/ethnic variability in genetic and biological factors may play important roles in who survives cancer (Wong, Ettner, Boscardin, & Shapiro,

2009). However, large epidemiological studies suggest a dramatic reduction in mortality differences between Blacks and Whites when the two groups receive equivalent treatments for their cancers (Bach et al., 2002).

Cancer-Related Mortality Rates among Blacks and Whites

Cancer is the second leading cause of death (following heart disease) in the United States for the all racial/ethnic groups identified by the Center for Disease Control and Prevention (National Center for Health Statistics [NCHS], 2008). However, the mortality rate (about 223 per 100,000) among people who self-identify as Black is substantially higher than among members of any other racial/ethnic group. According to the most recent data on causes of deaths in the United States (Siegel, Ward, Brawley, & Jemal, 2011), the overall mortality rate due to cancer among Blacks is about 25% higher than the mortality rate among Whites. The specific cancers we address in this article (breast and prostate) provide even more striking examples of this disparity. Although Black women are slightly less likely to develop breast cancer than White women, the mortality rate due to breast cancer is about 40% higher among Black than White women (Siegel et al., 2011). Black men are about 1.4 times as likely to develop prostate cancer as are White men, but Blacks are about 2.4 times as likely to die of prostate cancer as are Whites (NCHS, 2008; Siegel et al., 2011). In other words, the Black–White disparity in deaths due to prostate cancer is substantially greater than the Black–White difference in the incidence of prostate cancer. The data on 5-year survival rates following a diagnosis of cancer tell the same story. Among people who have breast or prostate cancer, Blacks have lower 5-year survival rates than do Whites (NCHS, 2008). Siegel et al. (2011) succinctly summarize the consequences of cancer health disparities, "The elimination of educational and racial disparities could potentially have avoided about 37% of the premature cancer deaths among individuals aged 25–64 years in 2007 alone." (p. 212.)

A very large literature also exists showing that SES is a strong predictor of overall health status (Gallo, Espinosa de los Monteros, & Shivpuri, 2009; NCHS, 2008). With specific regard to cancer, a number of individual studies (Hussain, Altieri, Sundquist, & Hemminki, 2008; Yu, 2009) show higher rates of cancer mortality among poorer and less-educated people.

The question then becomes why are Blacks and lower SES individuals more likely to die from cancer? One well-documented cause is that, for a host of reasons, minority group members and low SES individuals are usually less likely to be screened for certain cancers (e.g., breast and colorectal) (Ponce et al., 2004; Smith-Bindman et al., 2006) and their cancers are often diagnosed at more advanced stages than is the case for higher SES individuals and or Whites (Centers for Disease Control and Prevention [CDC], 2005). There is no doubt that screening disparities are a major cause of disparities in mortality (Smith-Bindman et al.,

2006), but it must be noted that, at least for some cancers, disparities in mortality rates remain even when stage at diagnosis of cancer is controlled (Jemal et al., 2004). This finding appears to support the core assumption of this article: in particular, for breast and prostate cancers, treatment disparities play a major role in the disparities in mortality rates between Blacks and Whites.

Black–White Disparities in Information Exchange during Oncology Interactions

It is estimated that about 75% of medical interactions in which Black patients participate are "racially discordant;" that is, the patient is Black and the physician is not (Penner, Albrecht, Orom, Coleman, & Underwood, 2010a). On the other hand, for White patients, only about 20% of their medical interactions are racially discordant. There is a large body of research showing that, relative to racially concordant medical interactions, racially discordant medical interactions are less positive and productive (Penner et al., 2010a). To be more specific, racially discordant medical interactions are shorter in length (Cooper-Patrick et al., 1999), less patient-centered (Johnson, Roter, Powe, & Cooper, 2004), and characterized by less positive affect (Johnson et al., 2004). These interactions involve fewer attempts at relationship building (Siminoff, Graham, & Gordon, 2006) and less patient participation in decision making (Koerber, Gajendra, Fulford, BeGole, & Evans, 2004). Furthermore, racially discordant medical interactions are more likely to be verbally dominated by the physician (Johnson, Saha, Arbelaez, Beach, & Cooper, 2004). Finally, Oliver, Goodwin, Gotler, Gregory, and Strange (2001) found that White physicians spent significantly less time planning treatment, providing health education, assessing health knowledge, engaging in informal conversation, and answering questions with Blacks as compared to White patients.

We could not locate data on the percentage of oncology interactions that are racially discordant, but it is likely that this percentage is at least as high as it is for primary care interactions, given that fewer than 2% of oncologists in the United States are Black (Newman, Pollock, & Johnson-Thompson, 2003). The research literature on outcomes of racially discordant cancer interactions is much smaller than the literature on racially discordant primary care interactions, but it also seems reasonable to assume that the outcomes do not meaningfully differ from those noted earlier. A study by Gordon, Street, Sharf, Kelly, and Souchek (2006a) supports this conclusion. These authors examined the relative levels of trust of Black and White lung cancer patients before and after a visit with an oncologist. As others have found, there was no previsit Black–White difference in patient trust in physicians, but there was a postvisit difference, with trust becoming significantly lower among Blacks. Black patients' postvisit trust was significantly associated their perceptions of how informative, supportive, and participatory the oncologist was.

Our own work on disparities in oncology interactions takes a slightly different tack than Gordon et al. (2006a). We are specifically interested in information exchange in oncology interactions. Our research is predicated on the assumption that most patients want as much information as possible about their cancer (Hack, Degner, & Parker, 2005) and that their preferred source of information is their physician (Arora et al., 2007; Rutten, Arora, Bakos, Aziz, & Rowland, 2005). Effective information exchange, with the goal of having a patient understand and be understood, is associated with increased patient satisfaction and involvement. Effective information exchange also increases involvement in the consultation and in decision making, satisfaction with treatment choices, improved ability to cope at all stages of cancer, reductions in anxiety and uncertainty, improved communication with family members, and reduced disruption in their quality of life (Arora, 2003; Epstein & Street, 2007; Griggs et al., 2007a; Hack et al., 2005). This body of research suggests that effective information exchange during an oncology interaction is critical to patients deriving maximum benefit from a visit to an oncologist and making the best decision regarding their own care.

Most people who visit an oncologist, especially at a cancer hospital, likely already have at least a strong suspicion that they have cancer. What they are less likely to know is how serious the cancer is, whether it can be treated, and what treatment options are available and recommended for their cancer. Given the complexity of most cancers and cancer treatments, treatment decisions are rarely easy. Patients are often presented with more than one treatment option, the outcomes of treatments are often uncertain, and the treatments can be complex and may involve adherence to a complex regimen. Treatment decisions become even harder when a patient is asked to enroll in a clinical trial. A clinical trial is often the best treatment available for a cancer (National Comprehensive Cancer Network [NCCN], 2008), but the regimens may be complex and difficult for lay people to understand. Thus, it seems reasonable to assume that patients will make the best treatment decisions when the information exchange has been effective; that is, when patients have provided and received the appropriate information relevant to their illness, and when they understand the information they received.

Our theoretical model argues that the effective exchange of information during oncology interactions results in high "convergence" between the participants (Albrecht, Penner, Cline, Eggly, & Ruckdeschel, 2009). Convergence occurs when there is a shared perspective regarding what was said and not said during the interaction, understanding of what was said, and agreement that the conclusions or courses of actions that result from the interaction are correct and/or should be followed. Ongoing work by Eggly, Penner, Albrecht and colleagues strongly suggests that there are racial/ethnic disparities in the quality of exchange of information in oncology interactions and thus disparities in the level of convergence that result from these interactions.

One aspect of information exchange that Eggly and colleagues have investigated is patient question asking in oncology interactions (Eggly et al., 2006, 2011; Eggly, Penner, Harper, Ruckdeschel, & Albrecht, 2007). The research is based on prior findings that patients' preferred way to gain information about their cancer diagnosis, prognosis, and treatment is to ask questions of their oncologists (Hesse, Arora, Burke-Bedford, & Finney, 2009).

Some of Eggly and her colleagues' work concerns Black–White disparities in question asking. Findings from prior research suggest that the total frequency of questions asked by patients and the proportion of direct questions relative to the total frequency of questions are both related to patients gaining more information (Cegala, McClure, Marinelli, & Post, 2000; Cegala, Street, & Clinch, 2007; Roter, 1984; Gordon, Street, Sharf, & Souchek, 2006b). Eggly et al. (2011) and a team of trained coders observed a large number of video recorded oncology interactions to identify and classify patient and companion questions as either direct (i.e., questions that directly solicit a response, such as "Will I lose my hair?") or indirect (i.e., questions that imply a desire for information, such as "I wonder if I'll lose my hair like my sister did."). They examined the total frequency of patient questions and the relative frequency of direct to total patient questions. Blacks asked fewer questions per interaction, and the proportion of direct questions was significantly smaller among Black than White patients. These relationships remained significant when Eggly et al. controlled for patients' age, education, and income.

There is, however, an additional source of Black–White disparities in information exchange that merits consideration: the impact of patients' companions. Findings from our own research (e.g., Eggly et al., 2011; Eggly et al., 2006) demonstrate that companions are active participants in oncology interactions, asking at least as many questions as patients. Eggly et al. (2011) found that patients and companions together asked over twice as many questions as patients alone. This finding leads us to a second source of Black–White disparities in information exchange—the likelihood of having companions present in the interaction.

Over the 8 years we have been studying medical interactions in cancer hospitals in racially/ethnically diverse areas, we have consistently found that Black patients are significantly less likely to bring a companion to oncology interactions than are White patients. Other researchers have found a similar phenomenon (Gordon et al., 2006b; Street & Gordon, 2008). For example, in Eggly et al.'s (2011) sample of 109 cancer interactions, 86% of the White patients brought a companion, but only 40% of the Black patients brought a companion. Pilot data from a more recent study show the same pattern; Whites were about twice as likely to bring a companion as Blacks. As a result, we find that across the interactions we study almost twice as many questions are asked on behalf of Whites in oncology interactions as are asked on behalf of Blacks. This may not only affect the amount of information Black oncology patients receive during the interaction, but because they are more likely to be alone, it is less likely that Blacks will have someone who can provide social and emotional support as well as assist them with exchanging information with the oncologist.

Thus, with regard to getting information from oncology interactions, Black patients are at a disadvantage in two ways: they ask fewer questions overall, they ask a smaller proportion of direct questions, and because they are much less likely than White patients to have a companion with them in the interaction, fewer questions are asked on their behalf.

Our data do not allow us to speculate on the reasons for the persistent racial difference in the presence of companions during oncology interactions. However, Brondolo, Libereti, Rivera, & Walsemann (2012) suggest that racism at various levels (e.g., institutional, internalized) may undermine Blacks' ability to "form, maintain, and benefit from peer relationships," thus reducing the social capital available to Blacks. It seems possible that the relative dearth of companions who accompany Black cancer patients may provide an example of this process. This would seem to be an interesting line of research to explore.

In a study that we have just completed, we more directly investigated disparities in information exchange in oncology interactions. We studied 65 new cancer patients, their physicians, and the person who accompanied patients to the interactions in a cancer center in Detroit. Immediately after the first interaction with the oncologist, we administered a questionnaire in which we asked all three participants about whether five specific topics were discussed during the interaction; if a topic was discussed, what the physician said about the topic; and finally, how well the patient understood what the physician said. Although our convergence model views the patient–companion, companion–physician, and patient–companion dyads as very important aspects of overall convergence (Albrecht et al., 2009), here we only consider our preliminary findings only on patient–physician dyads and any Black–White disparities in the information exchange within these dyads.

The first issue we examined was whether there were racial/ethnic disparities in the topics that were actually discussed. We assessed agreement among participants (i.e., patients, companions, physicians) regarding whether the following five topics related to cancer were discussed: diagnosis, prognosis, metastasis (i.e., spread), treatment, and side effects associated with treatment. There were no Black–White disparities with regard to whether patients and physicians had discussed diagnosis, prognosis, treatment of the cancer, and metastasis. However, we found a significant Black–White disparity in whether they discussed side effects during interactions in which both the physician and patient reported having discussed treatment. In those interactions where patients and physicians agreed on what had or had not been discussed, when patients were White, side effects were discussed in 97% of the interactions, but when patients were Black, side effects were discussed in only 62%% of the interactions (Eggly et al., 2010).

This finding is consistent with findings from an earlier study by Penner, Eggly, Harper, Albrecht, and Ruckdeschel (2007). In this study, rather than obtaining self-reports, trained coders observed video recordings of oncology interactions with patients who were being asked to enroll in a clinical trial. Coders counted the number of side effects oncologists mentioned and the number of messages they delivered about other aspects of clinical trials (e.g., the fact that patients would receive treatment even if they did not enroll in a particular trial). The results indicated that the oncologists mentioned at least one side effect of the trial treatment regimen during 77% of their interactions with White patients; in contrast, they mentioned side effects during only 44% of interactions with Black patients. Furthermore, in those interactions where patients received some information about side effects and related aspects of the trials, oncologists provided significantly more information about side effects and other aspects of the trial to White than to Black patients.

An ongoing linguistic analysis of a subset of these video recorded interactions by our colleague, Ellen Barton, is showing similar results. Using a quite different methodology, Barton calculated the time per minute oncologists spent telling their patients about various aspects of clinical trials. Barton found that oncologists spent about twice as much time talking about risks associated with the trial with White patients (about 29 seconds per minute) as they did with Black patients (about 14 seconds per minute) (Barton & Marback, 2009).

Returning to our study of self-reports of information exchange in patient–physician dyads, our findings did not show any Black–White disparities in terms of patient–physician agreement regarding what the oncologist said about the specific topics. We did, however, find that Black patients reported significantly less understanding of what physicians said about their diagnosis than did White patients. We also found some other patient characteristics associated with disparities in information exchange. For example, we found that older and less-educated patients were more likely to disagree with physicians with regard to what was said about the severity of side effects. Similarly, relative to other patients, patients who were older had less education reported they understood less of what the physician had told them.

In summary, research, including our own studies, provides substantial empirical evidence of racial/ethnic disparities in patient information seeking during oncology clinical interactions, in the amount of information oncologists actually provided (especially about side effects), and in patient understanding of the information provided. (For similar findings, see Gordon et al., 2006b.)

Thus far, we have considered communication disparities in oncology interactions. Next, we turn directly to disparities in cancer treatments. Specifically, we consider Black–White disparities in the treatment of breast cancer and of prostate cancer. These are two cancers that can, with proper treatment, often be cured and/or people typically survive them for a very long time.

Black–White Disparities in the Treatment of Breast Cancer

As already mentioned, breast cancer mortality rates are worse among Black women than among White women (Siegel et al., 2011). Cancer researchers have identified several factors that may contribute to these outcomes. Relative to White women, Black women often have more aggressive disease (Gordon, 2003; Thomson, Hole, Twelves, Brewster, & Black, 2001), more advanced disease at the time of initial diagnosis (Naik et al., 2003); a higher incidence of obesity, which is associated with a worse prognosis in breast cancers (Daling et al., 2001; Petrelli, Calle, Rodriguez, & Thun, 2002); and higher rates of other illnesses (Calle et al., 2002; Fleming, Pursley, Newman, Pavlov, & Chen, 2005). However, as is true with other cancers, the higher mortality rates among Black women remain even when these factors are controlled (Griggs, Sorbero, Stark, Heininger, & Dick, 2003).

These facts persuaded Griggs and her colleagues to study possible disparities in the treatment of breast cancer. Griggs and her colleagues are not, of course, the first or the only researchers to study ethnic disparities in the treatment of breast cancer. There is considerable evidence that patient race/ethnicity is associated with disparities in the probability of surgery, use of radiation, and use of chemotherapy. Black women (and lower SES women) receive poorer quality care in all these areas (Bach, Cramer, Warren, & Begg, 1999; Michalski & Nattinger, 1997). However, it is difficult in these studies to determine the relative role of patients and oncologists in contributing to these disparities. Indeed, some researchers have hypothesized that these treatment disparities reflect the effects of patient attitudes and behaviors regarding their treatment choices and adherence to treatment regimens. This perspective is consistent with other research that has identified ethnic differences in health-related beliefs, attitudes, and behaviors (Smedley et al., 2003).

The work of Griggs and her colleagues has more directly examined how oncologists' treatment decisions may affect the kinds of treatment women receive for breast cancer, specifically the levels and kinds of chemotherapy given to breast cancer patients. Specifically, Griggs and her associates have studied decisions about the amount of a drug (dose level) to be administered in adjuvant chemotherapy. Because we expect that most readers of this journal may not be familiar with treatments for breast cancer, a brief explanation of adjuvant chemotherapy is in order.

Chemotherapy can be used to treat breast cancer before surgery, typically to reduce the size of a tumor; this is called primary systemic (or neoadjuvant) chemotherapy. Chemotherapy that is given after apparently successful breast surgery is called adjuvant chemotherapy. In this case, no cancer can be detected, but chemotherapy is intended to reduce the probability of a recurrence of the cancer. Adjuvant chemotherapy, if properly administered, can quite substantially reduce the risk of breast cancer recurrence (Early Breast Cancer Trialists' Collaborative Group, 2005). If an oncologist decides that a patient is an appropriate candidate for adjuvant chemotherapy, he/she must decide on the correct medications and dose for this patient. With regard to dose, there are widely accepted clinical guidelines. These guidelines are primarily based on body surface area, which is calculated using the patient's height and weight and expressed in square meters (Griggs, Sorbero, & Lyman, 2005). The dose level is extremely important because there is substantial evidence that adjuvant chemotherapy doses that are 85% or less of the standard or recommended guidelines are substantially less effective in the prevention of the recurrence of breast cancer (Bonadonna & Valagussa, 1981; Bonadonna, Valagussa, Moliterni, Zambetti, & Brambilla, 1995).

In a series of prospective and retrospective studies, Griggs and her associates (Griggs et al., 2003, 2005, 2007a, 2007b) asked whether women from certain groups are at an increased risk of receiving reduced doses of adjuvant chemotherapy. Importantly, Griggs et al. (2003) have examined data on the initial doses that oncologists plan to give their patients, because decisions about initial dose levels reflects a physician's dose selection independent of patient's side effects in response to previous chemotherapy cycles. (Initial dose level decisions are also strongly associated with dose intensity over the entire course of treatment.) Griggs et al.'s logic is that, by using initial planned doses as their primary outcome measure, they are able to eliminate or minimize the influence of patient's physical or psychological reactions to a chemotherapy regimen on oncologists' decisions about the best chemotherapy regimen for that patient.

In the first of these studies, Griggs et al. (2003) examined the medical records of almost 500 women treated at 10 different treatment sites in two geographical areas. Patient SES was not assessed on an individual basis; rather the researchers used patients' addresses and census tract data to determine the SES characteristics of the neighborhood in which a patient lived.

Griggs and her colleagues used established guidelines to determine what dose should be recommended for each patient, based on her height and weight and resultant body surface area. The actual dose level selected by the oncologist was divided by the recommended dose. If the resultant ratio was 1.0, the individual oncologist's selection was exactly the same as the recommended dose. Based on the research cited earlier on dose–response effectiveness, a ratio of 0.80 or less (i.e., 80% or less of the recommended dose) was considered an instance of under dosing. In addition to this measure, the researchers also examined the recommended duration of adjuvant chemotherapy for each patient to the duration actually chosen by the oncologist and computed a comparable ratio. They also multiplied the planned dose by the planned duration to obtain an estimate of the total amount of chemotherapy planned for a patient.

Griggs et al. compared the doses planned for Black and for White patients. Because there were a number of differences between Black and White patients that might affect the dosing decisions, Griggs et al. controlled for factors such as tumor characteristics, other medical conditions, obesity, SES, and whether a patient had insurance. Even when these variables were controlled, Black women were significantly more likely to be under dosed than White women. That is, the ratio of planned to recommended dose was significantly lower for Black patients than for White patients. Only 61% of the Black patients received a dose proportion of 0.80 (i.e., 80% of the recommended dose) or greater; in contrast, 72% of the White patients received a dose this great or greater. There were no disparities in the planned duration of treatment, but there were disparities when planned dose was multiplied by duration. The total planned dose for Black patients was significantly less than for White patients. In this study, patients who lived in census tracts with income above the sample median were also less likely to have first cycle dose reductions.

Subsequent studies by Griggs and her colleagues have replicated and extended the findings with regard to patient ethnicity and SES. For example, Griggs et al. (2007b) conducted a prospective study on women about to start adjuvant chemotherapy and found a marginal effect ($p < .06$) for patient race/ethnicity; as before, Blacks were more likely to be under dosed than Whites. Significant effects were also found for SES. Lower SES patients were significantly more likely to receive less than 85% of the recommended dose than were higher SES patients.

Finally, Griggs et al. (Griggs et al., 2007a) looked at disparities in the kinds of drugs used in chemotherapy regimens. These authors compiled an exhaustive list of the recommended chemotherapy regimens (i.e., specific drugs and drug combinations) for adjuvant chemotherapy; then they examined the regimens actually used with 957 breast cancer patients. If a regimen was not included in the list, it was considered "nonstandard." Griggs et al. found that, whereas 11% of the White patients from a national sample received a chemotherapy regimen that differed from the standard, recommended chemotherapy regimens for breast cancer, 19% of the Black patients received nonstandard chemotherapy. In this study, Griggs et al. also found that patient education and age were also associated with treatment disparities. People who had less education and were older were more likely to receive nonstandard chemotherapies.

In summary, across four different studies, Griggs et al. found that Black breast cancer patients were more likely to be underdosed or given nonstandard chemotherapy regimens than were White breast cancer patients. The results are not just statistically significant; these findings also have clear implications for mortality rates among Black breast cancer patients. As already mentioned, reductions in chemotherapy doses at the level identified by Griggs et al. as nonstandard (less than 85% of the recommended dose), result in a much higher incidence of breast cancer recurrence (Goldhirsch & Gelber, 1994; Morrow, Siegel, Boone, Lawless, & Carter, 2002). Of course, this all begs the question of why there is this treatment disparity. Again, we defer a discussion of this question until the last section in this article and turn to disparities in the treatment of prostate cancer.

Black–White Disparities in the Treatment of Prostate Cancer

Blacks are more likely than Whites to die of most cancers; however, the largest Black–White differences in mortality/survival rates are for prostate cancer (Allen, Kennedy, Wilson-Glover, & Gilligan, 2007). Blacks are more than twice as likely to die from prostate cancer than are Whites (Siegel et al., 2011). Blacks are more likely to be diagnosed with a higher grade (more aggressive) and/or a higher stage (more advanced) prostate cancer than are Whites (Hoffman et al., 2001; Underwood et al., 2005). Survival differences between Black and White men with prostate cancer are partially due to Blacks having a more advanced stage at diagnosis and differences in tumor characteristics, but treatment disparities also explain survival differences between Black and White men diagnosed with equal disease (Bach et al., 2002; Wong et al., 2009).

In this section, we consider the research on Black–White disparities in the treatment of prostate cancer. As we did in the previous section on breast cancer, we begin with a brief introduction to prostate cancer diagnosis and treatment. Although many men do die of prostate cancer (9% of all cancer-related deaths), few men with prostate cancer die within 5 years of diagnosis; rather, the majority of men diagnosed with prostate cancer ultimately die of other causes. However, some men either are diagnosed with or go on to develop metastatic prostate cancer (i.e., the cancer spreads), which has a much lower 5-year survival rate than localized disease (33.5% vs. 99.3%) (Jemal et al., 2004).

The aggressiveness of the cancer is graded from a 2 to 10 on a scale called the Gleason score. Among patients with clinically localized prostate cancer, mortality varies significantly with a patient's age and where the cancer falls on this scale; younger age and higher Gleason scores are significantly associated with greater mortality risk (Albertsen, Hanley, & Fine, 2005). Of course, mortality rates are even higher among men whose cancer has spread beyond the prostate region (Jemal et al., 2004).

The recommended treatment options for prostate cancer vary and depend on a number of factors. These include the aggressiveness and amount of cancer at diagnosis, a patient's age and overall medical condition, and the patient's treatment preferences (NCCN, 2009). If the prostate cancer is relatively slow-growing and/or patient is older, it is fairly common to engage in "watchful waiting," also referred to as "active surveillance" (Bastian et al., 2009). This option means that initially the patient does not receive any "definitive" treatment (e.g., surgery, radiation, or some combination); rather his cancer is closely monitored to see how rapidly it grows. If it appears that cancer is beginning to grow or spread, then definitive treatments intended to cure the cancer are generally started (Zeliadt et al., 2006).

Definitive treatments include surgery, radiation, and cryotherapy (destroying the cancer by freezing it). These treatments may have different side effects, some of which can be significant (e.g., incontinence, erectile dysfunction) (Sanda et al., 2008). Also, there is professional disagreement as to the relative effectiveness of treatments. Thus, there may be substantial subjectivity in patient and physician decisions about whether, when and how to treat prostate cancer. This subjectivity, at least theoretically, increases the probability of treatment disparities based on nonmedical factors. The third and fourth authors of this article, Underwood and Orom, and others have examined Black–White disparities in prostate cancer treatments.

We begin with the decision to treat. Shavers and her colleagues (Shavers et al., 2004a) have looked at the relative frequency of watchful waiting (i.e., no definitive treatment) among newly diagnosed Black and White prostate cancer patients. Shavers et al. found that after controlling for factors such as patient age, comorbidities, stage of the cancer, and life expectancy, Black men were still about 1.4 times more likely to receive watchful waiting than were White men. Among the Black men, those with more comorbidity and less education (based on census tract data) were more likely to receive watchful waiting; no similar effects were found among the White men in the study. In a follow-up study, Shavers et al. (2004b) looked at medical care among Black and White men who were receiving watchful waiting. In general, Black men received less medical monitoring and had longer median times from diagnosis to receipt of a medical monitoring visit or procedure than did White men. Furthermore, during the 60 months following their diagnosis, 6% of the Black men did not receive any medical monitoring visits or procedures. In contrast, only 1% of the White men had no medical monitoring visits or procedures during this same time period. Controlling for sociodemographic or clinical variables did not reduce this difference. (It is also worth noting that Shavers et al. found the same kinds of disparity between White and Hispanic men.)

Next, we consider possible disparities among men who receive definitive treatment for their localized prostate cancer. As we have already mentioned, there are professional disagreements as to which specific definitive treatments are more effective in treating prostate cancer. However, there is general agreement that once prostate cancer begins to progress, treatment is better than no treatment (Wong et al., 2006).

There are substantial differences in the overall treatment rates for Black and White men with prostate cancer. Schapira, McAuliffe, and Nattinger (1995), using a subset of the National Cancer Institute's national cancer database (Surveillance

Epidemiology End Results [SEER]), Altekruse et al., 2010), found that Black men were half as likely as White men to receive definitive therapy (surgery or radiation) for their prostate cancer. Harlan, Brawley, Pommerenke, Wali, and Kramer (1995) examined the entire SEER database from 1984 to 1991 and found that among men 50–69 who were diagnosed with localized prostate cancer, 67% of Black men and 80% of White men received a radical prostatectomy (i.e., surgical removal of the prostate). In a study of men in the Detroit area with prostate cancer, Schwartz et al. (2009) found that among men whose cancer had spread beyond the prostate, Black men were twice as likely as White men (44–22%) not to receive definitive treatment for their cancer. In this context, it is important to note that if Black men receive the same treatment for the same grade and stage prostate cancer as do Whites, the two groups' survival rates are the same (Underwood et al., 2004a).

Schwartz et al. (2009) also analyzed the causes of mortality in their sample. Among both men with localized cancer and those whose cancer had spread outside the prostate region, variables such as patient age and tumor grade accounted for about 10% of the Black–White variability in mortality. Black–White differences in SES also contributed to differences in mortality. But even after these two classes of variables were controlled, Black–White disparities in treatment still accounted for significant additional variability in mortality rates. Thus, reducing the Black–White treatment disparities would substantially reduce mortality rates among Black men with prostate cancer.

Underwood and his colleagues (Underwood et al., 2004b) have more directly explored the relationship between patient race/ethnicity and treatments received. The primary question asked by these investigators was whether Black–White treatment disparities differed as a function of the grade or severity of their cancer. Underwood et al. used the SEER database to obtain treatment data on 140,000 men diagnosed with clinically localized prostate cancer (i.e., cancer that had not spread to other parts of the body). Although they were interested in treatment disparities among White, Black, and Hispanic men, we will focus primarily on the Black–White disparities they identified. These researchers used prostate cancer grade at diagnosis to classify the aggressiveness of the men's cancer and divided the type of treatment the men received into a definitive treatment group or a nondefinitive treatment group (watchful waiting or hormonal therapy).

In their analysis, Underwood et al. controlled for the patients' marital status, age at diagnosis, and region of the country of diagnosis. They used White men diagnosed with moderate-grade prostate cancer as the standard for comparison with other groups. Among men diagnosed with well-differentiated (low risk) prostate cancer, all racial/ethnic groups were less likely to receive definitive therapy compared to White men diagnosed with moderate-grade prostate cancer (i.e., the standard). This would be expected because men diagnosed with well-differentiated prostate cancer have a low risk of dying from prostate cancer even if they do not receive definitive treatment (Lu-Yao et al., 2009). Among men diagnosed with poorly differentiated grade (high risk) prostate cancer, Whites were just as likely to receive definitive treatment as were White men diagnosed with moderate-grade prostate cancer. In contrast, Black men with high-risk cancer were 50% less likely than White men with moderate-grade cancer to receive definitive treatment. This finding is extremely important because, compared to men diagnosed with moderately differentiated prostate cancer, men diagnosed with poorly differentiated prostate cancer are 2.5 times more likely to die from prostate cancer when not receiving nondefinitive treatment Lu-Yao et al., 2009). No Black–White differences in receiving definitive treatment were noted among men diagnosed with well-differentiated grade (low risk) prostate cancer. However, among men diagnosed with moderate-grade prostate cancer, Black men were 36% less likely to receive definitive treatment than their White counterparts.

In summary, Underwood and colleagues' findings indicate that there are Black–White disparities in the treatment of prostate cancer and that these disparities actually increase as men are diagnosed with more aggressive cancers. Other research (e.g., Zeliadt, Potosky, Etzioni, Ramsey, & Penson, 2004) shows that these treatment disparities cannot be explained by differences in patients' SES or the presence of other illnesses (i.e., comorbidities) that might affect treatment decisions.

Causes of Black–White Cancer Treatment Disparities

In this final section, we consider some possible explanations of Black–White disparities in the quality of communication and information exchange during oncology interactions and in the treatments provided to Black and White cancer patients. As far as we are aware, there is presently a dearth of research that directly and explicitly addresses the causes of disparities in the treatment of cancer. Therefore, we place cancer treatment within the framework of research on Black–White disparities in treatment for medical problems in general and extrapolate from this research to disparities in cancer. Our discussion of possible causes uses the same organizational framework as the 2003 IOM report on general health care disparities (Smedley et al., 2003).

In this report, the Institute of Medicine (IOM) panel proposed three related causes of Black–White disparities in health care. The first of these was at the system level: because of the way health care is financed in the United States, there may be differences in the overall quality of health care Blacks and Whites receive. One source of this disparity may be disparities in health insurance. Currently, for most people under 65, health care is paid for directly by patients or indirectly through private insurance companies, whose fees are paid by employers and/or patients. In the United States, the best health care usually occurs when the payer is a private insurance company (Smedley et al., 2003). Whereas 71% of Whites are covered by such plans, only 54% of Blacks have such coverage (NCHS, 2008).

There is also evidence to suggest that medical facilities with a high percentage of Black patients may provide relatively poorer care to all of their patients. For example, using a sample of over 140,000 Medicare patients, Barnato, Lucas, Staiger, Wennberg, and Chandra (2005) found that "Blacks went to hospitals that had lower rates of evidence-based medical treatments, higher rates of cardiac procedures, and worse risk-adjusted mortality after acute myocardial infarction" (p. 303). It seems very unlikely that Blacks (or anyone else) actually choose to go to lower quality hospitals. It seems much more likely that perhaps because of segregated housing patterns, limited means of transportation, and other similar social and physical barriers, Black patients are essentially forced to choose a health care facility on the basis of proximity and convenience rather than on their perceptions of the quality of care the facility provides.

A system-level explanation such as health care financing may have some intuitive appeal, but, at best, it provides only a partial explanation of health care disparities. Numerous studies find disparities in health status exist even when Blacks and Whites have the same insurance plans and use the same health care systems and medical facilities (Smedley et al., 2003). For example, Trivedi, Zaslavsky, Schneider, and Ayanian (2006) examined whether the quality of patients' health plans or their race/ethnicity was a better predictor of the patients' health status. They examined the health records of over 430,000 patients with chronic diseases, enrolled in 151 different health plans, each of which was independently rated for quality. The researchers found no relation between the overall quality of a health plan and the relative health status of Black and White patients. However, they did find very large health status disparities among Black and White patients enrolled in the same health plans.

Furthermore, health care system disparities do not explain the disparities in the quality of communication during racially discordant and racially concordant medical interactions that we have discussed. Most of the studies we cited in our earlier discussion were conducted in facilities where the same physicians saw Black and White patients in the same setting. Thus, while system-level factors almost certainly contribute to health disparities, there are clearly additional causes that we need to consider.

This brings us to the second possible cause, which the IOM called patient-level factors. Greatly simplified, the IOM panel proposed that certain patient attitudes and behaviors might negatively affect the outcomes of medical interactions and, thus, the health status of Black patients. There are many kinds of patient-related variables that might affect the health status of Black patients, but we limit our discussion to ways in which Black patients' experiences as members of a stigmatized racial/ethnic group and as targets of prejudice and discrimination might affect the quality of their medical interactions with non-Black providers and outcomes of these interactions. As we discuss some relevant research findings, we remind the reader that for most Black patients, medical interactions are racially discordant (Penner et al., 2010a).

We begin with Black patients' experiences with and resultant perceptions of the health care system in the United States. Malat and Hamilton (2006) reported that 57% of Blacks in a national survey said that discrimination occurs "often" or "very often" in their interactions with White physicians. Other surveys find that Blacks are significantly more likely than Whites to believe that their race negatively affects their health care (Thompson, Valdimarsdottir, Winkel, Jandorf, & Redd, 2004) and that Blacks are less trusting of their physicians than are Whites (Halbert, Armstrong, Gandy, & Shaker, 2006).

Independent of these predispositions, there is reason to believe that the dynamics of interracial interactions may influence medical encounters between Black patients and Whites health care providers. Specifically, Dovidio et al. (2008) proposed that when Blacks and Whites interact, because of a desire not to be perceived as prejudiced, many Whites pay great attention to and try to shape conscious intentions and controllable behaviors that might communicate racial bias. However, Whites may still behave differently with Blacks than with Whites on dimensions that are less controllable (e.g., nonverbal behaviors) and Blacks, because of their minority status and certain sociohistorical factors (e.g., less social power) may be more attentive to such behaviors than are Whites (Richeson & Shelton, 2005). For example, Dovidio, Kawakami, and Gaertner (2002) had Black confederates, trained to act the same across all interactions, and naïve White participants interact in interracial dyads. Following the interactions, both parties rated the White person's friendliness during the interaction. Dovidio et al. found that the White participants' ratings of their own friendliness during the interaction correlated significantly with their (more controllable) verbal behaviors during the interactions, but the Black confederates' ratings of the White participants' friendliness were correlated with the Whites' nonverbal behaviors during the interaction. Importantly, this latter rating of the Whites' friendliness was also correlated with the Whites' own implicit attitudes toward Blacks. This finding is consistent with other research that shows Blacks are better able than Whites to detect both explicit and implicit racial bias in Whites and more accurate than Whites in identifying the emotions of people from a different racial/ethnic group (Pearson et al., 2008; Richeson & Shelton, 2005). If we extrapolate from these studies in nonmedical settings to racially discordant medical interactions, these findings suggest that Black and White participants in the same medical interaction could leave the interaction with very different impressions of the other person's thoughts and feelings during the interactions. Their respective impressions would quite reasonably affect their subsequent reactions to the interaction.

It is also possible that some of the negative outcomes of racially discordant medical interactions we previously discussed (Eggly et al., 2011; Gordon et al.,

2006a) may reflect the influence of the Black patients' racial identity and their past experiences with racism. That is, such experiences may affect their own verbal and nonverbal behaviors and providers' responses during and after the interactions.

There is also some evidence that specific kinds of race-related attitudes and beliefs may affect racially discordant medical interactions and their outcomes. One is trust of the provider and the health care system in general. As noted earlier, overall Blacks are less trusting of the health care system than are Whites. O'Malley, Sheppard, Schwartz, and Mandelblatt (2004) studied the factors that affected Black women's usage of preventive services (e.g., cancer screenings). They found that higher trust in the health care provider was significantly associated with greater use of recommended preventive services; this relationship remained after controlling for the effects of insurance status and patient characteristics. (Also see Street, O'Malley, Cooper, & Haidet, 2008)

Another important factor is perceived discrimination. Bird and Bogart (2001) found poorer adherence to antiretroviral medications among Black patients who perceived that they were the targets of discrimination. More recently, Penner et al. (2009) measured perceived past discrimination among low income Black patients just prior to their visit with a physician at a primary care facility. They examined the correlation between the reported frequency of past discrimination with patients' reactions to the medical interactions and their compliance with physician recommendations. The more past discrimination the Black patients reported experiencing, the less satisfied they were with the interactions, the less likely they were to report adherence with the physicians' recommendations at 4 and 16 weeks after the interaction and the poorer their health at 4 and 16 weeks. A mediational analysis indicated that the relationship between perceived discrimination and health at 16 weeks was significantly mediated by adherence to the physicians' recommendations.

In summary, we believe that patient-level factors (i.e., patients' experiences, attitudes, and behaviors) play a direct and indirect role in the quality of the medical care they receive. However, we strongly caution against blaming the victim; in this case, the patient. As Penner et al. (2009) noted, distrust and perceptions of racism and racial discrimination among Blacks are primarily rooted in personal experiences of discrimination. Racism and racial discrimination in America are still pervasive, presenting a challenge to Blacks on a regular basis. Thus, we must emphasize that the root of this possible cause of medical treatment disparities is ultimately the subtle and sometimes not-so-subtle racism Blacks confront on an individual, social, and institutional level that are reflected in their attitudes, beliefs, and behaviors. Accordingly, solutions to treatment disparities may require some interventions directed at individual patients, but ultimately what is required are interventions targeting health care providers, the health care system, and society in general as well. In this context, we again refer the reader to the article by Brondolo et al. (2012). It suggests other, but in our view, complementary mechanisms through which racism may diminish the quality of Black–White interactions.

The third and final cause of racial disparities identified by the IOM report was at the level of the provider. This factor involves decisions and behaviors exhibited by health care professionals that may result in Blacks receiving poorer health care than Whites. The IOM committee explicitly proposed that provider stereotyping of and bias toward minority group members may produce poorer treatment for minority group patients. This proposal elicited strong reactions from health care providers (Epstein, 2005), who argued that the overwhelming majority of health care providers reject overt and blatant forms of racial prejudice in both their personal and professional lives. We have no reason to dispute this claim; however, as we know, contemporary prejudice and stereotyping can be expressed in subtle and indirect ways that escape provider awareness. It is these more subtle forms of racism that the IOM Committee suggested play a major role in Black–White disparities in health care.

The social psychology research literature on the effects of subtle or implicit/automatic forms of racial prejudice on behaviors toward Blacks would strongly suggest that provider bias does indeed affect medical interactions and treatment decisions (Penner et al., 2010a). However, only a small number of studies have directly investigated this relationship using experimental paradigms. One example of such research on Black–White treatment disparities was conducted by Schulman et al. (1999). Primary care physicians viewed video tapes of actors playing the role of patients complaining about chest pain. The gender and ethnicity of the patients (Black or White) were systematically manipulated. Schulman et al. found that Black women were significantly less likely to be referred for further testing than were White men. However, it must be noted that a more recent study using standardized patients (i.e. actors) showing symptoms of coronary heart disease failed to produce any evidence that patient race influenced diagnosis or treatment recommendations (Arber et al., 2006).

van Ryn and associates (van Ryn, 2002; van Ryn, Burgess, Malat, & Griffin, 2006; van Ryn & Burke, 2000) proposed a social–cognitive model of how patient race/ethnicity influences physicians' treatment decisions. Specifically, these authors posited that perceived patient ethnicity constitutes a potent means whereby physicians place patients in social categories, which activate implicit and explicit stereotypes about individuals who belong to these categories. These stereotypes influence physicians' interpretations of patients' symptoms, which then affect physicians' decisions about diagnosis and treatment. Consistent with this model, van Ryn et al. found that physicians stereotyped Black cardiac patients as less educated and less likely to comply with medical recommendations than Whites. These stereotypes mediated physicians' decisions about the suitability of Black patients for coronary bypass surgery. (Also see Bogart, Catz, Kelly, & Benotsch, 2001).

Finally, two recent studies have specifically focused on how providers' implicit attitudes affect treatment decisions and medical decisions. Green et al. (2007) first assessed physicians' explicit and implicit attitudes toward Blacks and Whites. Following this assessment, they presented the physicians with vignettes about hypothetical emergency room patients with symptoms of serious heart problems. The patients in the vignettes were either Black or White. The physicians showed no bias against Blacks on the measure of explicit or overt bias. However, on the implicit measure (the *Implicit Association Test*), physicians' attitudes were more negative toward Blacks than Whites and they were more likely to associate uncooperativeness with Blacks than Whites. More importantly, Green et al. (2007) found that physicians' implicit biases were strongly associated with their recommendations to give patients the appropriate treatment; physicians who were more implicitly biased were less likely to recommend the appropriate treatment for Black patients.

Finally, Penner et al. (2010b) studied how physician explicit and implicit anti-Black bias affected their own and their patients' reactions to primary care medical interactions. In a primary care facility, we measured physicians' explicit and implicit anti-Black bias prior to patient interactions. Then following the interactions, we measured the physicians' and their Black patients' reactions to one another and the interaction. We found some evidence that physicians' explicit and implicit bias affected how much they involved patients in treatment decisions and perceived closeness to the patient. However, the major effects of physicians' implicit bias were seen in their patients' reactions to the physicians. Of special interest were patient responses to physicians who fit the profile of aversive racists (Dovidio & Gaertner, 2004; Gaertner & Dovidio, 1986); that is, relative to the other physicians, these physicians scored quite low in explicit prejudice, but quite high in implicit prejudice. Patients reacted most negatively to these physicians; specifically, patients of these physicians reported less satisfaction, less perceived closeness, and lower estimates of warmth and friendliness than patients of the other groups of physicians. Other research has suggested that the patient responses we measured are associated with longer term medical outcomes of physician–patient interactions in general and oncology interactions in particular (Epstein & Street, 2007). Specifically, more negative patient reactions to interactions have been found to be significantly correlated with poorer patient outcomes related to the interactions. Finally, in a subsequent analysis (Hagiwara, Penner, Eggly, & Albrecht, 2011), we found that patients talked significantly less when they interacted with aversive racist physicians than with other physicians.

Summary/Conclusion

There are substantial and important Black–White disparities in the quality of communication and information exchange during oncology interactions and in the quality of the treatments Black and White cancer patients receive. To be sure, there are many instances in which there are no Black–White disparities in these interactions and treatments, but when there is a disparity, it is without exception Black patients who are disadvantaged, relative to the Whites. As we noted in the introduction to this article, most research on health care disparities, including our own, has focused on Black–White disparities in the United States. But as we also noted earlier, health care disparities due to some social or group characteristic is not what the Nobel Laureate Gunnar Myrdal once called an "American Dilemma."

Among major industrial countries, the United States is unique in the extent to which its health care system is privatized. There is, of course, ample evidence that structural differences in the quality of health care systems available to patients contribute substantially to health disparities (Smedley et al., 2003). Thus, the financial underpinnings of a country's health care system can play a major role in health disparities. However, public health data from a large number of countries suggest that disadvantaged ethnic/racial minorities systematically experience worse health and receive poorer health care than members of majority ethnic/racial groups throughout the world, across political systems, geographic regions, and health care financing systems. Thus, we would argue that the basic processes responsible for the disparities in cancer care for Blacks in the United States are probably operative around the world, although certainly they may differ in the specific forms they take and the extent to which they exist. Moreover, it is extremely important to recognize that the consequences of health care disparities extend beyond possible emotional and psychological distress in patients who experience these kinds of inequities. Consider, for example, Bach et al.'s (2002) work on cancer-related deaths in the United States. After an extensive meta-analysis, Bach et al. concluded that an unknown, but certainly substantial portion of higher mortality and lower survival rates among Blacks with cancer, relative to Whites with this disease, is due to preventable Black–White health care disparities. Indeed, when cancer treatment disparities were controlled in the meta-analysis, the differences in mortality/survival became very small. Given that these disparities are preventable, it is the responsibility of professionals who provide and study health care to strive to reduce these life-threatening disparities.

References

Albertsen, P. C., Hanley, J. A., & Fine, J. (2005). 20-year outcomes following conservative management of clinically localized prostate cancer. *Journal of the American Medical Association, 293*(17), 2095–2101. doi:10.1001/jama.293.17.2095.

Albrecht, T. L., Penner, L. A., Cline, R. J., Eggly, S. S., & Ruckdeschel, J. C. (2009). Studying the process of clinical communication: Issues of context, concepts, and research directions. *Journal of Health Communication, 14*(Suppl 1), 47–56. doi:10.1080/10810730902806794.

Allen, J. D., Kennedy, M., Wilson-Glover, A., & Gilligan, T. D. (2007). African-American men's perceptions about prostate cancer: Implications for designing educational interventions. *Social Science and Medicine*, *64*(11), 2189–2200. doi:10.1016/j.socscimed.2007.01.007.

Altekruse, S. F, Huang, L., Cucinelli, J. E, McNeel, T. S., Wells K. M., & Oliver, M. N. (2010). Spatial patterns of localized-stage prostate cancer incidence among white and black men in the southeastern United States, 1999–2001. *Cancer Epidemiological Biomarkers and Prevention*, *19*, 1460–467. doi:10.1158/1055-9965.EPI-09-1310.

Arber, S., McKinlay, J., Adams, A., Marceau, L., Link, C., & O'Donnell, A. (2006). Patient characteristics and inequalities in doctors' diagnostic and management strategies relating to CHD: A video-simulation experiment. *Social Science and Medicine*, *62*(1), 103–115. doi:10.1016/j.socscimed.2005.05.028.

Arora, N. K. (2003). Interacting with cancer patients: The significance of physicians' communication behavior. *Social Science and Medicine*, *57*(5), 791–806.

Arora, N. K., Hesse, B. W., Rimer, B. K., Viswanath, K., Clayman, M. L., & Croyle, R. T. (2007). Frustrated and confused: The American public rates its cancer-related information-seeking experiences. *Journal of General Internal Medicine*. *23*(3), 223–228. doi:10.1007/s11606-007-0406-y.

Bach, P. B., Cramer, L. D., Warren, J. L., & Begg, C. B. (1999). Racial differences in the treatment of early-stage lung cancer. *New England Journal of Medicine*, *341*(16), 1198–1205. doi:10.1056/NEJM 199910143411606.

Bach, P. B., Schrag, D., Brawley, O. W., Galaznik, A., Yakren, S., & Begg, C. B. (2002). Survival of blacks and whites after a cancer diagnosis. *Journal of the American Medical Association*, *287*(16), 2106–2113. doi:10.1001/jama.287.16.2106.

Barnato, A. E., Lucas, F. L., Staiger, D., Wennberg, D. E., & Chandra, A. (2005). Hospital-level racial disparities in acute myocardial infarction treatment and outcomes. *Medical Care*, *43*(4), 308–319.

Barton, E., & Marback, R. (2009). Bodies of the urban public, *Wayne State University Humanities Center Symposium on the Representation of Health and Disease in the City*, Detroit.

Bastian, P. J., Carter, B. H., Bjartell, A., Seitz, M., Stanislaus, P., Montorsi, F., Stief, C. G., Schröder F. (2009). Insignificant prostate cancer and active surveillance: From definition to clinical implications. *European Urology*, *55*(6), 1321–1330. doi:10.1016/j.eururo.2009.02.028.

Bird, S. T., & Bogart, L. M. (2001). Perceived race-based and socioeconomic status (SES)-based discrimination in interactions with health care providers. *Ethnicity and Disease*, *11*(3), 554–563.

Bogart, L. M., Catz, S. L., Kelly, J. A., & Benotsch, E. G. (2001). Factors influencing physicians' judgments of adherence and treatment decisions for patients with HIV disease. *Medical Decision Making*, *21*(1), 28–36. doi:10.1177/0272989X0102100104.

Bonadonna, G., & Valagussa, P. (1981). Dose-response effect of adjuvant chemotherapy in breast cancer. *New England Journal of Medicine*, *304*(1), 10–15.

Bonadonna, G., Valagussa, P., Moliterni, A., Zambetti, M., & Brambilla, C. (1995). Adjuvant cyclophosphamide, methotrexate, and fluorouracil in node-positive breast cancer: The results of 20 years of follow-up. *New England Journal of Medicine*, *332*(14), 901–906. doi:10.1056/NEJM199504063321401.

Braveman, P. (2006). Health disparities and health equity: Concepts and measurement. *Annual Review of Public Health*, *27*, 167–194. doi:10.1146/annurev.publhealth.27.021405.102103.

Brondolo, E., Libertti, M., Rivera, L., & Walsemann, K. M. (2012). Racism and social capital: The implications for social and physical well being. *Journal of Social Issues*, *68*(2), 358–384. doi: 10.1111/j.1540-4560.2011.01752.x

Byrd, W. M., & Clayton, L. A. (2000). *An American health dilemma: Race, medicine, and healthcare in the United States 1900–2000*. New York: Routledge.

Byrd, W. M., & Clayton, L. A. (2002). *An American health dilemma: A medical history of African Americans and the problem of race*. New York: Routledge.

Calle, E. E., Rodriguez, C., Jacobs, E. J., Almon, M. L., Chao, A., McCullough, M. L., Feigelson, H. S., & Thun, M. J. (2002). The American Cancer Society Cancer Prevention Study II Nutrition Cohort: rationale, study design, and baseline characteristics. *Cancer*, 94, 2490–2501.

Cegala, D. J., McClure, L., Marinelli, T. M., & Post, D. M. (2000). The effects of communication skills training on patients' participation during medical interviews. *Patient Education and Counseling*, *41*(2), 209–222.

Cegala, D. J., Street, R. L., Jr., & Clinch, C. R. (2007). The impact of patient participation on physicians' information provision during a primary care medical interview. *Health Communication*, *21*(2), 177–185.

Centers for Disease Control and Prevention. (2005). Breast cancer screening and socioeconomic status–35 metropolitan areas, 2000 and 2002. *Mortality and Morbidity Weekly Report*, *54*(9), 981–985.

Cooper-Patrick, J. J., Gonzales, J. J., Vu, H. T. R., Powe, N. R., Nelson, C., & Ford, D. E. (1999). Race, gender, and partnership in the patient-physician relationship. *Journal of the American Medical Association*, *282*, 583–589.

Daling, J. R., Malone, K. E., Doody, D. R., Johnson, L. G., Gralow, J. R., & Porter, P. L. (2001). Relation of body mass index to tumor markers and survival among young women with invasive ductal breast carcinoma. *Cancer*, *92*(4), 720–729. doi:10.1002/1097-0142(20010815) 92:4 3.0.CO;2-T.

Dilley, J. A., Simmons, K. W., Boysun, M. J., Pizacari, B. A., & Stark, M. J. (2010). Demonstrating the importance and feasibility of including sexual orientation in public health surveys: Health disparities in the Pacific Northwest. *American Journal of Public Health*, *100*, 460–467. doi:10.2105/AJPH.2007.130336.

Dorling, D., Mitchell, R., & Pearce, J. (2007). The global impact of income inequality on health by age: An observational study. *British Medical Journal*, *335*, 833–834. doi:10.1136/bmj.39349.507315.DE.

Dovidio, J. F., & Gaertner, S. (2004). Aversive racism. In M. P. Zanna (Ed.), *Advances in experimental social psychology* (Vol. *36*, pp. 1–51). San Diego: Academic Press.

Dovidio, J. F., Kawakami, K., & Gaertner, S. L. (2002). Implicit and explicit prejudice and interracial interaction. *Journal of Personality and Social Psychology*, *82*(1), 62–68. doi:10.1037/0022-3514.82.1.62.

Dovidio, J. F., Penner, L. A., Albrecht, T. L., Norton, W. E., Gaertner, S. L., & Shelton, J. N. (2008). Disparities and distrust: The implications of psychological processes for understanding racial disparities in health and health care. *Social Science and Medicine*, *67*(3), 478–486. doi:10.1016/j.socscimed.2008.03.019.

Early Breast Cancer Trialists' Collaborative Group. (2005). Effects of chemotherapy and hormonal therapy for early breast cancer on recurrence and 15-year survival: An overview of the randomised trials. *Lancet*, *365*, 1687–1717. doi:10.1016/S0140-6736(05)66544-0.

Eggly, S., Harper, F. W. K., Penner, L., Gleason, M., Foster, T., & Albrecht, T. L. (2011). Variation in question asking during cancer clinical interactions: A potential source of disparities in access to information *Patient Education and Counseling*, *82*, 63–68. doi:10.1016/j.pec.2010.04.008.

Eggly, S., Penner, L. A., Greene, M., Harper, F. W., Ruckdeschel, J. C., & Albrecht, T. L. (2006). Information seeking during "bad news" oncology interactions: Question asking by patients and their companions. *Social Science and Medicine*, *63*(11), 2974–2985. doi:10.1016/j.socscimed.2006.07.012.

Eggly, S., Penner, L. A., Harper, F. W., Ruckdeschel, J. C., & Albrecht, T. L. (2007). Question asking by black and white patients and companions during clinical trial offers. *Proceedings of American Association of Cancer Researchers Science of Cancer Health Disparities in Racial/Ethnic Minorities and the Medically Underserved*, Atlanta, GA.

Eggly, S. Penner, L. A, Harper, F. W. K., Zhdanova, L, Gonzalez, R., & Albrecht, T. L. (2010) Perceptions of information provided by oncologists in clinical interactions with black and white patients/companions. *Proceedings of the Conference of the American Association for Cancer Research Science of Cancer Health Disparities in Racial/Ethnic Minorities and the Medically Underserved*, Washington, DC.

Epstein, R. A. (2005). Disparities and discrimination in health care coverage: A critique of the Institute of Medicine study. *Perspectives in Biology and Medicine*, *48*(1 Suppl), S26–41.

Epstein, R. M., & Street, R. L. J. (2007). *Patient-centered communication in cancer care: Promoting healing and reducing suffering*. Bethesda, MD: National Cancer Institute.

Fleming, S. T., Pursley, H. G., Newman, B., Pavlov, D., & Chen, K. (2005). Comorbidity as a predictor of stage of illness for patients with breast cancer. *Medical Care*, *43*(2), 132–140. doi:10.1097/00005650-200502000-00006.

Frohlich, K. L., Ross, N., & Richmond, C. (2006). Health disparities in Canada today: Some evidence and a theoretical framework. *Health Policy*, *79*, 132–143. doi:10.1016/j.healthpol. 2005.12.010.

Gallo, L. C., Espinosa de los Monteros, K., & Shivpuri, S. (2009). Socioeconomic status and health: What is the role of reserve capacity? *Current Directions in Psychological Science*, *18*(5), 269–274. doi:10.1111/j.1467-8721.2009.01650.x.

Gaertner, S. L., & Dovidio, J. F. (1986). The aversive form of racism. In J. F. Dovidio & S. L. Gaertner (Eds.), *Prejudice, discrimination, and racism* (pp. 61–89). Orlando, FL: Academic Press.

Goldhirsch, A., & Gelber, R. D. (1994). Understanding adjuvant chemotherapy for breast cancer. *New England Journal of Medicine*, *330*(18), 1308–1309.

Gordon, H. S., Street, R. L., Jr., Sharf, B. F., Kelly, P. A., & Souchek, J. (2006a). Racial differences in trust and lung cancer patients' perceptions of physician communication. *Journal of Clinical Oncology*, *24*(6), 904–909. doi:10.1200/JCO.2005.03.1955.

Gordon, H. S., Street, R. L., Jr., Sharf, B. F., & Souchek, J. (2006b). Racial differences in doctors' information-giving and patients' participation. *Cancer*, *107*(6), 1313–1320. doi:10.1002/cncr.22122.

Gordon, N. H. (2003). Socioeconomic factors and breast cancer in black and white Americans. *Cancer and Metastasis Reviews*, *22*(1), 55–65. doi:10.1023/A:1022212018158.

Green, A. R., Carney, D. R., Pallin, D. J., Ngo, L. H., Raymond, K. L., Iezzoni, L. I., & Banaji, M. R. (2007). Implicit bias among physicians and its prediction of thrombolysis decisions for black and white patients. *Journal of General Internal Medicine*, *22*(9), 1231–1238. doi:10.1007/s11606-007-0258-5.

Griggs, J. J., Culakova, E., Sorbero, M. E., Poniewierski, M. S., Wolff, D. A., Crawford, J., Dale, D. C., & Lyman, G. H. (2007a). Social and racial differences in selection of breast cancer adjuvant chemotherapy regimens. *Journal of Clinical Oncology*, *25*(18), 2522–2527. doi:10.1200/JCO.2006.10.2749.

Griggs, J. J., Culakova, E., Sorbero, M. E., van Ryn, M., Poniewierski, M. S., Wolff, D. A., Dale, D. C., & Lyman, G. H. (2007b). Effect of patient socioeconomic status and body mass index on the quality of breast cancer adjuvant chemotherapy. *Journal of Clinical Oncology*, *25*(3), 277–284. doi:10.1200/JCO.2006.08.3063.

Griggs, J. J., Sorbero, M. E., & Lyman, G. H. (2005). Undertreatment of obese women receiving breast cancer chemotherapy. *Archives of Internal Medicine*, *165*(11), 1267–1273. doi:10.1001/archinte.165.11.1267.

Griggs, J. J., Sorbero, M. E., Stark, A. T., Heininger, S. E., & Dick, A. W. (2003). Racial disparity in the dose and dose intensity of breast cancer adjuvant chemotherapy. *Breast Cancer Research and Treatment*, *81*(1), 21–31. doi:10.1023/A:1025481505537.

Hack, T. F., Degner, L. F., & Parker, P. A. (2005). The communication goals and needs of cancer patients: A review. *Psycho-Oncology*, *14*(10), 831–847. doi:10.1002/pon.949.

Hagiwara, N. Penner, L. A., Eggly, S., & Albrecht, T. L. (2011). Perceived discrimination, implicit bias, and adherence to physician recommendations. *The Science of Research on Discrimination and Health Conference*, Washington, DC.

Halbert, C. H., Armstrong, K., Gandy, O. H., Jr., & Shaker, L. (2006). Racial differences in trust in health care providers. *Archives of Internal Medicine*, *166*(8), 896–901.

Harlan, L., Brawley, O., Pommerenke, F., Wali, P., & Kramer, B. (1995). Geographic, age, and racial variation in the treatment of local/regional carcinoma of the prostate. *Journal of Clinical Oncology*, *13*(1), 93–100.

Hesse, B. W., Arora, N. K., Burke-Bedford, B. E., & Finney, R. L. J. (2009). Information support for cancer survivors. *Cancer*, *112*, (11 Suppl), 2529–2540. doi:10.1002/cncr.23445.

Hoffman, R. M., Gilliland, F. D., Eley, J. W., Harlan, L. C. Stephenson, R. A., Stanford, J. L., Albertson, P. C., Hamilton, A. S., Hunt, W. C., & Potosky, A. L. (2001). Racial and ethnic differences in advanced-stage prostate cancer: The Prostate Cancer Outcomes Study. *Journal of National Cancer Institute*, *93*(5), 388–395. doi:10.1093/jnci/93.5.388.

Hussain, S. K., Altieri, A., Sundquist, J., & Hemminki, K. (2008). Influence of education level on breast cancer risk and survival in Sweden between 1990 and 2004. *International Journal of Cancer, 122*(1), 165–169. doi:10.1002/ijc.23007.

Jemal, A., Clegg, L. X., Ward, E., Ries, L. A., Jamison, P. M., Wingo, P. A., Howe, H. L., Anderson, R. N., & Edwards, B. K. (2004). Annual report to the nation on the status of cancer, 1975–2001, with a special feature regarding survival. *Cancer, 101*(1), 3–27. doi:10.1002/cncr.20288.

Johnson, R. L., Roter, D., Powe, N. R., & Cooper, L. A. (2004). Patient race/ethnicity and quality of patient-physician communication during medical visits. *American Journal of Public Health, 94*(12), 2084–2090.

Johnson, R. L., Saha, S., Arbelaez, J. J., Beach, M. C., & Cooper, L. A. (2004). Racial and ethnic differences in patient perceptions of bias and cultural competence in health care. *Journal of General Internal Medicine, 19,* 101–110.

Koerber, A., Gajendra, S., Fulford, R. L., BeGole, E., & Evans, C. A. (2004). An exploratory study of orthodontic resident communication by patient race and ethnicity. *Journal of Dental Education, 68*(5), 553–562.

Linehan, C., Walsh, P. N., van Schrojenstein Lantman-de Valk, H. M. J., Kerr, M. P., & Dawson, F. (2009). Are people with intellectual disabilities represented in European public health surveys? *Journal of Applied Research in Intellectual Disabilities, 22,* 409–420. doi:10.1111/j.1468-3148.2009.00521.x.

Lu-Yao, G. L., Albertsen, P. C., Moore, D. F., Shih, W., Lin, Y., DiPaola, R. S., Barry, M. J., Zietman, A., O'Leary, M., Walker-Corkery, E., & Yao, S. L. (2009). Outcomes of localized prostate cancer following conservative management. *Journal of the American Medical Association, 302*(11), 1202–1209. doi:10.1001/ jama.2009.1348.

Malat, J., & Hamilton, M. A. (2006). Preference for same-race health care providers and perceptions of interpersonal discrimination in health care. *Journal of Health and Social Behavior, 47*(2), 173–187. doi:10.1177/002214650604700206.

Michalski, T. A., & Nattinger, A. B. (1997). The influence of black race and socioeconomic status on the use of breast-conserving surgery for Medicare beneficiaries. *Cancer, 79*(2), 314–319. doi:10.1002/(SICI)1097-0142(19970115)79:23.0.CO;2-3.

Mobaraki, A. E., & Söderfeldt, B. (2010). Gender inequality in Saudi Arabia and its role in public health. *Eastern Mediterranean Health Journal, 16,* 113–118.

Morrow, T., Siegel, M., Boone, S., Lawless, G., & Carter, W. (2002). Chemotherapy dose intensity determination as a quality of care measure for managed care organizations in the treatment of early-stage breast cancer. *American Journal of Medical Quality, 17*(6), 218–224. doi:10.1177/106286060201700604.

Naik, A. M., Joseph, K., Harris, M., Davis, C., Shapiro, R., & Hiotis, K. L. (2003). Indigent breast cancer patients among all racial and ethnic groups present with more advanced disease compared with nationally reported data. *American Journal of Surgery, 186*(4), 400–403. doi:10.1016/S0002-9610(03)00282-4.

National Center for Health Statistics. (2008). *Health United States 2008, with chartbook on trends in the health of Americans.* Hyattsville, MD: US Government Printing Office.

National Comprehensive Cancer Network. (2008). *Clinical Trials.* (Retrieved October 15, 2009 from http://www.nccn.org/professionals/physicianguidelines.asp).

National Comprehensive Cancer Network. (2009). (Retrieved May 2, 2010 from www.nccn.org).

Newman, L. A., Pollock, R. E., & Johnson-Thompson, M. C. (2003). Increasing the pool of academically oriented African-American medical and surgical oncologists. *Cancer, 97*(1 Suppl), 329–334. doi:10.1002/cncr.11862.

Obeidat, N. A., Pradel, F. G., Zuckerman, I. H., Trovato, J. A., Palumbo, F. B., DeLisle, S., & Mullins, C. D. (2010). Racial/ethnic and age disparities in chemotherapy selection for colorectal cancer. *American Journal of Managed Care, 16,* 515–522.

O'Malley, A. S., Sheppard, V. B., Schwartz, M., & Mandelblatt, J. (2004). The role of trust in use of preventive services among low-income African-American women. *Preventive Medicine, 38*(6), 777–785. doi:10.1016/j.ypmed.2004.01.018.

Oliver, M. N., Goodwin, M. A., Gotler, R. S., Gregory, P. M., & Stange, K. C. (2001). Time use in clinical encounters: Are African-American patients treated differently? *Journal of the National Medical Association, 93*(10), 380–385.

Pearson, A. R., West, T. V., Dovidio, J. F., Powers, S. R., Buck, R., & Henning, R. (2008). The fragility of intergroup relations: Divergent effects of delayed audiovisual feedback in intergroup and intragroup interaction. *Psychological Science, 19*(12), 1272–1279. doi:10.1111/j.1467-9280.2008.02236.x.

Penner, L. A., Albrecht, T. L., Orom, H., Coleman, D. K., & Underwood, W., III. (2010a). Health and health care disparities. In J. F. Dovidio, M. Hewstone, P. Glick, & V. M. Esses (Eds.), *The Sage handbook of prejudice, stereotyping and discrimination* (pp. 472–490). New York: Sage.

Penner, L. A., Dovidio, J. F., Edmondson, D., Dailey, R. K., Markova, T., Albrecht, T. L., & Gaertner, S. L. (2009). The experience of discrimination and Black-White health disparities in medical care. *Journal of Black Psychology, 35*(2), 180–203. doi:10.1177/0095798409333585.

Penner, L. A., Dovidio, J. F., West, T. V., Gaertner, S., Albrecht, T., Dailey, R. K., & Markova, T. (2010b). Aversive racism and medical interactions with black patients: A field study. *Journal of Experimental Social Psychology, 46*, 436–410. doi:10.1016/j.jesp.2009.11.004.

Penner, L. A., Eggly, S., Harper, F. W. K., Albrecht, T. L., & Ruckdeschel, J. C. (2007). Patient attributes and information provided about clinical trials. *Poster presented at the American Association of Cancer Researchers Science of Cancer Health Disparities in Racial/Ethnic Minorities and the Medically Underserved*, Atlanta, GA.

Petrelli, J. M., Calle, E. E., Rodriguez, C., & Thun, M. J. (2002). Body mass index, height, and postmenopausal breast cancer mortality in a prospective cohort of US women. *Cancer Causes Control, 13*(4), 325–332.

Ponce, N. A., Babey, S. H., Etzioni, D., Spencer, B. A., Brown, E. R., & Chawla, N. (2004). *Cancer screening in California: Findings from the 2001 California Health Interview Survey*. Los Angeles: UCLA Center for Health Policy Research.

Richeson, J. A., & Shelton, J. N. (2005). Brief report: Thin slices of racial bias. *Journal of Nonverbal Behavior, 29*(1), 75–86. doi:10.1007/s10919-004-0890-2.

Roa, B. B., Boyd, A. A., Volcik, K., & Richards, C. S. (1996). Ashkenazi Jewish population frequencies for common mutations in BRCA1 and BRCA2. *Nature Genetics, 14*(2), 185–187. doi:10.1038/ng1096-185.

Rostila, M. (2010). Birds of a feather flock together–and fall ill? Migrant homophily and health in Sweden. *Sociology of Health & Illness, 32*, 382–399. doi:10.1111/j.1467-9566.2009.01196.x.

Roter, D. L. (1984). Patient question asking in physician-patient interaction. *Health Psychology, 3*(5), 395–409. doi:10.1037/0278-6133.3.5.395.

Rutten, L. J., Arora, N. K., Bakos, A. D., Aziz, N., & Rowland, J. (2005). Information needs and sources of information among cancer patients: A systematic review of research (1980–2003). *Patient Education and Counseling, 57*, 250–261.

Salami, M. A., Etukakpan, B., & Olapade-Olaopa, O. (2007). Update on prostate cancer in black men. *Journal of Men's Health & Gender, 4*(4), 456–463.

Sanda, M. G., Dunn, R. L., Michalski, J., Sandler, H. M., Northouse, L., Hembroff, L., Lin, X., Greenfield, T. K., Litwin, M. S., Saigal, C. S., Mahadevan, A., Klein, E., Kibel, A., Pisters, L. L., Kuban, D., Kaplan, I., Wood, D., Ciezki, J., Shah, N., & Wei, J. T. (2008). Quality of life and satisfaction with outcome among prostate-cancer survivors. *New England Journal of Medicine, 358*(12), 1250–1261. doi:10.1056/NEJMoa074311.

Schapira, M. M., McAuliffe, T. L., & Nattinger, A. B. (1995). Treatment of localized prostate cancer in African-American compared with Caucasian men. Less use of aggressive therapy for comparable disease. *Medical Care, 33*(11), 1079–1088.

Schulman, K. A., Berlin, J. A., Harless, W., Kerner, J. F., Sistrunk, S., Gersh, B. J., Dubé, R., Taleghani, C. K., Burke, J. E., Williams, S., Eisenberg, J. M., Ayers, W., & Escarce, J. J. (1999). The effect of race and sex on physicians' recommendations for cardiac catheterization. *New England Journal of Medicine, 340*(8), 618–626. doi:10.1056/NEJM199902253400806.

Schwartz, K. L., Powell, I. J., Underwood, W., III, George, J., Yee, C., & Banerjee, M. (2009). Interplay of race, socioeconomic status and treatment on survival of prostate cancer patients. *Urology, 74*(6), 1296–1302. doi:10.1016/j.urology.2009.02.058.

Shavers, V. L., Brown, M., Klabunde, C. N., Potosky, A. L., Davis, W., Moul, J., & Fahey, A. (2004a). Race/ethnicity and the intensity of medical monitoring under 'watchful waiting' for prostate cancer. *Medical Care, 42*(3), 239–250.

Shavers, V. L., Brown, M. L., Potosky, A. L., Klabunde, C. N., Davis, W. W., Moul, J. W., et al. (2004b). Race/ethnicity and the receipt of watchful waiting for the initial management of prostate cancer. *Journal of General Internal Medicine, 19*(2), 146–155. doi:10.1111/j.1525-1497.2004.30209.x.

Siegel, S., Ward, E., Brawley, O., & Jemal, A. (2011). Cancer statistics, 2011. *CA: A Cancer Journal for Clinicians, 61*(4), 212–236. doi:10.3322/caac.20121.

Siminoff, L. A., Graham, G. C., & Gordon, N. H. (2006). Cancer communication patterns and the influence of patient characteristics: Disparities in information-giving and affective behaviors. *Patient Education and Counseling, 62*(3), 355–360. doi:10.1016/j.pec.2006.06.011.

Smedley, B. D., Stith, A. Y., & Nelson, A. R. (2003). *Unequal treatment: Confronting racial and ethnic disparities in health care.* Washington, DC: National Academies Press.

Smith-Bindman, R., Miglioretti, D. L., Lurie, N., Abraham, L., Barbash, R. B., Strzelczyk, J., Dignan, M., Barlow, W. E., Beasley, C. M., & Kerlikowske, K. (2006). Does utilization of screening mammography explain racial and ethnic differences in breast cancer. *Annals of Internal Medicine, 144*(8), 541–553.

Street, R. L., & Gordon, H. S. (2008). Companion participation in cancer consultations. *Psycho-oncology, 17*(3), 244–251. doi:10.1002/pon.1225.

Street, R. L., Jr., O'Malley, K. J., Cooper, L. A., & Haidet, P. (2008). Understanding concordance in patient-physician relationships: Personal and ethnic dimensions of shared identity. *Annals of Family Medicine, 6*(3), 198–205. doi:10.1370/afm.821.

Thomson, C. S., Hole, D. J., Twelves, C. J., Brewster, D. H., & Black, R. J. (2001). Prognostic factors in women with breast cancer: Distribution by socioeconomic status and effect on differences in survival. *Journal of Epidemiology and Community Health, 55*(5), 308–315. doi:10.1136/jech.55.5.308.

Thompson, H. S., Valdimarsdottir, H. B., Winkel, G., Jandorf, L., & Redd, W. (2004). The Group-Based Medical Mistrust Scale: Psychometric properties and association with breast cancer screening. *Preventive Medicine, 38*(2), 209–218. doi:10.1016/j.ypmed.2003.09.041.

Trivedi, A. N., Zaslavsky, A. M., Schneider, E. C., & Ayanian, J. Z. (2006). Relationship between quality of care and racial disparities in Medicare health plans. *Journal of the American Medical Association, 296*(16), 1998–2004. doi:10.1001/jama.296.16.1998.

Underwood, W., III, Jackson, J., Wei, J. T., Dunn, R., Baker, E., Demonner, S., & Wood, D.P. (2005). Racial treatment trends in localized/regional prostate carcinoma: 1992–1999. *Cancer, 103*(3), 538–545. doi:10.1002/cncr.20796.

Underwood, W., III, Wei, J., Rubin, M. A., Montie, J. E., Resh, J., & Sanda, M. G. (2004a). Postprostatectomy cancer-free survival of African Americans is similar to non-African Americans after adjustment for baseline cancer severity. *Urologic Oncology, 22*(1), 20–24. doi:10.1016/S1078-1439(03)00119-4.

Underwood, W., De Monner, S., Ubel, P., Fagerlin, A., Sanda, M. G., & Wei, J. T. (2004b). Racial/ethnic disparities in the treatment of localized/regional prostate cancer. *Journal of Urology, 171*(4), 1504–1507.

van Ryn, M. (2002). Research on the provider contribution to race/ethnicity disparities in medical care. *Medical Care, 40*(1 Suppl), 140–151.

van Ryn, M., Burgess, D., Malat, J., & Griffin, J. (2006). Physicians' perceptions of patients' social and behavioral characteristics and race disparities in treatment recommendations for men with coronary artery disease. *American Journal of Public Health, 96*(2), 351–357. doi:10.2105/AJPH.2004.041806.

van Ryn, M., & Burke, J. (2000). The effect of patient race and socio-economic status on physicians' perceptions of patients. *Social Science and Medicine, 50*(6), 813–828. doi:10.1016/S0277-9536(99)00338-X.

van Ryn, M., & Saha, S. (2011). Exploring unconscious bias in disparities research and medical education. *Journal of the American Medical Association, 306*, 995–996. doi:10.1001/jama.2011.1275.

Wong, M. D., Ettner, S. L., Boscardin, W. J, & Shapiro, M. F. (2009). The contribution of cancer incidence, stage at diagnosis and survival to racial differences in years of life expectancy. *Journal of General Internal Medicine, 24*(4), 475–481. doi:10.1007/s11606-009-0912-1.

Wong, Y. N., Mitra, N., Hudes, G., Localio, R., Schwartz, J. S., Wan, F., Montagnet, C., & Armstrong, K. (2006). Survival associated with treatment vs observation of localized prostate cancer in elderly men. *Journal of the American Medical Association, 296*(22), 2683–2693. doi:10.1001/jama.296.22.2683.

Yu, X. Q. (2009). Socioeconomic disparities in breast cancer survival: Relation to stage at diagnosis, treatment and race. *Biomed Central Cancer, 9,* 364. doi:10.1186/1471-2407-9-364.

Zeliadt, S. B., Potosky A. L., Etzioni, R., Ramsey, S. D., & Penson, D. F. (2004). Racial disparity in primary and adjuvant treatment for nonmetastatic prostate cancer: SEER-Medicare trends 1991 to 1999. *Urology, 64,* 1171–1176.

Zeliadt, S. B., Ramsey, S. D., Penson, D. F., Hall, I. J., Ekwueme, D. U., Stroud, L., et al. (2006). Why do men choose one treatment over another? A review of patient decision making for localized prostate cancer. *Cancer, 106*(9), 1865–1874. doi:10.1002/cncr.21822.

LOUIS A. PENNER received his PhD in Social Psychology from Michigan State University. He is a Professor in the Population Studies and Disparities Research Program at the Karmanos Cancer Institute and the Department of Oncology at Wayne State University. He is also a Faculty Associate at the Institute for Social Research, University of Michigan. He is a past President of SPSSI.

SUSAN EGGLY received her PhD in communication studies from Wayne State University and is currently an Associate Professor in the Wayne State University Department of Oncology and in Population Studies and Disparities Research Program at the Karmanos Cancer Institute.

JENNIFER J. GRIGGS received her MD from the University of Buffalo. She is an Associate Professor of Medicine at the University of Michigan Medical School, where she is the Director of the Breast Cancer Survivorship Program.

WILLIE UNDERWOOD, III, received his MD and MSc degrees from State University of New York, Upstate Medical Center, and his MPH from the University of Michigan. He is an Associate Professor of Urology at Roswell Park Cancer Institute.

HEATHER OROM received her PhD in personality and social psychology from the University of Illinois, Chicago. She completed her postdoctoral training at Wayne State University's Institute of Gerontology and Karmanos Cancer Institute and is currently an Assistant Professor of Community Health and Health Behavior at SUNY at Buffalo.

TERRANCE L. ALBRECHT received her PhD in Communication from Michigan State University. She is Associate Center Director for Population Sciences at the Karmanos Cancer Institute in Detroit and Leader of the Population Studies and Disparities Research Program. She is Professor and Division Director in the Department of Oncology, Wayne State University School of Medicine.

Journal of Social Issues, Vol. 68, No. 2, 2012, pp. 358–384

Racism and Social Capital: The Implications for Social and Physical Well-Being

Elizabeth Brondolo* **and Madeline Libretti**
St. John's University

Luis Rivera
Rutgers University

Katrina M. Walsemann
University of South Carolina

Racism can be manifest at the cultural, institutional and individual levels, and can exert effects at the intrapersonal level if targeted individuals internalize attitudes toward their own racial/ethnic groups. The general aim of this article is to examine the ways in which all levels of racism undermine the development of peer relations, one component of social capital; and consequently affect the health and well-being of targeted individuals. The evidence suggests that cultural racism inculcates attitudes that may foster race-related social distancing; institutional racism isolates individuals from the opportunities to develop the skills needed to develop cross race-relations and promotes engagement with peers who exhibit antisocial behavior; interpersonal racism may erode the quality of routine interpersonal exchanges and engender anxiety about interacting with cross-race peers; and internalized racism may undermine the benefits of cross-race peer interactions. To the degree that racism affects the ability to form, maintain and benefit from peer relationships, it can contribute to racial disparities in economic, social and health-related outcomes and undermine the types of social cohesion that promote national unity.

Racism has been defined broadly as "the processes, norms, ideologies, and behaviors that perpetuate racial inequality" (Gee, Ro, Shariff-Marco, & Chae, 2009, p. 130). The systems that perpetuate racial inequality can be viewed as

---

*Correspondence concerning this article should be addressed to Elizabeth Brondolo, St. John's University, 8000 Utopia Parkway, Queens, NY 11439 [e-mail: brondole@stjohns.edu]

358

reinforcing race-based social ostracism, in which phenotypic or cultural characteristics are used to target individuals for social exclusion, unfair treatment, and harassment (Brondolo, Brady, Libby, & Pencille, 2011a). Racism can be manifest at the cultural, institutional and interpersonal levels, and can exert effects at the intrapersonal level as well, if targeted individuals internalize attitudes toward their own racial/ethnic group (Harrell, 2000; Krieger, 1999; Zárate, 2009). The aim of this article is to examine the ways in which all levels of racism affect access to economic opportunities, health and well-being by undermining the development of social capital.

Social capital is a broad construct. Definitions have encompassed both the skills and supports emerging from direct personal relations as well as the consequences of those relationships for access to economic, political and personal resources (Coleman, 1988; Moore, Shiell, Hawe, & Haines, 2005; Portes, 1998; Putnam, 1995). To provide a specific focus for this review, we examine one component of social capital—peer relationships; and identify the ways in which different levels of racism affect the development of both same-race and cross-race peer relationships.

We focus on peer relationships because they provide the context in which individuals develop the abilities and the motivation needed to function in a wide variety of personal and professional domains. Peers who are classmates or coworkers can support intellectual engagement, share knowledge and skills, and provide the social connections that create economic opportunity. Peers who are romantic partners, friends, and neighbors satisfy fundamental needs for belonging and can support the development of social norms and habits, including those necessary for physical and psychological health (Saegert, Warren, & Thompson, 2001; Smith & Christakis, 2008; Umberson, Crosnoe, & Reczek, 2010). Strong cross-race peer relationships create the type of social cohesion that promotes national unity (Braddock & Gonzalez, 2010).

We propose that peer relationships can be considered a potential mediator of the effects of racism on economic opportunity, health, and well-being. As we will review, the literature suggests that cultural, institutional, interpersonal and internalized racism affect peer relationships through a variety of pathways. In turn, racism-related effects on the development of peer relationships contribute to racial disparities in economic outcomes and health status.

Examining the effects of racism on peer relationships is consistent with the theme of this volume which focuses on the role of subtle racism in shaping racial disparities in key domains, including health care, employment, and criminal justice (Bendick & Nunes, 2012; Kang, 2012; Pager & Western, 2012; Penner et al., 2012). As Kang (2012) points out, we are more likely to take action in cases in which the perpetrators' expression of racial bias is explicit and intentional or when the consequences of prejudicial attitudes or discriminatory behavior are direct, proximal and largely attributable to racial bias. But as the articles in this volume will demonstrate, racial bias can also exert harmful effects when it is subtle. Here we are defining subtle to include episodes in which the race-based maltreatment is not conscious or intentional or when the consequences occur at points much later in time than the initial episode of race-based maltreatment.

For this review, we include literature across the disciplines of sociology and psychology, investigating the effects of cultural, institutional, interpersonal, and internalized racism on peer relationships. Although the bulk of the published literature on the effects of racism has focused on the experiences of African Americans and on interactions between Black and White individuals, we include studies of other groups where possible. Also, we note there is little consensus on the best terms to use to distinguish among these groups based on phenotypic characteristics, since both both scientific and political factors influence the use of these labels. In this article, we use the term Black to refer to individuals of African descent. We also use race and ethnicity interchangeably.

Most, but not all of the research we examine addresses the effects of racism on peer relations within the United States. Because this is a relatively new area of research, this article presents a selective rather than a comprehensive review of the literature in any one area. In each section, we examine subtle manifestations of each level of racism, and examine the consequences of exposure for the development of same-race and cross-race peer relationships. In doing so, we include cases in which the effects are temporally far removed from the original acts of race-based maltreatment or operating through other variables and mechanisms (Gee, Walsemann, & Brondolo, 2012; Myers, 2009). Identifying and articulating the different pathways through which racism can influence fundamental peer relationships is valuable for the development of more comprehensive models of the determinants of racial disparities in health and economic outcomes.

Cultural Racism

Helms has defined cultural racism as "societal beliefs and customs that promote the assumption that the products of White culture (e.g., language, traditions, appearance) are superior to those of non-White cultures" (Helms, 1990, p. 49, Powell, 2000). More generally, cultural racism reflects the dissemination of attitudes about the relative rights, privileges, and status that should be afforded to different racial/ethnic groups. These attitudes are communicated in a variety of forums.

The status of or respect for members of a particular culture can be communicated through public recognition of highly valued representatives of the group (e.g., the official celebration of Martin Luther King Day) or when there is a formal acknowledgement of the traditions, icons, and holidays associated with the group.

The failure to publicly acknowledge or recognize the valued representatives, icons, or traditions of a particular cultural group can be considered a form of cultural discrimination or racism (Sue et al., 2007).

Cultural racism can also be expressed in the ways in which members of different race or ethnic groups are depicted in mass media formats, (i.e., widely used forms of communication, including film, television, advertisements, newspapers and magazines, and the internet). Mass media presentations serve as a primary method for communicating stereotypes about race/ethnic group members. These presentations establish norms about the behaviors associated with group membership, and strengthen existing attitudes toward race/ethnic group members (Dalisay & Tan, 2009; Gilens, 1996; Mastro & Kopacz, 2006). In turn, these presentations can influence viewers' beliefs about the degree to which group members merit full social inclusion (Dovidio, 2009).

Viewers tend to believe that movies and TV shows communicate a social reality (i.e., the emotional truths about human nature and social relationships), even when they recognize that the situational details are fictional. Therefore, individuals presented in the media are often regarded as social role models, illustrating the types of values and behaviors that are believed to be normative or acceptable for that group (Tan, Fujioka, & Tan, 2000). When members of a particular racial or ethnic group are portrayed as displaying values that are unfamiliar or perceived as deviating from the mainstream, viewers tend to develop negative attitudes toward group members (Mastro & Kopacz, 2006).

Investigators studying race and the media have examined the ways in which mainstream media constrains the roles to which members of different groups are assigned (Entman & Rojecki, 2001) or communicates conscious and nonconscious biases toward members of different groups. For example, a recent study reported that nonverbal expressions of positive regard (e.g., smiling, etc.) were made more often to White than Black individuals viewed on TV programs, even though overt verbal expressions of regard did not differ by race (Weisbuch, Pauker, & Ambady, 2009). The investigators demonstrated that these variations in nonverbal behavior affected attitudes toward Black and White individuals, even when the viewers were unaware of these influences.

There has been extensive research on racial bias in news reporting (Bjornstrom, Kaufman, Peterson, & Slater, 2010; Dixon, Azocar, & Casas, 2003; Maddox, 2004; Mastro, Lapinski, Kopacz, & Behm-Morawitz, 2009). Studies have indicated that in TV news, Blacks are less likely (and Whites are more likely) to be portrayed as victims of crimes in comparison to the actual rate at which they are victimized (Dixon et al., 2003). Some, although not all studies of TV coverage suggest that the proportion of news stories featuring Blacks (versus Whites or members of other races) as perpetrators is greater than the proportion of crimes committed by Black individuals (Bjornstrom et al., 2010; Dixon & Linz, 2000; Poindexter, Smith, & Heider, 2003).

There is growing evidence that media portrayals affect our beliefs and attitudes toward minority groups, potentially influencing the desire of Whites to increase social distance from Black individuals and members of other racial or ethnic groups (Clawson & Trice, 2000; Dixon et al., 2003; Gilens, 1996). For example, Dixon reports that the amount of time individuals spent watching network news was positively correlated with the endorsement of stereotypes about Black Americans, including beliefs that Blacks are intimidating, hostile, and violent or beliefs consistent with modern racism, such as the idea that "Blacks push themselves where they are not wanted" (Dixon, 2008, p. 328). However, experimental studies have not consistently found these effects (Dixon & Azocar, 2007). To our knowledge, there has been no research explicitly examining the effects of different types of media presentations on the formation of same-race and cross-race friendships.

Mechanisms

Recent research suggests that cultural racism, in particular biased media presentations, may affect attitudes toward different race/ethnic groups through social-cognitive processes, including priming, stereotype activation, and social tuning (Dixon & Maddox, 2005; Dixon & Azocar, 2007). Through priming, repeated exposure to TV may strengthen the link between phenotype and stereotype. When primes for race-related stereotypes are presented (and even simply seeing a person of that ethnic/racial group can serve as a prime), then the schema network linked to these stereotypes is activated (Dovidio, 2009) and can affect judgments about phenotypically similar individuals (Monahan, Shtrulis, & Givens, 2005). For example, Monahan et al. (2005) report that when brief film presentations activate stereotypes about different kinds of Black women (e.g., "mammies" or "welfare queens"), viewers are more likely to impose characteristics associated with that stereotype onto unrelated Black women. Specifically, when viewers observed a clip depicting a Black "welfare queen," they were more likely to view other unrelated Black women as lazy or complaining (Monahan et al., 2005).

The process of social tuning may lead viewers to modify their own attitudes to conform to those held by members of their race or ethnic group. For example, when White individuals display subtle signs of dislike for Blacks on TV, White viewers may either perceive an affirmation of their existing views or modify their views to match. Social contagion processes may further reinforce these stereotypes as attitudes are communicated to wide audiences (Dovidio, 2009).

In sum, there is evidence of race-related biases in the presentation of members of racial and ethnic groups on TV news and entertainment programs and in the communication of attitudes toward members of these groups. This form of cultural racism has the potential to reduce the social capital of the individuals belonging to race/ethnic groups whose members are routinely presented exhibiting negative behavior consistent with stereotypes about the group (D. E. Mastro & Kopacz, 2006). For example, when minority group members are presented as violent, lazy or uneducated, majority group members may perceive all members of the group as potentially dangerous (Bonilla-Silva, 1997; Mastro & Kopacz, 2006). The failure to accurately depict Blacks as victims as well as perpetrators of crimes can create a subtle dehumanization of Black individuals, suggesting that they are capable of aggression, but do not feel the same type of pain as others (Dixon & Maddox, 2005; Mastro et al., 2009). Consequently, majority group viewers may perceive minority group members as fundamentally different or unfamiliar, increasing interracial anxiety and making contact more threatening, and ultimately strengthening the desire to increase social distance (Blascovich, Mendes, Hunter, Lickel, & Kowai-Bell, 2001; Pettigrew & Tropp, 2000). These episodes of bias have effects that are subtle as well, since some studies have suggested that viewers are unaware of the effects of watching these presentations on their attitudes toward members of different groups (Weisbuch et al., 2009).

In future research it will be important to more explicitly and thoroughly investigate the ways in which cultural racism drives the desire to achieve social distance from other race groups. To direct both policy and intervention efforts, it will be necessary to understand if and how cultural racism promotes race-based interpersonal maltreatment, residential segregation, and the internalization of negative stereotypes.

Institutional Racism

Institutional racism refers to the specific policies and/or procedures of institutions (i.e., government, business, schools, churches, etc.) which consistently result in unequal treatment for particular groups (Better, 2002; Gee et al., 2009; Griffith, Childs, Eng, & Jeffries, 2007; Lea, 2000). For the purposes of this article, we will focus on one highly salient example of institutional racism—residential racial segregation. Residential segregation refers to "the degree to which groups of people categorized on a variety of scales (race, ethnicity, income) occupy different space within urban areas" (Kramer & Hogue, 2009, p. 179). Across all income groups, Blacks tend to live in more racially segregated areas than do Whites. However, race-based residential segregation is most pronounced among individuals with low levels of income and education (LaVeist, 2003; Williams & Mohammed, 2009).

Residential segregation reflects both the extent to which Black individuals were and are ostracized by other groups on an individual level, as well as housing and land use policies that institutionalized these prejudicial attitudes and discriminatory behavior (Emerson, Yancey, & Chai, 2001; Fossett, 2006; Kramer & Hogue, 2009). In a population-based study assessing preferences for housing, Emerson et al. (2001) reports that Whites are very reluctant to live in areas with increasing numbers of Blacks, independent of the effects of crime, housing value, and educational quality of the schools. Prejudices held at an individual level were codified at an institutional level through Federal housing policies enacted in the post-World War II period (Seitles, 1998; Stuart, 2000). Subsequent fair housing laws made this explicit racism illegal. However, a number of other factors, including school district fragmentation, contributed to persistent residential segregation, even when these factors were not initially or directly motivated by racial bias.

The fragmentation of educational districts has been defined as the number of distinct educational districts for a given population. As Bischoff reports New Jersey has 616 school districts for 8.5 million residents, whereas Florida has 67 for 16 million residents (Bischoff, 2008). This fragmentation is a function of numerous factors, including population distributions, preferences for local control of schools, local zoning regulations, and other forces driving the competition for tax revenues. Although the policies that promote fragmentation may have arisen independently of racial considerations, several (Bischoff, 2008; Clotfelder, 2004; Urquiola, 2005), although not all studies (Hoxby, 2000), suggest that one side effect of greater school district fragmentation is increasing residential racial segregation. Individuals choose residential neighborhoods that provide the best services which they can afford, increasing the competition for (and driving up the costs of) housing in areas with high performing schools.

The patterns of racial residential segregation associated with fragmentation are further enforced by the individual level choices made by families searching for a new home. A recent multilevel analysis of school choice and residential relocation suggests that, holding all other variables constant, individual families make choices about where to live based on the percentage of African American and Latino students attending the local schools (Lankford & Wyckoff, 2006). Parents appear to use these percentages as a proxy for school quality. Fewer White families who plan to use public schools will choose to reside in a district housing many Black or Latino students. Instead, they are more likely to choose private schools or to avoid relocating to that area. This further deprives the school district of a student body diverse in economic and social resources.

In turn, racial segregation at the school and neighborhood level has long-term effects on the development of interracial relationships. Braddock and Gonzales (2010) report that early neighborhood segregation is associated with a greater desire for social distance from individuals of a different race/ethnicity, and school segregation during the early grades is associated with a greater desire to have same race neighbors, although there was some variability among ethnic groups (Braddock & Gonzalez, 2010). In another analysis of a national sample of Black and White students, Stearns (2010) reports that racial isolation in high school predicts more racial isolation in the workforce 10 years later (Stearns, 2010).

Racial isolation in the workplace is particularly problematic, since a study of referrals for employment in blue-collar business suggests that about one quarter of all referrals in the businesses studied come from social networks consisting of friends and relatives (Mouw, 2002). When social networks continue to be racially segregated, Black individuals have more limited access to employment opportunities in firms that employ large numbers of White individuals. This perpetuates a cycle in which Black individuals have limited ability to gain access to more integrated neighborhoods and business networks (Mouw, 2002; Wells, Holme, Revilla, & Atanda, 2005).

It is difficult to fully estimate the effects of residential racial segregation without considering the effects of reduced socioeconomic and social resources and increased psychosocial stressors that arise, at least partly, as a function of this segregation (Ceballo & McLoyd, 2002; Massey, 2008; Williams & Mohammed, 2009). Neighborhood disadvantage has been demonstrated to have negative effects on the development of peer relationships early in the lifespan. Specifically, most, although not all studies indicate that neighborhood disadvantage is associated with higher rates of association with peers engaged in antisocial behavior (Brody et al., 2001; Criss, Shaw, Moilanen, Hitchings, & Ingoldsby, 2009; Leventhal & Brooks-Gunn, 2000). These relationships are found in both White and Black children, and have been replicated in both urban and rural/suburban settings (Brody et al., 2001). Neighborhood violence also affects other aspects of children's relationships, with boys living in high violence neighborhoods tending to seek out friendships with others who are no longer attending school or attend different schools. These friendships may enable children to feel more protected in their environment, but may not support the development of a broader range of social skills or academic engagement (Harding, 2008).

Mechanisms

Research on the mechanisms through which institutional racism, particularly residential racial segregation affects the development of peer relations is still in its early stages (Criss et al., 2009), but some evidence suggests that the effects may be mediated by the lack of opportunities to develop certain social competencies and the existence of barriers to the emotional support necessary to exercise these competencies in a range of social situations. For example, perpetuation theory suggests that early racial isolation inhibits the development of the social skills and confidence required to negotiate relationships with individuals from other ethnicities (Braddock & Gonzalez, 2010). For minority students, racial isolation limits access to peer networks and adult mentors who can facilitate access to educational and work opportunities, consequently making it less likely that they will acquire the skills needed to succeed (Stearns, 2010).

The relationship of neighborhood disadvantage to child and adolescent peer relationships are mediated partly by neighborhood effects on the development of another dimension of social capital: parent–child relationships. In most cross-sectional and longitudinal studies, neighborhood economic disadvantage has been associated with lower levels of warm or consistent parenting (Criss et al., 2009; Klebanov, Brooks-Gunn, & Duncan, 1994; Kohen, Leventhal, Dahinten, & McIntosh, 2008; Pinderhughes, Nix, Foster, Jones, & The Conduct Problems Prevention Research Group, 2001). Perceived neighborhood dangerousness was associated with lower levels of supportive parenting (Criss et al., 2009) and higher levels of harsh parenting (Pinderhughes et al., 2001).

It is important to note that low SES neighborhoods have negative effects on consistent and warm parenting across racial/ethnic groups. One study reported that race differences (e.g., differences between White and Black Americans) in parenting warmth were no longer significant when neighborhood characteristics were controlled (Pinderhughes et al., 2001). This suggests that impairments in parenting relationships are a function primarily of responses to environmental barriers and demands, rather than a function of parenting practices indigenous to a particular ethnic group.

In sum, institutional racism, manifested as racial and economic neighborhood segregation, seems to contribute to difficulties in the development of a wide range of peer relationships across the lifespan, including children's and adolescents' friendships within their neighborhoods (Brody et al., 2001; Harding, 2008) and interracial relationships, both in school and in the workplace (Braddock & Gonzalez, 2010; Stearns, 2010). Although it is now illegal to engage in explicit or overt institutional racial bias in access to schools, employment, housing or mortgages (and other areas of public life), subtle forms of institutional racism can continue to influence the development of interpersonal relationships. The examples of institutional racism we have discussed here can be considered examples of subtle racism, in part, because the effects of discrimination on peer relationships are subtle. The effects are often seen not only at the time of exposure, but also long after the initial discriminatory acts; the consequences change over the course of development; and they are modified by the presence of other psychosocial processes that may co-occur with racial bias. For example, the effects of these initially explicit discriminatory acts (e.g., redlining, discriminatory housing policy) may persist, even across generations, in the form of residential racial segregation. In turn, residential racial segregation may contribute to different friendship choices, limiting the development of social skills in childhood and adolescence and the development of a network of educational and occupational colleagues in adulthood. The effects of residential racial segregation on peer relationships may also be a function of other psychosocial stressors associated with neighborhood disadvantage (e.g., low income, crime, disorder, harsh parenting behaviors, etc.). However, the degree to which individuals are exposed to these stressors is, in part, a function of the effects of individual and institutional level racism on housing choice. Further research is needed to understand the forces driving residential segregation and to clarify the effects of segregation itself versus the effects of neighborhood disadvantage on the development of same-race and cross-race peer relationships.

Interpersonal Racism

Individual-level racism refers to episodes of race or ethnicity-related maltreatment that occur to the individual. Interpersonal racism is a component of individual-level racism and has been defined as "directly perceived discriminatory interactions between individuals whether in their institutional roles or as public and private individuals" (Krieger, 1999, p. 301). Perceived or self-reported racism is a subset of these experiences and includes those episodes of maltreatment that are directly perceived by the individual and attributed to racial bias (Paradies, 2006; Utsey & Ponterotto, 1996). However, race-based maltreatment can also have negative effects, even if the targeted individual does not directly or immediately attribute the maltreatment to racial bias.

Interpersonal racism can take place in a number of different contexts, including work, public places, the criminal justice system, or social and personal venues (e.g., church, restaurants, or home) (Ryan, Gee, & Griffith, 2008). During episodes of interpersonal racism in each of these contexts, stereotypes held by the perpetrator are activated by the targeted individual's phenotypic or cultural characteristics. These stereotypes, and not the targeted individual's unique characteristics, influence the perpetrator's perceptions of and responses to the target (Wout, Murphy, & Steele, 2010).

Specific types of interpersonal race-based maltreatment include social distancing or social exclusion, discrimination at work or school, stigmatization, and physical threat and harassment (Brondolo et al., 2005a; Contrada et al., 2001). Social distancing can include verbal and nonverbal behavior that communicates rejection or exclusion. Some of these events can be explicit when they directly include references to the individual's ethnicity as a cause for the rejection. Other acts can be more subtle, and include avoiding eye contact during a meeting, failing to invite individuals to join social or work events, and ignoring requests for help (Henkel, Dovidio, & Gaertner, 2006; Sue et al., 2008). Subtle social distancing can be perceived as discriminatory, if the targeted individuals see that they are treated as less valuable (i.e., treated less warmly) than majority group members (Brondolo et al., 2011; Leary, 2005; Walton & Cohen, 2007).

Discrimination at work can take the form of reduced opportunities for employment, promotion, collaboration, or professional development. In addition to explicit statements that make clear the racial bias of the perpetrator, interpersonal can be expressed in more subtle ways, communicated through lowered expectations, decreased opportunities for collaboration or mentorship, or feedback that is either over or under accommodating (Walton & Cohen, 2007).

In episodes of stigmatization, the target may receive explicit or implicit messages that communicate the notion that he or she conforms to a negative stereotype associated with the group (i.e., is lazy, pushy, or alien, etc.). Most importantly, outcast or stigmatized individuals do not receive the same protections against verbal or physical attack (Williams, Forgas, Hippel, & Zadro, 2005). Given the history of violence against many minority groups, attacks against person or property are often considered episodes of racism, even in the absence of a clear mention of race (Carter, 2007).

Exposure to racism or ethnic discrimination is a part of everyday life for many Americans (Feagin & Sikes, 1994; Landrine & Klonoff, 1996). Several studies of Black Americans indicate that 80–100% of participants reported some experience of racism in their lifetimes (Klonoff & Landrine, 1999; Krieger & Sidney, 1996; Landrine & Klonoff, 1996; Peters, 2004). Our studies of different groups of Latino and Asian Americans find similar effects. We investigated episodes of racism experienced during the previous week among 449 Black and Latino adults (Brondolo, Brady, Libby, & Pencille, 2011a). In this convenience sample, 74% of the participants reported at least one racial incident in the past week, and 55% reported three or more incidents.

There are limited data on the effects of interpersonal racism on the development of peer relations, but there is consistent evidence that lifetime experiences of discrimination affect reactions to routine social exchanges (Brondolo et al., 2005b; Brondolo et al., 2008; Broudy et al., 2007; Ong, Fuller-Rowell, & Burrow, 2009; Taylor, Kamarck, & Shiffman, 2004). We have demonstrated that individuals exposed to higher levels of racism over the course of their lives were more likely to view new episodes of race-based maltreatment as threatening and harmful (Brondolo et al., 2005b). Past exposure to racism also influenced the individual's view of routine social interactions. In one study, we asked a multi-ethnic community sample of adults to complete diaries every 30 minutes to report on their moods and their day-to-day social interactions. Individuals who had higher levels of exposure to racism over the course of their lifetimes reported feeling more harassed, unfairly treated, or ignored during their routine social interactions (Broudy et al., 2007). These effects were significant and substantial even after controlling for a set of personality characteristics including defensiveness, hostility, cynicism, and anxiety, as well as comprehensive measures of socioeconomic status. We have recently replicated those findings in another larger sample of Black and Latino(a) adults (Brondolo et al., 2008). Similar associations of everyday maltreatment and daily diary ratings of social interactions have been reported by Taylor et al. (2004) and Ong et al. (2009) (Ong et al., 2009; Taylor et al., 2004).

Mechanisms

Interpersonal racism may have pervasive effects on peer relationships through the process of stress proliferation (Ong et al., 2009; Pearlin, Aneshensel, & LeBlanc, 1997) According to stress proliferation theories, exposure to one type of stressor directly and indirectly results in exposure to other stressors. Since social distancing or rejection can encompass a range of experiences, from partial inclusion to outright rejection, a broad range of interpersonal interchanges may become potential racial stressors (Broudy et al., 2007; Richeson & Shelton, 2005).

Experiences of racism can also increase other race-related stress processes including identity-related concerns, stereotype threat, stereotype confirmation concern, and stigma sensitivity (Contrada et al., 2001; Cross, 1991; Helms, 1990; Sellers & Shelton, 2003). For example, prospective studies suggest that exposure to racism increases the salience or centrality of race in personal identity (Quintana, 2007; Sellers & Shelton, 2003). This heightened attention to race-related matters facilitates the priming of race-related stereotypes and heightens concerns about stereotype threat. Therefore, even small doses of race-related maltreatment can serve as stressors, capable of eliciting distress.

The relationship of perceived racism to indices of psychological distress, including depressive symptoms and negative mood, is well documented (Brondolo, Gallo, Myers, & Hector, 2009b). These effects have been seen in studies conducted in the United States and internationally, and the effects of racism on psychological distress have been demonstrated in Asian, Black, Latino, and many other racial/ethnic groups (Kwok et al., 2011). Race-related maltreatment is alienating (Mendoza-Denton, Downey, Davis, Purdie, & Pietrzak, 2002), and alienation is painful and dispiriting under any circumstances. When it is caused by responses to characteristics that are immutable and outside of one's control (i.e., one's phenotype), the unfairness can lead to persistent anger and other indices of negative mood (Brondolo et al., 2008, 2011). In turn, persistent symptoms of stress and depression may impair the quality of interactions with others (Brody et al., 2008; Cutrona, Russell, Hessling, Brown, & Murry, 2000; Cutrona et al., 2005).

Racism may also hinder the development of interracial peer relationships by fostering interracial anxiety. At least in the initial stages, interracial relationships are difficult for both interaction partners (Blascovich et al., 2001). Anxiety acts as a barrier to initiating interracial interactions for both Blacks and Whites (Richeson & Shelton, 2007). For example, individuals high in prejudice are less likely to have interracial friendships during the first year of college (Schofield, Hausmann, Ye, & Woods, 2010). Both Whites students who report higher levels of anxiety about interactions with Black students and Black students who report higher levels of concern about being targeted for race-based rejection are less likely to initiate inter-racial interactions (Mendoza-Denton et al., 2002). Minority students are more likely to develop friendships with White students who already have a diverse group of friends, since they may expect that these individuals will be less biased in their interactions (Wout et al., 2010).

Concerns about confirming stereotypes can undermine routine social exchanges, as illustrated by new research on impression management strategies (Bergsieker, Shelton, & Richeson, 2010). Bergseiker et al. report that in inter-racial exchanges participants may communicate at cross-purposes, with Latino and Black individuals attempting to regulate perceptions of competence; whereas White individuals try to regulate perceptions of warmth.

Interracial anxiety may also play a role in the trajectory of relationships. Among freshman roommates, daily experiences of anxiety brought same-race roommates closer together. In contrast, in pairs composed of students of different races/ethnicities, experiences of anxiety were associated with an erosion of the relationship. Consequently, cross-race pairs were less likely to choose to live together again (Shelton, Trail, West, & Bergsieker, 2010).

In sum, interpersonal racism can be expressed in both overt and subtle ways, with subtle racism communicated through differences in nonverbal behavior and tone of voice. The effects of exposure to interpersonal discrimination can be subtle as well. Consistent with stress proliferation theories, previous exposure to racism is associated with both more frequent interpersonal conflict and more intensely negative interactions in a variety of settings (Brondolo et al., 2008; Broudy et al., 2007; Ong et al., 2009). A portion of these effects appears to be mediated by ongoing symptoms of depression and negative mood, potentially creating a feedback cycle in which exposure to race-based maltreatment degrades the experience of other social relationships, preventing recovery from the initial stress exposure. Interpersonal racism may also set in motion other psychological processes, including inter-racial anxiety that appears to decrease the willingness of individuals of all races to initiate and maintain interracial friendships (Mendoza-Denton et al., 2002; Richeson & Shelton, 2007; Schofield, Hausmann, Ye, & Woods, 2010). As the basic research on the mechanisms linking interpersonal racism to the development of peer relationships develops, new efforts to design interventions are needed.

Internalized Racism

Internalized racism is defined as "the acceptance, by marginalized racial populations, of the negative societal beliefs and stereotypes about themselves" (Williams & Williams-Morris, 2000, p. 255). Individuals may or may not be aware of their own acceptance of these negative beliefs. Internalized racism can also be expressed via a rejection of the cultural practices of one's own ethnic or racial group. Some conceptualizations of internalized racism have also encompassed the internalization of distress associated with exposure to racism. When race-related stereotypes are absorbed into the self-concept of a stigmatized individual, the individual is considered to be self-stereotyping (Hogg & Turner, 1987; Simon & Hamilton, 1994). Positive self-stereotyping may increase allegiance to one's ingroup; whereas negative self-stereotyping may decrease self-esteem, among other negative effects.

Some measures of internalized racism (e.g., the Nadolinazation scale) or of Black identity ask about explicit or conscious acceptance of racial stereotypes

(Helms, 1996; Sellers, Copeland-Linder, Martin, & Lewis, 2006; Taylor & Grundy, 1996). Recent research has employed the use of the Implicit Association test (Greenwald, McGhee, & Schwartz, 1998; Greenwald et al., 2002) to test implicit or nonconscious incorporation of stereotypes about one's cultural group into one's self-concept (Lun, Sinclair, & Cogburn, 2009). Lun et al. (2009) demonstrate that, when primed to think about the self, individuals respond more quickly to both positive and negative stereotypical attributes about their group versus words unrelated to their group or to nonwords. They demonstrate that in tests with young White participants who were primed to think about the self, both words related to positive stereotypes about Whites (e.g., successful, rich) and words related to negative stereotypes (e.g., materialistic, racist) were processed more quickly than words related to stereotypes about Blacks or nonwords (Lun et al., 2009).

Obtaining an estimate of the prevalence of self-stereotyping is challenging, but there is now fairly convincing evidence that some low status groups show implicit out-group (i.e., high status) group preferences (Jost, Banaji, & Nosek, 2004). Specifically, in several studies using implicit attitudes measures, a proportion of African American students reveal warmer implicit attitudes and preferences for European Americans versus African Americans.

There is very limited data explicitly linking internalized racism or self-stereotyping to the quality or quantity of peer relationships. One study reports that internalized racism, measured with the Nadolization scale, was associated with reduced marital satisfaction in Black couples (Taylor, Wright, Moghaddam, & Lalonde, 1990).

There is also indirect evidence that suggests that racial self-stereotyping may harm the development of other close relationships, including cross race friendships (Sinclair, Hardin, & Lowery, 2006). These studies suggest that individuals are often well aware of the stereotypes others hold about their group, and consistent with the notion of social tuning, they modify their behavior to conform to other people's expectations. In one study, Sinclair et al. (2006) asked Black participants to interact with a White experimental confederate and led the Black participants to believe the White student held prejudicial beliefs about the academic competence of Black students. The Black students performed more poorly when they wanted to be affiliated with the White student than when they did not. Therefore, the desire to develop friendships with other race individuals may come at a cost to one's self esteem and regard for one's group (Sinclair et al., 2006).

Mechanisms

There has been very little research directly examining the mechanisms through which internalized racism and self-stereotyping affects the development of peer relationships. The bulk of the data has concerned determinants of self-stereotyping, including theories about the role of cultural racism in developing these stereotyped notions and system justification motives, among other models (Jost et al., 2004).

One recent line of evidence suggests some potential explanations for maintenance of self-stereotyping. Seibt and Forster (2004) suggest that negative self-stereotypes can serve a protective function by inducing a prevention focus in certain situations likely to evoke stereotype threat (Seibt & Förster, 2004). Specifically, holding negative stereotypes can make individuals more cautious and analytic in order to avoid the potential consequences of exhibiting the characteristics associated with negative stereotypes.

Shared reality theory also explains some of the persistence of negative self-stereotypes (Sinclair et al., 2006). Sharing similar perceptions (i.e., a shared reality) confirms a sense of belonging. Since individuals are aware of the perceptions of others, the desire to belong and share common perceptions may override the aversion to endorsing negative self-stereotypes. In part this may explain concerns expressed among some minority individuals when other minority individuals initiate connections with others outside of their race group (Cohen & Garcia, 2005; Walton & Cohen, 2007).

In sum, internalized racism is subtle both in its manifestations (i.e., it is often measured by assessing implicit and not explicit attitudes) and its effects (e.g., including self-esteem or attitudes toward same- and different-race others). There is very limited research on internalized racism or self-stereotyping on the development or maintenance of social relationships. However, existing data suggest that exposure to racism may create concerns about presenting a genuine self in relationships both with same- and cross-race peers. When individuals wish to develop a relationship with an individual of a different race who they perceive as holding prejudicial beliefs, they may modify their own beliefs and actions to conform to the other's expectations.

Summary and Conclusions

Multidisciplinary research documents the presence of racial and ethnic biases at the cultural, institutional and individual/interpersonal levels. When beliefs about racial or ethnic groups are widely disseminated and automatically accepted (i.e., seen as the way things are), and when individuals experience discriminatory behavior on a routine basis or are racially segregated, then prejudicial beliefs can become incorporated into one's self-concept and lead to the development of internalized racism (Bonilla-Silva, 1997; Jost et al., 2004). The different levels of racism act both separately and jointly to create barriers to the development and maintenance of social capital and to social and physical well-being (Brondolo et al., 2011).

Interracial interactions are critical for access to economic and social resources and political power in the United States. Yet racism at multiple levels constrains the development of cross-race peer relationships (Braddock II & Gonzalez, 2010). Cultural racism influences the depictions of social interactions presented in the media, affecting the degree to which individuals of different ethnic groups are seen as desirable choices for relationships as colleagues, friends, or neighbors (Entman & Rojecki, 2001). Institutional racism in the form of residential segregation limits opportunity for the types of contact that can disconfirm racial biases or build the social skills necessary to interact with peers of a different race or ethnicity (Stearns, 2010). On an interpersonal level, fears of rejection or judgment deter participants of all races from taking the risks involved in initiating new cross-race relationships. Concerns about confirming stereotypes create further obstacles to maintaining these relationships (Mendoza-Denton et al., 2002; Richeson & Shelton, 2007). Minor anxiety-producing conflicts erode cross-race relationships, even as they build closeness among same-race peers (Shelton et al., 2010).

Relationships with peers within the local environment serve as a context for the development of social competencies and health behaviors. These relationships are also affected by racism. Institutional racism in the form of neighborhood disadvantage increases the likelihood that children and teens will socialize with peers engaged in antisocial behaviors; highly violent neighborhoods may lead children to choose friends for protection rather than for common interests (Brody et al., 2008; Harding, 2008). Interpersonal and internalized racism may undermine the quality of interactions with close relations or other community members (Broudy et al 2007; Taylor, 1990).

These findings are not meant to imply that individuals experiencing racism cannot form meaningful and supportive peer relationships. Friendships can blossom in a wide variety of circumstances. Instead, this review is intended to underscore the pressures on peer relationships that are faced by individuals who are targeted for discrimination. These pressures are often outside the individual's awareness or control, and yet they can affect the development of relationships crucial for social, economic and physical well-being.

Mechanisms

Each level of racism may affect interpersonal processes through different mechanisms. Cultural racism appears to affect attitudes and behaviors toward others through a variety of social-cognitive processes, including priming, modeling, schema creation and social tuning. Racial group members portrayed in all forms of media serve as social role models, influencing the beliefs of media consumers about members of other racial and ethnic groups (Dovidio, 2009).

Institutional racism, in the form of residential racial segregation may act by creating barriers to the development of and support for pro-social competencies (Leventhal & Brooks-Gunn, 2000; Sampson et al., 2002).

Institutional, interpersonal and internalized racism may affect peer relationships through processes related to stress proliferation (Brondolo et al., 2011; Ong et al., 2009; Pearlin et al., 1997). Race-related maltreatment is itself a stressor, and there is good evidence that race-related stress increases the risk for exposure to other types of interpersonal stressors (Brondolo et al., 2011; Ong et al., 2009). Disadvantaged neighborhoods present a wide range of both race and non race-related stressors, including exposure to crowding, toxins, and noise and offering very minimal facilities for rest and recovery (Brondolo, 2011b). There is some evidence that internalized racism is associated with perceived stress, as well (Tull, Sheu, Butler, & Cornelious, 2005).

Implications for Health and Well-Being

Exposure to the stress of racism is a likely contributor to the development of symptoms of depression and other negative mood states. In turn, these moods are likely to affect peer relationships. Data from studies of both institutional and interpersonal racism suggest that symptoms of depression and negative mood serve as a common pathway undermining parent–child and other interpersonal relationships (Brody et al., 2008; Broudy et al., 2007; C. E. Cutrona et al., 2000; C. E. Cutrona et al., 2005). Depressive symptoms may sap the energy needed for constructive engagement, and in turn, impairments in social relationship can further exacerbate the mental health effects of stress exposure.

The effects of racism on peer relationships may also have important implications for physical health outcomes. The effect of racism on a range of health outcomes has been well documented (Paradies, 2006; Pascoe & Richman, 2009; Williams & Mohammed, 2009; Brondolo, Love, Pencille, Schoenthaler, & Ogedegbe, 2011). The effects of racism on peer relations may mediate or possibly compound the direct effects of racism on health. We can consider these possibilities in more detail by examining obesity and smoking.

Institutional racism, in the form of residential segregation and neighborhood disadvantage is associated with barriers to healthy eating and physical activity, increasing risk for obesity among neighborhood residents (Dubowitz et al., 2008; Kwate, 2008; Lee & Cubbin, 2002). Recent data suggests that having close friends who are overweight increases the likelihood of being overweight oneself, although there are some gender differences in these effects (Smith & Christakis, 2008). Residential racial segregation may increase the likelihood that individuals have close relationships with obese peers, increasing each individual's risk for obesity. The concentration of obese individuals in racially segregated neighborhoods may affect risk by potentially changing expectations about the inevitability of obesity among other mechanisms (Hebl, King, & Perkins, 2009; Yancey et al., 2009).

Interpersonal or individual level racism has been consistently associated with cigarette smoking (Borrell et al., 2007; Landrine, Klonoff, Corral, Fernandez, &

Roesch, 2006). Negative mood states increase risk for smoking, and racism increases the risk for experiencing negative mood states (Landrine, Klonoff, Corral, Fernandez, & Roesch, 2006). Having friends who smoke increases risk for smoking, especially among adolescents (Smith & Christakis, 2008). Given the high prevalence of exposure to racism among minority group members, they are likely to have peers who have been exposed to racism. Racism may act to influence the individual's risk for smoking, and the effects may be intensified through interactions with peers whose own exposure to racism may increase the likelihood that they smoke as well.

Implications for Interventions

The effects of racism on interpersonal relations are subtle and can operate outside of conscious awareness. For example, the effects of nonverbal expressions of lower regard influenced TV viewers' attitudes toward Blacks, even when they were not aware of these effects (Weisbuch, Pauker, & Ambady, 2009). Negative messages can be embedded within more overtly friendly behavior (Biernat, Sesko, & Amo, 2009). Black individual's perceptions of another person's capacity for bias are shaped quickly, often based on less than a minute's worth of observation (Richeson & Shelton, 2005).

Consequently, it will be important to educate both majority and minority group members about the nature of these subtle or nonconscious processes, helping them to understand the ways these nonconscious attitudes and subsequent behaviors are shaped by cultural experiences. It may be particularly helpful to provide education about the ways in which differences in sociocultural and personal history can translate into differences in the perception and meaning of nonverbal and verbal aspects of social exchange (Avery, Hebl, Richeson, & Ambady, 2009; Oyserman, Sorensen, Reber, & Chen, 2009).

Efforts to intervene are less likely to succeed if all levels of racism are not adequately addressed. For example, there is a wealth of research demonstrating that stereotype threat inhibits performance (Steele, 1999). There have been successful efforts to reduce stereotype threat and thereby improve performance in a particular domain (e.g., on academic tests), by making members of a stigmatized group aware of other group members who have performed well in that domain (Marx, Stapel, & Muller, 2005). However, there can be side effects to the promotion of achievement among members of minority groups. Members of stigmatized groups who violate stereotypes associated with their group, (i.e., do well on tasks that are not associated with their group) face interpersonal backlash, including criticism and sabotage (Phelan & Rudman, 2010). Without efforts that address institutional and cultural racism and change expectations, it will be difficult for targeted individuals to receive greater peer support.

But despite the complexity of the problem, recent evidence suggests several encouraging trends. First, political and social pressures have resulted in modifications of the presentations of minority group members in the media. More TV shows feature minority group members in a range of social positions and family relationships (Smith & Christakis, 2008). Business media have made substantial changes in the degree to which they portray Black Americans in positions of power and influence (Stevenson, 2007). As stereotyped portrayals of Black Americans are less widely disseminated, they appear to lose their power to activate prejudicial attitudes and discriminatory behavior (Monahan et al., 2005). New efforts to understand the role of stereotype threat and interracial anxiety provide guidance for specific interventions that can allow majority group individuals to move past race-related anxiety and initiate effective collaborative relationships (Avery et al., 2009; Oyserman et al., 2009). Changes to the physical environment, including the development of shared spaces such as community gardens, have been demonstrated to promote positive social interactions (Shinew, Glover, & Parry, 2004). New research, as illustrated by the articles in this volume, is beginning to explicate the specific pathways through which subtle racism can affect health care interactions (Penner, 2012) or employment opportunities (Bendick & Nunes, 2012; Pager & Western, 2012). This type of mechanistic research can provide specific targets for intervention.

It would be hard to overestimate the importance of peer relationships for health, well-being, and prosperity. Social forces, including racism, which have adverse effects on the development of peer relationships warrant attention. A failure to address the effects of racism on peer relationships can contribute to significant social problems across society. Barriers to the formation of cross-race relationships contribute to the persistence of prejudicial beliefs and discriminatory behavior, and undermine social cohesion. Race-related stress further undermines all types of peer relations, depriving all individuals of the support they may need to face other challenges.

Although the majority of the studies we reviewed were conducted on U.S. samples, the effects of racism on the development of peer relationships are likely to be seen in other countries as well. The manifestations of cultural, institutional, and interpersonal racism may differ across societies. However, the outcomes of racism (i.e., social exclusion or marginalization) are likely to be similar and to have similar effects on the development of cross-race relationships.

Mechanistic research can facilitate efforts to reduce the expression of racial bias and its effects. Investigators are increasingly able to identify the specific types of beliefs, nonverbal behaviors, social interactions, public policies and environments that undermine peer relations. This knowledge can motivate and direct interventions both to reduce exposure to discrimination and to support the development of the types of peer relationships that promote health and create economic and social opportunities for all.

References

Avery, D. R., Hebl, M. R., Richeson, J. A., & Ambady, N. (2009). It does not have to be uncomfortable: The role of behavioral scripts in black-white interracial interactions. *Journal of Applied Psychology, 94*(6), 1382–1393. doi:10.1037/a0016208.

Bendick, M., Jr., & Nunes, A. P. (2012). Developing the research basis for controlling bias in hiring. *Journal of Social Issues, 68*(2), 238–262. doi:10.1111/j.1540-4560.2011.01747.x

Bergsieker, H. B., Shelton, J. N., & Richeson, J. A. (2010). To be liked versus respected: Divergent goals in interracial interactions. *Journal of Personality & Social Psychology, 99*(2), 248–264. doi:10.1037/a0018474.

Better, S. (2002). *Institutional racism: A primer on theory and strategies for social change*. Chicago: Rowman & Littlefield.

Biernat, M., Sesko, A. K., & Amo, R. B. (2009). Compensatory stereotyping in interracial encounters. *Group Processes & Intergroup Relations, 12*(5), 551–563. doi:10.1177/1368430209337469.

Bischoff, K. (2008). School district fragmentation and racial residential segregation: How do boundaries matter?. *Urban Affairs Review, 44*(2), 182–217. doi:10.1177/1078087408320651.

Bjornstrom, E. E. S., Kaufman, R. L., Peterson, R. D., & Slater, M. D. (2010). Race and ethnic representations of lawbreakers and victims in crime news: A national study of television coverage. *Social Problems, 57*(2), 269–293. doi:10.1525/sp.2010.57.2.269.

Blascovich, J., Mendes, W. B., Hunter, S. B., Lickel, B., & Kowai-Bell, N. (2001). Perceiver threat in social interactions with stigmatized others. *Journal of Personality & Social Psychology, 80*(2), 253–267. doi:10.1037//0022-3514.80.2.253.

Bonilla-Silva, E. (1997). Rethinking racism: Toward a structural interpretation. *American Sociological Review, 62*(3), 465–480.

Borrell, L. N., Jacobs Jr, DR, Williams, D. R., Pletcher, M. J., Houston, T. K., & Kiefe, C. I. (2007). Self-reported racial discrimination and substance use in the coronary artery risk development in adults study. *American Journal of Epidemiology, 20*, 1–12. doi:10.1093/aje/kwm180.

Braddock II, J., Henry, & Gonzalez, A. D. C. (2010). Social isolation and social cohesion: The effects of K-12 neighborhood and school segregation on intergroup orientations. *Teachers College Record, 112*(6), 1631–1653.

Brody, G. H., Chen, Y., Kogan, S. M., Murry, V. M., Logan, P., & Luo, Z. (2008). Linking perceived discrimination to longitudinal changes in African American mothers' parenting practices. *Journal of Marriage and Family, 70*(2), 319–331. doi:10.1111/j.1741-3737.2008.00484.x.

Brody, G. H., Ge, X., Conger, R., Gibbons, F. X., Murry McBride, V., Gerrard, M., & Simons, R. L. (2001). The influence of neighborhood disadvantage, collective socialization, and parenting on African American children's affiliation with deviant peers. *Child Development, 72*(4), 1231–1246.

Brondolo, E., Brady Ver Halen, N., Pencille, M., Beatty, D., & Contrada, R. J. (2009a). Coping with racism: A selective review of the literature and a theoretical and methodological critique. *Journal of Behavioral Medicine, 32*(1), 64–88.

Brondolo, E., Brady, N., Libby, D. J., & Pencille, M. (2011a). Racism as a psychosocial stressor. In A. Baum, & R. J. Contrada (Eds.), *Handbook of stress science: Biology, psychology, and health* (pp. 167–184). New York: Springer.

Brondolo, E., Brady, N., Thompson, S., Tobin, J. N., Cassells, A., Sweeney, M., McFarlane, D., Contrada, R. (2008). Perceived racism and negative affect: Analyses of trait and state measures of affect in a community sample. *Journal of Social & Clinical Psychology, 27*(2), 150–173.

Brondolo, E., Gallo, L. C., Myers, H. F., & Hector, F. (2009b). Race, racism and health: Disparities, mechanisms, and interventions. *Journal of Behavioral Medicine, 32*(1), 1–8.

Brondolo, E., Kelly, K. P., Coakley, V., Gordon, T., Thompson, S., Levy, E., Gordon, A., Tobin, J. N., Sweeney, M., Contrada, R. (2005a). The perceived ethnic discrimination questionnaire: Development and preliminary validation of a community version. *Journal of Applied Social Psychology, 35*(2), 335–365.

Brondolo, E., Lackey, S., & Love, E. (2011b). Race, racism & health: Evaluating racial disparities in hypertension to understand the links between racism and health status. In A. Baum, T. A.,

Revenson, & J. E. Singer (Eds.), *Handbook of health psychology*, 2nd edition (pp. 569–594). New York: Psychology Press.

Brondolo, E., Love, E. E., Pencille, M., Schoenthaler, A., & Ogedegbe, G. (2011). Racism and hypertension: A review of the empirical evidence and implications for clinical practice. *American Journal of Hypertension, 24*(5), 518–529. doi:10.1038/ajh.2011.9.

Brondolo, E., Thompson, S., Brady, N., Appel, R., Cassells, A., Tobin, J. N., & Sweeney, M. (2005b). The relationship of racism to appraisals and coping in a community sample. *Ethnicity & Disease, 15*(4 Suppl 5), S5–14-19.

Broudy, R., Brondolo, E., Coakley, V., Brady, N., Cassells, A., Tobin, J., & Sweeney, M. (2007). Perceived ethnic discrimination in relation to daily moods and negative social interactions. *Journal of Behavioral Medicine, 30*(1), 31–43.

Carter, R. T. (2007). Racism and psychological and emotional injury: Recognizing and assessing race-based traumatic stress. *The Counseling Psychologist, 35*(1), 13–105. doi:10.1177/0011000006292033.

Ceballo, R., & McLoyd, V. C. (2002). Social support and parenting in poor, dangerous neighborhoods. *Child Development, 73*(4), 1310–1321.

Clawson, R. A., & Trice, R. (2000). Poverty as we know it: Media portrayals of the poor. *Public Opinion Quarterly, 64*(1), 53–64.

Clotfelder, C. (2004). *After brown: The rise and retreat of school desegregation.* Princeton, NJ: Princeton University Press.

Cohen, G. L., & Garcia, J. (2005). "I am us": Negative stereotypes as collective threats. *Journal of Personality and Social Psychology, 89*(4), 566–582.

Coleman, J. S. (1988). Social capital in the development of human capital: The ambiguous position of private schools. Paper presentation at the Annual Conference of the National Association of Independent Schools (New York, NY, February 15–26, 1988).

Contrada, R. J., Ashmore, R. D., Gary, M. L., Coups, E., Egeth, J. D., Sewell, A., Goyal, T. (2001). Measures of ethnicity-related stress: Psychometric properties, ethnic group differences, and associations with well-being. *Journal of Applied Social Psychology, 31*, 1775–1820.

Criss, M. M., Shaw, D. S., Moilanen, K. L., Hitchings, J. E., & Ingoldsby, E. M. (2009). Family, neighborhood, and peer characteristics as predictors of child adjustment: A longitudinal analysis of additive and mediation models. *Social Development, 18*(3), 511–535. doi:10.1111/j.1467-9507.2008.00520.x.

Cross, W. E. J. (1991). *Shades of black: Diversity in African American identity.* Philadelphia, PA: Temple University Press.

Cutrona, C. E., Russell, D. W., Hessling, R. M., Brown, P. A., & Murry, V. (2000). Direct and moderating effects of community context on the psychological well-being of African American women. *Journal of Personality and Social Psychology, 79*(6), 1088–1101. doi:10.1037/0022-3514.79.6.1088.

Cutrona, C. E., Russell, D. W., Brown, P. A., Hessling, R. M., Clark, L. A., & Garder, K. A. (2005). Neighborhood context, personality, and stressful life events as predictors of depression among African American women. *Journal of Abnormal Psychology, 114*(1), 3–15. doi:10.1037/0021-843x.114.13.

Dalisay, F., & Tan, A. (2009). Assimilation and contrast effects in the priming of Asian American and African American stereotypes through TV exposure. *Journalism & Mass Communication Quarterly, 86*(1), 7–22.

Dixon, T. L. (2008). Network news and racial beliefs: Exploring the connection between national television news exposure and stereotypical perceptions of African Americans. *Journal of Communication, 58*(2), 321–337. doi:10.1111/j.1460-2466.2008.00387.x.

Dixon, T. L., & Azocar, C. L. (2007). Priming crime and activating blackness: Understanding the psychological impact of the overrepresentation of blacks as lawbreakers on television news. *Journal of Communication, 57*(2), 229–253. doi:10.1111/j.1460-2466.2007.00341.x.

Dixon, T. L., Azocar, C. L., & Casas, M. (2003). The portrayal of race and crime on television network news. *Journal of Broadcasting & Electronic Media, 47*(4), 498–523.

Dixon, T. L., & Linz, D. (2000). Overrepresentation and underrepresentation of African Americans and Latinos as lawbreakers on television news. *Journal of Communication, 50*(2), 131–154. doi:10.1111/j.1460-2466.2000.tb02845.x.

Dixon, T. L., & Maddox, K. B. (2005). Skin tone, crime news, and social reality judgments: Priming the stereotype of the dark and dangerous black criminal. *Journal of Applied Social Psychology*, *35*(8), 1555–1570. doi:10.1111/j.1559-1816.2005.tb02184.x.

Dovidio, J. F. (2009). Racial bias: Unspoken but heard. *Science*, *326*(5960), 1641–1642. doi:10.1126/science.1184231.

Dubowitz, T., Heron, M., Bird, C. E., Lurie, N., Finch, B. K., Basurto-Dávila, R. & Escarce, J. J. (2008). Neighborhood socioeconomic status and fruit and vegetable intake among whites, blacks, and Mexican Americans in the United States. *The American Journal of Clinical Nutrition*, *87*(6), 1883–1891.

Emerson, M. O., Yancey, G., & Chai, K. J. (2001). Does race matter in residential segregation? Exploring the preferences of white Americans. *American Social Review*, *66*(6), 922–935.

Entman, R. M., & Rojecki, A. (2001). *The black image in the white mind: Media and race in America*. Chicago, IL US: University of Chicago Press.

Feagin, J. R., & Sikes, M. P. (1994). Living with racism: The black middle-class experience. Boston: Beacon Press.

Fossett, M. (2006). Ethnic preferences, social distance dynamics, and residential segregation: Theoretical explorations using simulation analysis. *The Journal of Mathematical Sociology*, *30*(3), 184. doi:10.1080/00222500500544052.

Gee, G. C., Ro, A., Shariff-Marco, S., & Chae, D. (2009). Racial discrimination and health among Asian Americans: Evidence, assessment, and directions for future research. *Epidemiologic Reviews*, *31*, 130–151.

Gee, G., Walseman, K.M, & Brondolo, E. (2012). A lifecourse perspective on racism and health-inequities. *American Journal of Public Health*, *102*(5), 967–974.

Gilens, M. (1996). Race and poverty in America: Public misperceptions and the American news media. *Public Opinion Quarterly*, *60*(4), 515–541. doi:10.1086/297771.

Greenwald, A. G., McGhee, D. E., & Schwartz, J. L. K. (1998). Measuring individual differences in implicit cognition: The implicit association test. *Journal of Personality and Social Psychology*, *74*(6), 1464–1480. doi:10.1037/0022-3514.74.6.1464.

Greenwald, A. G., Banaji, M. R., Rudman, L. A., Farnham, S. D., Nosek, B. A., & Mellott, D. S. (2002). A unified theory of implicit attitudes, stereotypes, self-esteem, and self-concept. *Psychological Review*, *109*(1), 3–25. doi:10.1037/0033-295X.109.1.3.

Griffith, D. M., Childs, E. L., Eng, E., & Jeffries, V. (2007). Racism in organizations: The case of a county public health department. *Journal of Community Psychology*, *35*(3), 287–302.

Harding, D. J. (2008). Neighborhood violence and adolescent friendships. *International Journal of Conflict and Violence*, *2*(1), 28–55.

Harrell, S. P. (2000). A multidimensional conceptualization of racism-related stress: Implications for the well-being of people of color. *American Journal of Orthopsychiatry*, *70*(1), 42–57.

Hebl, M. R., King, E. B., & Perkins, A. (2009). Ethnic differences in the stigma of obesity: Identification and engagement with a thin ideal. *Journal of Experimental Social Psychology*, *45*(6), 1165–1172. doi:10.1016/j.jesp.2009.04.017.

Helms, J. E. (1996). Toward a methodology for measuring and assessing racial identity as distinguished from ethnic identity. In G. Sodowsky, & J. Imparaa (Eds.), *Multicultural assessment in counseling and clinical psychology* (pp. 143–192). Lincoln, NE: Buros Institute of Mental Measurement.

Helms, J. E. (1990). An overview of Black racial identity theory. In J. E. Helms (Ed.), *Black and White racial identity: Theory, research, and practice* (pp. 9–32). Westport, Conn: Praeger.

Henkel, K. E., Dovidio, J. F., & Gaertner, S. L. (2006). Institutional discrimination, individual racism, and hurricane katrina. *Analyses of Social Issues and Public Policy (ASAP)*, *6*(1), 99–124. doi:10.1111/j.1530-2415.2006.00106.x.

Hogg, M. A., & Turner, J. C. (1987). Intergroup behaviour, self-stereotyping and the salience of social categories. *British Journal of Social Psychology*, *26*(4), 325–340.

Hoxby, C. (2000). Does competition among public schools benefit students and taxpayers? *American Economic Review*, *90*(5), 1209–1238.

Jost, J. T., Banaji, M. R., & Nosek, B. A. (2004). A decade of system justification theory: Accumulated evidence of conscious and unconscious bolstering of the status quo. *Political Psychology*, *25*(6), 881–919. doi:10.1111/j.1467–9221.2004.00402.x.

Kang, J. (2012). The missing quadrants of anti-discrimination. *Journal of Social Issues, 68*(2), 314–327. doi:10.1111/j.1540-4560.2011.01750.x

Klebanov, P. K., Brooks-Gunn, J., & Duncan, G. J. (1994). Does neighborhood and family poverty affect mothers' parenting, mental health and social support?. *Journal of Marriage and the Family, 56*(441), 441–455.

Klonoff, E. A., & Landrine, H. (1999). Cross-validation of the schedule of racist events. *Journal of Black Psychology, 25*(2), 231–254. doi:10.1177/0095798499025002006.

Kohen, D. E., Leventhal, T., Dahinten, V. S., & McIntosh, C. N. (2008). Neighborhood disadvantage: Pathways of effects for young children. *Child Development, 79*(1), 156–169. doi:10.1111/j.1467–8624.2007.01117.x.

Kramer, M. R., & Hogue, C. R. (2009). Is segregation bad for your health? *Epidemiologic Review, 31*(1), 178–194. doi:10.1093/epirev/mxp001.

Krieger, N. (1999). Embodying inequality: A review of concepts, measures, and methods for studying health consequences of discrimination. *International Journal of Health Services, 29*, 295–352.

Krieger, N., & Sidney, S. (1996). Racial discrimination and blood pressure: The CARDIA study of young black and white adults. *American Journal of Public Health, 86*(10), 1370–1378.

Kwate, N. O. A. (2008). Fried chicken and fresh apples: Racial segregation as a fundamental cause of fast food density in black neighborhoods. *Health & Place, 14*(1), 32–44. doi:10.1016/j.healthplace.2007.04.001.

Kwok, J., Atencio, J., Ullah., Crupi, D., Roth, A., Chaplin, W., & Brondolo, E. (2011). The perceived ethnic discrimination questionnaire–community version: Validation in a multi-ethnic asian sample. *Cultural Diversity and Ethnic Minority Psychology, 17*(3), 271–282

Landrine, H., & Klonoff, E. A. (1996). The schedule of racist events: A measure of racial discrimination and a study of its negative physical and mental health consequences. *Journal of Black Psychology, 22*, 144–168.

Landrine, H., Klonoff, E. A., Corral, I., Fernandez, S., & Roesch, S. (2006). Conceptualizing and measuring ethnic discrimination in health research. *Journal of Behavioral Medicine, 29*(1), 79–94. doi:10.1007/s10865–005-9029—0.

Lankford, H., & Wyckoff, J. (2006). The effect of school choice and residential location on the racial and economic segregation of students. In T. Gronberg, & D. Jansen (Eds.), *Advances in applied microeconomics* (Vol. 14, pp. 185–240). Kidington, Oxford: Elsevier.

LaVeist, T. A. (2003). Racial segregation and longevity among African Americans: An individual level analysis. *Health Services Research, 38*(6), 1719–1734.

Lea, J. (2000). The macpherson report and question of institutional racism. *Howard Journal of Criminal Justice, 39*(3), 219–233. doi:10.1111/1468-2311.00165.

Leary, M. R. (2005). Varieties of interpersonal rejection. In K. D. Williams, J. P. Forgas & W. von Hippel (Eds.), *The social outcast: Ostracism, social exclusion, rejection, and bullying* (pp. 35–51). New York, NY: Psychology Press.

Lee, R. E., & Cubbin, C. (2002). Neighborhood context and youth cardiovascular health behaviors. *American Journal of Public Health, 92*(3), 428–36.

Leventhal, T., & Brooks-Gunn, J. (2000). The neighborhoods they live in: The effects of neighborhood residence on child and adolescent outcomes. *Psychological Bulletin, 126*(2), 309–37. doi:10.1037/0033-2909.126.2.309.

Lun, J., Sinclair, S., & Cogburn, C. (2009). Cultural stereotypes and the self: A closer examination of implicit self-stereotyping. *Basic & Applied Social Psychology, 31*(2), 117–127. doi:10.1080/01973530902880340.

Maddox, K. B. (2004). Perspectives on racial phenotypicality bias. *Personality & Social Psychology Review, 8*(4), 383–401. doi: 10.1207/s15327957pspr0804_4.

Marx, D. M., Stapel, D. A., & Muller, D. (2005). We can do it: The interplay of construal orientation and social comparisons under threat. *Journal of Personality & Social Psychology, 88*(3), 432–446. doi:10.1037/0022-3514.88.3.432.

Massey, D. S. (2008). Origins of economic disparities: The historical role of housing segregation. In J. H. Carr, N. K. Kutty (Ed.), Segregation: The rising cost for America (pp. 39–80). New York, NY: Routledge

Mastro, D. E., & Kopacz, M. A. (2006). Media representations of race, prototypicality, and policy reasoning: An application of self-categorization theory. *Journal of Broadcasting & Electronic Media, 50*(2), 305–322.

Mastro, D.E., Lapinski, M. K., Kopacz, M. K., & Behm-Morawitz, E. (2009). The influence of exposure to depictions of race and crime in TV news on viewer's social judgments. *Journal of Broadcasting & Electronic Media, 53*(4), 615–635. doi:10.1080/08838150903310534.

Mendoza-Denton, R., Downey, G., Davis, A., Purdie, V. J., & Pietrzak, J. (2002). Sensitivity to status-based rejection: Implications for African American students' college experience. *Journal of Personality and Social Psychology, 83*(4), 896–918. doi:10.1037/0022–3514.83.4.896.

Monahan, J. L., Shtrulis, I., & Givens, S. B. (2005). Priming welfare queens and other stereotypes: The transference of media images into interpersonal contexts. *Communication Research Reports, 22*(3), 199–205. doi:10.1080/00036810500207014.

Moore, S., Shiell, A., Hawe, P., & Haines, V. A. (2005). The privileging of communitarian ideas: Citation practices and the translation of social capital into public health research. *American Journal of Public Health, 95*(8), 1330–1337.

Mouw, T. (2002). Are black workers missing the connection? The effect of spatial distance and employee referrals on interfirm racial segregation. *Demography, 39*(3), 507–529.

Myers, H. F. (2009). Ethnicity- and socio-economic status-related stresses in context: An integrative review and conceptual model. *Journal of Behavioral Medicine, 32*(1), 9–19. doi:10.1007/s10865-008-9181-4.

Ong, A. D., Fuller-Rowell, T., & Burrow, A. L. (2009). Racial discrimination and the stress process. *Journal of Personality and Social Psychology, 96*(6), 1259–1271. doi:10.1037/a0015335.

Oyserman, D., Sorensen, N., Reber, R., & Chen, S. X. (2009). Connecting and separating mind sets: Culture as situated cognition. *Journal of Personality and Social Psychology, 97*(2), 217–235. doi:10.1037/a0015850.

Pager, D., & Western, B. (2012). Identifying discrimination at work: The use of field experiements. *Journal of Social Issues, 68*(2), 221–237. doi:10.1111/j.1540-4560.2011.01746.x

Paradies, Y. (2006). A systematic review of empirical research on self-reported racism and health. *International Journal of Epidemiology, 35*, 888–901.

Pascoe, E. A., & Richman, L. S. (2009). Perceived discrimination and health: A meta-analytic review. *Psychological Bulletin, 135*(4), 531–554. doi:10.1037/a0016059.

Pearlin, L. I., Aneshensel, C. S., & LeBlanc, A. J. (1997). The forms and mechanisms of stress proliferation: The case of AIDS caregivers. *Journal of Health and Social Behavior, 38*, 223–236.

Penner, L. A., Eggly, S., Griggs, J. J., Underwood, W., III., Orom, H., & Albrecht, T. L. (2012). Life-threatening disparities: The treatment of black and white cancer patients. *Journal of Social Issues, 68*(2), 328–357. doi:10.1111/j.1540-4560.2011.01751.x

Peters, R. M. (2004). Racism and hypertension among african americans. *Western Journal of Nursing Research, 26*(6), 612–631. doi:10.1177/0193945904265816.

Pettigrew, T. F., & Tropp, L. R. (2000). Does intergroup contact reduce prejudice: Recent meta analytic findings. In S. Oskamp (Ed.), *Reducing prejudice and discrimination* (pp. 93–114). Mahwah, NJ: Lawrence Erlbaum.

Phelan, J. E., & Rudman, L. A. (2010). Reactions to ethnic deviance: The role of backlash in racial stereotype maintenance. *Journal of Personality & Social Psychology, 99*(2), 265–281. doi:10.1037/a0018304.

Pinderhughes, E. E., Nix, R., Foster, E. M., Jones, D., & The Conduct Problems Prevention Research Group. (2001). Parenting in context: Impact of neighborhood poverty, residential stability, public services, social networks, and danger on parental behaviors. *Journal of Marriage and Family, 63*, 941–953. doi:10.1111/j.1741-3737.2001.00941.x.

Poindexter, P. M., Smith, L., & Heider, D. (2003). Race and ethnicity in local television news: Framing, story assignments, and source selections. *Journal of Broadcasting & Electronic Media, 47*, 524–536.

Portes, A. (1998). Social capital: Its origins and applications in modern sociology. *Annual Review of Sociology, 24*(1), 1–24.

Powell, R. (2000). Overcoming cultural racism: The promise of multicultural education. *Multicultural Perspectives, 2*(3), 8–14. doi:10.1207/S15327892MCP0203_03.

Putnam, R. D. (1995). Bowling alone: America's declining social capital. *Journal of Democracy, 6*(1), 65–78.

Quintana, S. M. (2007). Racial and ethnic identity: Developmental perspectives and research. *Journal of Counseling Psychology, 54*(3), 259–270. doi:10.1037/0022-0167.54.3.259.

Richeson, J. A., & Shelton, N. J. (2005). Brief report: Thin slices of racial bias. *Journal of Nonverbal Behavior, 29*(1), 75–86. doi:10.1007/s10919-004-0890-2.

Richeson, J. A., & Shelton, N. J. (2007). Negotiating interracial interactions: Costs, consequences, and possibilities. *Current Directions in Psychological Science, 16*(6), 316–320. doi:10.1111/j.1467-8721.2007.00528.x.

Ryan, A. M., Gee, G. C., & Griffith, D. (2008). The effects of perceived discrimination and diabetes management. *Journal of Health Care for the Poor and Underserved, 19*, 149–163.

Saegert, S., Warren, M. R., & Thompson, J. (2001). *Social capital and poor communities.* New York: Russell Sage.

Sampson, R. J., Morenoff, J. D., & Gannon-Rowley, T. (2002). Assessing "neighborhood effects": Social processes and new directions in research. *Annual Review of Sociology, 28*, 443–478. doi:10.1146/annurev.soc.28.110601.141114.

Schofield, J. W., Hausmann, L. R. M., Ye, F., & Woods, R. L. (2010). Intergroup friendships on campus: Predicting close and casual friendships between white and African American first-year college students. *Group Processes & Intergroup Relations, 13*(5), 585–602. doi:10.1177/1368430210362437.

Seibt, B., & Förster, J. (2004). Stereotype threat and performance: How self-stereotypes influence processing by inducing regulatory foci. *Journal of Personality & Social Psychology, 87*(1), 38–56. doi:10.1037/0022-3514.87.1.38.

Seitles, M. (1998). The perpetuation of residential racial segregation in America: Historical discrimination, modern forms of exclusion, and inclusionary remedies. *Journal of Land Use and Environmental Law, 14*(1), 89–123.

Sellers, R. M., Copeland-Linder, N., Martin, P. P., & Lewis, R. L. (2006). Racial identity matters: The relationship between racial discrimination and psychological functioning in African American adolescents. *Journal of Research on Adolescence, 16*(2), 187–216. doi:10.1111/j.1532-7795.2006.00128.x.

Sellers, R. M., & Shelton, N. J. (2003). The role of racial identity in perceived racial discrimination. *Journal of Personality and Social Psychology, 84*(5), 1079–1092. doi:10.1037/0022-3514.84.5.1079.

Shelton, J. N., Trail, T. E., West, T. V., & Bergsieker, H. B. (2010). From strangers to friends: The interpersonal process model of intimacy in developing interracial friendships. *Journal of Social & Personal Relationships, 27*(1), 71–90. doi:10.1177/0265407509346422.

Shinew, K. J., Glover, T. D., & Parry, D. C. (2004). Leisure spaces as potential sites for interracial interaction: Community gardens in urban areas. *Journal of Leisure Research, 36*(3), 336–355.

Simon, B., & Hamilton, D. L. (1994). Self-stereotyping and social context: The effects of relative in-group size and in-group status. *Journal of Personality and Social Psychology, 66*(4), 699–711. doi:10.1037/0022-3514.66.4.699.

Sinclair, S., Hardin, C. D., & Lowery, B. S. (2006). Self-stereotyping in the context of multiple social identities. *Journal of Personality and Social Psychology, 90*(4), 529–542. doi:10.1037/0022-3514.90.4.529.

Smith, K. P., & Christakis, N. A. (2008). Social networks and health. *Annual Review of Sociology, 34*(1), 405–429. doi:10.1146/annurev.soc.34.040507.134601.

Stearns, E. (2010). Long-term correlates of high school racial composition: Perpetuation theory reexamined. *Teachers College Record, 112*(6), 1654–1678.

Steele, J. R. (1999). Teenage sexuality and media practice: Factoring in the influences of family, friends, and school. *Journal of Sex Research, 36*(4), 331–341. doi:10.1080/00224499909552005.

Stevenson, T. H. (2007). A six-decade study of the portrayal of African Americans in business print media: Trailing, mirroring, or shaping social change? *Journal of Current Issues & Research in Advertising, 29*(1), 1–14.

Stuart, G. (2000). *Segregation in the Boston metropolitan area at the end of the 20th century.* Los Angeles, CA: Civil Rights Project. Retrieved from: http://civilrightsproject.ucla.edu/research/

metro-and-regional-inequalities/metro-boston-equity-initiative-1/segregation-in-the-boston-metropolitan-area-at-the-end-of-the-20th-century.

Sue, D. W., Capodilupo, C. M., Torino, G. C., Bucceri, J. M., Holder, A. M. B., Nadal, K. L., & Esquilin, M. (2007). Racial microaggressions in everyday life: Implications for clinical practice. *American Psychologist, 62*(4), 271–286. doi:10.1037/0003-066X.62.4.271.

Sue, D. W., Nadal, K. L., Capodilupo, C. M., Lin, A. I., Torino, G. C., & Rivera, D. P. (2008). Racial microaggressions against black Americans: Implications for counseling. *Journal of Counseling & Development, 86*(3), 330–338. doi: 10.1002/j.1556-6678.2008.tb00517.x.

Tan, A., Fujioka, Y., & Tan, G. (2000). Television use, stereotypes of African Americans and opinions on affirmative action: An affective model of policy reasoning. *Communication Monographs, 67*(4), 362–371. doi:10.1080/03637750009376517.

Taylor, D. M., Wright, S. C., Moghaddam, F. M., & Lalonde, R. N. (1990). The personal/group discrimination discrepancy: Perceiving my group, but not myself, to be a target for discrimination. *Personality and Social Psychology Bulletin, 16*(2), 254–262. doi:10.1177/0146167290162006.

Taylor, J., & Grundy, C. (1996). Measuring black internalization of white stereotypes about African Americans: The nadanolitization scale. In R. L. Jones (Ed.), *The handbook of tests and measurements for black populations* (pp. 217–226). Hampton, VA: Cobb & Henry.

Taylor, J. (1990). Relationship between internalized racism and marital satisfaction. *Journal of Black Psychology, 16*(2), 45–53. doi:10.1177/00957984900162004.

Taylor, T. R., Kamarck, T. W., & Shiffman, S. (2004). Validation of the Detroit area study discrimination scale in a community sample of older African American adults: The Pittsburgh healthy heart project. *International Journal of Behavioral Medicine, 11*(2), 88–94.

Tull, E. S., Sheu, Y. T., Butler, C., & Cornelious, K. (2005). Relationships between perceived stress, coping behavior and cortisol secretion in women with high and low levels of internalized racism. *Journal of the National Medical Association, 97*(2), 206–212.

Umberson, D., Crosnoe, R., & Reczek, C. (2010). Social relationships and health behavior across the life course. *Annual Review of Sociology, 36*(1), 139–157. doi:10.1146/annurev-soc-070308-120011.

Urquiola, M. (2005). Does school choice lead to sorting? Evidence from tiebout variation. *American Economic Review, 95*(4), 1310–1326.

Utsey, S. O., & Ponterotto, J. G. (1996). Development and validation of the index of race-related stress (IRRS). *Journal of Counseling Psychology, 43*(4), 490–501. doi:10.1037/0022-0167.43.4.490.

Walton, G. M., & Cohen, G. L. (2007). A question of belonging: Race, social fit and achievement. *Journal of Personality and Social Psychology, 92*(1), 82–96. doi:10.1037/0022-3514.92.1.82.

Weisbuch, M., Pauker, K., & Ambady, N. (2009). The subtle transmission of race bias via televised nonverbal behavior. *Science, 326*(5960), 1711–1714. doi:10.1126/science.1178358.

Wells, A. S., Holme, J. J., Revilla, A. T., & Atanda, A. K. (2005). *How desegregation changed us: The effects of racially mixed schools on students and society.* Teacher's College: Columbia University: Harvard University Press.

Williams, D. R., & Mohammed, S. A. (2009). Discrimination and racial disparities in health: Evidence and needed research. *Journal of Behavioral Medicine, 32*, 20–47. doi:10.1007/s10865-008-9185-0.

Williams, D. R., & Williams-Morris, R. (2000). Racism and mental health: The African American experience. *Ethnicity & Health, 5*, 243–268. doi:10.1080/135578500200009356.

Williams, K. D., Forgas, J. P., Hippel, W. V., & Zadro, L. (2005). The social outcast: An overview. In K. D. Williams, J. P. Forgas & W. von Hippel (Eds.), *The social outcast: Ostracism, social exclusion, rejection, and bullying* (pp. 1–16). New York, NY: Psychology Press.

Wout, D. A., Murphy, M. C., & Steele, C. M. (2010). When your friends matter: The effect of white students' racial friendship networks on meta-perceptions and perceived identity contingencies. *Journal of Experimental Social Psychology, 46*(6), 1035–1041. doi:10.1016/j.jesp.2010.06.003.

Yancey, A. K., Cole, B. L., Brown, R., Williams, J. D., Hillier, A., Kline, R. S., & McCarthy, W. J. (2009). A cross-sectional prevalence study of ethnically targeted and general audience outdoor obesity-related advertising. *The Milbank Quarterly, 87*(1), 155–184. doi:10.1111/j.1468-0009.2009.00551.x.

Zárate, M. A. (2009). Racism in the 21st century. In T. D. Nelson (Ed.), *Handbook of prejudice, stereotyping, and discrimination* (pp. 387–406). New York, NY: Psychology Press.

ELIZABETH BRONDOLO is a Professor in the Department of Psychology at St. John's University and Director of the Social Stress and Health Research Unit. She received her PhD in Clinical Psychology from Rutgers University in 1989. Her research focuses on the relationship of social stressors, including racism and work stress, on cardiovascular and mental health.

MADELINE LIBRETTI is a Graduate Student in Psychology at St. John's University and will receive her Master's degree in May 2012. She is a member of the Social Stress and Health Research Unit.

LUIS RIVERA is an Assistant Professor in the Department of Psychology and the Principal Investigator of the Rutgers Implicit Social Cognition (RISC) lab at Rutgers, The State University of New Jersey, Newark. He earned his PhD in Social Psychology at the University of Massachusetts, Amherst, in 2006. His research focuses on the social cognitive processes that underlie the expression of stereotyping and prejudice and how such processes affect stigmatized individuals' self-concept, health, and performance.

KATRINA M. WALSEMANN is an Assistant Professor in the Department of Health Promotion, Education, & Behavior at The University of South Carolina. Her research focuses on understanding how social inequalities and various contexts (e.g., schools and communities) can influence health and racial health disparities during key developmental transitions and across the life course.

Journal of Social Issues, Vol. 68, No. 2, 2012, pp. 385–398

Intergroup Disparities and Implicit Bias:
A Commentary

Emily L. Fisher* and Eugene Borgida

University of Minnesota

Despite changing societal norms that are less tolerant of overt discrimination, demonstrable disparities between racial and gender groups remain. The contributors to this impressive special issue document and offer explanations for these disparities in employment and professional contexts, and with regard to disparate outcomes associated with the legal system, and in medical and health care contexts. In our commentary, we examine these aggregate-level disparities and the individual-level explanatory accounts proposed for their existence. The evidence that these papers present is often enough to rule out alternative explanatory accounts, and implicit bias remains a viable account for disparities that, to varying degrees, fit with the available data and the claim that implicit biases are contributing to an understanding of ongoing real-world disparities. As such, we believe that implicit bias research will continue to play a crucial role in understanding and hopefully reducing these aggregate-level disparities in employment, legal, and health care domains.

Despite changing societal norms that are less tolerant of overt discrimination, disparities between racial and gender groups remain. The authors in this special issue document these disparities and explain how and why they have been perpetuated. Contemporary discrimination persists in a range of domains that have very real and serious consequences for members of disadvantaged groups; the focus on employment, legal, and health care disparities provides some exemplars of an insidious problem. In our commentary, we examine these aggregate-level disparities and the explanatory accounts for their existence proposed by the distinguished set of contributors to this special issue. We ask: which accounts have been conclusively dismissed, and which remain viable contenders for the cause of group-based disparities? We pursue this discussion in the context of the three

---

*Correspondence regarding this article should be addressed to Emily L. Fisher, Department of Psychology, Hobart & William Smith Colleges, Geneva, NY 14456; e-mail: fisher@hws.edu.

domains that characterize the papers included in the special issue: disparities in employment and professional contexts, disparate outcomes associated with the legal system, and medical and health care disparities.

Disparities in Professional and Employment Contexts

Cikara, Rudman, and Fiske (2012) examine gender differences in academics' publication rates in the *Journal of Personality and Social Psychology* (*JPSP*). They suggest that men publish in *JPSP* for a longer portion of their careers and do so more frequently, and the investigators seek to determine what factors could account for this gap. A variety of factors are examined, including gender bias, differences in research quality, effort or persistence, family demands, and institutional status of the author's PhD-granting institution as well as current place of employment. However, the data they collect do not support most of these explanatory accounts. When there are gender differences in these variables, the benefit(s) often went to the man. For instance, when examining authors' persistence, Cikara et al. note that negotiating with editors led to more publications for men, but there was no such effect for women. Similarly, marriage and family demands were actually associated with more *JPSP* articles for men, but had no effect for women. The women in this sample had received their PhDs from (on average) more prestigious institutions than the men, so this variable cannot account for the publication gap. After each of the accounts are examined and dismissed, the one remaining explanatory account is a subtle gender bias within the field. Cikara et al. are careful to note that they do not have the kind of direct evidence for this bias needed to establish this account for the disparity, but when other potential accounts are dismissed, it is hard to avoid attributing this gap to anything else.

The other two groups of contributors to the employment contexts section of this special issue concern themselves with employment disparities that affect a wider range of career types: they focus on racial disparities in hiring job applicants. Pager and Western (2012) provide detailed documentation of the existence of such disparities. The authors present results of two field studies which used a technique called "matched pair testing" in which pairs of testers with different racial status but equivalent qualifications apply for the same actual job openings. With such experimental controls to rule out any confounding factors that could affect employment attainment, they were able to demonstrate that employers appear to use different evaluation standards for White and minority applicants. Case studies of some of their tester pairs indicate that employers are not categorically denying opportunities to minorities; rather, they simply seem to allow a bit more flexibility in their evaluation of White applicants and maintain stricter standards in the evaluation of minority applicants. These data clearly establish that discrimination (in the form of fewer interviews and job offers for minorities compared to equally qualified White candidates) occurs at the aggregate level, and imply that racial bias must be an explanatory factor to be taken seriously. However, this type of data does not allow one to draw conclusions about any particular employer's reasons for discriminating, since "even a non-discriminatory employer, when forced to choose between two equally qualified candidates, will choose the white applicant in half of all cases" (Pager & Western, 2012, p. 233). Once again, it is impossible to rule out implicit bias as an account for a demonstrable disparity, but the data do not yet allow us to rule it in with causal certainty.

Bendick and Nunes (2012) concur with Pager and Western that hiring bias exists, and also espouse the power of matched pair testing for documenting these disparities without the need to generalize from laboratory results. They review the psychological literature supporting two potential accounts for this disparity. First, stereotypes about a racial outgroup (whether explicit or implicit) can automatically affect impression formation, memory, and other processes that influence judgments of people. Second, when an applicant is a member of the employer's own racial group, ingroup preferences can bias judgments in favor of the applicant. Bendick and Nunes note that the hiring process can be especially vulnerable to these biases because of the characteristics of the situation: there is limited individuating information available about a job applicant, decisions are often made under time pressure, and (compared to other employment decisions such as promotions) there is less of a chance to reexamine a decision and correct for errors. Because race and gender hiring and pay disparities exist even when controlling for a myriad of factors that could influence employers' decisions, automatic stereotyping and ingroup favoratism cannot be ruled out as accounts for such disparities. Bendick and Nunes praise and advocate for the matched pair testing technique insofar as it provides powerful evidence that the disparity needs to be addressed. But what this methodology ultimately cannot overcome is the need to infer what is happening inside employers' minds: it cannot inform us of the psychological processes underlying the hiring bias.

In sum, when evaluating the conclusions that all of these authors reach, one common theme clearly emerges. Implicit bias cannot be definitively ruled out as a cause of these group-based disparities. When researchers examine other accounts for the disparities discussed throughout this special issue, they can provide evidence demonstrating that each of these explanations cannot scientifically account for the gaps. However, it is almost a truism in science that we can disprove hypotheses, but we can never really prove them. Thus, as good scientists, none of the contributors to this issue leap to conclusions from their data to claim that implicit bias must be the cause of the disparity. Many strongly suspect that it is, but are impressively circumspect about the extent to which their data allow them to definitively rule it in for all situations. Ruling out *and* ruling in explanations can both help us to tighten and strengthen the causal reasoning about the role of implicit bias in these disparities.

Disparities in the Legal Context

A second set of disparities examined in this special issue involves the legal system, and the experience of racial groups in various legal contexts. For example, Sadler, Correll, Park, and Judd (2012) point out that minorities are incarcerated and shot at by police at rates disproportionate to their numbers in the general population. It may be that minorities simply commit a disproportionate number of crimes, and Sadler et al. admit that evidence regarding the veracity of this claim is mixed. However, it may also be that police officers' behavior is affected by the stereotype that associates minorities with criminal activity. To test this hypothesis, they review recent theoretical developments that rely on the "shooter bias" paradigm (Correll, Park, Judd, & Wittenbrink, 2002; Correll et al., 2007) and present three new studies that extend this methodology. The extant literature demonstrates that police tend to associate Blacks with weapons, based on their reaction times and accuracy on the shooter bias task. Sadler et al. (2012) teach us that this "shooter bias" extends to Latino targets as well, and that police officers' explicit endorsement of stereotypes about racial tendencies to commit crimes relates to the officers' performance on the shooter bias task. These new data reinforce the idea that police officers may have an automatic association with violence for some racial minorities, so we cannot rule out this bias as an account for the disparities in the tendency to suspect members of certain races that go beyond actual base rates of criminality. However, as Sadler et al. point out, their data cannot empirically establish the reasons for this association. Perhaps the association could be a reflection of the officer's experiences on the job, or it could be factoring into self-fulfilling prophecies during officers' interactions with minorities (i.e., officers expect a minority suspect to be more violent and therefore unintentionally treat the suspect in a way that provokes him or her to then react more violently). Thus, more research is needed before we claim that the "shooter bias" is due to police officers' prejudice, although this account cannot be dismissed.

Disparities in Health Care Contexts

In this section of the special issue on health care contexts, Eggly, Griggs, Orom, Penner, and Underwood (2012) document several alarming racial disparities in medical treatments: Black patients receive less information from their oncology doctors than White patients do, Black breast cancer patients are less likely to receive the proper doses for chemotherapy and other drug regimens, and Black prostate cancer patients are less likely to undergo surgery or other definitive treatments for their cancer. Each of these disparities contributes to differential survival and mortality rates for Black and White patients with cancer. Eggly et al. examine several potential explanations for these disparities. At the systemic level, racial disparities could be due to broader gaps in socioeconomic status and access to public health services that correlate with race. If Blacks are less likely to be insured, and tend to go to poorer quality hospitals, then one would expect poorer outcomes. Disparities could also be due to patient factors: Black patients might be less likely to trust their doctors and thus be more likely to be medically noncompliant. Finally, there could be provider-level factors at play. The physicians themselves could fall prey to subtle prejudices and stereotypes that lead them to treat patients differently based on race. However, evidence discounts the first of these accounts. When Eggly et al. examine the issue at the systemic level, they find that disparities cannot just be due to socioeconomic differences because race-based disparities persist even when controlling for such factors. For instance, even when Blacks and Whites are on the same insurance plan, their health outcomes are not equal. Although there is evidence that patients' trust of their doctors and perceptions of discrimination do predict the degree to which they adhere to treatment plans and seek preventive care, Eggly et al. caution against blaming the victim in this case. After all, Black patients' attitudes may very well reflect an understandable reaction to the institutional and everyday racism that they face in society. So even if patient attitudes are part of the explanation for health disparities, they cannot be the ultimate cause. This leaves us with physicians' attitudes as an account for health disparities, and evidence does suggest that physician bias may well play a role. Several recent studies (Green et al., 2007; Penner et al., 2010) suggest that physicians do hold implicit biases that affect their treatment recommendations and that patients respond negatively to physicians who can be classified as aversive racists (i.e., they have negative implicit attitudes despite explicit attitudes that are egalitarian). Eggly et al. also highlight differences in doctor–patient interactions. For Blacks, these interactions are much more likely to be interracial interactions than they are for Whites, and research in medical settings (Penner, Albrecht, Orom, Coleman, & Underwood, 2009) suggests that such interactions are shorter and less positive. In sum, Eggly et al. do not rule out physician bias (especially as it leads to doctor–patient communication problems as an account for racial disparities in cancer treatments).

Another disparity in the health context is highlighted in this issue: racial disparities in social capital and well being. For example, Brondolo, Libretti, Riviera, and Walsemann (2012) review findings at different levels of analysis which suggest that racism adversely affects the development and durability of cross-race peer relationships (a key component, they argue, of social capital). In particular, Brondolo et al. discuss the ways in which racism could be a psychological stressor that constrains and limits the social capital of minorities, which in turn makes them more vulnerable to disease (as well as to other disparate economic and social outcomes) relative to members of groups that do not face racism regularly. Although they maintain that many other factors contribute to social and physical well being, they review data that support a connection between racism indicators of social capital, and cardiac health. For instance, there is a relationship between experiencing racism and risk factors for cardiac disease such as depression and smoking. Brondolo et al. are not yet ready to claim that racism is an indisputable factor in cardiac health (i.e., racism may mediate the direct effects of racism on health outcomes), but they do suggest that it is an important area for further research. Implicit bias as an explanatory account for such health care disparities, or as an account for disparities in the employment context, has generated considerable scientific scrutiny. Some of these issues and concerns, discussed briefly in the next section, focus on the use of the Implicit Association Test (IAT) as a measure of implicit bias.

Implicit Bias and Intergroup Disparities

Despite (or perhaps because of) the novel and important claims that implicit bias research can make, the study of implicit bias has attracted its fair share of controversy, especially with regard to measures of implicit bias. As this special issue demonstrates, implicit bias is a potential factor in many important contexts, and its effects have been examined from a variety of methodologies and perspectives. Nevertheless, critics sometimes conflate certain measures and methods (most notably, the Implicit Association Test or IAT; Greenwald, McGhee, & Schwartz, 1998) with the scientific study of implicit bias, more generally. We briefly turn our focus to two recent examples that highlight this controversy and point in the direction that research needs to go in order to most effectively understand implicit bias in non-laboratory contexts. Both are cases in which psychological journals have published commentaries from critics of the IAT and implicit bias research along with responses from proponents of such research. These exchanges have highlighted the concerns that implicit bias research raises as well as attempts to address such concerns. Studying this debate can illuminate some relevant concerns for this issue's theme of the realities of contemporary discrimination and reveals the degree to which social scientists have reached consensus regarding implicit bias as a scientific account for discriminatory actions.

Major Criticisms of Implicit Bias Research

In a recent issue of *Research in Organizational Behavior*, Tetlock and Mitchell's (2009) latest critique of the IAT and implicit bias research (see also Arkes & Tetlock, 2004; Mitchell & Tetlock, 2006; Tetlock & Arkes, 2004; Tetlock, Mitchell, & Murray 2008) focuses on three broad criticisms of such research programs. First, they question the construct validity of the IAT and propose that other factors, such as familiarity with the stimuli, anxiety over the test, sympathy for disadvantaged groups, or cognitive dexterity, may actually be what the IAT is measuring (rather than levels of prejudice, per se). They also suggest that the IAT's test-retest reliability and its varying correlations with explicit measures of attitudes indicate a high degree of error variance among individuals' scores.

Another point of contention for Tetlock and Mitchell (2009) is the psychometric issue of whether a person with a given IAT score will be more or less likely to discriminate. This criticism is based on arguments such as Blanton and Jaccard's (2006) discussion of "arbitrary metrics": it is unknown, they argue, how a given reaction time will map out onto observable behavior. They also propose that the size of the IAT's correlations with behavioral measures will lead to incredibly high rates of false positives (i.e., a nonprejudiced person being accused of prejudice based on "failing" the IAT).

Finally, they take on the question of external validity, and argue that implicit bias research will not generalize to real workplaces given the differences between such situations and the typical psychology laboratory. This point of view is shared by other IAT skeptics; for instance, Landy's (2008) target article in *Industrial and Organizational Psychology: Perspectives on Science and Practice* focuses on the application of laboratory-based stereotyping research to real-life employment decision making, and concludes that it is often inappropriate to make inferential leaps between these contexts. He outlines numerous differences between the typical lab study and an employment setting, mainly focused around the lack or presence of individuating information, and the degree of accountability (Lerner & Tetlock, 1999). Because individuating information has been shown, theoretically and empirically, to decrease the tendency to rely on stereotypes (e.g., Fiske & Neuberg, 1990; Kunda & Sinclair, 1999), and people in the real world tend to have individuating information about their subordinates, Landy (2008) argues (but does not establish empirically) that stereotyping will have only a small or insignificant effect on real-world decision making in complex organizations.

Specific Attempts to Address These Criticisms

Such criticisms have not gone unanswered (e.g., Borgida, Deason, Kim, & Fiske, 2008; Jost et al., 2009; Kang, 2012). Some of this debate has actually stimulated scientific work to clarify and improve the status of the IAT (Greenwald, Poehlman, Uhlmann, & Banaji, 2009; Nosek, Greenwald & Banaji, 2005, 2007). Moreover, many psychologists accept the basic claims of implicit bias or implicit prejudice and are concerned about their implications for society. For instance, Jost et al. (2009) paint a picture that puts Tetlock and Mitchell (2009) in the role of the global warming skeptics of the implicit bias world—a minority railing against sound scientific consensus. Jost et al. (2009) make the case that the IAT is just one methodology to emerge from decades' worth of empirical evidence and theoretical development in social and cognitive psychology; one that has evolved in an evidence-based way. Questioning the explanatory and predictive power of implicit racial attitudes, they argue, would be tantamount to dismissing much of modern psychology: much established knowledge about social cognition would need to be similarly disregarded on the basis of Tetlock and Mitchell's (2009) stance. Moreover, even in the applied setting of the courtroom, scientific testimony about implicit bias and stereotyping is routinely accepted (Borgida et al., 2008).

Several commentaries provide support for the IAT's validity and reliability in a variety of contexts. Rudman (2008; see also Greenwald, Poehlman, Uhlmann, & Banaji, 2009; Nosek, Greenwald, & Banaji, 2007) provides an overview of the IAT's validity as demonstrated by a wealth of research. Although early versions of the IAT were somewhat more influenced by constructs unrelated to bias such as cognitive skill, its scoring procedure has been reevaluated and updated to make it more robust to extraneous variance and more validly associated with implicit emotional conditioning (Nosek et al., 2007). The IAT's predictive validity has also been demonstrated in a wide range of contexts with many real-world behaviors, such as doctors' treatment recommendations for patients (Eggly et al., 2012; Green et al., 2007), shooter biases (Glaser & Knowles, 2008; Sadler et al., 2012), evaluations of racial minority targets (Amodio & Devine, 2006; Rudman & Lee, 2002), and actual hiring decisions (Rooth, 2010). In contrast to Landy's (2008) critique that the IAT only predicts micro-level behaviors in laboratory settings, work on the IAT's validity has expanded to include the prediction of more macro-behaviors in real-world samples (Greenwald, 2008; Jost et al., 2009). Other researchers have worked to establish the IAT's construct validity through neurological and psychophysiological correlates. For instance, IAT scores are associated with amygdala activation when exposed to other-race photos (Phelps et al., 2000) and with physiological stress markers during interracial encounters (Mendes, Gray, Mendoza-Denton, Major, & Epel, 2007).

Despite criticisms that the IAT is not relevant outside of the laboratory (Landy, 2008) many studies that use the IAT or other measures of implicit bias are conducted in such applied settings, providing corroboration for the implicit bias account using real-world behaviors and a variety of samples. For instance, Jost et al. (2009; see also Greenwald, 2008) highlight 10 recent studies that administered IATs to diverse samples of professionals, from doctors and nurses to police officers and employment recruiters. In each of these cases, IAT scores predicted a potentially discriminatory behavioral outcome. For example, Rooth (2010) asked employment recruiters to complete an IAT. An audit study sending resumes to these same recruiters (in response to actual job openings in a Swedish city) revealed an association between implicit bias and a preference to call back applicants with a Swedish surname over a Turkish surname.

Regardless of any debate over IAT validity, the broader point that is often lost amidst the methodological and ideological cacophony is that considerable implicit bias research goes beyond the IAT and uses methods that have been regarded with less criticism. The IAT, after all, is only one of several families of implicit bias measures that have been adapted from social cognition research more broadly; others include affective priming or linguistic analysis (Fazio & Olson, 2003). Research using these types of techniques also finds that implicit bias predicts a variety of behavioral outcomes in intergroup domains. The "shooter bias" paradigm (Correll et al., 2002; Sadler et al., 2012) offers a method that relies on reactions to ambiguously threatening targets and demonstrates the extent to which people's judgments are in line with racial stereotypes. Other research paradigms move discrimination research entirely outside of the laboratory and into the field. As several of the special issue authors discuss, audit studies are a prime example of this research (Bendick & Nunes, 2012; Pager & Westen, 2012; see also Leslie, King, Bradley, & Hebl, 2008; Pager, 2003; Pager & Quillian, 2005). Researchers can send resumes or confederates to apply for open positions. This strategy allows for the applicants to have equivalent qualifications for the job, yet vary on group membership. When the applicant with one group membership receives more interviews or job offers than the applicant with another group membership, managers' bias against that group is more likely to be the only explanation for the discrepancy. Similarly, work outcome studies use employers' data on salaries, promotions, or other outcomes, and perform multivariate analyses to control for legitimate causes of variance (Leslie et al., 2008). When disparities between groups remain despite such controls, the results are regarded as evidence of discrimination or bias in employment decisions and enhance our ability to rule in or rule out implicit bias as a causal account for the disparities in question.

Another way to address criticisms of IAT and implicit bias research is by challenging the critics' assumptions about the context of discrimination. For instance, Landy (2008) believes that such research is overblown because stereotyping effects often diminish in the presence of individuating information about a person in complex work contexts. Thus, in a real-life employment situation, such individuating information is likely to take precedence over categorical stereotypes. However, this perspective ignores the many obstacles to using such individuating information in the real world. As Bendick & Nunes (2012) demonstrate, hiring decisions are frequently made in an environment in which very little individuating information is available: a résumé or brief interview may not provide much information about a job candidate. Moreover, if that applicant's group membership activates any stereotypes for the hiring decision maker, those stereotypes are likely to affect the very manner in which that person interprets and evaluates any individuating information about the applicant that is available. Thus, contrary to skeptics' claims, this position suggests that stereotypes can be *particularly* powerful in such hiring decisions.

Critics often claim that the IAT is best at predicting small effects or micro-behaviors in lab settings, and less useful for predicting behaviors that would be typically considered discrimination (Landy, 2008; Mitchell & Tetlock, 2006). This outdated belief has been addressed and qualified by recent evidence (Greenwald, 2008; Nosek, Greenwald, & Banaji, 2007). But the broader point is that, even if this claim were true, we would argue that discrimination in micro-behaviors (in lab and/or non-lab contexts) should not be dismissed so casually. When aggregated over time, a career's worth of micro-actions can add up to much larger effects on a person's employment status (Reskin, 2002). Managers may want to be egalitarian and fair in their decision making, but often the conditions under which they are working involve time pressures and distractions. These are exactly the conditions that would impair an explicit commitment to nonprejudice and increase the likelihood that implicit biases and stereotypes would be influential (Chugh, 2004). Decades of psychological research suggests that interviewers can negatively influence the person being evaluated without being aware of doing so, i.e., they create a self-fulfilling prophecy (e.g., Word, Zanna, & Cooper, 1974). This process allows a manager to believe in his or her objectivity when evaluating candidates yet still make a decision that was influenced by implicit bias. Although we agree that the IAT can predict more than these spontaneous, automatic behaviors, we believe their power ought not to be dismissed so quickly.

Links between Implicit Bias and Behavior

Two other important common themes emerge from the set of articles in this special issue. One such theme is that the contributors to this issue routinely draw connections between the constructs that they study and real-world behaviors. Some have noted the trend in social psychology to focus more on self-report or reaction time measures when collecting data (Baumeister, Vohs, & Funder, 2007). As various papers in this special issue suggest, such data are valuable on their own, but they can be richer and more informative when used in conjunction with data on actual behavioral outcomes. A survey of the empirical work in this special issue reveals research on a range of behaviors from scheduling a job interview to prescribing a medical treatment to reacting to a criminal suspect. Such a strong effort to use a variety of measures to represent the complex forces at work in social situations where discrimination may occur is a significant development. Moreover, the results from behavioral studies complement those using more strictly laboratory-based research paradigms and bolster various claims about the relationship between stereotyping, prejudice, and discrimination. From a scientific standpoint, such a multimethod approach is encouraging because it increases our level of certainty about the connections between a mental process such as implicit bias and a behavioral outcome such as disparate treatment of a minority group member (e.g., Leslie et al., 2008). For psychology in general, such research responds to the call for more behavioral research to enrich the field (Baumeister et al., 2007).

Bridging the Divide between Individual and Aggregate Levels of Analysis

The other important common theme in this collection of articles is that they examine individual and aggregate-level accounts for the disparities in question.

Both levels of analysis are important to consider, as is the *relationship* between the aggregate and individual levels of analysis. As we discussed earlier, the debate over implicit bias often hinges on whether the aggregate-level research establishes prejudice as a causal force at the individual level of analysis (Tetlock & Mitchell, 2009). As the papers included in this special issue highlight, the connection between individual-level accounts and aggregate-level disparities in different social domains is complicated and often likely to be established indirectly and inferentially than by more direct empirical evidence. Kang (2012), for example, in thinking about these issues in a legal context, develops four "quadrants" that can be derived by crossing an axis of *specificity* (i.e., scientific and nonscientific facts can be specific or general), and an axis that involves a *temporal perspective* (i.e., an ex ante or future-oriented actions, or a ex post time orientation that emphasizes actions that already have taken place).

Kang's approach would suggest that there are two ways to account for discriminatory actions that allegedly have taken place: for example, to use the IAT as a "prejudice polygraph" to address these specific claims (an approach that even the developers of the IAT have not advocated) or to rely upon general scientific facts, presented in the form of a social framework analysis (Monahan, Walker, & Mitchell, 2008) to address specific discrimination claims (see Fiske & Borgida, 2008). When it comes to accounting for ex ante events, Kang similarly argues that science can be deployed in two different ways: to use, for example, the IAT as a selection tool to screen out potentially biased employees before discriminatory actions occur, or to use a foundational framework of consensus scientific facts to assess whether a proposed public policy should be adopted. More generally, Kang's analysis suggests that there are clearly different ways to think about the connection between aggregate-level disparities and the individual or psychological level of analysis. It is crucial to distinguish between the availability and applicability of specific versus general scientific facts, and whether such facts are being appropriately used to understand actions that have taken place or might take place in the future. In other words, Kang's "quadrants" approach is a more nuanced approach to thinking about the validity of individual-level accounts for aggregate-level disparities. Kang's analysis, along with related work by other legal scholars (e.g., Faigman, 2010; Mitchell, Monahan, & Walker, 2011), thus has tremendous potential to guide future empirical work.

Conclusion

While it is important to acknowledge the ongoing debate over the IAT's validity, we do not believe this controversy is sufficient reason to dismiss implicit bias as an account for real-world racial and gender disparities in various social contexts. The contributors to this special issue consider implicit bias and other accounts for disparities in legal, professional, or employment contexts, or in health care contexts. The evidence that these papers present is often enough to rule out alternative hypotheses, but implicit bias remains as an account for disparities that, to varying degrees, fits with the available data. Moreover, implicit bias research is not synonymous with the IAT: evidence of bias emerges through a variety of research methods, including but not limited to the IAT. Taken together, the research included in this terrific special issue represents a strong body of evidence in support of the claim that implicit biases are contributing to an understanding of ongoing real-world disparities. As such, we believe that implicit bias research will continue to play a crucial role in understanding and hopefully reducing these aggregate-level disparities as they surface in employment, legal, and health care domains.

References

Amodio, D. M., & Devine, P. G. (2006). Stereotyping and evaluation in implicit race bias: Evidence for independent constructs and unique effects on behavior. *Journal of Personality and Social Psychology, 91*, 652–661. doi: 10.1037/0022-3514.91.4.652.

Arkes, H., & Tetlock, P. E. (2004). Attributions of implicit prejudice, or "Would Jesse Jackson 'fail' the Implicit Association Test?" *Psychological Inquiry, 15*, 257–278. doi:10.1207/s15327965pli1504_01.

Baumeister, R. F., Vohs, K. D., & Funder, D. C. (2007). Psychology as the science of self-reports and finger movements: What ever happened to actual behavior? *Perspectives on Psychological Science, 2*, 396–405. doi:10.1111/j.1745-6916.2007.00051.x.

Bendick, M., & Nunes, A. P. (2012). Developing the research basis for controlling bias in hiring. *Journal of Social Issues, 68*(2), 238–262. doi: 10.1111/j.1540-4560.2011.01747.x

Blanton, H., & Jaccard, J. (2006). Arbitrary metrics in psychology. *American Psychologist, 61*, 27–41. doi:10.1037/0003-066X.61.1.27.

Borgida, E., Deason, G., Kim, A., & Fiske, S. T. (2008). Stereotyping research and employment discrimination: Time to see the forest for the trees. *Industrial and Organizational Psychology, 1*, 405–408. doi: 10.1111/j.1754-9434.2008.00074.x.

Brondolo, E., Libretti, M., Riviera, L., & Walsemann, K. (2012). Racism and the development of social capital. *Journal of Social Issues, 68*(2), 358–384. doi: 10.1111/j.1540-4560.2011.01752.x

Chugh, D. (2004). Societal and managerial implications of social cognition: Why milliseconds matter. *Social Justice Research, 17*, 203–222. doi:10.1023/B:SORE.0000027410.26010.40.

Cikara, M., Rudman, L., & Fiske, S. T. (2012). Discrimination by a thousand cuts? Accounting for gender differences in top-ranked publication rates in social psychology. *Journal of Social Issues, 68*(2), 263–285. doi: 10.1111/j.1540-4560.2011.01748.x

Correll, Park, J., Judd, C. M., & Wittenbrink, B. (2002). The police officer's dilemma: Using ethnicity to disambiguate potentially threatening individuals. *Journal of Personality and Social Psychology, 83*, 1314–1329. doi:10.1037/0022-3514.83.6.1314.

Correll, J., Park, B., Judd, C. M., Wittenbrink, B., Sadler, M. S., & Keesee, T. (2007). Across the thin blue line: Police officers and racial bias in the decision to shoot. *Journal of Personality and Social Psychology, 92*, 1006–1023. doi: 10.1037/0022-3514.92.6.1006.

Eggly, S., Griggs, J. J., Orom, H., Penner, L. A., & Underwood, W. (2012). Life-threatening disparities: The treatment of Black and White cancer patients. *Journal of Social Issues, 68*(2), 328–357. doi: 10.1111/j.1540-4560.2011.01751.x

Faigman, D. L. (2010). Evidentiary incommensurability: A preliminary exploration of the problem of reasoning from general scientific data to individualized legal decision-making. *Brooklyn Law School, 75*, 1–22.

Fazio, R. H., & Olson, M. A. (2003). Implicit measures in social cognition research: Their meaning and use. *Annual Review of Psychology, 54*, 297–327. doi: 10.1146/annurev.psych.54.101601.14522.

Fiske, S. T., & Borgida, E. (2008). Providing expert knowledge for the legal system: Social science in an adversary context. *Annual Review of Law and Social Science, 4*, 123–148.

Fiske, S. T., & Neuberg, S. L. (1990). A continuum of impression formation from category-based to individuating processes: Influences of information and motivation on attention and interpretation. In M. Zanna (Ed.), *Advances in experimental social psychology* (Vol. *23*, pp. 1–74). New York: Academic Press.

Glaser, J., & Knowles, E. D. (2008). Implicit motivation to control prejudice. *Journal of Experimental Social Psychology, 44*, 164–172. doi: 10.1016/j.jesp.2007.01.002.

Green, A. R., Carney, D. R., Pallin, D. J., Ngo, L. H., Raymond, K. L., Iezzoni, L.I., & Banaji, M. R. (2007). Implicit bias among physicians and its prediction of thrombolysis decisions for Black and White patients. *Journal of General Internal Medicine, 22*, 1231–1238. doi: 10.1007/s11606-007-0258-5.

Greenwald, A. G. (2008). Landy is correct: Stereotyping can be moderated by individuating the outgroup and by being accountable. *Industrial and Organizational Psychology, 1*, 430–435. doi: 10.1111/j.1754-9434.2008.00082.x.

Greenwald, A. G., McGhee, D. E., & Schwartz, J. L. K. (1998). Measuring individual differences in implicit cognition: The Implicit Association Test. *Journal of Personality and Social Psychology, 74*, 1464–1480. doi: 10.1037/0022-3514.74.6.1464.

Greenwald, A. G., Poehlman, T. A., Uhlmann, E. L., & Banaji, M. R. (2009). Understanding and using the Implicit Association Test III. Meta-analysis of predictive validity. *Journal of Personality and Social Psychology, 97*, 17–41. doi: 10.1037/a0015575.

Jost, J. T., Rudman, L. A., Blair, I. V., Carney, D. R., Dasgupta, N., Glaser, J., & Hardin, C. D. (2009). The existence of implicit bias is beyond reasonable doubt: A refutation of ideological and methodological objections and executive summary of ten studies that no manager should ignore. *Research in Organizational Behavior, 29*, 39–69. doi: 10.1016/j.riob.2009.10.001.

Kang, J. (2012). The missing quadrants of anti-discrimination: Going beyond the "prejudice polygraph". *Journal of Social Issues, 68*(2), 314–327. doi: 10.1111/j.1540-4560.2011.01750.x

Kunda, Z., & Sinclair, L. (1999). Motivated reasoning with stereotypes: Activation, application and inhibition. *Psychological Inquiry, 10*, 12–22. doi: 10.1207/s15327965pli1001_2.

Landy, F. (2008). Stereotypes, bias, and personnel decisions: Strange and stranger. *Industrial and Organizational Psychology, 1*, 379–392. doi: 10.1111/j.1754-9434.2008.00071.x.

Leslie, L. M., King, E. B., Bradley, J. C., & Hebl, M. R. (2008). Triangulation across methodologies: All signs point to persistent stereotyping and discrimination in organizations. *Industrial and Organizational Psychology, 1*, 399–404. doi: 10.1111/j.1754-9434.2008.00073.x.

Mendes, W. B., Gray, H. M., Mendoza-Denton, R., Major, B., & Epel, E. S. (2007). Why egalitarianism might be good for your health: Physiological thriving during stressful intergroup encounters. *Psychological Science, 18*, 991–998. doi: 10.1111/j.1467-9280.2007.02014.x.

Mitchell, G., Monahan, J., & Walker, L. (2011). Beyond context: Social facts as case-specific evidence. *Emory Law Review, 60*, 1109–1155.

Mitchell, G., & Tetlock, P. E. (2006). Antidiscrimination law and the perils of mindreading. *Ohio State Law Journal, 67*, 1180–1192.

Monahan, J., Walker, L., & Mitchell, G. (2008). Contextual evidence of gender discrimination: The ascendance of "social frameworks." *Virginia Law Review, 94*, 1715–1749.

Nosek, B. A., Greenwald, A. G., & Banaji, M. R. (2005). Understanding and using the Implicit Association Test: II. Method variables and construct validity. *Personality and Social Psychology Bulletin, 31*, 166–180. doi: 10.1177/0146167204271418.

Nosek, B. A., Greenwald, A. G., & Banaji, M. R. (2007). The Implicit Association Test at age 7: A methodological and conceptual review. In J. A. Bargh (Ed.), *Social psychology and the unconscious: The automaticity of higher mental processes* (pp. 265–292). New York: Psychology Press.

Pager D. (2003). The mark of a criminal record. *American Journal of Sociology, 108*, 937–975. doi: 10.1086/374403.

Pager, D., & Quillian, L. (2005). Walking the talk: What employers say versus what they do. *American Sociology Review, 70*, 355–380. doi: 10.1177/000312240507000301.

Pager, D., & Western, B. (2012). Identifying discrimination at work: The use of field experiments. *Journal of Social Issues, 68*(2), 221–237. doi: 10.1111/j.1540-4560.2011.01746.x

Penner, L. A., Albrecht, T. L., Orom, H. A., Coleman, D., & Underwood, W. III. (2009). The role of prejudice, stereotyping, and discrimination in Black-White health disparities in the United States. In J. F. Dovidio, M. Hewstone, P. Glick & V. M. Esses (Eds.), *Handbook of prejudice, stereotyping, and discrimination*. London: Sage.

Penner, L., Dovidio, J. F., West, T. V., Gaertner, S., Albrecht, T., Dailey, R. K., & Markova, T. (2010). Aversive racism and medical interactions with black patients: A field study. *Journal of Experimental Social Psychology, 46*, 436–440. doi: 10.1016/j.jesp.2009.11.004.

Phelps, E. A., O'Connor, K. J., Cunningham, W. A., Gatenby, J. C., Funayama, E. S., Gore, J. C., & Banaji, M. R. (2000). Amygdala activation predicts performance on indirect measures of racial bias. *Journal of Cognitive Neuroscience, 12*, 729–738. doi: 10.1162/089892900562552.

Reskin, B. (2002). Rethinking employment discrimination and its remedies. In M. F. Guillen, R. Collins, P. England, & M. Meyer (Eds.), *New directions in economic sociology* (pp. 218–244). New York: Sage.

Rooth, D. O. (2010). Automatic associations and discrimination in hiring: Real world evidence. *Labour Economics, 17*, 523–534. doi:10.1016/j.labeco.2009.04.005.

Rudman, L. A. (2008). The validity of the Implicit Association Test is a scientific certainty. *Industrial and Organizational Psychology, 1*, 426–429. doi:10.1111/j.1754-9434.2008.00081.x.

Rudman, L. A., & Lee, M. R. (2002). Implicit and explicit consequences of exposure to violent and misogynous rap music. *Group Processes and Intergroup Relations, 5*, 133–150. doi:10.1177/1368430202005002541.

Sadler, M. S., Correll, J., Park, B., & Judd, C. M. (2012). The world is not black and white: Racial bias in the decision to shoot in a multiethnic context. *Journal of Social Issues, 68*(2), 286–313. doi: 10.1111/j.1540-4560.2011.01749.x

Tetlock, P. E., & Arkes, H. (2004). The implicit-prejudice exchange: Islands of consensus in a sea of controversy. *Psychological Inquiry, 15*, 311–321.

Lerner, J. S., & Tetlock, P. E. (1999). Accounting for the effects of accountability. *Psychological Bulletin, 125*, 255–275. doi:10.1037/0033-2909.125.2.255.

Tetlock, P. E., Mitchell, G., & Murray, T. L. (2008). The challenge of debiasing personnel decisions: Avoiding both under-and overcorrection. *Industrial and Organizational Psychology: Perspectives on Science and Practice, 1*(4), 439–443. doi:10.1111/j.1754-9434.2008.00084.x.

Tetlock, P. E., & Mitchell, G. (2009). Implicit prejudice and accountability systems: What must organizations do to prevent discrimination? *Research in Organizational Behavior, 29*, 3–38. doi:10.1016/j.riob.2009.10.002.

Word, C. O., Zanna, M. P., & Cooper, J. (1974). The nonverbal mediation of self-fulfilling prophecies in interracial interaction. *Journal of Experimental Social Psychology, 10*, 109–120. doi:10.1016/0022-1031(74)90059-6.

EMILY L. FISHER is now an Assistant Professor of psychology at Hobart and William Smith Colleges. She received her PhD in social psychology from the University of Minnesota, Twin Cities, in 2011, with an interdisciplinary specialty in political psychology. Her research focuses on intergroup relations, with a particular focus on the role of social capital in structuring intergroup attitudes.

EUGENE BORGIDA is a Professor of psychology and law, and Morse-Alumni Distinguished Professor of psychology at the University of Minnesota. He is a fellow of the APS and the APA, and Past President of SPSSI. He has served on the Board of Directors for the Association of Psychological Science (APS) and the Social Science Research Council (SSRC). Borgida's research interests include social cognition, attitudes and persuasion, psychology and law, and political psychology.

Journal of Social Issues, Vol. 68, No. 2, 2012, pp. 399–412

Contemporary Discrimination in the Lab and Field: Benefits and Obstacles of Full-Cycle Social Psychology

Nilanjana Dasgupta[*]
University of Massachusetts

Jane G. Stout
University of Colorado

This article highlights the necessity of applying evidence-based social psychological research to identify the causes and consequences of implicit bias as they occur in the real world. We first outline a number of benefits that emerge from complementing controlled laboratory experiments with field studies chief among them is that the latter bolster external validity and the applicability of laboratory research to real-world settings where social problems are rooted. Second, we briefly (1) highlight where in the process of decision-making discrimination might occur, as demonstrated by field studies (i.e., when do perceivers' implicit attitudes get translated into action) and (2) identify some underlying causes. Finally, we speculate about possible remedies for implicit bias in the real world, some of which have been tested in prior research whereas others are yet to be tested.

The existence of large structural inequalities between social groups in employment, healthcare, housing, education, and treatment in the judicial system have been widely noted and debated in the past few decades (Badgett, 1996; Daniels, 2001; Ellis & Riggle, 1996; Leonhardt, 2002; Portwood, 1995; Raudenbush & Kasim, 1998; Ridgeway, 1997; Rubenstein, 1996; Stohlberg, 2002). The causes of these disparities are, no doubt, manifold depending on the specific area of social life under scrutiny. Nevertheless, one particular causal factor has attracted the attention of social psychologists because it often remains a viable explanation even when other causes have been ruled out: namely, the effect of group-based

---

[*]Correspondence concerning this article should be addressed to Nilanjana Dasgupta, Department of Psychology, University of Massachusetts, Tobin Hall, 135 Hicks Way, Amherst, MA 01003 [e-mail: dasgupta@psych.umass.edu].

399

stereotypes on decision-making such as deciding who to hire or promote in the workplace, what medical treatments to offer patients in clinics and hospitals, who to sell or rent a home to, who is a criminal versus an innocent civilian, and how much punishment is fair in the justice system.

Given the long history of empirical research on stereotyping and prejudice in social psychology, and the scientific evidence that has accumulated as a result, our field is well-placed to apply evidence-based research to identify the causes and consequences of group-based inequalities as they occur in the real world. This type of research that crosses over from lab to field and back to the lab is what Cialdini (1980) called "full-cycle social psychology" whereby everyday observation of events and phenomena is used both at the beginning and end of the research process. When used in the beginning, real-world events help to identify important phenomena and social problems worthy of empirical investigation. When used in the middle or end of the research process, events in the real world check the validity of experimental findings. If there was ever an urgent need for social psychological research to create a "full cycle" between everyday social problems and laboratory research, it is here—in investigating the potential role of subtle stereotypes and prejudice in creating or magnifying structural inequalities.

A contemporary discovery of social psychology that can illuminate seemingly intractable structural inequalities is that people's everyday decisions and actions can be influenced subtly by stereotypes, preferences, and biases, without their awareness or control, even when they exhibit no overt bigotry. In other words, even people who report egalitarian attitudes toward disadvantaged out-groups may subtly (or implicitly) favor some groups and be biased against others in ways that are consistent with societal stereotypes (Dasgupta, 2004, 2008; Dovidio, Kawakami, Smoak, & Gaertner, 2008; Greenwald & Banaji, 1995; Nosek et al., 2007). Sometimes these implicit biases get expressed without the individual's full awareness; at other times they are expressed in situations involving time pressure, distraction, and cognitive load, where it is difficult to control and edit one's judgments and decisions in real time, even if one is aware of potential bias. Importantly, implicit biases in one's thoughts are known to affect one's decisions, actions, and judgments, producing discriminatory effects whether or not they were consciously intended by the decision-maker (Dasgupta, 2004, 2008; Greenwald, Poehlman, Uhlmann, & Banaji, 2009).

Although meticulous lab experiments initially led to important discoveries about implicit bias in attitudes and actions, the Achilles heel of this work was concern about external validity. That is, how do we know that evidence obtained from lab research about implicit bias is actually responsible for structural inequalities observed in employment, healthcare, housing, and law enforcement in the real world? This is where field research provides a beautiful complement to laboratory experiments.

Benefits of Field Studies Illustrated in This Special Issue

Field Studies Conducted at the Actual Site of a Social Problem Directly Identify the Causes

Quasi-experimental studies conducted in field settings can be more compelling than lab studies if they illuminate social inequality at the actual site of the problem (e.g., when a study is conducted in the workplace or in a healthcare facility rather than in a lab) and if study participants represent the population to which the findings need to be generalized (e.g., when study participants are human resource professionals or healthcare providers rather than college students). Three articles in this issue (Bendick & Nunes, 2012; Pager & Western, 2012; Penner et al., 2012) fit nicely in this category. The first two articles describe field studies investigating whether hiring decisions for entry level retail positions as well as professional and managerial positions are influenced by implicit bias using matched-pair testing. This is a technique where equally qualified (i.e., "matched") applications are sent to employers in response to job advertisements—the applications are identical on all job-relevant attributes except for the person's group membership (race, gender, age, sexuality, disability, etc., depending on the specific type of stereotype under investigation). Of course, these applications don't belong to real applicants but are created by researchers in order to investigate whether equally qualified applicants will be equally likely to receive callbacks and be hired or whether callbacks and hiring rates will vary based on group membership. The beauty of this research design is threefold: (1) any difference in hiring rates can be confidently attributed to bias against the target group rather than any other quality of the job applicant; (2) decision-makers in these studies are real human resource professionals who make these types of decisions in their professional life; and (3) the study was conducted in a real workplace where participants thought they were making hiring decisions about actual applicants rather than simulating such decisions. Results of these studies consistently show that job applicants from historically excluded groups had a 20–40% chance of not being hired or receiving callbacks every time they applied for a job.

If this type of study had been conducted in a lab setting, the hiring situation would have been a simulation and most likely participants would have been convenience samples of undergraduate students rather than human resource professionals (Dasgupta & Hunsinger, 2008; Henry, 2008; McGuire, 1967; Sears, 1986). Although the results of such lab studies often converge with matched-pair field studies and other field studies (e.g., Bertrand & Mullainathan, 2004; Correll, Benard, & Paik, 2007; Davison & Burke, 2000; Hebl, Foster, Mannix, & Dovidio, 2002), there are reasons to think that the translation from lab findings to the field may not always be perfect. For example, one might argue that because students are novices whereas human resource professionals are experts who have done this job for many years, the latter may be less prone to implicit bias in hiring than the former (cf. Dasgupta & Hunsinger, 2008). Alternatively, one might argue that because real hiring decisions are consequential whereas experimental simulations are not, decision-makers may be more careful and thorough in their decision-making in the former situation than the latter. For these reasons, it is particularly persuasive to demonstrate that implicit bias occurs in real life and is responsible for structural inequality rather than showing bias in lab situations that are several times removed from real-world settings.

Moving to a very different domain, one often finds race differences in health-care delivery but in order to understand where and why that happens, field studies conducted in real healthcare facilities are needed with real doctors as participants. Penner and colleagues (2012) provide an excellent review of many such field studies. Their review demonstrates that race bias is evident in several stages of the healthcare delivery pipeline. First, studies that analyzed conversations between real doctors and patients found that the amount of information provided by doctors to their patients especially about treatment side effects was significantly less when patients were Black rather than White. In mirror image fashion, the amount of information sought by patients and their understanding of the information was significantly lower when they were Black than White.

Other studies examined doctors' treatment decisions in the case of patients diagnosed with low-grade prostate cancer. One relatively common treatment recommendation in this case is to engage in "watchful waiting" or "active surveillance" without any definitive treatment. Interestingly, even after controlling for factors such as patient age, comorbidities, stage of the cancer, and life expectancy, Black men were significantly more likely to undergo watchful waiting than were White men. Moreover, when comparing medical care among Black and White men who were receiving watchful waiting, Black men tended to receive less medical monitoring and had longer median times from diagnosis to receipt of a medical monitoring visit or procedure than did White men.

Yet other studies compared the quality of chemotherapy treatment given to Black versus White breast cancer patients and found that even after controlling for all possible confounding factors, Black women were more likely to be under-dosed or receive nonstandard chemotherapy compared to the treatments given to equivalent White women. This discrepancy has grave implications for mortality rates because underdosed chemotherapy treatment results in higher incidence of cancer recurrence. The import of these health disparity studies is that participants in these studies were real doctors making decisions about real patients in real hospitals and clinics (not simulated medical treatments). Equally importantly, this form of discrimination cannot be ethically investigated in lab experiments thus field studies offer a rare opportunity.

Recruiting Samples from the Site of a Social Problem Illustrates the Ubiquity of Implicit Bias

It is particularly compelling when research reveals evidence of implicit bias in specific real-world domains using study participants who make important (often life-and-death) decisions in that domain—thus, any evidence of implicit bias in decision-making from these studies can be directly connected to societal-level disparities in that domain. Some of these studies use standard experimental designs to avoid potential confounding variables. When results of these studies converge with other lab studies that use student samples, it provides reassuring evidence that the phenomena we study in the lab do indeed map onto the real world. For example, consider a study by Green et al. (2007) summarized in Penner et al. (2012). This study examined whether physicians' implicit and explicit attitudes about race predicted treatment recommendations they gave to a potential patient who showed symptoms of coronary artery disease. The patients in this case were not real, but fictitious individuals in matched vignettes identical in all respects except for their race (Black or White man). Results showed that on average, physicians were more likely to recommend thrombolysis for the White patient than for the Black patient (even when they believed the Black patient was suffering from coronary artery disease). More importantly, physicians who were more implicitly biased in terms of their racial attitudes were less likely to recommend thrombolysis for Black patients but instead more likely to recommend the same treatment for White patients. These results remained significant even after adjusting for physicians' demographic characteristics, their explicit racial attitudes, and their confidence in thrombolysis effectiveness. The general finding that implicit bias predicts discriminatory behavior has been demonstrated in many lab studies using student samples, but it is particularly powerful to see this type of finding in a hospital setting with physicians as participants. These data clearly reveal how implicit bias can have life-or-death consequences for others.

The idea that implicit bias can have life-or-death consequences has also been illustrated in other lab and field studies on shooter bias (Correll, Park, Judd, & Wittenbrink, 2007a; Correll et al., 2007b; Sadler, Correll, Park, & Judd 2012). Shooter bias is the phenomenon wherein stereotypes linking Black men to criminality operate implicitly in perceivers' mind and bias their rapid decisions to shoot or not shoot target individuals in a simulated law enforcement game. The original findings using convenience samples of undergraduate students found that people were more likely to accidentally "shoot" unarmed Black than White men. This bias was also seen in the degree of hesitation people exhibited (i.e., the amount of time it took them to make a decision). Sadler, Correll, Park, and Judd (2012) and Correll et al (2007b) replicate the same finding using police officers as participants who are experts in law enforcement rather than undergraduates or other civilians who are novices. Although the shooter task is a simulation rather than examining actual records of police shootings, these types of studies show that findings from convenience samples can be replicated using professional police officers.

Studies that Compare Multiple Social Groups Illuminate Similarities and Differences among Groups Targeted by Implicit Bias

One weakness of many lab experiments is that they simplify the independent variables of interest into two or three conditions. Applied to the domain of prejudice research this means that experiments typically compare binary targets (e.g., reactions to Black vs. White individuals); however, these results are often overgeneralized to all minority groups. Of course, lab experiments do not have to be constrained by such a narrow definition of minority versus majority, but because the experimental method encourages simplification of variables into neat factorial designs (e.g., 2 × 2 factorials), comparisons of multiple ethnic minorities within the same experiment are rare. Sadler and colleagues offer just such a study that investigated how varying target groups (Black, Asian, Latino, and White) in the shooter paradigm influenced police officers' simulated shooting behavior as they tried to decide whether the target was armed or unarmed under time pressure.

Sadler et al.'s (2012) results showed interesting undiscovered effects about shooter bias. Recall that past research in this domain has shown that when comparing Black and White targets both civilians and police officers are faster to correctly "shoot" armed Black than White men and were slower to not shoot unarmed Black than White men, indicating a propensity to perceive Black men as perpetrators. Sadler and colleagues' study compared police officers' responses to Black, Latino, Asian, and White targets who were sometimes armed and other times unarmed. Results showed that police officers showed more shooter bias against Blacks and Latinos compared to Whites and Asians. They also showed more shooter bias against Whites than Asians, which fits with the idea that violent criminality is not part of the Asian stereotype in the United States. Third, police officers who overestimated violent crime in their region of the country showed more shooter bias against Latinos (but not African Americans) and less bias against Whites. Finally, contact (probably negative contact) with African Americans predicted more shooter bias against Black men. These findings illustrate that variations in the expectations associated with specific target groups change the likelihood of implicit bias.

Field Studies with External Validity Can Be Applied Directly to Legal Issues

One important benefit of field research is that it moves closer to the actual site of social problems and by doing so it can make a more persuasive case that the data apply directly to a particular area of the law that one is seeking to remedy (e.g., employment discrimination). From the perspective of legal scholars and practitioners, lab experiments raise two concerns. First, because lab experiments are conducted in carefully controlled settings that often involve mental simulations rather than real events they may lack ecological validity. Second, the fact that experiments often use student samples raise concerns about external validity. For these reasons, legal scholars and practitioners who are interested in applying social psychological findings on implicit bias to law and policy may experience a niggling doubt—are these findings really applicable to real-world events? By using participants drawn from the site of the problem (doctors, nurses, human resource decision-makers) and by conducting the study at that very site, field studies nip this doubt in the bud.

Kang's (2012) article in this issue nicely highlights three ways in which evidence about implicit bias from field and lab studies might promote legal change. First, these studies can spotlight critical issues in a legal case by providing general facts relevant to deciding whether or not a law has been broken. For example, evidence that group-based disparities can emerge in healthcare delivery implicitly, without the decision-maker's conscious intention or animus, might provide a social framework or a lens through which the facts of a particular legal case can be analyzed.

Second, field research on implicit bias may prevent instances of bias before they happen. For instance, learning about this type of research in one's own profession might bring the message closer to home; people in a given profession may come to understand how easily stereotypes can bias their own professional judgments despite good intentions. Moreover, personal experience with implicit attitude measures may serve as a consciousness-raising device by allowing individuals to discover their own implicit bias. As an example, imagine the experience of physicians in Green et al.'s 2007 study who learned about their own implicit racial attitudes after taking the Implicit Association Test. Their personal experience as study participants might encourage individual physicians to set up structured remedies to ensure that they treat patients the same way regardless of group membership (e.g., by using structured interviews, anonymous initial screening of patient treatment records, periodic comparison of patients' treatment records, etc.).

Finally, the most ambitious application of implicit bias research in the legal arena is that it provides an opportunity to raise questions about assumptions underlying specific laws having to do with discrimination in light of evidence from the mind sciences, thereby potentially changing the substance of law. For instance, we know from many lab and field studies that implicit biases are malleable—repeated exposure to likeable and competent members of underrepresented groups significantly reduces implicit prejudice and stereotyping of those groups (Dasgupta & Asgari, 2004; Dasgupta & Greenwald, 2001; Dasgupta & Rivera, 2008).

These findings imply that increasing the diversity of otherwise homogeneous environments by recruiting admirable and competent members of underrepresented groups is likely to benefit majority group members in that environment by changing their implicit attitudes and beliefs. This knowledge provides an opportunity to reframe the affirmative action debate—as a program that is not solely directed at benefiting minority group members. Rather, the recruitment of underrepresented individuals as part of affirmative action programs is likely to also benefit the majority group because the recruited individuals become debiasing agents whose presence changes the thoughts and actions of the majority.

In sum, field studies make it possible to observe bias as it occurs in the real world. If we hope to remedy these biases, it is necessary to identify the locations and underlying causes of such biases. In the sections that follow, we highlight some locations and underlying causes that emerge from field studies followed by potential remedies for implicit bias in the real world.

Identifying Multiple Locations in the Social Structure Where Implicit Bias Occurs and Possible Causes

In order to rectify group-based disparities as they occur in the real world, we first need to locate where in a social structure implicit bias occurs and why it occurs. To that end, Penner and colleagues (2012) take the case of race disparities in oncology treatment and identify three reasons why such disparities occur: (1) healthcare providers' attitudes and stereotypes, (2) patients' expectations of how they will be treated, and (3) structural inequality in the healthcare system.

One reason why Black cancer patients might suffer higher mortality rates than their White peers is that physicians' implicit racial attitudes and stereotypes about their patients' race or ethnicity, which might bias their treatment plan. Specifically, research suggests that physicians sometimes implicitly assume that Black patients are less educated than White patients and less likely to adhere to medical treatment plans (Van Ryn & Burke, 2000); these stereotypic assumptions predict their treatment decisions. In addition to stereotypes, other research shows that physicians who hold anti-Black implicit attitudes are less likely to recommend appropriate treatment to Black patients suffering from cardiovascular diseases (Green et al., 2007). However, these physicians' explicit (or conscious) attitudes about race did not predict their treatment decisions.

A second reason for group disparities in healthcare has to do with patients' perceptions of their physicians. Penner and colleagues cite research indicating that Black patients perceive greater racial discrimination in healthcare compared to their White peers and, not surprisingly, feel less trust toward White physicians. Importantly, Black patients' perceptions of past discrimination in the healthcare system are associated with lower adherence to medical treatment recommendations and, in turn, poorer health (e.g., Penner et al., 2010). In contrast, positive expectations about healthcare providers are associated with greater adherence to, and satisfaction with, one's healthcare (Bogart, Bird, Walt, Delahanty, & Figler, 2004). Along the same lines, the more patients trust their providers, the more likely they are to follow prescribed preventative measures (O'Malley, Sheppard, Schwartz, & Mandelblatt, 2004).

Finally, a third reason for race disparities in health suggested by Penner and colleagues has to do with structural disparities in healthcare delivery as a function of social class and the fact that racial minorities are overrepresented in low socioeconomic segments of the American population. Because healthcare is distributed through employment and its quality is contingent on the quality of employment, individuals of low socioeconomic status (SES) suffer from low-quality healthcare. Further, individuals of low SES must rely on hospitals and clinics in their neighborhoods, which likely have low-quality facilities. Thus, race disparities in health may be due to structural factors, perceiver (i.e., physician) factors and also target (i.e., patient) factors.

Possible Remedies

Given the evidence that discrimination occurs in the real world, what actions should be taken to remedy this discrimination? We suggest that both perceivers and targets of discrimination can play an active role in reducing the prevalence of group-based discrimination. For example, both parties might benefit from being made aware of the role of implicit bias in creating group disparities. Greater awareness might make perceivers more mindful of the subtle impact of bias on their judgments and actions and activate corrective processes. At the same time, greater awareness might make targets of discrimination more able to deflect bias by disproving stereotypes when they become aware of it.

Awareness of Implicit Bias Enhances Perceivers' Motivation to Correct

From the perceiver's end (e.g., medical practitioners, law enforcement officers), individuals who hold explicit egalitarian beliefs may benefit from learning that despite their explicit egalitarian attitudes, implicit stereotypes and biases may influence their decisions and behavior in unintended ways. Explicitly low prejudiced individuals are particularly likely to feel compunction at the possibility of their own unintended bias and subsequently motivated to monitor and correct such bias in the future (Monteith, 1993; Monteith & Mark, 2005, 2009). Indeed, Dasgupta and Rivera (2006) found that although many people hold implicit anti-gay bias, among those who were consciously motivated to be egalitarian such biased attitudes do not translate into biased behavior toward a gay person. In contrast, among individuals who were not motivated to be egalitarian, strong antigay implicit attitudes did indeed predict more biased behavior.

A Priori Decision-Making Strategies Reduce Perceivers' Implicit Bias

Once individuals are aware of potential bias and motivated to control it, the next step is to develop concrete strategies to implement. In law enforcement and shooter bias, recent work has found that individuals can improve their accuracy on the Shooter Task by developing implementation intentions to ignore goal-irrelevant stimuli (e.g., race of perpetrator) or by adopting a conscious goal to shoot only when appropriate and to avoid shooting when inappropriate (Mendoza, Gollwitzer, & Amodio, 2010).

At an organizational level, implementing specific strategies for hiring and promotion have been found to reduce implicit bias. For example, research in employment suggests that the use of highly structured interviews can reduce if not eliminate group-based hiring bias (e.g., McCarthy, Van Iddekinge, & Campion, 2010; Sacco, Scheu, Ryan, & Schmitt, 2003). Specifically, hiring bias against pregnant women was alleviated by the use of structured rather than unstructured interviews (Bragger, Kutcher, Morgan, & Firth, 2002). Gender disparity in the composition of orchestras was reduced by the use of "blind auditions" for orchestras whereby most major orchestras now use a screen during auditions to hide the identity of the musician. An audit study showed that blind auditions increased the probability of female musicians advancing into final rounds of auditions and being eventually hired (Goldin & Rouse, 2000). Together, these techniques identify means of achieving greater impartiality in hiring decisions which can be put to good use in other professions.

Finally, when targets of implicit bias become aware of such bias toward themselves or their in-group, sometimes they may be able to use this knowledge as power by playing an active role in deflecting or remedying implicit bias. For example, women who become aware of gender disparities in negotiated salaries and raises (Kray & Thompson, 2005) may become motivated to negotiate salaries and raises for themselves more actively. Similarly, as suggested by Cikara, Rudman, and Fiske (2012), female social psychologists who become aware that gender disparity in the publication rate in the field's leading journal is partially due to the fact that male authors appeal editorial decisions more often than female authors, may choose to use that strategy when appropriate. In the healthcare domain, once Black patients become aware of race disparities in healthcare and the specific reasons responsible for it, they might opt to actively initiate discussions about their medical treatment options with their physicians, which in turn might enhance their health outcomes. This "knowledge as power" approach gives targets of discrimination some agency and control to deflect or remedy implicit bias. Needless to say, this must be accompanied by other remedies that involve the perceiver and larger social structure.

Conclusion

In conclusion, field studies provide direct evidence of implicit bias in action in everyday life and equally importantly, illuminates where and why such bias occurs. We suggest that these field studies when coupled with laboratory experiments provide an excellent example of full-cycle social psychology which is a powerful research tool that identifies important social problems and possible remedies.

References

Badgett, M. V. L. (1996). Employment and sexual orientation: Disclosure and discrimination in the workplace. In A. L. Ellis & E. D. B. Riggle (Eds.), *Sexual identity on the job: Issues and services* (pp. 29–52). New York, NY: Haworth Press.

Bendick, M., Jr., & Nunes, A. P. (2012). Developing the research bias is for controlling bias in hiring. *Journal of Social Issues, 68*(2), 238–262. doi:10.1111/j.1540-4560.2011.01747.x

Bertrand, M., & Mullainathan, S. (2004). Are Emily and Greg more employable than Lakisha and Jamal? A field experiment on labor market discrimination. *The American Economic Review, 94*, 991–1013. doi:10.1257/0002828042002561.

Bogart, L., Bird, S., Walt, L., Delahanty, D., & Figler, J. (2004). Association of stereotypes about physicians to health care satisfaction, help-seeking behavior, and adherence to treatment. *Social Science & Medicine, 58*, 1049–1058. doi:10.1016/S0277-9536(03)00277-6.

Bragger, J. D., Kutcher, E., Morgan, J., & Firth, P. (2002). The effects of structured interview on reducing bias against pregnant job applicants. *Sex Roles, 46*, 215–226. doi:10.1023/A:1019967231059.

Cialdini, R. B. (1980). Full-cycle social psychology. *Applied Social Psychology Annual, 1*, 21–47.

Cikara, M., Rudman, L., & Fiske, S. (2012). Dearth by a thousand cuts? Accounting for gender differences in top-ranked publication rates in social psychology. *Journal of Social Issues, 68*(2), 263–285. doi:10.1111/j.1540-4560.2011.01748.x

Correll, J., Park, B., Judd, C., & Wittenbrink, B. (2007a). The influence of stereotypes on decisions to shoot. *European Journal of Social Psychology, 37*, 1102–1117. doi:10.1002/ejsp.450.

Correll, J., Park, B., Judd, C., Wittenbrink, B., Sadler, M., & Keesee, T. (2007b). Across the thin blue line: Police officers and racial bias in the decision to shoot. *Journal of Personality and Social Psychology, 92*, 1006–1023. doi:10.1037/0022-3514.92.6.1006.

Correll, S. J., Benard, S., & Paik, I. (2007). Getting a job: Is there a motherhood penalty? *American Journal of Sociology, 112*, 1297–1338. doi: 10.1086/511799.

Daniels, L. A. (2001). *State of Black America 2000*. New York: National Urban League.

Dasgupta, N. (2004). Implicit ingroup favoritism, outgroup favoritism, and their behavioral manifestations. *Social Justice Research, 17*, 143–169. doi:10.1023/B:SORE.0000027407.70241.15.

Dasgupta, N. (2008). Color lines in the mind: Unconscious prejudice, discriminatory behavior, and the potential for change. In A. Grant-Thomas & G. Orfield (Eds.), *Twenty-first century color lines: Multiracial change in contemporary America*. Philadelphia, PA: Temple University Press.

Dasgupta, N., & Asgari, S. (2004). Seeing is believing: Exposure to counterstereotypic women leaders and its effect on automatic gender stereotyping. *Journal of Experimental Social Psychology, 40*, 642–658. doi:10.1016/j.jesp.2004.02.003.

Dasgupta, N., & Greenwald, A. G. (2001). On the malleability of automatic attitudes: Combating automatic prejudice with images of admired and disliked individuals. *Journal of Personality and Social Psychology, 81*, 800–814. doi:10.1037/0022-3514.81.5.800.

Dasgupta, N., & Hunsinger, M. (2008). The opposite of a great truth is also true: When do student samples help versus hurt the scientific study of prejudice? *Psychological Inquiry, 19*, 90–98. doi:10.1080/10478400802049860.

Dasgupta, N., & Rivera, L. M. (2006). From automatic anti-gay prejudice to behavior: The moderating role of conscious beliefs about gender and behavioral control. *Journal of Personality and Social Psychology, 91*, 268–280. doi:10.1037/0022-3514.91.2.268.

Dasgupta, N., & Rivera, L. M. (2008). When social context matters: The influence of long-term contact and short-term exposure to admired outgroup members on implicit attitudes and behavioral intentions. *Social Cognition, 26*, 54–66. doi:10.1521/soco.2008.26.1.112.

Davison, H., & Burke, M. (2000). Sex discrimination in simulated employment contexts: A meta-analytic investigation. *Journal of Vocational Behavior, 56*, 225–248. doi: 10.1006/jvbe.1999.1711.

Dovidio, J. F., Kawakami, K., Smoak, N., & Gaertner, S. L. (2008). The nature of contemporary racial prejudice: Insight from implicit and explicit measures of attitudes. In R. E. Petty, R. H. Fazio & P. Briñol (Eds.), *Attitudes: Insights from the new implicit measures* (pp. 165–192). New York, NY: Psychology Press.

Ellis, A. L., & Riggle, E. D. B. (1996). *Sexual identity on the job: Issues and services*. New York, NY: Haworth Press.

Goldin, C., & Rouse, C. (2000). Orchestrating impartiality: The impact of "blind" auditions on female musicians. *The American Economic Review, 90*, 715–741.

Green, A. R., Carney, D. R., Pallin, D. J., Ngo, L. H., Raymond, K. L., Iezzoni, A. I., & Banaji, M. R. (2007). Implicit bias among physicians and its prediction of thrombolysis decisions for black and white patients. *Journal of General Internal Medicine, 22*, 1231–1238. doi:10.1007/s11606-007-0258-5.

Greenwald, A., & Banaji, M. (1995). Implicit social cognition: Attitudes, self-esteem, and stereotypes. *Psychological Review, 102*, 4–27. doi:10.1037/0033-295X.102.1.4.

Greenwald, A., Poehlman, T., Uhlmann, E., & Banaji, M. (2009). Understanding and using the Implicit Association Test: III. Meta-analysis of predictive validity. *Journal of Personality and Social Psychology, 97*, 17–41. doi: 10.1037/a0015575.

Hebl, M. R., Foster, J. B., Mannix, L. M., & Dovidio, J. F. (2002). Formal and interpersonal discrimination: A field study of bias toward homosexual applicants. *Personality and Social Psychology Bulletin, 28*, 815–825. doi:10.1177/0146167202289010.

Henry, P. (2008). College sophomores in the laboratory redux: Influences of a narrow data base on social psychology's view of the nature of prejudice. *Psychological Inquiry, 19*, 49–71. doi:10.1080/10478400802049936.

Kang, J. (2012). The missing quadrants of anti-discrimination: Going beyond the "prejudice polygraph." *Journal of Social Issues, 68*(2), 314–327. doi:10.1111/j.1540-4560.2011.01748.x

Kray, L., & Thompson, L. (2005). Gender stereotypes and negotiation performance: An examination of theory and research. *Research in organizational behavior: An annual series of analytical essays and critical reviews* (Vol. 26, pp. 103–182). US: Elsevier Science/JAI Press.

Leonhardt, D. (2002, May). Wide Racial Disparities Found in Costs of Mortgages. *New York Times*, p. 23.

McCarthy, J., Van Iddekinge, C., & Campion, M. (2010). Are highly structured job interviews resistant to demographic similarity effects? *Personnel Psychology, 63*, 325–359. doi:10.1111/j.1744-6570.2010.01172.x.

McGuire, W. J. (1967). Some impending reorientations in social psychology: Some thoughts provoked by Kenneth Ring. *Journal of Experimental Social Psychology, 3*, 124–139. doi: 10.1016/0022-1031(67)90017-0.

Mendoza, S., Gollwitzer, P., & Amodio, D. (2010). Reducing the expression of implicit stereotypes: Reflexive control through implementation intentions. *Personality and Social Psychology Bulletin, 36*, 512–523. doi:10.1177/0146167210362789.

Monteith, M. (1993). Self-regulation of prejudiced responses: Implications for progress in prejudice-reduction efforts. *Journal of Personality and Social Psychology, 65*, 469–485. doi:10.1037/0022-3514.65.3.469.

Monteith, M. J., & Mark, A. Y. (2005). Changing one's prejudiced ways: Awareness, affect, and self-regulation. *European Review of Social Psychology*, *16*, 113–154. doi:10.1080/10463280500229882.

Monteith, M. J., & Mark, A. Y. (2009). The self-regulation of prejudice. In T. D. Nelson (Ed.), *Handbook of prejudice, stereotyping, and discrimination* (pp. 507–523). New York, NY: Psychology Press.

Nosek, B. A., Smyth, F. L., Hansen, J. J., Devos, T., Lindner, N. M., Ranganath, K. A., Smith, C. T., Olson, K. R., Chugh, D., Greenwald, A. G., & Banaji, M. R. (2007). Pervasiveness and correlates of implicit attitudes and stereotypes. *European Review of Social Psychology*, *18*, 36–88. doi: 10.1080/10463280701489053.

O'Malley, A. S., Sheppard, V. B., Schwartz, M., & Mandelblatt, J. (2004). The role of trust in use of preventive services among low-income African-American women. *Preventive Medicine*, *38*, 777–785. doi:10.1016/j.ypmed.2004.01.018.

Pager, D., & Western, B. (2012). Identifying discrimination at work: The use of field experiments. *Journal of Social Issues*, *68*(2), 221–237. doi:10.1111/j.1540-4560.2011.01746.x

Penner, L., Dovidio, J. F., West, T. V., Gaertner, S., Albrecht, T., Dailey, R. K., & Markova, T. (2010). Aversive racism and medical interactions with black patients: A field study. *Journal of Experimental Social Psychology*, *46*, 436–440. doi:10.1016/j.jesp.2009.11.004.

Penner, L. A., Eggly, S., Greggs, J. J., Underwood, W., III, Orom, H., & Albrecht, T. L. (2012). Life-threatening disparities: The treatment of black and white cancer patients. *Journal of Social Issues*, *68*(2), 328–357. doi:10.1111/j.1540-4560.2011.01751.x

Portwood, S. G. (1995). Employment discrimination in the public sector based on sexual orientation: Conflicts between research evidence and the law. *Law and Psychology Review*, *19*, 113–152.

Raudenbush, S. W., & Kasim, R. M. (1998). Cognitive skill and economic inequality: Findings from the National Adult Literacy Survey. *Harvard Educational Review*, *68*, 33–79.

Ridgeway, C. L. (1997). Interaction and the conservation of gender inequality: Considering employment. *American Sociological Review*, *62*, 218–235. doi:10.2307/2657301.

Rubenstein, W. B. (1996). Lesbians, gay men, and the law. In R. C. Savin-Williams & K. M. Cohen (Eds.), *The lives of lesbians, gays, and bisexuals: Children to adults* (pp. 331–344). Orlando, FL: Harcourt Brace.

Sacco, J. M., Scheu, R. R., Ryan, A. M., & Schmitt, N. (2003). An investigation of race and sex similarity effects in interviews: A multilevel approach to relational demography. *Journal of Applied Psychology*, *88*, 852–865. doi:10.1037/0021-9010.88.5.852.

Sadler, M. S., Correll, J., Park, B., & Judd, C. M. (2012). The world is not black and white: Racial bias in the decision to shoot in a multiethnic context. *Journal of Social Issues*, *68*(2), 286–313. doi:10.1111/j.1540-4560.2011.01749.x

Sears, D. (1986). College sophomores in the laboratory: Influences of a narrow data base on social psychology's view of human nature. *Journal of Personality and Social Psychology*, *51*, 515–530. doi:10.1037/0022-3514.51.3.515.

Stohlberg, S. G. (2002, March). Minorities get inferior care, even if insured, study finds. *The New York Times*, p. 1.

Van Ryn, M., & Burke, J. (2000). The effect of patient race and socio-economic status on physicians' perceptions of patients. *Social Science and Medicine*, *50*, 813–828. doi: 10.1016/S0277-9536(99)00338-X.

NILANJANA DASGUPTA is an Associate Professor of Psychology at the University of Massachusetts. Her research focuses on prejudice, stereotyping, and the self-concept, with emphasis on the ways in which societal expectations subtly influence people's attitudes and behavior toward others and, in the case of disadvantaged groups, influence their self-concept, as well as professional and personal life decisions. She is interested in identifying how implicit bias might be reduced by changing the structure of local environments and, in contrast, how such bias might get magnified by specific negative emotions. Dr. Dasgupta has translated her research to shed light on real-world problems by examining the effect of implicit bias on women in science and engineering, on employment discrimination and on law enforcement decisions. She is involved in several collaborations with legal scholars, judges, K-12 teachers, school principals, and education practitioners. Her research reported in this article was supported by a CAREER Award from the National Science Foundation (BCS 0547967), a second NSF grant (BCS-0921096), and a grant from the National Institute of Mental Health (R03 MH66036-01).

JANE G. STOUT earned her PhD in social psychology from the University of Massachusetts, Amherst, in 2011. She is currently a Postdoctoral Fellow at the University of Colorado, Boulder, funded by the Research and Evaluation on Education in Science and Engineering (REESE) program of the National Science Foundation. She is interested in the ways in which gender stereotypes constrain women's self-concept and the conditions that release those constraints.

Journal of Social Issues, Vol. 68, No. 2, 2012, pp. 413–415

Introduction to Michelle Fine's SPSSI Kurt Lewin Award Address

Susan Opotow
John Jay College of Criminal Justice and The Graduate Center the City University of New York

In *Loss and desire in New Jersey* (2009), Michelle Fine writes:

> My psychological researcher/activist genes come from Kurt Lewin by way of Morton Deutsch, with wonderful contributions from existential philosopher Maxine Greene. Trained in experimental social psychology, with deep roots in the lab, I was well schooled in the theory and practice of action research, work groups, force field theory and the mid-century version of social psychology designed for social change. (p. 99)

I am thrilled to introduce Michelle Fine, Distinguished Professor of Psychology at the Graduate Center of the City University of New York, SPSSI's 2011 Kurt Lewin Awardee. Michelle's work is visionary, passionate, poetic, inspiring, and brilliant. Her research on the psychology of justice is powerful—intellectually and practically—because of its simultaneous attention to micro and macro levels of analysis. Consistent with Lewin's tenet that social behavior is a function of the person and environment, her work takes a top-down, situational perspective that considers politics and societal institutions as significant contexts for social living. At the same time, she takes the individual seriously and is especially attentive to people, young and aged, whose well-being and lives are tenuous.

Michelle Fine's research has shaped theory and method to the field and, in Lewin's spirit, has had significant implications for practice. She sees social issues as related to each other in "circuit of dispossession"—interactions among such social issues as joblessness, schooling, health care, incarceration, and poverty.

Michelle is astonishingly productive, but it is the high quality of her empirical research, her incisive analyses, and broad influence of her work that are outstanding. She has written many books, including now-classic works on race, class, and gender; research methods; and education. She has provided expert testimony to legislative bodies throughout the USA. And she has written scores of oft-cited book chapters, journal articles, and monographs that integrate psychological research and social action.

Her expertise as a social scientist, activist, and community member are contagious. Like Lewin, her students engage in high quality, influential, and innovative social justice research, practice, and teaching and themselves are making significant contributions to our field. Michelle's influence extends well beyond psychology into education, cultural and women's studies, sociology, and criminal justice. Her innovative and significant work places her as a highly respected public intellectual.

Michelle Fine comes to the Lewin legacy in spirit as well as genealogically via Morton Deutsch. The generation that knew Kurt Lewin personally describe him in ways that are uncannily similar to Michelle—as a seminal and inspiring mentor, as bubbling with infectious enthusiasm; as having restless curiosity, fertile ideas, and genius for the team approach; as having a zestful approach to life; as furthering science and humanitarian goals; as taking a broad multidisciplinary approach; as mounting courageous attacks on significant problems; as integrating the scientific approach with humanitarian values; and as having a warm heart and a lively sense of the possible that underlies his uncommonly fertile scientific imagination (cf., Hartley, 1962; MacLeod, 1958; Smith, 1965).

Faye Crosby, the Chair of the 2011 Lewin Award committee wrote:

> In selecting you for this award [SPSSI's premier career recognition, Distinguished Research on Social Issues], the committee noted your inspirational career combining activism and scholarship in a manner that best embodied the spirit and essence of the SPSSI mission. Your abiding, long term commitment to these twin goals of superb scholarship and dedication to action, community based research made your selection a most enjoyable task for the committee.

On behalf of the Lewin Committee and The Society for the psychological Study of Social Issues, I delighted to present you, dear colleague and friend, with this plaque that reads—

Michelle Fine—In recognition of your outstanding contributions to the development and integration of psychological research and social action.

References

Fine, M. (2009) Loss and desire in New Jersey. In J. G. Ponterrotto, L.A. Suzuki, J. M. Casas, C.M. Alexander (Eds.), *Handbook of multicultural counseling* (pp. 99–105). Beverly Hills: Sage Publications.

Hartley, E.L. (1962). Presentation to Robert M. MacIver, *Journal of Social Issues, 18*(2), 85–87. doi: 10.1111/j.1540-4560.1962.tb02202.x

MacLeod, R.B. (1958). Kurt Lewin Memorial Award [to Dorwin Cartwright]. *Journal of Social Issues, 14*, 1–2. doi: 10.1111/j.1540-4560.1958.tb02185.x

Smith, B.M. (1965). Kurt Lewin Memorial Address: Introduction [Kenneth B. Clark]. *Journal of Social Issues, 21*, 1–3. doi: 10.1111/j.1540-4560.1965.tb00501.x

SUSAN OPOTOW is a Professor at John Jay College of Criminal Justice and The Graduate Center the City University of New York. Her work examines the narrowing and widening of the scope of justice within a variety of social contexts including environmental conservation and during war and the post war period. She was the 2008–2009 president of the Society for the Psychological Study of Social Issues. She is a Fellow of the American Psychological Association, the 2008 recipient of the Morton Deutsch Conflict Resolution, and the 2011 awardee of the American Psychological Foundation Lynn Stuart Weiss Lecture. She is Editor of *Peace and Conflict: Journal of Peace* Psychology and Secretary of the International Society of Justice Research.

Journal of Social Issues, Vol. 68, No. 2, 2012, pp. 416–438

Resuscitating Critical Psychology for "Revolting" Times

Michelle Fine*

The Graduate Center of the City University of New York

Playing with the doubled use of the term "revolting"—as an adjective to describe the repulsive inequality gaps that litter the globe and as a delightful gerund to capture the thrilling days of global collective protest—this Lewin address muses about social psychology's debt in politically difficult times of massive inequality and sustained oppression. I venture back to the 1930s for inspiration, reviewing the writings of Lewin, Jahoda, and Dollard, as well as the research of W.E.B. Du Bois in the early 1900s and Ignacio Martín-Baró toward the latter part of the 1900s, to understand how social psychologists have intervened theoretically and empirically to contest injustice, inspire solidarity, and advance more just social arrangements. Calling for research that both documents the collateral damage of neoliberalism and generates alternative visions of democracy and justice, the second half of the article sketches a critical participatory action research project conducted with urban youth, which was designed to challenge both the strategic disinvestment in the public sphere and the concomitant conservatizing pressures on our methods of social inquiry, raising questions about "evidence-based practice" and the current marketing of Randomized Clinical Trials as the "gold standard."

As I edit my summer Lewin Address for publication in the *Journal of Social Issues*, the world is trembling with the thrills of global revolutions. On October 15, 2011, inspired by Arab Spring, Spanish "indignants," Greek Protests, Occupy Wall Street, and the courage of resistance in communities across the globe, millions of people in more than 950 cities across 82 countries took to the streets demanding economic and racial justice. The 99% link across racial/ethnic, gender, sexuality, (dis)ability, religion, nation, North/South, and across zip codes. Laborers in hard hats sit alongside young women in hijab, teachers, farmers, retired police officers, laid-off lawyers, formerly incarcerated mothers, and unemployed Wall Street investors chanting, "They got bailed out, we got sold out." Building a

---

*Correspondence concerning this article should be addressed to Michelle Fine, The Graduate Center, CUNY 365 Fifth Avenue, New York, NY 10016 [e-mail: mfine@gc.cuny.edu].

416

solidarity movement within and across place, these protesters are refusing narrow constructions of identities and are instead cultivating a collective praxis of solidarity, critique, and desire, in the radical activities of organizing and protest, in place and across the globe. They are indeed revolting against inequality gaps, global and national policies that protect the wealthiest 1% and corporations while taxing the poor. And while it may not be foremost on their minds, they are contesting, by their actions, the ways in which human desires for justice, collectivity, and solidarity have been neglected and empirically obfuscated in academic psychology.

In this essay, I resurrect the embers and long for a sustained critical social psychology that engages in interdisciplinary discussions of and inquiry with social movements and solidarities, group relations, and dedicated interdependence; a social psychology that challenges the dominant belief that self-interest and self-protection are basic human motives. I fear as a discipline, at least in the United States, we have forged a program of research that normalizes motives that may characterize the behavior of the 1% but neglects the yearnings of most (see Deutsch, 1985). This is more than a sampling problem. This is what critical psychologist Teo (2010) would call epistemological violence.

We are in the Fall of Occupy Wall Street after the Spring of Arab awakening. The world is spinning, fueled with profoundly social psychological dynamics of radical possibility. It's time that we, as a discipline, reenter critical discussions of what could be and resist reinscribing what is. Fortunately, we stand on the shoulders of a long and radical, if buried, history of SPSSI members who have contested dominant economic and racial arrangements, who have cultivated strategic relationships between the academy and resistance movements, who have embodied a collective spirit of critical public science within social movements for justice.

In this essay, the ironies of language will be put to radical use. Playing with the doubled use of the term *revolting*—as an adjective to describe the repulsive inequality gaps that litter the globe and as a delightful gerund to capture the thrilling days of global collective protest—this Lewin address muses about social psychology's debt in politically difficult times of massive inequality and sustained oppression. It is time to contest revolting inequities with revolting epistemologies.

Lewin Lecture, August 2011

As an academic daughter of Morton Deutsch, I am honored to deliver the Lewin Address for 2011. In these very hard times for the world, the nation and particularly poor working class and immigrant communities, I offer a love song to social psychology in the subjunctive, social psychology as it must be, as so many SPSSI ancestors envisioned and practiced our discipline. Although it is a time-honored tradition, I will not belabor the crisis in social psychology that has so richly filled the air at Lewinian lectures for decades, except to say that the critique narrated 30 years ago by Marie Jahoda ripples still throughout social psychology in the United States and Europe.

In 1981, Jahoda wrote, "mainstream social psychology is often no longer social, treats people like objects rather than persons and where it does not, limits its concern to the cognitively rational and consistent; it has not tackled the circulate causality between individual and group" (1981, p. 215). More than a quarter century later, Robert Cialdini, an experimental and field researcher and a past associate editor of JPSP, published a short essay in *Perspectives on Psychological Science* to explain why he decided to take early retirement. "Truth be told, as a discipline, we've become lax in our responsibilities to the public . . . they deserve to know the pertinence of our research . . . they've paid for that research." (Cialdini, 2009, p. 5)

Perhaps it has always been this way, but the forces surrounding and impinging on the field of social psychology today are a contradictory and confusing swirl of political, economic, and intellectual winds, signaling perhaps an important moment to pause for disciplinary reflection on our intellectual debt in these critical times.

As a subdiscipline, social psychology was born and has long teetered delicately on an edge; a scholarly double helix of person and social, field and lab, numbers and stories, politics and bodies, and social critique and engagement. We seem to both enjoy and suffer in the contentious dialectics of "crisis." Indeed a sense of disciplinary crisis has historically instigated some of the most significant turns in the field (Stainton-Rogers, 2009). At the moment, however, I fear our delicate twinning is fraying. The romantic in me believes that because of sturdy braiding and hybrid roots, social psychology may be one of the few disciplines with the history, intellect, heart, and courage to research the complex and circuited lives of persons nestled within global and local inequality gaps and to generate compelling evidence relevant to social theory, policy, and social movements; to offer a counter-story to the dominant narrative of motivated self-interest, defensive identity politics, and the inevitability of inequality gaps. But I'm worried.

In 1939, Kurt Lewin argued that in order to research complex lives situated in complex political circumstances, social psychologists would have to overcome what he saw as major difficulties:

(1) "integrating—vast areas of divergent facts and aspects . . . cultural, historical, sociological, psychological, and physical facts . . .

(2) treating—these facts on the basis of their interdependence,

(3) handling—both historical and systematic problems,

(4) handling—problems related to groups as well as to individuals,

(5) handling—all 'sizes' of objects or patterns (. . . problems of a nation . . . as well as a play group of three children),

(6) Problems of 'atmosphere' . . .

(7) Experimental social psychology will have to find a way to bring the large size patterns into a framework small enough for the technical possibilities of experimentation." (1997, pp. 264–265)

To Lewin's list, I would add a few additional challenges in the contemporary political landscape. The world today is plagued by growing and hardening inequality gaps; the explicit protection of elite power; a psychic numbing to crisis, oppression and violence; an ideological valorization of individualism and freedom tithed to a cumulative sense of powerlessness. People are flooded with "science" and facts, much of it purchased by corporations or conservative think tanks. Critical voices for democracy, interdependence, racial justice, solidarity movements, public radio, television, and public science are severely underfunded and thereby muted.

The world deserves an engaged critical social psychology (see Fox, Prilletensky, & Austin, 2009; Martín-Baró, 1994; Stainton-Rogers, 2009; Torre & Fine, 2011; Torre, Fine, Stoudt, & Fox, 2012) to take up the tasks that Lewin sketched: to theorize and study the membranes that link/separate people in contentious sociopolitical contexts; reframe individual issues in the social landscape of historic, political, economic, and cultural topography; to document the dynamic interdependence of inequality gaps, tithing wealth and poverty, oppression and security, health and despair, and to pierce what Morton Deutsch has called the "slumber of complacency" among those who think they are doing just fine while others suffer (Bhatia, 2011; Deutsch, 1974; Fine & Sirin, 2007; Fox & Prilletensky, 2009; Opotow, 2011; Stoudt, Fine, & Fox, 2012). These are hard times to strategize an intellectual and political path through our increasingly conservative discipline, psychology. Yet I find wisdom and courage in the writings of social psychologists who responded so boldly 75 years ago to the shifting political, economic, and scientific winds of the post-Depression era.

Through the Nostalgic Lens of a Rear View Mirror

For inspiration, we travel back to the 1930s (see Rutherford, Unger, & Cherry, 2011 for a volume of historic essays on SPSSI). Just coming out of the Great Depression, Franklin Delano Roosevelt—controversial though he was—was railing against what he called "economic royalists" who were hording capital and draping their lust for control and profit in the language of patriotism and democracy. This was an astonishing moment for social policy formulation. Secretary of the Department of Labor Francis Perkins, the first female cabinet appointment, was ushering in New Deal policies to tighten the structural weave of our collective fabric, including social security, child labor, and minimum wage laws. Recall that in the 30s the highest marginal tax rate was over 80% even as racism remained a relatively uncontested national tradition. So what were social psychologists writing about?

In the late 1930s, the social psychologies of group life, collective action and cohesion were enjoying a Renaissance (Danzinger, 2007). Critical intellectuals chronicled the psychic erosion produced by structural oppression and, at the same time, documented the dynamic circuitry linking privilege and oppression. A small group of social psychologists tuned their scholarship toward documenting and intervening in the messy spaces between lives in struggle, lives in comfort, and oppressive political regimes. Two social psychological classics were underway, ethnographies archiving the material, psychological, and existential weight of cumulative injustice. John Dollard first published *Class and Caste in a Southern Town* in 1937, a detailed and searing investigation of race and class relations in the South, whereas Marie Jahoda, Paul Lazarsfeld, and Hans Zeisel published *Marienthal*, a social psychological analysis of everyday life in a community outside of Vienna where villagers suffered individually and collectively from what was called the Worldwide Economic Crisis (1933; see also Torre, Fine, Stoudt, & Fox, 2012).

These writers penned bold texts on the collateral damage of fascism, economic and racial oppression on everyday lives and communities. Both sacrificed much for their intellectual, political, and ethical convictions. While Dollard enjoyed a faculty appointment in Psychology and African American Studies at Yale, he apparently, "paid a price for his unusual interdisciplinary interests: academic departments tend[ed] to look with disfavor on those who depart from the common mold, and he did not become a voting full professor in the department of psychology at Yale until age 52" (Ewen, 1998, p. 507). Marie Jahoda, as her obituary tells us, was "a staunch anti-fascist, [who] came into collision with the repressive Austrian government even before Hitler's Anschluss, was imprisoned between 1936 and 1937.... She also ran the secret radio station, Radio Rotes Wien, under Richard Crossman at the Ministry of Information." (1981, p. 98, reprinted 2003).

Crafting scholarship at the interdisciplinary nexus of the social and the psychological, Jahoda and Dollard, like Du Bois (1913) before them and Martín-Baró (1994) since, worked across interdisciplinary boundaries, integrated a range of methods and theoretical frameworks, and produced works intentionally accessible and accountable to communities within and beyond the academy. They struggled to capture the damage of oppression and at the same time to honor the humanity of those exiled beyond the borders of social inclusion. They bent their science, like light, to refract a sense of collective responsibility among those with privilege. They worked elegantly at the hyphen of critical science and political resistance.

And on the radio, in 1939, one could hear Billie Holiday singing *Strange Fruit*, a painful depiction of tangled lives, written by a Jew, sung by a Black woman,

> strange fruit hanging from the poplar trees . . .
> Scent of magnolias sweet and fresh,
> then a sudden smell of burning flesh –

By the late 30s, popular culture, politics, and critical scholarship were beginning to realize and reveal the troubling entanglements of progress for some and violence for others. And a number of psychologists were among the critical voices contesting the inhumane consequences of inequality and cumulative oppression, entering the fray of political debate, refusing the false promise of neutrality.

Swelling Inequality Gaps in the 2010s

Today we witness a(nother) chapter of U.S. history in which rising inequality gaps refract through racial, ethnic, class, as well as gendered disparities. The Center on Budget and Policy Priorities reports that the income share of the top 1% of the nation has reached its highest level since 1928 (Feller & Stone, 2009).

The wealth gaps of today parallel those of the 1930s. Yet, unlike the New Deal era, today's federal and state ideologies and policies are explicitly engineered toward preserving and strengthening inequality gaps, protecting the wealth and status of the rich and corporations and dismantling the social supports that have [unevenly and inadequately] been in place for poor, working class, and middle-class families.

U.S. policy makers seem to have turned away from a vision of human rights, justice and a multiracial democracy. Slashing the very safety nets Perkins helped to stitch together, in 2011 knives are wielded by Republicans but also Democrats, building firewalls between elites and the remaining 99%; constructing exit ramps for a few "deserving" poor, and securing concrete criminalized containers for the remainder. Deportations under the Obama administration have been authorized at rates that surpass the Bush administration. School systems and public school educators are being defunded, demonized, privatized, and resegregated. Student loans saddle college graduates with average debt in excess of $30,000. Housing foreclosures disproportionately exile middle-class African Americans from once integrated neighborhoods. Prison populations swell as racial and ethnic mass incarceration breeds profit. Legal scholar Alexander (2010) reports that more Black men now are in prison than were enslaved in 1850. Today our strange fruit has been outsourced to prisons, homeless shelters, sometimes the military, often on the streets and gathering in tent cities around the land.

Neoliberalism, this not so new but dizzying economic, political, racial, social, and psychological regime (Harvey, 2004) has been ushered in by a well-funded conservative social movement and accelerated by public policies which facilitate and justify the upward consolidation of wealth, control, and class power while undermining the social health of poor, working class, and increasingly middle-class communities. The strategic redesign of our gender, race/ethnicity, and class structure is being launched at the dangerous intersection of radical economic transformation in the private sector and severe cuts in the public sector.

In synchronized fashion, the social sciences are today undergoing parallel, and disturbing renovations. Reflecting, and I fear legitimating, the sorting, separating, and vision-constricting conventions of our time, mainstream academic social psychology in the United States and also across Europe has seemingly lost interest in studies of group life, interdependence, solidarity, and collective action. On July 7, 2011 a petition signed by prominent psychologists of the European Association of Social Psychologies (EASP) was sent to president of EASP and members of the executive committee, concerned that

"...European social psychology has become skewed in the direction of micro-individualistic-experimentalist approaches...moving away from the vision of its founders who envisioned a field that would be societally relevant, open to a variety of different perspectives, respectful of multiple methods and attentive to both micro and macro levels of analysis...a limited paradigm continues to dominate social psychological journals and professional meetings." (EASP petition signers, personal communication, July 4, 2011).

This turn away from a social psychology of macrointerests and shared fates aligns with a problematic ideological and political desire to have us all look away from the 1% and disattend to the privatization of all things public; to obsess empirically about the individual who is "damaged," "at risk," or "a potential terror," and to erase history and the structural politics that produce everyday life in wealthy and dispossessed communities in the United States and globally (Liebert, 2010; MacLeod & Bhatia, 2008). We are being asked to forget that the "haves" not only require but help to create the "have nots" and we are being funded to study how the latter group "copes," collapses or develops into "risk" threatening, or taxing, all of "us" with their needs (Liu, 2012) or madness (Liebert, 2010). There is a troubling social psychological shadow cast by these political turns.

As our nation invests in war(s), mass incarceration, human "insecurity" and deportation and refuses to equitably tax the wealthy and corporations, national, state, and local governments are slipping into austerity, retreating from social welfare across a vast range of fields including public education, libraries, welfare, civil service jobs, public transportation, and entitlement programs including Social Security, Medicare, and Medicaid. Accompanying these structural transformations lies a shadow discourse, operating ideologically and psychologically, through popular media and everyday talk, to privatize and individualize responsibility for the cause of social problems and for the solutions.

In 1959, C. Wright Mills wrote *The Sociological Imagination* in which he argued that the task of social science is to "translate private troubles into public issues." Today we are witnessing a deliberate counter-translation as public issues are exiled from the public sphere and returned to the province of private troubles. Indeed, the ideological valorization of the family—even the gay family—reflects the domestication of "private problems" as the province of the family. My concern here is with the cultural but also the scientific representations of public concerns as if they were personal troubles that could be stuffed back into the private zone of the home, or tracked down in a brain image.

As national, state, and local safety nets shred and the state shirks its responsibility for collective well-being, scrutiny intensifies on those who are most economically and politically marginalized who grow inflated with social responsibility for those persons, and those issues, the State has abandoned—elderly parents and children, housing security, inadequate schools and health care, unemployment, fears of deportation and incarceration (Fine & Carney, 2001; Fine & McClelland, 2007).

As social responsibilities drain downward, the effects are, however, uneven across race, ethnicity, class, and sexualities. A cultural splitting of responsibility, blame, and public humiliation occurs reminiscent of the writings of Klein (1932; Fine, 2010). Particularly during difficult economic times, when scapegoats are recruited for political deflection, the "good Other" is pitted against the "bad Other." Poor women, particularly women of color, who "fail" to fulfill ever mounting responsibilities are punished publicly, sometimes dragged into court and found guilty:

Grieving Mother Faces 36 Months in Jail for Jaywalking after Son is Killed by Hit-And-Run Driver

Nelson was crossing a busy Marietta, Georgia, street with her son and his two siblings when they were struck by a hit-and-run driver. Jerry Guy, later admitted he had been drinking and had taken painkillers the night of the accident. . . . Nelson had taken her children with her to shop for groceries and supplies for her upcoming birthday party. The working mother and college student regularly took public transportation . . . Nelson's apartment complex sits across the street from the bus stop, but the nearest crosswalk is three-tenths of a mile away . . . She crossed one side of the divided highway to the median, where she waited for a break in the traffic. Several people then crossed the street before Nelson thought it was safe. She waited with her kids. But when others started to move towards the road, Nelson's son must taken it as a cue it was time to go. She felt his grip on her hand loosen and he darted out into the road. She followed. Guy's car struck Nelson, her son and her daughter, and the boy died . . . As Guy was processed by Georgia's criminal justice system . . . the Atlanta Journal-Constitution ran a long story [which] mentioned Nelson and her son, pointing out that she hadn't been charged with any crime. Three days later, the Georgia Solicitor General's office charged Nelson with the three misdemeanors. Nelson, a black woman, was convicted by an all-white jury. She relies on public transportation; she is a pedestrian in a car-oriented Atlanta suburb. During jury questioning, none of the jurors who would eventually convict Nelson raised their hands when asked if they relied on public transportation. (Balko, 2011)

Cultural splitting places the burden of proof and the heel of punishment squarely on those long abandoned by the State.

We are living and working in a time of doubled shrinkage. The communities we study (with) are politically shrinking, as safety nets are shorn from beneath their feet. So too the dominant research designs and methods in psychology are being aggressively influenced to narrow the scientific gaze. A series of political, scientific, economic, and institutional forces constrict and curve the direction of our scholarship. Focusing on individual "risk," intergroup conflict, cognitive and neurological correlates of prejudice our scholarship subtly turns away from the messy intersections of structure, context, history, and the rich texture of lives. It is important for us to be mindful of these forces impinging on our theorizing, teaching, and our research practice. As Danzinger (2007) has argued, what we study and how we study are intimately bound such that "[there is a] close link that always exists between preconceptions about the object to be investigated and faith in the appropriateness of particular methods of investigation." Danzinger continues, "Methodology is not ontologically neutral."(p. 332)

To nudge this conversation further into the always awkward and equally urgent, tight quarters of "family feuds" within social psychology, I'll turn to the role of social psychology as a discipline, and social psychologists as researchers, to lift up for discussion how we are being recruited to help build a science that supports neoliberalism, by naturalizing intergroup conflict, prejudice, and identity threat and not solidarity; that fetishes the autonomous individual or artificial group as if dangling free from history and context; a science that privileges internal validity over external validity; a science easily deployed in applied settings to test single variable interventions, confirm the null hypothesis of "no effect" and legitimate the decision to "cut waste." Bear with me as I try to explain.

As governments declare austerity and try to root out public sector inefficiencies, there is a curious growth industry of accountability and evaluation systems funded handsomely with public dollars, designed to "cut waste," maximize efficiency, weed out corruption and greed, and "improve outcomes." While audit culture has many distinct features, two are significant for our discussion: Randomized Clinical Trials as the "gold standard" of social science and the associated mandate for "evidence-based practice" (and not practice-based evidence, Wallerstein, 2010; see Fine, 2012, in press on "evidence"). With these two simple moves of science, the fields we study, practice, and teach, and the ways in which we study, practice, and teach, shrink dangerously; as so much of Lewin's topography is deported from the gaze of social inquiry.

Randomized Clinical Trial as the Gold Standard

"Sometime during the ensuring quarter century or so, the humble search for improved methods of generating believable answers to pressing policy questions gave way to what many now perceive as methodological triumphalism. Much of the controversy surrounding randomized clinical trials (RCTs) seems to be an artifact of its most fervent advocates proclaiming the RCT as the 'gold standard' marking the apparent end of methodological history and of other researchers' uncritical acceptance of these exaggerated claims." (Barnett & Carter, 2010, p. 516)

Tracking the intensified popularity of experimental design in national legislation, state policies, and in the mandated evaluation language of major foundations, many roads lead back to the extremely well-funded Coalition for Evidence-Based Practice:

The Coalition for Evidence-Based Practice is a well-respected think tank involved with federal policy making and evaluation. On their website we learn that **"the Coalition seeks to increase government effectiveness through the use of rigorous evidence about what works** . . . in most areas of social policy—such as education, poverty reduction, and crime prevention—government programs often are implemented with little regard to evidence, costing billions of dollars yet failing to address critical social problems . . . a central theme of our advocacy, consistent with a recent National Academies recommendation, is that evidence of effectiveness generally cannot be considered definitive without ultimate confirmation in well-conducted randomized controlled trials." (http://coalition4evidence.org/wordpress/)

An internal evaluation of the Coalition (Herk, 2009) concludes that "the Coalition assisted the Institute for Educational Sciences . . . by having language supportive of RCTs placed in Senate and House Appropriations Committee reports over several years." (p. 5) Two years later a second evaluator praised the Coalition and recommended an even more ambitious agenda: "The coalition has been so effective an advocate across multiple social program areas, but . . . should move beyond the discretionary realm . . . into Medicare and Medicaid." (p. 4) Thanks to the Coalition, Wallace finds a "clear consensus . . . in Congress, the Office of management and Budget and federal departments . . . about the unusually high level of value and credibility that scientific, randomized controlled experiments have for increasing the effectiveness of social programs."

The arguments for evidence-based practice and RCTs are no doubt compelling; by all measures the Coalition has been enormously successful and self-described as nonpartisan. And yet this voice of rigor, experimentation and randomization doth protest a bit too much at a particularly vulnerable time in our nation's/globe's social well being.

In the field of economics and international development, there is serious concern over the rise of "randomistas" (Center for Global Development, 2009). Applied economists Barnett and Carter write that, "RCTs are invaluable tools for biophysical scientists, where the mechanisms involved are more mechanicals . . . A core pitfall is that experiments typically treat human beings as subjects, not as agents." (p. 525)

They moderate their critique when they explain, "The fact that RCTs are not appropriate for all questions is not a criticism of the methodology per se. However, *it becomes a serious problem when RCTs are seen as the way of knowing and the applicability of the RCT method, rather than the importance of the question being asked, seems to drive the research agenda.*" (p. 525)

Confession: I was trained as an experimental social psychologist. My first book was co-authored with Leonard Saxe and entitled *Social Experiments:*

Methods for an Experimenting Society (Saxe & Fine, 1981). In order to design a true experiment, even a quasi-experiment, one needs to select one or two standardized interventions as the focus of analysis and treat all other factors as irrelevant, controlled for or simply beyond the scope of the study. In the abstract, this makes perfect sense. The experimental logic is elegant and seductive. While the calls for randomization and standardized outcomes may be understandable, these designs white out the threatening landscape of structural injustice in which people are trying to get by, build lives and families. Designs that rely upon simple, decontextualized and standardized indicators generated by "experts" with neither experience nor histories of engagement in these fields, can also be enormously misleading when they exert undue influence on the shape of programs or funding decisions. As Donald Campbell warned 30 years ago, "The more any quantitative social indicator is used for social decision making, the more subject it will be to corruption pressures and the more apt it will be to distort and corrupt the social processes it is intended to monitor." (Campbell, 1976, p. 41)

To address the implications of the "gold standard" pressures on the ground, for those fragile community-based organizations that are trying to catch the affective overflow of human need bleeding through the fraying public safety net, let us consider the field of domestic violence, where the tensions of evaluation, expertise and experience are almost at a boil; where scientific privileging of internal validity is bumping dangerously into programmatic needs for external validity and local accountability.

In the field of violence against women, three terrible things are true: the problem is on the rise, the state sponsored programs/supports on the decline and scientific scrutiny embedded in evaluation mandates suffers from pin point vision on a set of indicators orthogonal to the well being of the women.

Over the past 18 months, Maria Torre and I at the Public Science Project (PSP) of the Graduate Center, CUNY (where researchers and activists gather to design participatory action research projects for social justice) have been asked by a small group of directors/advocates/participants in rural and urban domestic violence programs to convene "quiet" meetings to discuss openly how they might keep funding and strategically deal and ethically contend with accountability pressures. A number of the participants explained that increasingly federal agencies and foundations premise funding on programs' willingness to participate in a controlled experiment, by standardizing their programs in order to document "what works" and testing their interventions via the random assignment of women to intervention or control group to establish internal validity. They are also expected to document the impact of their programs, across sites, on varied standardized outcomes including: the number and percent of women who call the police, apply for Orders of Protection, leave their abusers permanently, improve parenting and self-efficacy skills and report lower depression scores. The logic is compelling and understandable. These are not evil privatizers crafting strategies to defund or delegitimize domestic violence programs. And yet the conventions of privileging of internal validity over external validity, and standardizing outcomes over time, community, and place, are deeply problematic.

Alisa Del Tufo, an Ashoka fellow who has worked for decades in urban New York City and now rural Vermont on domestic violence advocacy and policy explained the confusion and frustration that swells in the "gap" between foundation desires to know and practitioners' needs on the ground:

> One of the most absurd indicators of success for victims of intimate violence is the Order of Protection. In fact it is used as a litmus test to determine the "seriousness" of the violence and her intent to stay away from the abuser. What it most often does is open a woman up to a dizzying array of potentially negative consequences from deportation, loss of housing, child welfare investigations, custody disputes, extended time needed to attend court hearings, job loss, intensified intimidation from the abuser with little or no hope of real protection from authorities. It is little wonder that almost 20% of women murdered by their partners have Orders of Protection! And yet OP's are often a prerequisite to obtaining other services such as public housing, welfare to work waivers, satisfying child welfare investigations, and sometimes even shelter itself.

Over a series of meetings, the directors, advocates, and some of the women themselves, speaking off record, elaborated on the complexities of leaving or obtaining an Order of Protection or calling the police in the midst of recession, foreclosure and unemployment crises and profound structural insecurity. They detailed the knotty intimacies of violence, love, poverty, homelessness, and fear. They all seemed to know that the probability of intimate murder escalates after a woman leaves. An advocate working with women from Central America told us it's extremely difficult to apply for an Order of Protection, call police or leave if a woman is undocumented and he is a citizen. A woman working with orthodox Jewish women with many children, and another working with lesbian survivors of intimate violence, reminded us that many women can't turn to their families of origin for support. First Nation women told us that they struggle within community even talking about these issues, much less sending a Native man to "white man's prison." African American women know they risk losing custody of their children if they call the police, for fear of being charged with "engaging in domestic violence." Directors detailed the particular obstacles faced by women who have HIV, or a child is receiving services for special needs, or fears of more violence in her local shelter. These women are not against evidence or accountability. Indeed, they have been fighting for decades for strong programs, accountable to women, children, and communities. But they are rightly concerned about the new audit culture where "evidence" is gathered on simplistic, standardized interventions, assessed with narrow indicators, determined by persons far from experience or practice, with no attention to the rhythms of local context or the life-threatening dangers of State mandates. They are concerned that the need for "rigor" is legitimating the scientific occlusion of complex, devastating life spaces in which women are trying to carve lives of meaning and human security for themselves and their children (see APA Presidential Task Force on Evidence-Based Practice, 2006; Silverstein & Auerbach, 2009).

In these contexts—and these are the contexts of women, children, and men living in poverty in the United States—the elegance of the experimental design and standardized litmus-test indicators as the primary indicators of effectiveness, and as a passbook required for funding, may induce and legitimate a scientific dissociation from the complexities of living in poor, working, and middle-class America.

Sociologist Gay Tuchman calls this funding dynamic "coercive accountability." Alison Bernstein (2009), formerly of the Ford Foundation, describes it as "metric mania" induced by the corporatization of U.S. philanthropy, "the idea that an organization or its grants can only be effective when it arrays all the data that are known or can be measured by a metric and makes decisions based on that metric." Bernstein continues, "But the metric by its very nature only measures what can be measured, and thus it is a proxy or an incomplete indicator of what is actually happening. Real, lasting change can not be reduced to a single metric." (Bernstein, 2011, p. 38)

Almost 50 years ago, psychologist Allport forecast this tension when he offered a stern caution, not from the critical margins but from the absolute center of the discipline, about the dangerous consequences of theoretical and methodological shrinkage: "While the course of science moves toward ever larger abstractions, psychology seems headed in the opposite direction, the trend toward conceptual specialization, earning a reputation among other sciences for timidity and for a bagatelle of contributions irrelevant to human needs . . . eclecticism of theory is the recognition that human behavior may derive from many causes acting separately or conjointly . . . For investigators, a new categorical imperative: Do not forget what you have decided to neglect." (1964, p. 23)

Our disciplinary proclivity toward shrinkage is an historic problem of science and ethics; a betrayal of our bold SPSSI history.

In the remainder of this essay, I stand humbly on the shoulders of a significant strain of SPSSI researchers who have historically resisted the technical glide to the Right, by exploring and contesting lives marinating in inequality gaps; researchers who have forged paths of critical psychological science for the public good. These researchers have refused to fix (sic) the problem of injustice on the backs of those who suffer the consequences of oppression and have committed instead to document the wide landscape of human life, in comfort and pain, privilege and poverty, resilience and despair. They have allied their critical research projects with interdisciplinary scholars, activists, and policy makers. Ambitious? Indeed, this has been SPSSI's historic debt and signature.

The PSP: Critical Participatory Action Research

To ground my remarks on critical psychology in critical times, I want to briefly sketch the work of the PSP crafted in the legacy of Lewin's Center for Community Interrelations, housed at the Graduate Center of the City University of New York (www.publicscienceproject.org). Building on the theoretical legacy of critical scholars and activists including W.E.B. Du Bois, Claire Selltiz, Gloria Anzaldua, Morton Deutsch, Kurt Lewin, Carolyn & Muzafer Sherif, and Marie Jahoda in the United States (see Stainton-Rogers, 2009; Steinitz & Mishler, 2008; Torre & Fine, 2011; Torre, Fine, Stoudt, & Fox, 2012) and Fals-Borda (1979), Friere (1984), and Martín-Baró (1994) in Central and South America, PSP has launched projects investigating inequality gaps and human rights violations in schools, communities, and prisons (Fine, Burns, Torre, & Payne, 2007; Fine et al., 2003).

Rooted in the social psychology of justice studies (Deutsch, 1974; Jahoda, Lazarsfeld, & Zeisel, 1933; Lykes & Coquillon, 2009; Martín-Baró, 1994; Opotow, 2011; Saegert, Fields, & Libman, 2009; Stainton-Rogers, 2009; Steinitz & Mischler, 2008), our research projects are designed collaboratively to document, contest and reimagine the social psychological dynamics and consequences of circuits of dispossession and privilege: the policies, ideologies, institutional relationships, and social dynamics that move across place and over time to redistribute and naturalize the upward consolidation of wealth, control, and class power while undermining, destabilizing and containing low-income communities of color (Fine & Ruglis, 2008). In order to theorize how these circuits move through and across young bodies and communities, our research projects aim to be deeply historic, theoretical and participatory, committed to the study of circuits (not just "victims" or "perpetrators") of injustice and resistance, designed in collaboration with activists, organizers, interdisciplinary colleagues, and youth, who gather evidence for reconstructing theory, informing policy and feeding social movements and organizing campaigns. (Fox & Prillentensky, 2008). To whet the epistemological appetite of readers, below I offer a sketch of one PSP project, Polling for Justice (PFJ).

Polling for Justice

In the early spring of 2008, PFJ researchers—youth and adults—designed a citywide youth census to document young people's experiences of (in)justice in four sectors of public life: education, health care, criminal justice, and housing. The research was designed by a coalition of social psychologists, public health, human rights, education, and youth organizing groups. Together we:

(1) Built a participatory research team combining the expertise of diverse groups
     of urban youth, educators, lawyers, public health researchers, and social
     psychologists,
(2) (who) collectively designed a citywide youth survey to catalog, with quan-
     titative and qualitative measures, how differently positioned young people
     experience policies in education, health care, housing, and criminal justice,
(3) (so we could) map how circuits of dispossession, privilege, and resistance
     migrate across zip codes affecting the full landscape of youth development
     in New York City, attending closely to the intersections of race/ethnicity,
     class, gender, sexuality, immigration, disability, and neighborhood, so we
     could collectively
(4) co-produce articles, white papers, creative performances, testimony for city
     council, and youth newspaper articles to reveal the costs of inequality gaps
     and inspire a sense of shared fates with more privileged audiences and policy
     makers.

Recruited from youth organizations, schools, and via word of mouth,
40 youths (aged 14–21) came to the basement of the Graduate Center from public and private high schools, community-based organizations and court-appointed
programs all over New York City. Diverse by race, ethnicity, socioeconomic background, educational level, religion, sexuality, gender, disability, and immigration
status, the youth represented a range of educational experiences: from push-outs to
Advanced Placement classes, from detention rooms to student leadership. Alongside the young people were another 20 or so university faculty, graduate students,
community organizers, and public health professionals. Our first evening, the
embryo of PFJ was conceived.

In distinct corners of our meeting room, and then over a few weeks, multigen-
erational teams constructed sections of the PFJ survey, weaving together standardized measures with home-grown items to assess youth experiences with education
and schooling; safety, violence, and housing security; interactions with the criminal justice system; and the physical, psychological, sexual, and reproductive
health. Over the span of a year, on the streets, in youth programs and online, we
collected more than 1,100 survey responses from New York City youth, mirroring
the demographics of the New York City board of education student body (see Fox
et al., 2010).

PFJ design, sampling, instrument development, and data collection processes
were intensely participatory; so too were the statistical and qualitative analyses.
On Saturdays, we sponsored Stats-in-Action, throwing data up on a large screen
and inviting youth and adult researchers to suggest analyses across variables, demographics, communities, and even the open-ended data. As we sat on the couches
at the Graduate Center and reviewed the frequencies and racial/ethnic/gender cross

tabs on attitudes toward education, youth organizing, trust in teachers, aspirations, relations with family . . . we learned, to our delight, that most survey respondents reported high educational aspirations, strong hopes for the future, and a strong sense of civic engagement/desire to work with other young people to improve their communities. No racial or ethnic differences emerged on these indicators. We then moved into the more vexing sections of the survey, toward the items assessing youth interactions with police.

> In the last six months (never, once, twice, more than twice):
>
> I was given a summons/ticket by a police officer
> I was arrested
> I was given a second chance by police
> I was threatened and/or called a name by police
> I was helped by a police officer
> I was touched inappropriately by police (patted down)

The frequency counts, and then the intersectional cross tabs by race/ethnicity, borough, and by sexuality were extremely disturbing, at least to many of the adult researchers. The youth researchers knew intimately, from experience and witnessing, the extent of negative interactions with police in communities of color, but they were jazzed to document these patterns with the tools of social research, and eager to learn more. They wanted to know who was getting stopped, where and with what effects.

We superimposed the survey data onto maps of New York City and to capture the geography of negative and positive interactions with the police. We quickly saw that youth living in Brooklyn and Bronx (see Figure 1) as well as youth of color, males and youth identifying as lesbian, gay, bisexual, or questioning (LGBQ) (see Figure 2) reported the highest rates of negative interactions with police. Youth researchers extrapolated from personal to social, identifying their own neighborhoods in central Brooklyn and the South Bronx as having the highest concentration of negative interactions with police.

Because PFJ was designed in collaboration with youth organizers and human rights lawyers working on litigation to redress the overpolicing of youth, the descriptive and spatial evidence we gathered on negative police contact data prompted us to pursue further research necessary for legal testimony and policy development. We ventured out to the street corners that emerged as "hot spots" for negative police interactions and facilitated place-based data-driven focus groups with local youth, drawing on their experience, analysis, and community knowledge to help us unpack the quantitative evidence. We conducted a series of policy interviews with, for instance, a drug-court judge asking why the rates of negative youth-police interactions were so high in some communities. Without hesitation the Judge explained, "Overtime." She continued, "In communities that are already over-policed, police can pick up a group of students coming out of school, take them to the station. Often someone has a joint or a box cutter. Even if all charges

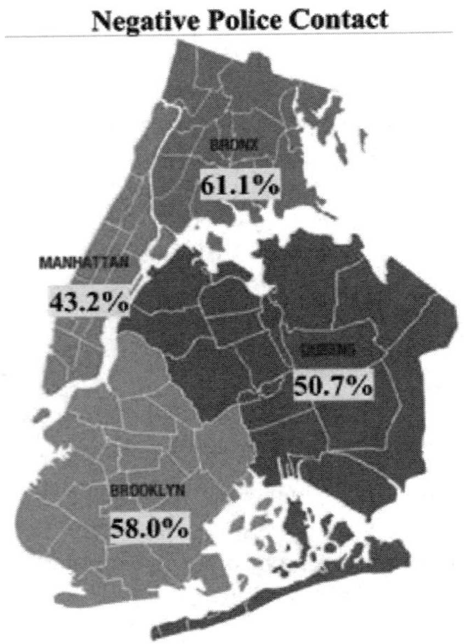

Fig. 1. Percentage of survey respondents reporting negative police contact (data from polling for justice, 2010, Michelle Fine PI).

were dismissed, the police earn over time. There's an economic motive." This response led us into the literatures and interviews with varied experts on stop and frisk, racial profiling, the Clean Hallways Act, trespassing tickets, overtime, and police quotas. Then, in coalition with a number of allied youth/activist organizations who were also involved with documenting the patterns and consequences of racialized stop and frisk, we co-hosted a metaanalysis of youth–police data from varied youth organizing groups to integrate our evidence for ongoing policy work and community education. We now co-sponsor with community allies a series of Research and Policy Salons called, "Growing Up Policed."

Our participatory commitments extended into our discussions of dissemination—to whom? How? For what? When? The PFJ team, particularly the young people, wanted to publish, distribute, and perform the findings to a wide range of audiences. While we had presented our findings at youth rallies, City Council and scholarly conferences in the United States, Canada, Cypress, and London, the youth researchers were eager to invent a palette of dissemination strategies that provoked more than empathy, more than tears and nods of the head. Following in the footsteps of the little known performance work of W.E.B. Du Bois (Dubois, 1913) who used pageantry, performance, and circus theater in order to explore alternative possibilities of African American history, we decided to translate empirical evidence into dramatic performance (see Fox & Fine, 2012).

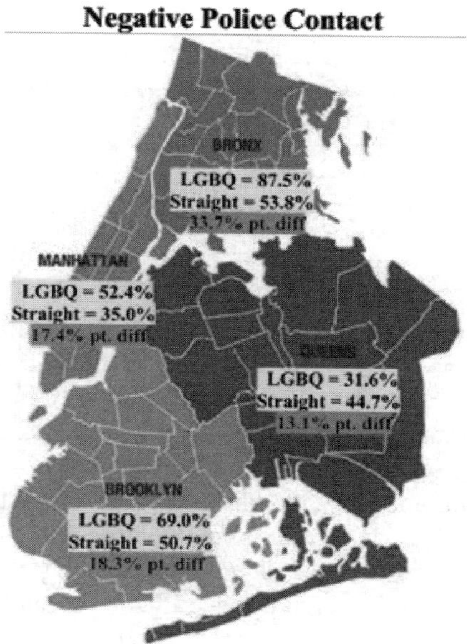

Fig. 2. LGBQ youth reporting negative police contact as compared with straight youth (data from polling for justice, 2010, Michelle Fine PI).

Maddy Fox, director of PFJ, has a long history with Theatre of the Oppressed (Boal, 2002) and Playback Theatre.

Here's an excerpt from the script performed in Halifax Canada. The youth researchers/performers opened on stage to an audience of 700 international "resilience" researchers, educating them first about the public policies now taken for granted in urban United States:

> **Did you know** that there are over 5,000 police in NYC schools?
>
> **Did you know** that in NYC we have to pass 5 standardized tests in order to graduate from high school? And now teacher tenure is tied to how well their students do on standardized tests.
>
> **Did you know** that in my first year of high school we had 100 people, and now there are only 30 graduating . . . we have a 45% graduation rate in NYC?
>
> **Did you know**, it's really no joke, 45.8 million U.S. citizens don't have health insurance? And, 1 in 6 New Yorkers are uninsured?
>
> But despite all of these things happening to us our survey found that: 69% of youth in our survey plan on getting a masters degree, doctoral degree or being a doctor or lawyer
>
> 90% of the youth of our survey feel somewhat or very hopeful about the future.
>
> 94% of students care about getting good grades in school, and 89% feel their teachers have high expectations of them and say that teachers help when they don't understand something.

Each piece of data was reenacted through dance, spoken text and/or a scripted scene woven with projected images of the data drawn from over 1,100 young people and personal testimonies we gathered from surveys and biographies. The youth researcher-performers then invited audience members to voice their reactions to the evidence—in the charts, the narratives, the movement work and the testimonies.

> I feel inspired by youth doing research;
> I'm outraged!
> I hear these experiences everyday from my students, and I don't know if anything can change.
> I feel ashamed when I know this is happening and I am doing nothing.

The youth researchers-performers created human sculptures of these reactions. Audience responses were now enfleshed on the stage—making visible circuits of dispossession and privilege, data and affect, performers and audience (Fox & Fine, 2012). The circuits of dispossession data provoked a circuit of shared fates, solidarity, and courage, even if just for a moment.

PFJ is a story within a story; an empirically driven participatory analysis of the scarring impacts of policy reform on the youth landscape of New York City, embedded in a public performance of research, resilience, and resistance. As a quantitative and qualitative research project, PFJ draws on the history, language, and weight of public science to contest policies that undermine poor communities of color, revealing the circuits of dispossession that link communities on the rise and communities in decline, and the circuits of resistance that mobilize across zip codes for justice. At the same time, PFJ draws on the wisdom of Carolyn and Muzafer Sherif, Marie Jahoda, John Dollard, Kurt Lewin, Kenneth Clark, Ignacio Martín-Baró, and others challenging fashionable pressures to study and represent poor youth through a lens of risk and inviting audiences, instead, to consider how we might review young people under siege through a lens of desire.

The critical design, analysis, and performances of PFJ have been nourished by a long line of SPSSI-based critical inquiry projects which have represented and humanized communities under siege, lighting up the circuits that connect "us" and "them" and cultivating research as a tool for social justice. Such critical inquiry is situated in a critical epistemology of solidarity, tuned with an assumption that humans desire justice for self and others (Drury & Reicher, 2000; Lykes & Mallone, 2009; Martín-Baró, 1994; Prilleltensky, 2010). Such a line of inquiry has long danced on the pages of SPSSI's journals, seasoned discussions at Council meetings, framed our research projects, been celebrated at our award deliberations and at our conferences. Perhaps this is a recessive strain of SPSSI, a "forgotten alternative," but it is vibrant and relentless.

After 75 years, SPSSI has much to be proud of, much to worry about, and a strong history of ancestors with chutzpa to guide us through difficult times. Just this past year, we have enjoyed the victories of public science as enacted by engaged social psychologists in the news . . . to name just a few Craig Haney's scholarship was foundational to the Supreme Court mandate that California reduction its prison population; Katie Cumiskey and her wife Robin were selected as one of three same sex married couples to testify against the Defense of Marriage Act in Congress; Ilan Meyer provided outstanding testimony in the Prop 8 same sex marriage case in California and social psychologist Nancy Cantor, president of Syracuse University, decided courageously to remove Syracuse from the American Association of Universities because the National Research Council (NRC) rankings, based on a narrow set of indicators, were swaying her institution away from its mission of public scholarship, diversity, and intellectual originality.

In each of these settings, critical psychologists have channeled the chutzpa of Asch's 1953 resisters who refused to conform. In courts, Congress, academic leadership positions, and in the popular media, these scholars provided empirical accounts contesting the prevailing "common sense" that prisons keep us safe, that marriage should be between a man and a woman or that test-driven ranking systems facilitate educational progress. By challenging the false consensus and intervening theoretically, empirically, and politically, they documented the devastation wrought by inequality gaps, refused to focus on only those most adversely affected and challenged the (in)justice of who loses and who gains. They have produced and assembled an archive of evidence on shared loss, shared gains, and braided fates, scholarship designed to be of use in campaigns for liberation and human rights. These are the everyday heroes of SPSSI.

Our challenge today is to theorize and document the social psychological dynamics of surviving, resisting, and transforming, with humanity, a global landscape scorched by voracious inequality gaps; gathering up evidence that links the local to the global; unemployment to fascism; strange fruits to perfumes; 1–99%; to uncover the common capillaries that carry presumptions of merit, health, and positive psychology to one side of Manhattan and deposit despair, risk, and need for containment 10 blocks north. We need a critical psychology that draws from varied methodological traditions—experiments, mapping, focus groups, archival methods, community surveys, interviews, and q-sorts; honors and theorizes how people make sense of their lives, identities, and relationships; create music, love, art, and science; how they grow babies and vegetables, and how they link arms to propel the very revolutions of solidarity circling the globe as we speak. These are profoundly social psychological questions; intensely critical and passionately committed to social change. Call me a romantic, but I think we are up to the task. Happy anniversary SPSSI, and thanks Kurt for leaving us a wide open (force) field of dreams.

References

Alexander, M. (2010). *The new Jim Crow: Mass incarceration in the age of colorblindness*. New York: The New Press.

Allport, G. (1964). The fruits of eclecticism: Bitter or sweet? *Acta Psychologica, 23*, 27–44.

APA Presidential Task Force on Evidence-Based Practice (2006). Evidence-based practice in psychology. *American Psychologist, 61*(4), 271–285.

Balko, R. (2011). Grieving Mother Faces 36 Months In Jail For Jaywalking After Son Is Killed By Hit-And-Run Driver. Huff Press. (Downloaded from http://www.huffingtonpost.com/radley-balko/raquel-nelson-jail-for jaywalking_b_905925.html 7/21/11). Accessed June 14, 2011.

Bernstein, A. (Fall 2011). Metrics mania: The growing corporatization of U.S. Philanthropy. *Thought and Action*, 33–41.

Bhatia, S. (2011). *Globalization and culture: Mimicry and identity in the new circuits of dispossession.* Invited paper. City University of New York, Department of Psychology, NY.

Boal, A. (2002). *Games for actors and non-actors* (2nd ed.). New York: Routledge.

Center for Global Development (2009). The rapid rise of randomistas and the trouble with RCTs. In D. Roodman's Blog, at blogs.cgdev.org/openbook/2009. Accessed January 20, 2011.

Cialdini, R. (2009). We have to break up. *Perspectives on Psychological Science*, *4*(1), 5–6. doi: 10.1111/j.1745-6924.

Campbell, D. T. (1976). *Assessing the impact of planned social change*. The Public Affairs Center, Dartmouth College, Hanover, NH.

Danziger, K. (1990).*Constructing the subject: Historical origins of psychological research*. New York: Cambridge University Press.

Deutsch, M. (1974). Awakening a sense of injustice. In M. Lerner & M. Ross (Eds.), *The quest for justice: Myth, reality, ideal*. Canada: Holt, Rinehart & Winston.

Deutsch, M. (1985). *Distributive justice: A social psychological perspective*. New Haven: Yale University Press.

Dollard, J. (1937) *Class and caste in a southern town*. New Haven: Yale University Press.

Drury, J., & Reicher, S. (2000). Collective action and psychological change: The emergence of new social identities. *British Journal of Social Psychology*, *39*(4), 579–604. doi:10.1348/014466600164642.

Du Bois, W. E. B. (1913). Introduction. *The Crisis Magazine*, *6*, 339–345.

Ewen, R. (1998). *An introduction to theories of personality*. Mahwah, NJ: Erlbaum.

Feller, A., & Stone, C. (2009). *Top 1 percent of Americans reaped two-thirds of income gains in last economic expansion. Income concentration in 2007 was at highest level since 1928, new analysis shows*. Washington, DC: Center on Budget and Policy Priorities.

Fine, M. (2010). The breast and the state: An analysis of good and bad nipples by gender, race, and class. *Studies in Gender & Sexuality*, *11*(1), 24–32.

Fine, M. (2012). Troubling calls for evidence: A critical race, class and gender analysis of whose evidence counts. *Feminism and Psychology*. *22*, 3–19.

Fine, M., Burns, A., Torre, M. E., & Payne, Y. (2007). How class matters: The geography of educational desire and despair in schools and courts. In L. Weis (Ed.), *The way class works: Matters: readings on school, family and the economy* (Chap. 16, pp. 225–242). New York: Routledge.

Fine, M., & Carney, S. (2001). Women, gender, and the law: Toward a feminist rethinking of responsibility. In R.Unger (Ed.), *Handbook of psychology and gender* (pp. 388–409). NY: McMillan Publishers.

Fine, M., & McClelland, S. (2007). The politics of teen women's sexuality: Public policy and the adolescent female body. *Emory Law Review*, *56*(4), 993–1038.

Fine, M., & Ruglis, J. (2008). Circuits of dispossession: The racialized and classed realignment of the public sphere for youth in the U.S. *Transforming Anthropology*, *17*(1), 20–33. doi:10.1111/j.1548-7466.2009.01037.x/ abstract.

Fine, M., & Sirin, S. (2007). Theorizing hyphenated selves: Researching marginalized youth in times of historical and political conflict. *Social and Personality Psychology Compass*, *1*(1), 16—38. doi:10.1111/ j.1751-9004.2007.

Fine, M., Torre, M. E., Boudin, K., Bowen, I., Clark, J., Hylton, D., Martinez, M., Missy, R., Rosemarie, A., Smart, P., & Upegui, D. (2003). Participatory action research: From within and beyond prison bars. Qualitative research in psychology: Expanding perspectives in methodology and design. In P. M. Camic, J. E. Rhodes, & L. Yardley(Eds.), (2003). *Qualitative research in psychology: Expanding perspectives in methodology and design* (pp. 173–198). Washington, DC: American Psychological Association, xvi, 315pp. doi:10.1037/10595-010.

Fox, D., Prilleltensky, I., & Austin, S. (Eds.). (2009). *Critical psychology* (2nd ed.). Los Angeles: Sage Publications.

Fox, M., & Fine, M. (2012). Circulating critical research: Reflections on performance and moving inquiry into action. In G. Cannella, & S. Steinberg (Eds.), *Critical qualitative research reader*. NY: Peter Lang Publishing.

Fox, M., Mediratta, K., Ruglis, J., Stoudt, B., Shah, S., & Fine, M. (2010). Critical youth engagement: Participatory action research and organizing. In L. Sherrod, J. Torney-Puta, & C. Flanagan (Eds.), *Handbook of research and policy on civic engagement with youth*. NJ: Wiley Press.

Harvey, D. (2004). A geographer's perspective on the new American imperialism. Conversations with history. Berkeley, CA: UC Institute of International Studies. [Electronic Document]. (Accessed May 10, 2007 from http://globetrotter.berkeley.edu/people4/Harvey/harvey-con.html).

Haug, F. (1992). *Beyond female masochism*. London: Verso.

Herk, M. (2009). The coalition for evidence based policy: Independent assessment submitted to W.T. Grant. www.coalition4evidence.org.2009.Accessed on January 11, 2011.

Jahoda, M. (1981). To publish or not to publish. *Journal of Social Issues, 37*(1), 208–220. doi:10.1111/j.1540-4560.1981.tb01064.x.

Jahoda, M., Lazarsfeld, P., & Zeisel, H. (1933). *Marienthal: The sociography of an unemployed community*. New Brunswick, NJ: Transaction Publishers.

Klein, M. (1984). The psycho-analysis of children (A. Strachey, Trans.), R. Money-Kyrle (Ed.), *The writings of Melanie Klein* (Vol. 2). New York: Free Press. (Original work published 1932).

Lewin, G. (Ed.). (1997). *Resolving social conflicts and field theory in social science*. Washington, DC: American Psychological Association.

Lewin, K. (1946). Action research and minority problems. *The Journal of Social Issues, 2*(4), 34–46. doi:10.1111/j.1540-4560.1946.tb02295.x.

Liebert, R. (2010). Synaptic peace-keeping: Of bipolar and securitization. *Women's Studies Quarterly Special Issue, Market, 38*(3&4), 325–342.

Liu, W. (2012). The dispossession of needs in neoliberal globalization: Life stories of Southeast Asian migrant workers in Taiwan. Manuscript in preparation.

Lykes, B. (2012). One legacy among many: The Ignacio Martin-Baro fund. *Peace and Conflict Journal, 18*(1), 88–95.

Lykes, M. B., & Coquillon, E.D. (2009). Psychosocial trauma, poverty and human rights in communities emerging from war. In D. Fox, I. Prilleltensky, & S. Austin (Eds.), *Critical psychology* (pp. 285–299). Los Angeles: Sage Publications. doi:10.1111/j.1540-4560.

Macleod, C., & Bhatia, S. (2008). Post colonial psychology. In C. Willig & W. Stainton-Rogers (Eds.), *Handbook of qualitative research in psychology* (pp. 576–590). London: Sage Press. doi:10.4135/9781848607927.

Martín-Baró, I. (1994). *Writings for a liberation psychology*. Cambridge, MA: Harvard University Press.

McClelland, S. (2010). Intimate justice. *Social and Personality Psychology Compass, 4*(9), 663–680. doi:10.1111/j.1751-9004.2010.00293.x.

McGarty, C. (2000). The citation impact factor in social psychology. *Current research in social psychology, 5*(1), 1–10.

Mills, C. W. (2000). *The sociological imagination* (40th Anniversary Ed.). New York: Oxford University Press.

Opotow, S. (2011). How this was possible: Interpreting the Holocaust. *Journal of Social Issues, 67*(1), 205–224. doi:10.1111/j.1540-4560.2010.01694.x.

Prilleltensky, I. (2010). Commitment, accountability and power. In G. Nelson & I. Prilleltensky (Eds.), *Community psychology: In pursuit of liberation and well-being* (2nd ed.). London: Palgrave.

Richie, B. (1996). *Compelled to crime*. New York: Routledge.

Rutherford, A., Unger, R., & Cherry, F. (2011). Reclaiming SPSSI's sociological past: Maria Jahoda and the immersion tradition in social psychology. *Journal of Social Issues, 67*(1), 42–58. doi:10.1111/j.1540-4560.2010.01678.x.

Saegert, S., Fields, D., & Libman, K. (2009). Deflating the dream: Radical risk and the neoliberalization of home ownership. *Journal of Urban Affairs, 31*(3), 297–317. doi:10.1111/j.1467-9906.2009.00461.x.

Saxe, L., & Fine, M. (1981). *Social experiments: Methods for design and evaluation*. Beverly Hills: Sage Publications.

Sherif, M. (1968). If the social scientist is to be more than a mere technician. *Journal of Social Issues, 24*, 41–61. doi:10.1111/j.1540-4560.1968.tb01468.x.

Silverstein, L., & Auerbach, C. (2009). Using qualitative research to develop culturally competent evidence based practice. *American Psychologist, 64*(4), 274–275.

Stainton-Rogers, W. (2009). Research methodology. In D. Fox, I. Prilleltensky, & S. Austin (Eds.), *Critical psychology* (pp. 335–354). Los Angeles: Sage Publications.

Steinitz, V., & Mishler, E. (2008). Critical psychology and the politics of resistance. In D. Fox, I. Prilleltensky, & S. Austin (Eds.), *Critical psychology* (pp. 391–409). Los Angeles: Sage Publications.

Stoudt, B., Fine, M., & Fox, M. (2011) Growing up policed in the age of aggressive policing policies. *New York Law School Law Review, 56*(12), 1331–1370.

Teo, T. (2010). What is epistemological violence in the empirical social sciences? *Social and Personality Psychology Compass, 4/5*, 295–303. doi:10.1111/j.1751-9004.2010.00265.x.

Torre, M. E., & Fine, M. (2011). A wrinkle in time. *Journal of Social Issues, 67*(1), 106–121. doi:10.1111/j.1540-4560.2010.01686.x.

Torre, M., Fine, M., Stoudt, B., & Fox, M. (2012). Critical participatory action research as public science. In P. Camic & H. Cooper (Eds.), *Handbook of research methods in psychology.* Washington, DC: American Psychological Association.

Tuchman, G. (2009). *Wannabe U: Inside the corporate university.* Chicago: University of Chicago Press.

Wallerstein, N. (2012). Community based participatory research as a path to equity. Chapel Hill, NC: Global Public Health Conference.

Wilkinson, R., & Pickett, K. (2009). *The spirit level: Why greater equality makes societies stronger.* New York: Bloomsbury Press.

MICHELLE FINE is a Distinguished Professor of Social Psychology, Women's Studies and Urban Education at the Graduate Center, CUNY and is a founding faculty member of the Public Science Project (PSP). A consortium of researchers, policy makers and community activists PSP produces critical scholarship "to be of use" in social policy debates and organizing movements for educational equity and human rights. Recent books and policy monographs include *Charter Schools and the Corporate Make-Over of Public Education* (Teachers College Press, 2012, with Michael Fabricant), *Revolutionizing Education: Youth Participatory Action Research in Motion* (with Julio Cammarota, Routledge, 2008), *Muslim-American Youth* (with Selcuk Sirin, New York University Press, 2008), and *Working Method: Social Research and Social Justice* (Routledge, 2004, with Lois Weis). "*Changing minds: The impact of college on women in prison,*" nationally recognized as the primary empirical basis for the contemporary college in prison movement (2001). Fine has provided expert testimony in a number of ground breaking legal victories including women's access to the Citadel Military Academy and in *Williams v. California*, a class action lawsuit for urban youth-of-color denied adequate education in California. Fine is the recipient of the 2012 Henry Murray Award, 2011 Kurt Lewin Award from the Society for the Psychological Study of Social Issues, and the 2010 Social Justice and Higher Education Award from the College and Community Fellowship for her work in prison. She was awarded the first Morton Deutsch Scholarship Award in 2005 and the Carolyn Sherif Award from the Division 35, Psychology of Women in 2001.